VOLUME 1

oncooking
techniques from expert chefs

CUSTOM EDITION

sarah r. labensky • alan m. hause

with Steven Labensky

Material selected from:
On Cooking: Techniques from Expert Chefs, Third Edition
by Sarah R. Labensky, Alan M. Hause, with Steven Labensky

Photographs by Richard Embery

Drawings by Stacey Winters Quattrone and William E. Ingram

Cover image courtesy of Photodisc/Getty Images, Inc.

Taken from:

On Cooking: Techniques from Expert Chefs, Third Edition
by Sarah R. Labensky and Alan M. Hause
Copyright © 2003, 1999, 1995 by Pearson Education, Inc.
Published by Prentice Hall
Upper Saddle River, New Jersey, 07458.

This special edition published in cooperation with Pearson Custom Publishing.

Printed in the United States of America

10 9 8 7 6 5

ISBN 0-536-73221-3

2006520060

SB

Please visit our web site at *www.pearsoncustom.com*

PEARSON CUSTOM PUBLISHING
75 Arlington Street, Suite 300, Boston, MA 02116
A Pearson Education Company

CONTENTS

PART 3   COOKING

PREFACE

Learning to cook is much more than simply learning to follow a recipe. Consequently, this is not a cookbook or a collection of recipes. It is a carefully designed text intended to teach you the fundamentals of the culinary arts and to prepare you for a rewarding career in the food service industry.

Many chapters have extensive illustrated sections identifying foods and equipment. Throughout the book, we emphasize culinary principles, not recipes (although we include more than 750 of them). Whenever possible, we focus on the general procedure highlighting fundamental principles and skills, whether it be for preparing a yeast bread or grilling a piece of fish. We discuss both the how and why of cooking. Only then are specific applications and sample recipes given.

Numerous hotel and restaurant chefs throughout the country have contributed recipes to this book, usually accompanied by photographs of the dishes as prepared in their kitchens. These recipes and illustrations allow you to explore different techniques and presentation styles.

In order to provide you with a sense of the rich traditions of cookery, informative sidebars on food history, chef biographies and other topics are scattered throughout the book. Also included are several short essays written by prominent culinarians on topics ranging from tempering chocolate to tasting spicy foods.

We wish you much success in your culinary career and hope that this text will continue to inform and inspire you long after graduation.

▶ A NOTE ON RECIPES

Recipes are important and useful as a means of standardizing food preparation and recording information. We include recipes that are designed primarily to reinforce and explain techniques and procedures presented in the text. Many recipe yields are intentionally low in order to be less intimidating to beginning cooks and more useful in small schools and kitchens.

All ingredients are listed in both U.S. and metric measurements. The metric equivalents are rounded off to even, easily measured amounts. So, you should consider these ingredient lists as separate recipes or formulas; do not measure some ingredients according to the metric amounts and other ingredients according to the U.S. amount or the proportions will not be accurate and the intended result will not be achieved.

Throughout this book, unless otherwise noted:

▶ *mirepoix* refers to a preparation of 2 parts onion, 1 part celery and 1 part carrot by weight

▶ *pepper* refers to ground black pepper, preferably freshly ground

▶ *butter* refers to whole, unsalted butter

▶ *milk* refers to whole or reduced fat (not nonfat) milk, and

▶ *TT* means "to taste"

A registered dietician analyzed all of the recipes in this book using nutritional analysis software that incorporates data from the U.S. Department of Agriculture, research laboratories and food manufacturers. The nutrient information provided here should be used only as a reference, however. A margin of error of approximately 20% can be expected because of natural variations in ingredients. Preparation techniques and serving sizes may also significantly alter the values of many nutrients. For the nutritional analysis, if a recipe offers a choice of ingredients, the first-mentioned ingredient is the one used. Ingredients listed as "to taste" (TT) and "as needed" are omitted from the analysis. Corn oil and whole milk are used throughout for "vegetable oil" and "milk," respectively. In cases of a range of ingredient quantities or numbers of servings, the average is used.

Throughout this book various recipes are marked with the pyramid symbol. This symbol identifies dishes that are particularly low in calories, fat, saturated fat or sodium; if appropriate, they may also be a good source of vitamins, protein, fiber or calcium.

Vegetarian dishes are indicated with a vegetable symbol. These recipes do not contain meat, fish, shellfish or poultry, but may contain dairy products and/or eggs. Vegetarian dishes are not necessarily low in calories, fat or sodium; nor are they automatically good sources of vitamins, protein, fiber or calcium.

 The World Wide Web icon appears next to end-of-chapter questions for discussion whose answers may be researched on the web.

Detailed procedures for standard techniques are presented in the text and generally are not repeated in each recipe (for example, "deglaze the pan" or "monté au beurre"). No matter how detailed the written recipe, however, we must assume that you have certain knowledge, skills and judgment.

Variations appear at the end of selected recipes. These variations give you the opportunity to see how one set of techniques or procedures can be used to prepare different dishes with only minor modifications.

You should also rely upon the knowledge and skills of your instructor for guidance. Although some skills and an understanding of theory can be acquired through reading and study, no book can substitute for repeated, hands-on preparation and observation.

▶ ACKNOWLEDGMENTS

This book would not have been possible without the assistance and support of many people. We are particularly indebted to Steve Labensky for his countless hours with a sharp pencil, his comments and criticism and his constant support. Special thanks to our photographer, Richard Embery, for his talent, professionalism and commitment to quality; and to Sharon Salomon, MS, RD, for preparation of the Nutrition chapter. The nutritional analysis for this edition was prepared by Mindy Hermann, MS, RD, whose thoroughness and prompt replies were greatly appreciated. Thanks also to Stacey Winters Quattrone and Bill Ingram for their artistry. We are also grateful to the many chefs, restaurateurs, writers and culinary professionals who provided recipes and essays for this book.

Alan would also like to thank his wife Chantal for her guidance, support, advice and patience throughout this project. He also thanks the many coworkers and friends who contributed to the success of the text including: Charlie Blonkenfeld, Tom Klarstrom, Reynalda Montes, Bryan Elliott, Rosalino Morales, Estela Morales, Margarita Nava, Gregoria Alvizo, Linda Proffitt, Marty van de Brug and Jimmy Curry.

Sarah especially wishes to thank Mississippi University for Women for granting her a break from her teaching duties. She would also like to thank her husband Dave Moline and her administrative assistant Cheryl Brown for their patience and for keeping the real world on track during this project.

The authors wish to thank the following companies for their generous donations of equipment and supplies: J.A. Henckels Zwillingswerk, Inc., All-Clad Metalcrafters, Inc. and Parrish's Cake Decorating Supplies, Inc. We also wish to thank Shamrock Foods Company, East Coast Seafood of Phoenix Inc., KitchenAid Home Appliances, Taylor Environmental Instruments, Hobart Corporation, Jeff and Sue Reising of Arizona Ostrich Fillet and Randy Dougherty of ISF International.

Finally, we wish to thank everyone involved in this project at Prentice Hall, including Vernon Anthony, Executive Editor; Linda Zuk, Production Editor; Marion Gottlieb, Associate Editor; Cheryl Asherman, Creative Director; Mary Carnis, Managing Editor; Adele Kupchik, Senior Production Editor; and Ryan DeGrote, Marketing Manager. We also remain indebted to Robin Baliszewski, Acquisitions Editor of the first edition and current President of Career, Health, Education & Technology Division, for her support and friendship.

The authors would also like to acknowledge the following reviewers for their comments and assistance with this third edition. The reviewers of *On Cooking* provided many excellent suggestions and ideas for improving the text. The quality of the reviews was outstanding and played a major role in the preparation of this revision. Their assistance and expertise is greatly appreciated.

Michael Baskette, CEC, CCE, AAC
American Culinary Federation
St. Augustine, FL

Carl A. Behnke, CEC
Purdue University
West Lafayette, IN

Brian C. Bergquist Ed.S., CFE, COI
University of Wisconsin-Stout
Menomonie, WI

Charlotte Britto, RD, FADA
San Joaquin Delta College
Stockton, CA

Scott H. Doughty
Newbury College
Brookline, MA

Nancy Graves
University of Houston
Houston, TX

William C. Jarvie
Johnson & Wales University
The Hospitality College
Providence, RI

Jerrold K. Leong
Oklahoma State University
Stillwater, OK

Brian McDonald, CEC, CCE
Asheville-Buncombe Technical
    Community College
Asheville, NC

Michael J. McGreal
Joliet Junior College
Joliet, IL

James W. Paul, II, CSC, CCE, FMP
Caroline Edenfield
Jim Morris, CCE
Joe Costa
The Art Institute of Atlanta—
    Culinary Arts
Atlanta, GA

Gary J. Prell, CEC, CCE, AAC
General Manager for the Colorado
    Convention Center & the Denver
    Performing Arts Complex
Denver, CO

Urbano Salvati, CEC
Brown Institute Le Cordon Bleu
Mendota Heights, MN

Raymond J. Wesolowski, CCC
Pennsylvania Culinary
Pittsburgh, PA

▶ ADDITIONAL CREDITS

We wish to extend our thanks to the many chefs and instructors who took the time to complete our general survey regarding introductory cooking textbooks. Their feedback has contributed greatly to the production of our text.

Henry Anderson, Macomb Community College; Mike Artlip, Kendall College; Allen Asch, University of Nevada–Las Vegas; Claire Berg, Brookdale Community College; Nancy Berkoff, Los Angeles Trade-Technical College; LeRoy Blanchard, Los Angeles Trade-Technical College; Char Britto, San Joaquin Delta College; Laura Bullen, College of Sequoias; Stephen Burgeson, Buffalo State College; Paul Cannamela, Erie Community College–City Campus; Michael Carmel, The Illinois Institute of Art; Jeanne Curtis, Newbury College; W. Haze Dennis, Mission College; Randy Doescher, Mitchell Technical Institute; Timothy Farley, Milwaukee Area Technical College; Andrew Feldman, Glendale Community College; Jo-Ann Foley, Sacramento City College; Gregory Forte, Utah Valley State College; Deborah Foster, Ball State University; Maureen Garfolo, Pennsylvania Culinary; Richard Ghiseli, Purdue University; Nancy Graves, University of Houston; Richard Grigsby, Florida Community College; Carol Gunter, Nicholls State University; Jeffrey Hamblin, Ricks College; John Harrison, Mercyhurst College–North East; Joe Harrold, Florida Community College at Jacksonville; John Head, Johnson County Community College; Carolyn Himes, Pueblo Community College; Roger Holden, Oakland Community College; Connie Holt, Widener University; James Hughes, Travel Institute of the Pacific; William Jarvie, Johnson & Wales University; Ken Jarvis, Anne Arundel Community College; Ron Jones, Atlantic Culinary Academy; Lisa Kennon, University of North Texas; Lind Kinney, University of Massachusetts; Jerrold Leong, Oklahoma State University; Wesley Luckhardt, Central Michigan University; Elaine Madden, Anne Arundel Community College; Brian McDonald, Asheville-Buncombe Technical Community College; Michael McGreal, Joliet Junior College; Robert Menne, Hennepin Technical College; Kenneth Morlino, Nashville State Tech; Robert Nelson, University of Delaware; Becky Noto, University of Louisiana at Lafayette; David Pavesic, Georgia State University; Jayne Pearson, Manchester Community College; Deborah Peterson, Victor Valley College; Rose Postel, East Carolina University; Mary Rhiner, Kirkwood Community College; Warren Sackler, Rochester Institute of Technology; Barbara Scheule, Kent State University; David Schneider, Macomb Community College; Doris Schomberg, Alamance Community College; Leslie Cory Shoemaker, Northern Michigan University; Nancy Simonds-Ruderman, Berkshire Community College; Beth Sonnier, El Centro College; Carl Statford, Manchester Community College; Jim Trebbien, Metro College–Omaha; Mary Trometter, Pennsylvania School of Technology; Keith Vonhoff, Joliet Junior College; Erich Wagner, Scottsdale Community College; Cliff Wener, College of Lake County; Raymond Weslowski, Pennsylvania Culinary; Mark Wright, Erie Community College; George Yackey, Grossmont College.

ONCOOKING

COOKERY IS BECOME AN ART,
A NOBLE SCIENCE; COOKS ARE GENTLEMEN.
—*Robert Burton, British author (1577—1640)*

PROFESSIONALISM

▶ discuss the development of the modern food service industry

▶ name key historical figures responsible for developing food service professionalism

▶ explain the organization of classic and modern kitchen brigades

▶ appreciate the role of the professional chef in modern food service operations

▶ understand the attributes a student chef needs to become a professional chef

▶ **cooking** (1) the transfer of energy from a heat source to a food; this energy alters the food's molecular structure, changing its texture, flavor, aroma and appearance; (2) the preparation of food for consumption

▶ **cookery** the art, practice or work of cooking

▶ **professional cooking** a system of cooking based on a knowledge of and appreciation for ingredients and procedures

Like any fine art, great cookery requires taste and creativity, an appreciation of beauty and a mastery of technique. Like the sciences, successful cookery demands knowledge and an understanding of basic principles. And like any successful leader, today's professional chefs must exercise sound judgment and be committed to achieving excellence in their endeavors.

This book describes foods and cooking equipment, explains culinary principles and cooking techniques and provides recipes using these principles and techniques. No book , however, can provide taste, creativity, commitment and judgment. For these, you must rely upon yourself.

▶ CHEFS AND RESTAURANTS

Cooks have produced food in quantity for as long as people have eaten together. For millennia, chefs have catered to the often elaborate dining needs of the wealthy and powerful, whether they be Asian, Native American, European or African. And for centuries, vendors in China, Europe and elsewhere have sold to the public foods that they prepared themselves or bought from others.

But the history of the professional chef is of relatively recent origin. Its cast is mostly French, and it is intertwined with the history of restaurants—for only with the development of restaurants during the late 18th and early 19th centuries were chefs expected to produce, efficiently and economically, different dishes at different times for different diners.

THE 18TH CENTURY—BOULANGER'S RESTAURANT

The word *restaurant* is derived from the French word *restaurer* ("to restore"). Since the 16th century, the word *restorative* had been used to describe rich and highly flavored soups or stews capable of restoring lost strength. Restoratives, like all other cooked foods offered and purchased outside the home, were made by guild members. Each guild had a monopoly on preparing certain food items. For example, during the reign of Henri IV of France (1553–1610), there were separate guilds for *rotisseurs* (who cooked *la grosse viande*, the main cuts of meat), *patissiers* (who cooked poultry, pies and tarts), *tamisiers* (who baked breads), *vinaigriers* (who made sauces and some stews, including some restoratives), *traiteurs* (who made ragouts) and *porte-chapes* (caterers who organized feasts and celebrations).

The French claim that the first modern restaurant opened one day in 1765 when a Parisian tavernkeeper, a Monsieur Boulanger, hung a sign advertising the sale of his special restorative, a dish of sheep feet in white sauce. His establishment closed shortly thereafter as the result of a lawsuit brought by a guild whose members claimed that Boulanger was infringing on their exclusive right to sell prepared dishes. Boulanger triumphed in court and later reopened.

Boulanger's establishment differed from the inns and taverns that had existed throughout Europe for centuries. These inns and taverns served foods prepared (usually off premises) by the appropriate guild. The food—of which there was little choice—was offered by the keeper as incidental to the establishment's primary function: providing sleeping accommodations or drink. Customers were served family style and ate at communal tables. Boulanger's contribution to the food service industry was to serve a variety of foods prepared on premises to customers whose primary interest was dining.

Several other restaurants opened in Paris during the succeeding decades, including the Grande Taverne de Londres in 1782. Its owner, Antoine Beauvilliers (1754–1817), was the former steward to the Comte de Provence, later King Louis XVIII of France. He advanced the development of the modern restaurant by offering his wealthy patrons a menu listing available dishes during fixed hours. Beauvilliers's impeccably trained wait staff served patrons at small, individual tables in an elegant setting.

The French Revolution (1789–1799) had a significant effect on the budding restaurant industry. Along with the aristocracy, guilds and their monopolies were generally abolished. The revolution also allowed the public access to the skills and creativity of the well-trained, sophisticated chefs who had worked in the aristocracy's private kitchens. Although many of the aristocracy's chefs either left the country or lost their jobs (and some their heads), a few opened restaurants catering to the growing urbanized middle class.

THE EARLY 19TH CENTURY—CARÊME AND *GRANDE CUISINE*

As the 19th century progressed, more restaurants opened, serving a greater selection of items and catering to a wider clientele. By mid-century, several large, grand restaurants in Paris were serving elaborate meals, decidedly reminiscent of the *grande cuisine* (also known as *haute cuisine*) of the aristocracy. **Grande cuisine**, which arguably reached its peak of perfection in the hands of Antonin Carême, was characterized by meals consisting of dozens of courses of elaborately and intricately prepared, presented, garnished and sauced foods. Other restaurateurs blended the techniques and styles of *grande cuisine* with the simpler foods and tastes of the middle class (*cuisine bourgeoisie*) to create a new cuisine simpler than *grande cuisine* but more than mere home cooking.

▶ *grande cuisine* the rich, intricate and elaborate cuisine of the 18th- and 19th-century French aristocracy and upper classes. It is based on the rational identification, development and adoption of strict culinary principles. By emphasizing the how and why of cooking, *grande cuisine* was the first to distinguish itself from regional cuisines, which tend to emphasize the tradition of cooking.

THE LATE 19TH CENTURY—ESCOFFIER AND *CUISINE CLASSIQUE*

Following the lead set by the French in both culinary style and the restaurant business, restaurants opened in the United States and throughout Europe during the 19th century. Charles Ranhofer (1836–1899) was the first internationally renowned chef of an American restaurant, Delmonico's in New York City. In 1893, Ranhofer published his "franco-american" encyclopedia of cooking, *The Epicurean*, containing more than 3500 recipes.

One of the finest restaurants outside France was the dining room at London's Savoy Hotel, opened in 1898 under the directions of Cesar Ritz (1850–1918) and Auguste Escoffier. Escoffier is generally credited with refining the *grande cuisine* of Carême to create *cuisine classique* or **classic cuisine**. By doing so, he brought French cuisine into the 20th century.

▶ *classic cuisine* a late 19th- and early 20th-century refinement and simplification of French *grande cuisine*. Classic (or classical) cuisine relies on the thorough exploration of culinary principles and techniques, and emphasizes the refined preparation and presentation of superb ingredients.

THE MID-20TH CENTURY—POINT AND *NOUVELLE CUISINE*

The mid 20th century witnessed a trend toward lighter, more naturally flavored and more simply prepared foods. Fernand Point was a master practitioner of this movement. But this master's goal of simplicity and refinement was carried to even greater heights by a generation of chefs Point trained: principally, Paul Bocuse, Jean and Pierre Troisgros, Alain Chapel, Francois Bise and Louis Outhier. They, along with Michel Guérard and Roger Vergé, were the pioneers of **nouvelle cuisine** in the early 1970s.

Their culinary philosophy was principled on the rejection of overly rich, needlessly complicated dishes. These chefs emphasized healthful eating. The ingredients must be absolutely fresh and of the highest possible quality; the

▶ *nouvelle cuisine* French for "new cooking"; a mid-20th-century movement away from many classic cuisine principles and toward a lighter cuisine based on natural flavors, shortened cooking times and innovative combinations

MARIE-ANTOIN (ANTONIN) CARÊME (1783–1833)

Carême, known as the "cook of kings and the king of cooks," was an acknowledged master of French grande cuisine. Abandoned on the streets of Paris as a child, he worked his way from cook's helper in a working-class restaurant to become one of the most prestigious chefs of his (or, arguably, any other) time. During his career, he was chef to the famous French diplomat and gourmand Prince de Talleyrand, the Prince Regent of England (who became King George IV), Tsar Alexander I of Russia and Baron de Rothschild, among others.

His stated goal was to achieve "lightness," "grace," "order" and "perspicuity" in the preparation and presentation of food. As a *patissier*, he designed and prepared elaborate and elegant pastry and confectionery creations, many of which were based on architectural designs. (He wrote that "the fine arts are five in number, namely: painting, sculpture, poetry, music, architecture–the main branch of which is confectionery.") As a showman, he garnished his dishes with ornamental hatelets (skewers) threaded with colorful ingredients such as crayfish and intricately carved vegetables, and presented his creations on elaborate socles (bases). As a *saucier*, he standardized the use of roux as a thickening agent, perfected recipes and devised a system for classifying sauces. As a *garde-manger*, Carême popularized cold cuisine, emphasizing molds and aspic dishes. As a culinary professional, he designed kitchen tools, equipment and uniforms.

As an author, he wrote and illustrated important texts on the culinary arts, including *Le*

Courtesy of Barbara Wheaton

Maitre d'hotel francais (1822), describing the hundreds of dishes he personally created and cooked in the capitals of Europe; *Le Patissier royal parisian* (1825), containing fanciful designs for *les pieces montées*, the great decorative centerpieces that were the crowning glory of grand dinners; and his five-volume masterpiece on the state of his profession, *L'Art de la cuisine au XIXe siecle* (1833), the last two volumes of which were completed after his death by his associate Plumerey. Carême's writings almost single-handedly refined and summarized five hundred years of culinary evolution. But his treatises were not mere cookbooks. Rather, he analyzed cooking, old and new, emphasizing procedure and order and covering every aspect of the art known as *grande cuisine*.

Carême died before age 50, burnt out, according to Laurent Tailhade, "by the flame of his genius and the coal of the spits." But this may have been the glory he sought, for he once wrote:

> Imagine yourself in a large kitchen at the moment of a great dinner. . . . [S]ee twenty chefs coming, going, moving with speed in this cauldron of heat, look at the great mass of charcoal, a cubic meter for the cooking of entrées, and another mass on the ovens for the cooking of soups, sauces, ragouts, for frying and the water baths. Add to that a heap of burning wood in front of which four spits are turning, one which bears a sirloin weighing 45–50 pounds, the other fowl or game. In this furnace everyone moves with speed; not a sound is heard, only the chef has a right to speak, and at the sound of his voice, everyone obeys. Finally, the last straw; for about half an hour, all windows are closed so that the air does not cool the dishes as they are being served. This is the way we spend the best years of our lives. We must obey even when physical strength fails, but it is the burning charcoal that kills us. . . . [C]harcoal kills us but what does it matter? The shorter the life, the greater the glory.

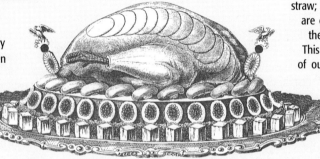

cooking methods should be simple and direct whenever possible. The accompaniments and garnishes must be light and contribute to an overall harmony; the completed plates must be elegantly designed and decorated. Following these guidelines, some traditional cooking methods have been applied to untraditional ingredients, and ingredients have been combined in new and previously unorthodox fashions. For chefs with knowledge, skill, taste and judgment, this works.

THE LATE 20TH CENTURY—AN AMERICAN CULINARY REVOLUTION

During the last 30 years or so, two distinct culinary trends have emerged in the United States: "the hotter, the better" and "fresh food, simply prepared."

AUGUSTE ESCOFFIER (1846–1935)

Escoffier's brilliant culinary career began at the age of 13 in his uncle's restaurant and continued until his death at the age of 89. Called the "emperor of the world's kitchens," he is perhaps best known for defining French cuisine and dining during La Belle Époque (the "Gay Nineties").

Unlike Carême, Escoffier never worked in an aristocratic household. Rather, he exhibited his culinary skills in the dining rooms of the finest hotels in Europe, including the Place Vendôme in Paris and the Savoy and Carlton Hotels in London.

Escoffier did much to enhance the *grande cuisine* that arguably reached its perfection under Carême. Crediting Carême with providing the foundation for great—that is, French—cooking, Escoffier simplified the profusion of flavors, dishes and garnishes typifying Carême's work. He also streamlined some of Carême's overly elaborate and fussy procedures and classifications. For example, he reduced Carême's elaborate system of classifying sauces into the five

families of sauces still recognized today. Escoffier sought simplicity and aimed for the perfect balance of a few superb ingredients. Some consider his refinement of *grande cuisine* to have been so radical as to credit him with the

development of a new cuisine referred to as *cuisine classique* (classic or classical cuisine).

His many writings include *Le Livre des menus* (1912), in which, discussing the principles of a well-planned meal, he analogizes a great dinner to a symphony with contrasting movements that should be appropriate to the occasion, the guests and the season, and *Ma cuisine* (1934), surveying *cuisine bourgeoisie*. But his most important contribution is a culinary treatise intended for the professional chef entitled *Le Guide culinaire* (1903). Still in use today, it is an astounding collection of more than 5000 classic cuisine recipes and garnishes. In it, Escoffier emphasizes the mastery of techniques, the thorough understanding of cooking, principles and the appreciation of ingredients—attributes he considered to be the building blocks professional chefs should use to create great dishes.

Escoffier was honored as a Chevalier of the French Legion of Honour in 1920 for his work in enhancing the reputation of French cuisine.

The first trend is due, in large part, to an unlikely source: the Immigration Act of 1965. Under its provisions, a large number of Asians immigrated to this country. They brought with them their rich culinary traditions and they ignited America's love affair with fiery hot cuisines. By the late 1970s, many Americans were no longer content with bland or overly salty pseudo-Chinese dishes such as chop suey and chow mein. They demanded authenticity and developed cravings for spicy dishes from Szechuan and Hunan provinces, Vietnam and Thailand. At the same time, Mexican food left the barrio and became mainstream. Burritos and tacos became routine menu items, while authentic regional Mexican dishes were sought out by middle America. Indeed, by the 1990s, people used more salsa than ketchup as a condiment.

During this same time period, restaurateurs and chefs began Americanizing the principles of French *nouvelle cuisine*. When Alice Waters opened Chez Panisse in Berkeley, California, in 1971, her goal was to serve fresh food, simply prepared. Rejecting the growing popularity of processed and packaged foods, Waters wanted to use fresh, seasonal and locally grown produce in simple preparations that preserved and emphasized the foods' natural flavors. Chez Panisse and the many chefs who passed through its kitchen launched a new style of cuisine that became known as **New American cuisine**. As Waters's culinary philosophy spread across the United States, farmers and chefs began working together to make fresh, locally grown foods available, and producers and suppliers began developing domestic sources for some of the high-quality ingredients that were once available only from overseas. Excellent foie gras from Long Island, New York, and goat cheese from Sonoma County, California, are just two examples.

By the mid-1980s, American chefs began to combine aspects of these two trends. Their work resulted in **fusion cuisine**. With fusion cuisine, ingredients or preparation methods associated with one ethnic or regional cuisine are combined with those of another. A fillet of Norwegian salmon might be grilled over hickory wood, then served on a bed of Japanese soba noodles with pesto cream

▶ **New American cuisine** a late-20th-century movement that began in California but has spread across the United States; it stresses the use of fresh, locally grown, seasonal produce and high-quality ingredients simply prepared in a fashion that preserves and emphasizes natural flavors

▶ **fusion cuisine** the blending or use of ingredients and/or preparation methods from various ethnic, regional or national cuisines in the same dish; also known as transnational cuisine

FERNAND POINT (1897–1955)

A massive man with a monumental personality, Point refined and modernized the classic cuisine of Escoffier. By doing so, he laid the foundations for *nouvelle cuisine*.

Point received his early training in some of the finest hotel-restaurant kitchens in Paris. In 1922, he and his family moved to Vienne, a city in southwest France near Lyon, and opened a restaurant. Two years later his father left the restaurant to Fernand, who renamed it *La Pyra-*

mide. During the succeeding years, it became one of the culinary wonders of the world.

Point disdained dominating sauces and distracting accompaniments and garnishes. He believed that each dish should have a single dominant ingredient, flavor or theme; garnishes must be simple and match "like a tie to a suit." Procedure was of great importance. He devoted equal efforts to frying an egg and creating the marjolaine (a light almond and hazelnut

spongecake filled with chocolate and praline buttercreams). His goal was to use the finest of raw ingredients to produce perfect food that looked elegant and simple. But simplicity was not easy to achieve. As he once said, "a bearnaise sauce is simply an egg yolk, a shallot, a little tarragon vinegar, and butter, but it takes years of practice for the result to be perfect."

sauce, for example, while duck confit prepared by the traditional French method is seasoned with lemongrass, ginger and chiles.

Along with this new interest in and appreciation for American ingredients and American tastes has come a new respect for American chefs. Many European and American food writers and pundits now consider American chefs to be among the best in the world, a fact they often triumph at the same time they express their concern about the general decline of French cuisine and the exodus of European chefs to America. In addition, the American public has taken food to heart.

Many chefs have been elevated to celebrity status; an entire cable television network is devoted to cooking. Bookstore and library shelves are jammed with cookbooks, and newspapers and magazines regularly review restaurants or report on culinary trends. With gourmet shops and cookware stores in most malls, cooking has become both a hobby and a spectator sport. All this has helped to inspire a generation of American teenagers to pursue careers behind the stove—and in front of the camera.

▶ INFLUENCES ON MODERN FOOD SERVICE OPERATIONS

From Monsieur Boulanger's humble establishment, a great industry has grown. Today, almost 850,000 public dining facilities operate in the United States alone. The dramatic growth and diversification of the food service industry is due in part to the Industrial Revolution and the social and economic changes it wrought, including the introduction of new technologies, foods, concerns and consumers.

NEW TECHNOLOGIES

Technology has always had a profound effect on cooking. For example, the development of clay and, later, metal vessels that could contain liquids and withstand as well as conduct heat offered prehistoric cooks the opportunity to stew, make soups and porridge, pickle and brine foods and control fermentation. But it was not until the rapid technological advances fostered by the Industrial Revolution that anything approaching the modern kitchen was possible.

One of the most important advancements was the introduction of the cast-iron stove. Prior to the 19th century, most cooking was done on spits or grills or in cauldrons or pots set on or in a wood- or coal-burning hearth. Hearthside cooking did not lend itself well to the simultaneous preparation of many items or to items requiring constant and delicate attention. With the introduction of cast-iron stoves during the 1800s (first wood- and coal-burning; by midcentury, gas; and by the early 20th century, electric), cooks could more comfortably and safely approach the heat source and control its temperatures. They were also able to efficiently prepare and hold for later use or service a multitude of smaller amounts of items requiring different cooking methods or ingredients, a necessity at a restaurant simultaneously catering to different diners' demands.

Also of great importance were developments in food preservation and storage techniques. For thousands of years, food had been preserved by sun-drying, salting, smoking, pickling, sugar-curing or fermenting. Although useful, these procedures destroy or distort the appearance and flavor of most foods. By the early 19th century, preserving techniques that had minimal effect on appearance and flavor began to emerge. For example, by 1800, the Frenchman François Appert successfully "canned" foods by subjecting foods stored in sterilized glass jars to very high heat. An early mechanical refrigerator was developed by the mid-1800s; soon reliable iceboxes, refrigerators and, later, freezers were available. During the 20th century, freeze-drying, vacuum-packing and irradiation became common preservation techniques.

While advancements were being made in preservation and storage techniques, developments in transportation technology were also underway. During the 19th century, steam-powered ships and railroads were able to bring foods quickly to market from distant suppliers. Indeed, by the 1870s, Chicago meatpackers were routinely supplying Europe with beef from the western Great Plains. During the 20th century, temperature-controlled cargo ships, trains, trucks and airplanes all were used as part of an integrated worldwide food transportation network. Combined with dependable food preservation and storage techniques, improved transportation networks have freed chefs from seasonal and geographic limitations in their choice of foods and have expanded consumers' culinary horizons.

Engineering advancements also have facilitated or even eliminated much routine kitchen work. Since the start of the Industrial Revolution, chefs have come to rely increasingly on mechanical and motorized food processors, mixers and cutters as well as a wealth of sophisticated kitchen equipment such as high-carbon stainless steel knife blades, infrared thermometers and induction cooktops.

NEW FOODS

Modern food preservation, storage and transportation techniques have made both fresh and exotic foods regularly available to chefs and consumers.

Advancements in agriculture such as the switch from organic to chemical fertilizers and the introduction of pesticides and drought- or pest-resistant strains have resulted in increased yields of healthy crops. Traditional hybridization techniques and, more recently, genetic engineering have produced new or improved grains and, for better or for worse, fruits and vegetables that have a longer shelf life and are more amenable to mass-production handling, storage and transportation methods.

Likewise, advancements in animal husbandry and aquaculture have led to a more reliable supply of leaner meat, poultry and fish. Moreover, foods found traditionally only in the wild (for example, game, wild rice and many mushrooms) are now being raised commercially and are routinely available.

Food preservation and processing techniques have also led to the development of prepackaged, prepared convenience foods, some of which are actually quite good. After careful thought and testing, today's chef can rely on some of these products. Doing so allows greater flexibility and more time to devote to other preparations.

NEW CONCERNS

Consumer concerns about nutrition and diet have fueled changes in the food service industry. Obviously, what we eat affects our health. Adequate amounts of certain nutrients promote good health by preventing deficiencies; good nutrition

---

A VERY BIG BUSINESS INDEED

The National Restaurant Association, which closely monitors the economic impact of the U.S. food service industry, issued the following statistics for 2001:

- Daily food service industry sales averaged $1.1 billion; annual sales were approximately $400 billion.
- More than 54 billion meals were eaten in restaurants and school and work cafeterias.
- The food service industry claimed approximately 45 percent of the U.S. food dollar.
- More than 11 million people were employed in the industry, making it the second-largest employer after the government.
- One-third of all American adults have worked in the food service industry at some time during their lives.

also helps prevent chronic diseases and increases longevity. Chefs should provide their customers with nutritious foods.

The public has long been concerned about food safety. Federal, state and local governments have helped promote food safety by inspecting and grading meats and poultry, regulating label contents for packaged foods and setting sanitation standards. All these standards, especially sanitation standards, affect the way foods are prepared, stored and served.

Concerns about nutrition and food safety have also resulted in renewed interest in organically grown fruits and vegetables and free-range-raised animals.

NEW CONSUMERS

▶ **global cuisine** foods (often commercially produced items) or preparation methods that have become ubiquitous throughout the world; for example, curries and French-fried potatoes

▶ **national cuisine** the characteristic cuisine of a nation

▶ **regional cuisine** a set of recipes based upon local ingredients, traditions and practices; within a larger geographical, political, cultural or social unit, regional cuisines are often variations of one another that blend together to create a national cuisine

▶ **ethnic cuisine** the cuisine of a group of people having a common cultural heritage, as opposed to the cuisine of a group of people bound together by geography or political factors

Demographic and social changes have contributed to the diversification of the food service industry by creating or identifying new consumer groups with their own desires or needs. By tailoring their menu, prices and décor accordingly, food service operations can cater to consumers defined by age (baby boomers and seniors, in particular), type of household (singles, couples and families), income, education and geography.

Since World War II, there has also been a rapid increase in the number and types of institutions providing food services. These include hospitals, schools, retirement centers, hotels and resorts (which may in turn have fine dining, coffee shop, banquet and room service facilities), factories and office complexes. Each of these institutions presents the professional chef with unique challenges, whether they be culinary, dietary or budgetary.

Through travel or exposure to the many books and magazines about food, consumers are becoming better educated and more sophisticated. Educated consumers provide a market for new foods and cuisines as well as an appreciation for a job well done.

Although some consumers may frequent a particular restaurant because its chef or owner is a celebrity or the restaurant is riding high on a crest of fad or fashion, most consumers choose a restaurant—whether it be a fast-food burger place or an elegant French restaurant—because it provides quality food at a cost they are willing to pay. To remain successful, then, the restaurant must carefully balance its commitment to quality with marketplace realities.

▶ THE FOOD SERVICE OPERATION

▶ **brigade** a system of staffing a kitchen so that each worker is assigned a set of specific tasks; these tasks are often related by cooking method, equipment or the types of foods being produced

To function efficiently, a food service operation must be well organized and staffed with appropriate personnel. This staff is sometimes called a **brigade**. Although a chef will be most familiar with the back-of-the-house or kitchen brigade, he or she should also understand how the dining room or front of the house operates.

THE CLASSIC KITCHEN BRIGADE

Escoffier is credited with developing the kitchen brigade system used in large restaurant kitchens. From the chaos and redundancy found in the private kitchens of the aristocracy, he created a distinct hierarchy of responsibilities and functions for commercial food service operations.

At the top is the *chef de cuisine* or *chef*, who is responsible for all kitchen operations, developing menu items and setting the kitchen's tone and tempo.

His or her principal assistant is the *sous-chef* (the under chef or second chef), who is responsible for scheduling personnel and replacing the chef and station chefs as necessary. The *sous-chef* also often functions as the *aboyeur* (expediter or announcer), who accepts the orders from the dining room, relays them to the various station chefs and then reviews the dishes before service.

The *chefs de partie* (station chefs) produce the menu items and are under the direct supervision of the chef or *sous-chef*. Previously, whenever a cook needed an item, he or his assistants produced it; thus several cooks could be making the same sauce or basic preparation. Under Escoffier's system, each station chef is assigned a specific task based on either the cooking method and equipment or the category of items to be produced. They include the following:

▷ The *saucier* (sauté station chef), who holds one of the most demanding jobs in the kitchen, is responsible for all sautéed items and most sauces.

▷ The *poissonier* (fish station chef) is responsible for fish and shellfish items and their sauces. This position is occasionally combined with the sauce station.

▷ The *grillardin* (grill station chef) is responsible for all grilled items.

▷ The *friturier* (fry station chef) is responsible for all fried items.

▷ The *rotisseur* (roast station chef) is responsible for all roasted items and jus or other related sauces. The grill and fry stations are sometimes subsumed into the roast station.

▷ The *potager* (soup station chef) is responsible for soups and stocks.

▷ The *legumier* (vegetable station chef) is responsible for all vegetable and starch items.

▷ The *potager* and *legumier* functions are often combined into a single vegetable station whose chef is known as the *entremetier*. *Entremets* were the courses served after the roast and usually comprised vegetables, fruits, fritters or sweet items (the sorbet served before the main course in some contemporary restaurants is a vestigial *entremet*).

▷ The *garde-manger* (pantry chef) is responsible for cold food preparations, including salads and salad dressings, cold appetizers, charcuterie items, pâtés, terrines and similar dishes. The *garde-manger* supervises the *boucher* (butcher), who is responsible for butchering meats and poultry (fish and shellfish are usually fabricated by the fish station chef), as well as the chefs responsible for hors d'oeuvre and breakfast items.

▷ The *tournant*, also known as the roundsman or swing cook, works where needed.

▷ The *patissier* (pastry chef) is responsible for all baked items, including breads, pastries and desserts. Unlike the several station chefs, the *patissier* is not necessarily under the *sous-chef*'s direct supervision. The *patissier* supervises the *boulanger* (bread baker), who makes the breads, rolls and baked dough containers used for other menu items (for example, *bouchées* and *feuilletés*); the *confiseur*, who makes candies and petits fours; the *glacier*, who makes all chilled and frozen desserts; and the *decorateur*, who makes showpieces and special cakes.

▷ Depending upon the size and needs of any station or area, there are one or more *demi-chefs* (assistants) and *commis* (apprentices) who work with the station chef or pastry chef to learn the area.

THE MODERN KITCHEN BRIGADE

Today, most food service operations use a simplified version of Escoffier's kitchen brigade.

The **executive chef** coordinates kitchen activities and directs the kitchen staff's training and work efforts. The executive chef plans menus and creates recipes. He or she sets and enforces nutrition, safety and sanitation standards and participates in (or at least observes) the preparation and presentation of menu items to ensure that quality standards are rigorously and consistently maintained. He or she is also responsible for purchasing food items and, often, equipment. In some food service operations, the executive chef may assist in designing the menu, dining room and kitchen. He or she trains the dining room staff so that

THE DINING ROOM

Like the back-of-the-house (that is, kitchen) staff, the front-of-the-house (that is, dining room) staff is also organized into a brigade. A traditional dining room brigade is led by the **dining room manager** (French *maître d'hotel* or *maître d'*), who generally trains all service personnel, oversees wine selections and works with the chef to develop the menu. He or she organizes the seating chart and may also seat the guests. Working subordinate to him or her are:

- The **wine steward** (French *chef de vin* or *sommelier*), who is responsible for the wine service, including purchasing wines, assisting guests in selecting wines and serving the wines.
- The **headwaiter** (French *chef de salle*), who is responsible for service throughout the dining room or a section of it. In smaller operations, his or her role may be assumed by the *maître d'* or a captain.

- The **captains** (French *chefs d'étage*), who are responsible for explaining the menu to guests and taking their orders. They are also responsible for any tableside preparations.
- The **front waiters** (French *chefs de rang*), who are responsible for assuring that the tables are set properly for each course, foods are delivered properly to the proper tables and the needs of the guests are met.
- The **back waiters** (French *demi-chefs de rang* or *commis de rang*, also known as dining room attendants or buspersons), who are responsible for clearing plates, refilling water glasses and other general tasks appropriate for new dining room workers.

Whether a restaurant uses this entire array of staff depends upon the nature and size of the restaurant and the type of service provided. With **American service**, there is one waiter (also called a server) who takes the order and brings the food to the table. The table is then cleaned by a dining room attendant. With **French service**, there are two waiters: a captain and a waiter. The captain takes the order, does the tableside cooking and brings the drinks, appetizers, entrées and desserts to the table. The waiter serves bread and water, clears each course, crumbs the table and serves the coffee. With **Russian service**, the entrée, vegetables and potatoes are served from a platter onto a plate by the waiter. With **buffet service**, usually found in specialty restaurants and some institutional settings such as schools and correctional facilities, diners generally serve themselves or are served by workers assigned to specific areas of the buffet. Restaurants offering buffet service generally charge by the meal; if they charge by the dish, they are known as cafeterias.

they can correctly answer questions about the menu. He or she may also work with food purveyors to learn about new food items and products, as well as with catering directors, equipment vendors, food stylists, restaurant consultants, public relations specialists, sanitation engineers, nutritionists and dietitians.

The executive chef is assisted by a **sous-chef** or **executive sous-chef**, who participates in, supervises and coordinates the preparation of menu items. His or her primary responsibility is to make sure that the food is prepared, portioned, garnished and presented according to the executive chef's standards. The sous-chef may be the cook principally responsible for producing menu items and supervising the kitchen.

Large hotels and conference centers with multiple dining facilities may have one or more **area chefs**, each responsible for a specific facility or function. There could be, for instance, a restaurant chef and a banquet chef. Area chefs usually report to the executive chef. Each area chef, in turn, has a brigade working under him or her.

Like Escoffier's station chefs, **line cooks** (or section cooks) are responsible for preparing menu items according to recipe specifications. Making the most of time, talent, space and equipment, the chef assigns responsibilities to each of the line cooks.

The **pastry chef** is responsible for developing recipes for and preparing desserts, pastries, frozen desserts and breads. He or she is usually responsible for purchasing the food items used in the bakeshop.

And, as in Escoffier's days, **assistants** and **apprentices** are assigned where needed in today's kitchens.

New styles of dining have created new positions since Escoffier's days. The most notable is the **short-order cook**, who is responsible for quickly preparing foods to order in smaller operations. He or she will work the broiler, deep-fat fryer and griddle as well as make sandwiches and even some sautéed items. Another is the **institutional cook**, who generally works with large quantities of prepackaged or prepared foods for a captive market such as a school, hospital or prison.

▶ THE PROFESSIONAL CHEF

Although there is no one recipe for producing a good professional chef, we believe that with knowledge, skill, taste, judgment, dedication and pride a student chef will mature into a professional chef.

KNOWLEDGE

Chefs must be able to identify, purchase, utilize and prepare a wide variety of foods. They should be able to train and supervise a safe, skilled and efficient staff. To do all this successfully, chefs must possess a body of knowledge and understand and apply certain scientific and business principles. Schooling helps. A professional culinary program should, at a minimum, provide the student chef with a basic knowledge of foods, food styles and the methods used to prepare foods. Student chefs should also have an understanding of sanitation, nutrition and business procedures such as food costing.

This book is designed to help you learn these basics. Many chapters have extensive sections identifying foods and equipment. Throughout this book, we emphasize culinary principles, not recipes. Whenever possible, whether it be preparing puff pastry or grilling a steak, we focus on the general procedure, highlighting fundamental principles and skills; we discuss both the how and why of cooking. Only then are specific applications and sample recipes given. We also want you to have a sense of the rich tradition of cookery, so informative sidebars on food history, chef biographies and other topics are scattered throughout the book.

In this way, we follow the trail blazed by Escoffier, who wrote in the introduction to *Le Guide culinaire* that his book is not intended to be a compendium of recipes slavishly followed, but rather his treatise should be a tool that leaves his colleagues "free to develop their own methods and follow their own inspiration; . . . the art of cooking . . . will evolve as a society evolves, . . . only basic rules remain unalterable."

As with any profession, an education does not stop at graduation. The acquisition of knowledge continues after the student chef joins the ranks of the employed. He or she should take additional classes on unique or ethnic cuisines, nutrition, business management or specialized skills. He or she should regularly review some of the many periodicals and books devoted to cooking, should travel and should try new dishes to broaden his or her culinary horizons. The professional chef should also become involved in professional organizations (see Appendix I) in order to meet his or her peers and exchange ideas.

SKILL

Culinary schooling alone does not make a student a chef. Nothing but practical, hands-on experience will provide even the most academically gifted student with the skills needed to produce, consistently and efficiently, quality foods or to organize, train, motivate and supervise a staff.

Many food service operations recognize that new workers, even those who have graduated from culinary programs, need time and experience to develop and hone their skills. Therefore, many graduates start in entry-level positions. Do not be discouraged; advancement will come, and the training pays off in the long run. Today, culinary styles and fashions change frequently. What does not go out of fashion are well-trained, skilled and knowledgeable chefs. They can adapt.

TASTE

No matter how knowledgeable or skilled the chef, he or she must be able to produce foods that taste great, or the consumer will not return. A chef can do so only if he or she is confident about his or her own sense of taste.

ON TASTE

Taste is composed of about ten thousand compounds. When we think of taste, we normally think in terms of the language we are familiar with and the foods we grew up with. The structure of our taste is formed very early, basically when we start eating baby food. As Westerners, we divide taste into four major groups: sweet, salty, bitter and sour. The Chinese include a fifth, hot (spicy), and Southeast Asians add aromatic and pungent. So there are actually seven or more types. Americans, however, largely rely on sweet and salty. They don't use sour and bitter very much. They certainly don't use hot very much. Nor do they use aromatic or strong pungent things like fish paste very often. We really use only about 30 percent of our palate. To compare this to sight, it's as if we are colorblind, unable to perceive and enjoy fully five out of every seven colors we see. This is why we sometimes have trouble "acquiring" a taste for ethnic foods.

Westerners have a lineal palate, which is set up on sweet and salty with very few counterpoints and harmonies. For instance, if you eat in the European manner, you usually begin with an appetizer, which may be salty or hot. Then you have soup, then a fish course, then a meat course, then a sweet. You are using different parts of your palate, but one after another, or linearly. Asian cuisines, however, use sweet, hot, bitter and sour at the same time. You're eating circularly. The meal is not a lineal progress to some point, like dessert. You may have already had fruit or a sweet in the meal, which is a much more satisfying and actually much more healthy way to eat. European food, like European art, is more concerned with finished form. Most ethnic things are concerned with process and expression.

You must train your mind to go after flavor characteristics and become involved in the process of eating. You must look for flavors in different parts of your mouth. Think about how quickly flavors appear in the mouth and how long the flavors are. Think about the finish. You must develop a very good sensitivity to the finish of the product; otherwise, you overseason and lose the compositional balance.

MARK MILLER, Chef/Owner, Red Sage, Washington, D.C.,
and Coyote Cafe, Santa Fe, NM

▶ **gastronomy** the art and science of eating well

▶ **gourmet** a connoisseur of fine food and drink

▶ **gourmand** a connoisseur of fine food and drink, often to excess

▶ **gourmet foods** foods of the highest quality, perfectly prepared and beautifully presented

Our total perception of taste is a complex combination of smell, taste, sight, sound and texture. All senses are involved in the enjoyment of eating; all must be considered in creating or preparing a dish. The chef should develop a taste memory by sampling foods, both familiar and unfamiliar. The chef should also think about what he or she tastes, making notes and experimenting with flavor combinations and cooking methods. But a chef should not be inventive simply for the sake of invention. Rather, he or she must consider how the flavors, appearances, textures and aromas of various foods will interact to create a total taste experience.

JUDGMENT

Selecting menu items, determining how much of what item to order, deciding whether and how to combine ingredients and approving finished items for service are all matters of judgment. Although knowledge and skill play a role in developing judgment, sound judgment comes only with experience. And real experience is often accompanied by failure. Do not be upset or surprised when a dish does not turn out as you expected. Learn from your mistakes as well as from your successes; only then will you develop sound judgment.

DEDICATION

Becoming a chef is hard work; so is being one. The work is often physically taxing, the hours are usually long and the pace is frequently hectic. Despite these pressures, the chef is expected to efficiently produce consistently fine foods that are properly prepared, seasoned, garnished and presented. To do so, the chef must be dedicated to the job.

The dedicated chef should never falter. The food service industry is competitive and depends upon the continuing goodwill of an often fickle public. One bad dish or one off night can result in a disgruntled diner and lost business. The chef should always be mindful of the food prepared and the customer served.

The chef must also be dedicated to his or her staff. Virtually all food service operations rely on teamwork to get the job done well. Good teamwork requires a positive attitude and dedication to a shared goal.

PRIDE

Not only is it important that the job be well done, but the professional chef should have a sense of pride in doing it well. Pride should also extend to personal appearance and behavior in and around the kitchen. The professional chef should be well-groomed and in uniform when working.

The professional chef's uniform consists of comfortable shoes, trousers (either solid white, solid black, black-and-white checked or black-and-white striped), a white double-breasted jacket, an apron and a neckerchief usually knotted or tied cravat style. The uniform has certain utilitarian aspects: Checked trousers disguise stains; the double-breasted white jacket can be rebuttoned to hide dirt, and the double layer of fabric protects from scalds and burns; the neckerchief absorbs facial perspiration; and the apron protects the uniform and insulates the body. This uniform should be worn with pride. Shoes should be polished; trousers and jacket should be pressed.

The crowning element of the uniform is the toque. A toque is the tall white hat worn by chefs almost everywhere. Although the toque traces its origin to the monasteries of the 6th century, the style worn today was introduced at the end of the 19th century. Most chefs now wear a standard six- or nine-inch-high toque, but historically, a cook's rank in the kitchen dictated the type of hat worn. Beginners wore flat-topped calottes; cooks with more advanced skills wore low toques and the master chefs wore high toques called dodin-bouffants. Culinary lore holds that the toque's pleats—101 in all—represent the 101 ways its wearer can successfully prepare eggs.

CONCLUSION

The art and science of cookery form a noble profession with a rich history and long traditions. With knowledge, skill, taste, judgment, dedication and pride, the student chef can become part of this profession. In this book, we provide you with the basic knowledge and describe the techniques in which you must become skilled. Dedicate yourself to learning this information and mastering your skills. Once you have done so, take pride in your accomplishments. Good luck.

QUESTIONS FOR DISCUSSION

1 Describe the kitchen brigade system. What is its significance in today's professional kitchens?

2 What are the roles of a chef, sous-chef and line cook in a modern kitchen?

3 Describe the differences in a meal prepared by Carême and one prepared by Point.

4 List and explain three technological advances affecting food preparation.

5 Discuss the societal changes that have contributed to diversification in the modern food service industry.

6 The newspapers in most large cities publish restaurant reviews. Use the Internet to find restaurant reviews from a city other than the one in which you live. Select one or two restaurants where you would like to dine the next time you visit that city. Why did you select these particular establishments?

7 The James Beard Foundation recognizes and honors outstanding American chefs each year. Who was James Beard? Which chefs are currently considered some of the most outstanding in the United States? Why?

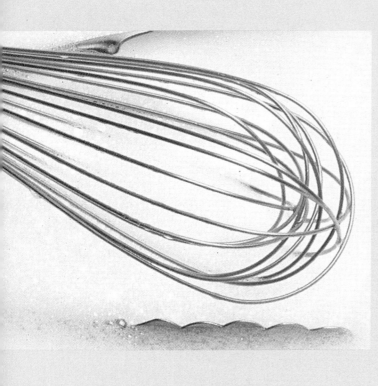

OUR LIVES ARE NOT IN THE LAP OF THE GODS, BUT IN THE LAP OF OUR COOKS.

—Lin Yutang, Chinese-American writer, in The Importance of Living, *1937*

2

FOOD SAFETY AND SANITATION

AFTER STUDYING THIS CHAPTER, YOU WILL BE ABLE TO:

▶ identify the causes of food-borne illnesses

▶ handle foods in a safe manner

▶ explain and follow a HACCP system

▶ take appropriate actions to create and maintain a safe and sanitary working environment

The U.S. Public Health Service identifies more than 40 diseases that can be transmitted through food. Many can cause serious illness; some are even deadly. Therefore, providing consumers with safe food is the food handler's most important responsibility. Unfortunately, food handlers are also the primary cause of food-related illnesses.

By understanding what causes food-borne illnesses and what can be done to prevent them, you will be better able to protect your customers. This chapter, however, is not meant to be a complete discussion of sanitation in food service operations. But it should alert you to practices that can result in food-borne illnesses.

Federal, state, county and municipal health, building and other codes are designed in part to ensure that food is handled in a safe and proper manner. Always consult your local health department for information and guidance. And always be conscious of what you can do to create and maintain a safe product as well as a safe environment for your customers, your fellow employees and yourself.

▶ **biological hazard** a danger to the safety of food caused by disease-causing microorganisms such as bacteria, molds, yeasts, viruses or fungi

▶ **chemical hazard** a danger to the safety of food caused by chemical substances, especially cleaning agents, pesticides and toxic metals

▶ **physical hazard** a danger to the safety of food caused by particles such as glass chips, metal shavings, bits of wood or other foreign matter

Sanitation refers to the creation and maintenance of conditions that will prevent food contamination or food-borne illness. **Contamination** refers to the presence, generally unintended, of harmful organisms or substances. Contaminants can be (1) biological, (2) chemical or (3) physical. When consumed in sufficient quantities, food-borne contaminants can cause illness or injury, long-lasting disease or even death.

Contamination occurs in two ways: direct contamination and cross-contamination. **Direct contamination** is the contamination of raw foods, or the plants or animals from which they come, in their natural settings or habitats. Chemical and biological contaminants such as bacteria and fungi are present in the air, soil and water. So foods can be easily contaminated by their general exposure to the environment: Grains can become contaminated by soil fumigants in the field, and shellfish can become contaminated by ingesting toxic marine algae.

Chemicals and microorganisms generally cannot move on their own, however. They need to be transported, an event known as **cross-contamination**. The major cause of cross-contamination is people. Food handlers can transfer biological, chemical and physical contaminants to food while processing, preparing, cooking or serving it. It is therefore necessary to view sanitation as the correction of problems caused by direct contamination and the prevention of problems caused by cross-contamination during processing and service.

▶ DIRECT CONTAMINATION

BIOLOGICAL CONTAMINANTS

▶ **microorganisms** single-celled organisms as well as tiny plants and animals that can be seen only through a microscope

Several **microorganisms**, primarily bacteria, parasites, viruses and fungi, can cause biologically based food-borne illnesses. By understanding how these organisms live and reproduce, you can better understand how to protect food from them.

BACTERIA

Bacteria, which are single-celled microorganisms, are the leading cause of food-borne illnesses. See Figure 2.1. Some bacteria are beneficial, such as those that aid in digesting food or decomposing garbage. Other bacteria spoil food, but without rendering it unfit for human consumption. These bacteria, called **putre-factives**, are not a sanitation concern. (Indeed, in some cultures, they are not even a culinary concern. Cultures differ on what constitutes "bad" meat, for example, and game is sometimes hung for a time to allow bacteria to grow.) The bacteria that are dangerous when consumed by humans are called **pathogenic**. These bacteria must be destroyed or controlled in a food service operation.

Most bacteria reproduce by binary fission: Their genetic material is first duplicated and the nucleus then splits, each new nucleus taking some of the cellular material with it. See Figure 2.2. Under favorable conditions each bacterium can divide every 15–30 minutes. Within 12 hours, one bacterium can become a colony of 72 billion bacteria, more than enough to cause serious illness.

Some rod-shaped bacteria are capable of forming spores. Spores are thick-walled structures used as protection against a hostile environment. The bacteria essentially hibernate within their spores, where they can survive extreme conditions that would otherwise destroy them. When conditions become favorable, the bacteria return to a viable state. This is important in food sanitation because heating or sanitizing techniques may not destroy bacterial spores.

Intoxications and Infections

Depending upon the particular microorganism, pathogenic bacteria can cause illnesses in humans in one of three ways: by intoxication, infection or toxin-mediated infection. See Table 2.1.

Botulism is a well-known example of an **intoxication**. Certain bacteria produce **toxins**, byproducts of their life processes. You cannot smell, see or taste toxins. Ingesting these toxin-producing bacteria by themselves does not cause illness. But when their toxins are ingested, the toxins can poison the consumer. Proper food-handling techniques are critical in preventing an intoxication because even if a food is cooked to a sufficiently high temperature to kill all bacteria present, the toxins they leave behind are usually not destroyed.

The second type of bacterial illness is an **infection**. Salmonella is an especially well-known example. An infection occurs when live pathogenic bacteria (infectants) are ingested. The bacteria then live in the consumer's intestinal tract.

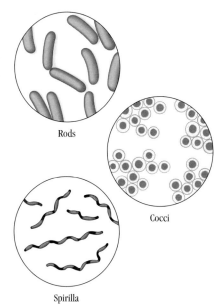

FIGURE 2.1 ▶ Bacteria can be classified by shape: Rods are short, tubular structures; cocci are discs, some of which form clusters; and spirilla are corkscrews.

▶ **pathogen** any organism that causes disease; usually refers to bacteria

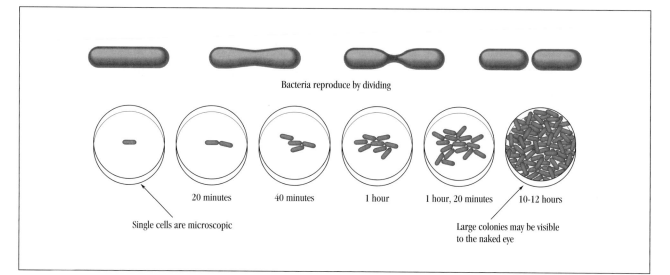

FIGURE 2.2 ▶ One bacterium divides into two; the two bacteria each divide, creating four; the four become 16 and so on. It takes only a very short time for one bacterium to produce millions more.

Table 2.1 CHARACTERISTICS OF BACTERIAL ILLNESSES

COMMON NAME	ORGANISM	FORM	COMMON SOURCES	PREVENTION
Staph	*Staphylococcus aureus*	Toxin	Starchy foods, cold meats, bakery items, custards, milk products, humans with infected wounds or sores	Wash hands and utensils before use; exclude unhealthy food handlers; avoid having foods at room temperature
Perfringens or CP	*Clostridium perfringens*	Cells and toxin	Reheated meats, sauces, stews, casseroles	Keep cooked foods at an internal temperature of 140°F (60°C) or higher; reheat leftovers to an internal temperature of 165°F (74°C) or higher
Botulism	*Clostridium botulinum*	Toxin, cells, spores	Cooked foods held for an extended time at warm temperatures with limited oxygen, rice, potatoes, smoked fish, canned vegetables	Keep cooked foods at an internal temperature of 140°F (60°C) or higher or 40°F (4°C) or lower; reheat leftovers thoroughly; discard swollen cans
Salmonella	*Salmonella*	Cells	Poultry, eggs, milk, meats, fecal contamination	Thoroughly cook all meat, poultry, fish and eggs; avoid cross-contamination with raw foods; maintain good personal hygiene
Strep	*Streptococcus*	Cells	Infected food handlers	Do not allow employees to work if ill; protect foods from customers' coughs and sneezes
E. coli or 0157	*Escherichia coli* 0157:H7 (enteropathogenic strains)	Cells and toxins	Any food, especially raw milk, raw vegetables, raw or rare beef, humans	Thoroughly cook or reheat items
Listeria	*Listeria monocytogenes*	Cells	Milk products, humans, deli meats	Avoid raw milk and cheese made from unpasteurized milk; keep storage areas clean

POTENTIALLY HAZARDOUS FOODS

A potentially hazardous food (PHF) is any food or food ingredient that will support the rapid growth of infectious or toxigenic microorganisms, or the slower growth of *Clostridium botulinum*. Potentially hazardous foods include the following:

- Food from an animal source (for example, meat, fish, shellfish, poultry, milk and eggs)
- Food from a plant that has been heat-treated (for example, cooked rice, beans, potatoes, soy products and pasta)
- Raw seed sprouts
- Cut melons
- Garlic in oil mixtures that are not acidified or otherwise appropriately modified at a processing plant
- Foods containing any of the preceding items (for example, custards, sauces and casseroles)

It is the living bacteria, not their waste products, that cause an illness. Infectants must be alive when eaten for them to do any harm. Fortunately, these bacteria can be destroyed by cooking foods to sufficiently high temperatures, usually 165°F (74°C) or higher.

The third type of bacterial illness has characteristics of both an intoxication and an infection, and is referred to as a **toxin-mediated infection**. Examples are *Clostridium perfringens* and *Escherichia coli* 0157:H7. When these living organisms are ingested, they establish colonies in human or animal intestinal tracts where they then produce toxins. These bacteria are particularly dangerous for young children, the elderly and the infirm.

Preventing Bacterial Intoxications and Infections

All bacteria, like other living things, need certain conditions in order to complete their life cycles. Like humans, they need food, a comfortable temperature, moisture, the proper pH, the proper atmosphere and time. The best way to prevent bacterial intoxications and infections is to attack the factors bacteria need to survive and multiply.

FOOD   Bacteria need food for energy and growth. The foods on which bacteria thrive are referred to as **potentially hazardous foods (PHF)**. They are generally high in protein and include animal-based products, cooked grains and some cooked vegetables. These foods and items containing these foods must be handled with great care.

THE FOOD-BORNE ILLNESS CRISIS IN AMERICA

America is confronted with a food-related health crisis of unprecedented proportions. The Centers for Disease Control and Prevention (CDC) have estimated that there are some 76 million incidents of food-related illness in the United States annually. Of these, an estimated 325,000 Americans are hospitalized and 5,000 die each year. Yet most Americans are unaware of this crisis and, indeed, many who suffer from food poisoning are not even aware of the cause. Symptoms may take a week or longer to appear, and victims frequently incorrectly attribute the distress and discomfort to stomach flu. It is not until the victims' afflictions become acute that tests are taken to determine the real cause. For those at risk—children, the elderly and anyone with a compromised immune system—this is frequently too late and the consequences can be deadly.

In his best-selling book, *Fast Food Nation*, Eric Schlosser points out that one cause for this increase in food-borne illnesses is the vast expansion of the meat-packing industry due to increased demand from the fast-food industry. Indeed, recent *E. coli* outbreaks have been traced to meat processors' operations, just as *Salmonella* has increasingly been traced to poultry operations.

While the health problems that Schlosser raises are important and should not be glossed over, they should not be exaggerated either. The Food Safety and Inspection Service (FSIS), a branch of the U.S. Department of Agriculture (USDA), has tested more than 26,000 samples of ground beef since 1996. Of these, only 25 tested positive for *E. coli* and none of these samples were associated with any outbreak of illness. Even if health problems in the meat-packing industry were somehow solved tomorrow, food-borne illnesses would likely still be on the rise. The Government Accounting Office has estimated that 85 percent of food-borne illnesses comes from fruits, vegetables, seafood and cheeses—not meat or poultry.

Schlosser also raises concerns about the fat and nutritional content of the food served in fast-food establishments. Obesity and high cholesterol can cause health problems, and consuming vast quantities of fast food can contribute to potential illness. However, for most Americans an occasional trip to McDonald's is not hazardous to their health. It just depends on the rest of their diet. And popular images to the contrary, fast-food establishments have a good record of cleanliness when compared with other restaurants—and particularly when compared with home kitchens.

In fact, food safety experts have concluded that the home is the number one place where food-borne illnesses originate. Indeed, most home kitchens would not pass food inspections that public facilities regularly pass with flying colors. And most cases of illnesses caused by *E. coli* and *Salmonella*, even those originating at meat and poultry packers, could have been averted if home cooks had followed basic health procedures: properly storing meat and poultry, frequently washing their hands, promptly disinfecting all areas touched by raw meat or poultry and correctly cooking foods at the appropriate high temperatures for the appropriate period of time.

Of course, food inspections need to be increased and conditions improved at some meat and poultry packing plants. However, while blaming particular elements in the food system may bring visibility to serious problems, contamination can occur at many points along the way in the food system. If this food-related health crisis is to be controlled, it must be approached systemically from the farm to the fork.

ANDREW F. SMITH teaches culinary history at the New School University and is the author of eight books on culinary topics. He is editor-in-chief of the forthcoming *Oxford Encyclopedia of American Food and Drink*.

TEMPERATURE Temperature is the most important factor in the pathogenic bacteria's environment because it is the factor most easily controlled by food service workers. Most microorganisms are destroyed at high temperatures. Freezing slows but does not stop growth, nor does it destroy bacteria.

Most bacteria that cause food-borne illnesses multiply rapidly at temperatures between 60°F and 120°F (16°C and 49°C). Therefore, the broad range of temperatures between 40°F and 140°F (4°C and 60°C) is referred to as the **temperature danger zone**. See Figure 2.3. By keeping foods out of the temperature danger zone, you decrease the bacteria's ability to thrive and reproduce.

To control the growth of any bacteria that may be present, it is important to maintain the internal temperature of food at 140°F (60°C) or above or 40°F (4°C) or below. Simply stated: *Keep hot foods hot and cold foods cold.* Potentially hazardous foods should be heated or cooled quickly so that they are within the temperature danger zone as briefly as possible. This is known as the **time-and-temperature principle**.

Keep hot foods hot. The high internal temperatures reached during proper cooking kill most of the bacteria that can cause food-borne illnesses. (See Table 2.2.) When foods are reheated, the internal temperature should quickly reach or exceed 165°F (74°C) in order to kill any bacteria that may have grown during storage. Once properly heated, hot foods must be held at temperatures of 140°F (60°C) or above. Foods that are to be displayed or served hot must be heated

THE TEMPERATURE DANGER ZONE

The temperature danger zone is a broad range of temperatures in which most of the bacteria that cause food-borne illnesses multiply rapidly. The *2001 Model Food Code* of the Food and Drug Administration (FDA) indicates that the temperature danger zone begins at 41°F (5°C) and ends at 140°F (60°C). Regulations in some localities state that the danger zone begins at 45°F (7°C) or ends at 130°F (54°C), however. Here we use the broader range recommended by the U.S. Department of Agriculture (USDA)—40°F to 140°F (4°C to 60°C)—since this provides a slightly greater margin of safety.

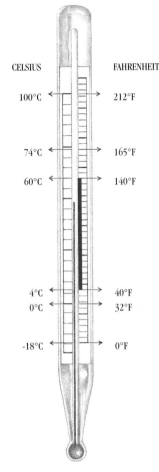

CELSIUS   FAHRENHEIT

100°C ←→ 212°F

74°C ←→ 165°F

60°C ←→ 140°F

4°C ←→ 40°F
0°C ←→ 32°F

-18°C ←→ 0°F

FIGURE 2.3 ▶ **The temperature danger zone**

rapidly to reduce the time within the temperature danger zone. When heating or reheating foods:

▷ Heat small quantities at a time.
▷ Stir frequently.
▷ Heat foods as close to service time as possible.
▷ Use preheated ingredients whenever possible to prepare hot foods.
▷ Never use a steam table for heating or reheating foods. Bring reheated food to an appropriate internal temperature (at least 165°F/74°C) before placing it in the steam table for holding.

Keep cold foods cold. Foods that are to be displayed, stored or served cold must be cooled rapidly. When cooling foods:

▷ Refrigerate semisolid foods at 40°F (4°C) or below in containers that are less than 2 inches deep. (Increased surface area decreases cooling time.)
▷ Avoid crowding the refrigerator; allow air to circulate around foods.
▷ Vent hot foods in an ice-water bath, as illustrated in Chapter 11, Stocks and Sauces.
▷ Prechill ingredients such as mayonnaise before preparing cold foods.
▷ Store cooked foods above raw foods to prevent cross-contamination.

Keep frozen foods frozen. Freezing at 0°F (−18°C) or below essentially stops bacterial growth but will not kill the bacteria. Do not place hot foods in a standard freezer. This will not cool the food any faster, and the release of heat can raise the temperature of other foods in the freezer. Only a special blast freezer can be used for chilling hot items. If one is not available, cool hot foods as mentioned earlier before freezing them. When frozen foods are thawed, bacteria that are present will begin to grow. Therefore:

▷ Never thaw foods at room temperature.
▷ Thaw foods gradually under refrigeration to maintain the food's temperature at 40°F (4°C) or less. Place thawing foods in a container to prevent cross-contamination from dripping or leaking liquids.
▷ Thaw foods under running water at a temperature of 70°F (21°C) or cooler.
▷ Thaw foods in a microwave only if the food will be prepared and served immediately.

TIME When bacteria are moved from one place to another, they require time to adjust to new conditions. This resting period, during which very little growth occurs, is known as the **lag phase** and may last from one to four hours. It is followed by the **log phase**, a period of accelerated growth, and then by the **stationary phase**, which lasts until the bacteria begin to crowd others within their colony, creating competition for food, space and moisture. This begins the **decline** or **negative growth phase**, during which bacteria die at an accelerated rate. See Figure 2.4.

Because of the lag phase, foods can be in the temperature danger zone for *very short periods* during preparation without an unacceptable increase in bacterial growth. Exposure to the temperature danger zone is cumulative, however, and should not exceed four hours total. The less time food is in the temperature danger zone, the less opportunity bacteria have to multiply.

MOISTURE Bacteria need a certain amount of moisture, which is expressed as water activity or A_w. Water it-

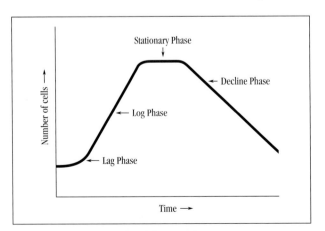

FIGURE 2.4 ▶ **Bacterial growth curve**

TABLE 2.2   RECOMMENDED INTERNAL COOKING TEMPERATURES

PRODUCT	TEMPERATURE
Beef, veal or lamb steaks, chops and roasts	Cook to 145°F/63°C
Egg dishes	Cook to 160°F/71°C; if the dish is uncooked, use only pasteurized eggs
Eggs	Cook until the yolk and white are firm OR cook to 145°F/63°C for 15 seconds if prepared for a customer's immediate order*
Fish	Cook until opaque and flakes easily OR cook to 145°F/63°C for 15 seconds*
Game, commercial	Cook to 165°F/74°C
Ground beef, veal, pork or lamb	Cook to 160°F/71°C
Ground turkey or chicken	Cook to 165°F/74°C
Pork, ham and bacon	Cook to 145°F/63°C for 15 seconds*
Poultry	Cook to 180°F/82°C (in thigh); 170°F/77°C (in breast)
Ratites and injected meats (commercially flavored with marinade or brine)	Cook to 155°F/68°C for 15 seconds*
Shellfish	Cook until opaque and firm; shells should open
Stuffing, stuffed meat, stuffed pasta and casseroles	Cook to 165°F/74°C

SOURCE: USDA Food Safety and Inspection Service
*FDA 2001 Model Food Code

self has an A_w of 1.0. Any food with an A_w of 0.85 or greater is considered potentially hazardous. Bacteria cannot flourish where the A_w is too low, usually below 0.85. This explains why dry foods such as flour, sugar or crackers are rarely subject to bacterial infestations. A low A_w only halts bacterial growth, however; it does not kill the microorganisms. When dried foods such as beans or rice are rehydrated, any bacteria present can flourish and the food may become potentially hazardous.

ACID/ALKALI BALANCE   Bacteria are affected by the **pH** of their environment. Although they can survive in a wider range, they prefer a neutral environment with a pH of 6.6 to 7.5. Growth is usually halted if the pH is 4.6 or less. So acidic foods such as lemon juice, tomatoes and vinegar create an unfavorable environment for bacteria. Simply adding an acidic ingredient to foods should not, however, be relied upon to destroy bacteria or preserve foods. The amount of acidity appropriate for flavoring is not sufficient to ensure the destruction of bacteria.

▶ **pH** a measurement of the acid or alkali content of a solution, expressed on a scale of 0 to 14.0. A pH of 7.0 is considered neutral or balanced. The lower the pH value, the more acidic the substance. The higher the pH value, the more alkaline the substance.

ATMOSPHERE   Bacteria need an appropriate atmosphere. Some bacteria, known as **aerobic**, thrive on oxygen, whereas others, known as **anaerobic**, cannot survive in its presence. Still others, known as **facultative**, can adapt and will survive with or without oxygen. Unfortunately, most pathogenic bacteria are facultative.

Canning, which creates an anaerobic atmosphere, destroys bacteria that need oxygen. But it also creates a favorable atmosphere for anaerobic and facultative bacteria. A complete vacuum need not be formed for anaerobic bacteria to thrive, however. A tight foil covering, a complete layer of fat, even a well-fitting lid can create an atmosphere sufficiently devoid of oxygen to permit the growth of anaerobic bacteria.

PARASITES

Parasites are tiny organisms that depend on nutrients from a living host to complete their life cycle. Animals, poultry, fish, shellfish and humans can all play host to parasites. Several types of very small parasitic worms can enter an

MAD COW DISEASE

During the past several years, medical authorities have found links between a disease in cattle called **bovine spongiform encephalopathy** (**BSE**, popularly known as "mad cow disease") and an extremely rare disease in humans called **new variant Creutzfeldt-Jakob disease** (**nvCJD**). Both BSE and nvCJD are slowly degenerative and invariably fatal diseases affecting the central nervous system. Researchers know that these diseases have unusually long incubation periods, but do not know exactly what causes them. They believe that BSE is spread in cattle through feed that has been made, in part, with processed ingredients from slaughtered animals that carried the unknown infectious agent. They also believe that nvCJD is probably contracted by eating meat or other products processed from infected animals. So far, the worst of the known BSE outbreaks has been confined to Europe, principally Great Britain, and even there only a few people have been diagnosed with nvCJD.

There have been no reported cases of BSE or nvCJD in the United States. For more than a decade, federal authorities have restricted the importation of certain species of live animals and products derived from them originating in countries suffering or suspected of suffering from outbreaks of BSE. They also actively monitor American meat-packing facilities for any signs of BSE in cattle waiting to be slaughtered, and long ago banned the sale of the type of feed associated with BSE in Europe.

Responsible government and nongovernmental authorities continue to assure the American public that it is safe to eat American beef.

animal through contaminated feed, then settle in the host's intestinal tract or muscles, where they grow and reproduce.

Trichinosis is caused by eating undercooked meat (usually game or pork) infected with trichina larvae. Although trichinosis has been virtually eradicated by grain-feeding hogs and testing them before slaughter, some cases still occur each year. Traditionally, it was thought that pork must be cooked to internal temperatures of 170°F (77°C) or higher to eradicate the larvae. This generally resulted in a dry, tough product. Scientists have now determined that trichina larvae are killed if held at 137°F (58°C) for 10 seconds. The FDA currently recommends cooking pork products to an internal temperature of 145°F (63°C) or above for 15 seconds. The National Livestock and Meat Board and the USDA recommend cooking all pork products to 160°F (71°C), however.

Anisakiasis is another illness caused by parasitic roundworms. *Anisakis* worms reside in the organs of fish, especially bottom feeders or those taken from contaminated waters. Raw or undercooked fish are most often implicated in anisakiasis. Fish should be thoroughly cleaned immediately after being caught so that the parasites do not have an opportunity to spread. Thorough cooking to a minimum internal temperature of 140°F (60°C) is the only way to destroy the larvae since they can survive even highly acidic marinades.

Cyclospora infections are caused by a single-celled parasite found in water or food contaminated by infected feces. Produce from undeveloped countries is a common source of *Cyclospora* parasites, as is untreated water. Avoiding such products is the best prevention method.

VIRUSES

Viruses cause other biologically based food-borne illnesses such as hepatitis A and the Norwalk virus. Viruses are among the smallest known forms of life. They invade the living cells of a host, take over those cells' genetic material, and cause the cells to produce more viruses.

Viruses do not require a host to survive, however. They can survive—but not multiply—while lying on any food or food contact surface. Unlike bacteria, viruses can be present on any food, not just a potentially hazardous food. The food or food contact surface simply becomes a means of transportation between hosts.

Unlike bacteria, viruses are not affected by the water activity, pH or oxygen content of their environment. Some, however, can be destroyed by temperatures higher than 176°F (80°C). Basically, the only way to prevent food-borne viral illnesses is to prevent contamination in the first place.

FOOT-AND-MOUTH DISEASE

Although humans are not susceptible to **foot-and-mouth disease** (**FMD**; also known as hoof-and-mouth disease), it could have a severe impact on our food supply. Foot-and-mouth disease affects animals with cloven hooves such as cattle, swine, sheep, goats and deer. Nearly 100 percent of the animals exposed to the virus ultimately become infected. The disease is rarely fatal, but those that survive are often debilitated and experience severe loss in milk or meat production.

Fortunately, there has not been a reported case of FMD in the United States for more than 70 years. But in recent years, there has been an FMD epidemic in Europe. Hundreds of thousands of cattle, pigs and sheep have been destroyed. Milk and meat production has declined and farmers and meat packers are suffering tremendous economic loses.

The U.S. government is taking steps to ensure that a similar outbreak does not take place here. It has temporarily prohibited the importation of certain animals and animal products from countries with infected animal populations. In addition, as the FMD virus can be transported by humans and on their clothes and possessions, travelers from countries with infected animal populations are prohibited from bringing with them most agricultural products, and they and their possessions can be subjected to varying degrees of decontamination procedures.

Hepatitis A often enters the food supply through shellfish harvested from polluted waters. The virus is carried by humans, some of whom may never know they are infected, and is transmitted by poor personal hygiene and cross-contamination. The actual source of contamination may be hard to establish, though, because it sometimes takes months for symptoms to appear.

The **Norwalk virus** is spread almost entirely by poor personal hygiene among infected food handlers. The virus is found in human feces, contaminated water or vegetables fertilized by manure. The virus can be destroyed by high cooking temperatures but not by sanitizing solutions or freezing. In fact, the Norwalk virus has even been found in ice cubes.

Foods most likely to transmit viral diseases are those that are not heated after handling. These include salads, sandwiches, milk, baked products, uncooked fish and shellfish and sliced meats. The best techniques for avoiding viral food-borne illnesses are to observe good personal hygiene habits, avoid cross-contamination and use only foods obtained from reputable sources.

FUNGI

Fungi are a large group of plants ranging from single-celled organisms to giant mushrooms. Fungi are everywhere: in the soil, air and water. Poisonous mushrooms, a type of fungus, can cause illness or death if consumed. The most common fungi, however, are molds and yeasts.

Molds

Molds are algaelike fungi that form long filaments or strands. These filaments often extend into the air, appearing as cottony or velvety masses on food. Large colonies of mold are easily visible to the naked eye. Although many food molds are not dangerous, and some are even very beneficial, rare types known as *mycotoxicoses* form toxins that have been linked to food-borne illnesses. For the most part, however, molds affect only the appearance and flavor of foods. They cause discoloration, odors and off-flavors.

Unlike bacteria, molds can grow on almost any food at almost any temperature, moist or dry, acidic or alkaline. Mold cells can be destroyed by heating to 140°F (60°C) for 10 minutes. Their toxins are heat resistant, however, and are not destroyed by normal cooking methods. Therefore, foods that develop mold should be discarded, and any container or storage area cleaned and sanitized.

Yeasts

Yeasts require water and carbohydrates (sugar or starch) for survival. As the organisms consume carbohydrates, they expel alcohol and carbon dioxide gas through a process known as **fermentation**. Fermentation is of great benefit in making breads and alcoholic beverages.

Although naturally occurring yeasts have not been proved to be harmful to humans, they can cause foods to spoil and develop off-flavors, odors and discoloration. Yeasts are killed at temperatures of 136°F (58°C) or above.

CHEMICAL CONTAMINANTS

Contamination of foods by a wide variety of chemicals is a very real and serious danger in which the public has shown a strong interest. Chemical contamination is usually inadvertent and invisible, making it extremely difficult to detect. The only way to avoid such hazards is for everyone working in a food service operation to follow proper procedures when handling foods or chemicals.

Chemical hazards include contamination with (1) residual chemicals used in growing the food supply, (2) food service chemicals and (3) toxic metals.

RESIDUAL CHEMICALS

Chemicals such as antibiotics, fertilizers, insecticides and herbicides have brought about great progress in controlling plant, animal and human diseases, permitting greater food yields and stimulating animal growth. The benefits derived from these chemicals, however, must be contrasted with the adverse effects on humans when they are used indiscriminately or improperly.

The danger of these chemicals lies in the possible contamination of human foods, which occurs when chemical residues remain after the intended goal is achieved. Fruits and vegetables must be washed and peeled properly to reduce the risk of consuming residual chemicals.

FOOD SERVICE CHEMICALS

A more common contamination problem involves the common chemicals found in most every food service operation. Cleaners, polishes, pesticides and abrasives are often poisonous to humans. Illness and even death can result from foods contaminated by such common items as bug spray, drain cleaner, oven cleaner or silver polish. These chemicals pose a hazard if used or stored near food supplies. Even improperly washing or rinsing dishes and utensils leaves a soap residue, which is then transmitted via food to anyone using the item.

To avoid food service chemical contamination, make sure all cleaning chemicals are clearly labeled and stored well away from food preparation and storage areas. Always use these products as directed by the manufacturer; never reuse a chemical container or package.

TOXIC METALS

Another type of chemical contamination occurs when metals such as lead, mercury, copper, zinc and antimony are dispersed in food or water. For example:

▶ Metals can accumulate in fish and shellfish living in polluted waters or in plants grown in soil contaminated by the metals.

▶ Using an acidic food such as tomatoes or wine in a zinc (galvanized) or unlined copper container causes metal ions to be released into the food.

▶ Antimony is used in bonding enamelware; it can be released into food when the enamel is chipped or cracked, so the use of enamelware is prohibited in food service facilities.

▶ Lead enters the water supply from lead pipes and solder, and is found in the glaze on some imported ceramic items.

Consuming any of these metals can cause poisoning.

To prevent metal contamination, use only approved food service equipment and utensils and re-tin copper cookware as needed. Never serve fish or shellfish that was illegally harvested or obtained from uninspected sources.

PHYSICAL CONTAMINANTS

Physical contaminants include foreign objects that find their way into foods by mistake. Examples include metal shavings created by a worn can opener, pieces of glass from a broken container, hair and dirt. Physical contaminants may be created by intentional tampering, but they are most likely the result of poor safety and sanitation practices or a lack of training.

▶ CROSS-CONTAMINATION

Generally, microorganisms and other contaminants cannot move by themselves. Rather, they are carried to foods and food contact surfaces by humans, rodents or insects. This transfer is referred to as cross-contamination.

Cross-contamination is the process by which one item, such as your finger or a cutting board, becomes contaminated and then contaminates another food or tool. For example, suppose a chef's knife and cutting board are used in butchering a potentially hazardous food such as a chicken, and the chicken was directly contaminated with salmonella at the hatchery. If the knife and board are not cleaned *and sanitized* properly, anything that touches them can also become contaminated. So even though cooking the chicken to an appropriate internal temperature may destroy the salmonella in the chicken, the uncooked salad greens cut on the same cutting board or with the same knife can contain live bacteria.

Cross-contamination can occur with bacteria or other microorganisms, chemicals, dirt and debris. Side towels are an especially common source of cross-contamination. If a cook uses a side towel to wipe a spill off the floor, then uses that same towel to dry his hands after visiting the restroom, he has recontaminated his hands with whatever bacteria or dirt was on the floor. Cross-contamination also occurs when raw foods come in contact with cooked foods. Never store cooked food below raw food in a refrigerator, and never return cooked food to the container that held the raw food. Cross-contamination can also occur easily from smoking, drinking or eating, unless hands are properly washed after each of these activities.

Even with proper hand washing, food service workers should strive to minimize direct contact with prepared food by using single-use gloves, clean tongs, tasting spoons, bakery tissue paper and other appropriate tools whenever possible.

REDUCING CROSS-CONTAMINATION

Cross-contamination can be reduced or even prevented by (1) personal cleanliness, (2) dish and equipment cleanliness and (3) pest management.

PERSONAL CLEANLINESS

To produce clean, sanitary food, all food handlers must maintain high standards of personal cleanliness and hygiene. This begins with good grooming.

Humans provide the ideal environment for the growth of microorganisms. Everyone harbors bacteria in the nose and mouth. These bacteria are easily spread by sneezing or coughing, by not disposing of tissues properly and by not washing hands frequently and properly. Touching your body and then touching food or utensils transfers bacteria. Human waste carries many dangerous microorganisms, so it is especially important to wash your hands thoroughly after visiting the restroom. An employee who is ill should not be allowed in the kitchen.

Current research shows that the human immunodeficiency virus (HIV), the causative agent of AIDS, is not spread by food. According to the Centers for Disease Control and Prevention (CDC), food service workers infected with HIV should not be restricted from work unless there is another infection or illness.

PROPER HAND-WASHING PROCEDURE

- Use hot running water.
- Wet hands and forearms.
- Apply an antibacterial soap.
- Rub hands and arms briskly with soapy lather for at least 20 seconds.
- Scrub between fingers and clean nails with a clean nail brush.
- Rinse thoroughly under hot running water.
- Reapply soap and scrub hands and forearms for another 5–10 seconds.
- Rinse again.
- Dry hands and arms using a single-use towel.
- Use the towel to turn off the water.
- Discard the towel in a trash receptacle.

You can do several things to decrease the risk of an illness being spread by poor personal hygiene:

▶ Wash your hands frequently and thoroughly. Gloves are not a substitute for proper hand washing.

▶ Keep your fingernails short, clean and neat. Do not bite your nails or wear nail polish.

▶ Keep any cut or wound antiseptically bandaged. An injured hand should also be covered with a disposable glove.

▶ Bathe daily, or more often if required.

▶ Keep your hair clean and restrained.

▶ Wear work clothes that are clean and neat. Avoid wearing jewelry or watches.

▶ Do not eat, drink, smoke or chew gum in food preparation areas.

DISH AND EQUIPMENT CLEANLINESS

One of the requirements for any food service facility is cleanability. But there is an important difference between *clean* and *sanitary*. **Clean** means that the item has no visible soil on it. **Sanitary** means that harmful substances are reduced to safe levels. Thus, something may be clean without being sanitary; the visible dirt can be removed, but disease-causing microorganisms can remain.

The cleaning of dishes, pots, pans and utensils in a food service operation involves both removing soil and sanitizing. Soil can be removed manually or by machine. Sanitizing can be accomplished with heat or chemical disinfectants.

Procedures for manually washing, rinsing and sanitizing dishes and equipment generally follow the three-compartment sink setup shown in Figure 2.5. The dishwasher must do the following:

1 Scrape and spray the item to remove soil.

2 Wash the item in the first sink compartment using an approved detergent. A brush or cloth may be used to remove any remaining soil.

3 Rinse the item in the second sink compartment using clear, hot water.

4 Sanitize the item in the third sink compartment by either:
   a. immersing it in 171°F (77°C) water for at least 30 seconds, or
   b. immersing it in an approved chemical sanitizing solution used according to the manufacturer's directions.

5 Empty, clean and refill each sink compartment as necessary, and check the water temperature regularly.

Food service items, dishes, silverware and utensils should always be allowed to air-dry, as towel-drying might recontaminate them.

▶ **clean** to remove visible dirt and soil

▶ **sanitize** to reduce pathogenic organisms to safe levels

▶ **sterilize** to destroy all living microorganisms

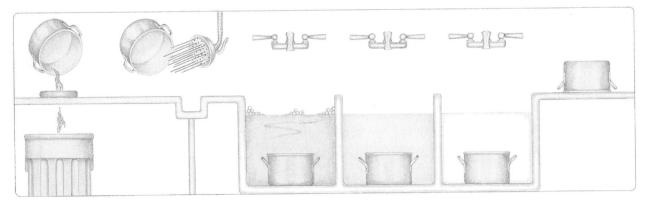

FIGURE 2.5 ▶ The three-compartment sink procedure—scrape, spray, wash, rinse, sanitize and air-dry each item.

Machine-washing dishes or utensils follows a similar procedure. The dishwasher should first scrape and rinse items as needed, then load the items into dishwasher racks so that the spray of water will reach all surfaces. The machine cleans the items with a detergent, then sanitizes them with either a hot-water rinse (at least 180°F/82°C) or a chemical disinfectant. When the machine cycle is complete, items should be inspected for residual soil, allowed to air-dry and stored in a clean area.

Work tables and stationary equipment must also be cleaned and sanitized properly. Equipment and surfaces, including floors, walls and work tables, should be easily exposed for inspection and cleaning and should be constructed so that soil can be removed effectively and efficiently with normal cleaning procedures. A thorough cleaning schedule should be implemented and closely monitored to prevent problems from developing.

The following points are important to the safety and cleanliness of any food service facility:

► Equipment should be disassembled for cleaning; any immersible pieces should be cleaned and sanitized like other items.

► All work tables or other food contact surfaces should be cleaned with detergent, then sanitized with a clean cloth dipped in a sanitizing solution. Combining 1 gallon (4 liters) of lukewarm water with 1 tablespoon (15 milliliters) of chlorine bleach makes an acceptable sanitizing solution. This solution must be replaced every two hours. Other chemical sanitizers should be prepared and used according to health department and manufacturer's directions.

► Surfaces, especially work surfaces with which food may come in contact, should be smooth and free of cracks, crevices or seams in which soil and microorganisms can hide.

► Floors should be nonabsorbent and should not become slippery when wet.

► Walls and ceilings should be smooth and light-colored so that soil is easier to see.

► Light should be ample and well located throughout food preparation and storage areas. All light bulbs should be covered with a sleeve or globe to protect surroundings from shattered glass.

A kitchen's design can also affect food safety and sanitation. Food preparation equipment should be arranged in such a way as to decrease the chances of cross-contamination. The workflow should eliminate crisscrossing and backtracking. Employees should be able to reach storage, refrigeration and cleanup areas easily. Dish- and pot-washing areas and garbage facilities should be kept as far from food preparation and storage areas as possible. Cleaning supplies and other chemicals should be stored away from foods.

PEST MANAGEMENT

Food can be contaminated by insects (for example, roaches and flies) and rodents (for example, mice and rats). These pests carry many harmful bacteria on their bodies, thus contaminating any surface with which they come in contact. An insect or rodent infestation is usually considered a serious health risk and should be dealt with immediately and thoroughly. Pests must be controlled by (1) building them out of the facility, (2) creating an environment in which they cannot find food, water or shelter, and (3) relying on professional extermination.

The best defense against pests is to prevent infestations in the first place by building them out. Any crack—no matter how small—in door frames, walls or window sills should be repaired immediately, and all drains, pipes and vents should be well sealed. Inspect all deliveries thoroughly, and reject any packages or containers found to contain evidence of pests.

Flies are a perfect method of transportation for bacteria because they feed and breed on human waste and garbage. Use screens or "fly fans" (also known as air curtains) to keep them out in the first place. Controlling garbage is also essential because moist, warm, decaying organic material attracts flies and provides favorable conditions for eggs to hatch and larvae to grow.

Pest management also requires creating an inhospitable environment for pests. Store all food and supplies at least 6 inches off the floor and 6 inches away from walls. **Rotate stock** often to disrupt nesting places and breeding habits. Provide good ventilation in storerooms to remove humidity, airborne contaminants, grease and fumes. Do not allow water to stand in drains, sinks or buckets, as cockroaches are attracted to moisture. Clean up spills and crumbs immediately and completely to reduce their food supply.

Despite your best efforts to build pests out and maintain proper housekeeping standards, it is still important to watch for the presence of pests. For example, cockroaches leave a strong, oily odor and feces that look like large grains of pepper. Cockroaches prefer to search for food and water in the dark, so seeing any cockroach on the move in the daylight is an indication of a large infestation.

Rodents (mice and rats) tend to hide during the day, so an infestation may be rather serious before any creature is actually seen. Rodent droppings, which are shiny black to brownish gray, may be evident, however. Rodent nests made from scraps of paper, hair or other soft materials may be spotted.

Should an infestation occur, consult a licensed pest control operator immediately. With early detection and proper treatment, infestations can be eliminated. Be very careful in attempting to use pesticides or insecticides yourself. These chemicals are toxic to humans as well as to pests. Great care must be used to prevent contaminating food or exposing workers or customers to the chemicals.

▶ **rotate stock** to use products in the order in which they were received; all perishable and semi-perishable goods, whether fresh, frozen, canned or dry, should be used according to the first in, first out (FIFO) principle

▶ HACCP SYSTEMS

Now that you understand what contaminants are and how they can be destroyed or controlled, it is necessary to put this information into practice during day-to-day operations. Although local health departments regularly inspect all food service facilities, continual self-inspection and control are essential for maintaining sanitary conditions.

Hazard Analysis Critical Control Points (HACCP) is proving to be an effective and efficient system for managing and maintaining sanitary conditions in all types of food service operations. Developed in 1971 for NASA to ensure food safety for astronauts, HACCP (pronounced HASS-ip) is a rigorous system of self-inspection. It focuses on the flow of food through the food service facility, from the decision to include an item on the menu through service to the consumer. A critical control point in that flow is any step during the processing of a food when a mistake can result in the transmission, growth or survival of pathogenic bacteria.

The HACCP process begins by identifying the steps and evaluating the type and severity of hazard that can occur. It then identifies what actions can be taken to reduce or prevent each risk of hazard. See Table 2.3. The activities that present the highest risk of hazard should be monitored most closely. For example, a cook's failure to wash his or her hands before handling cooked food presents a greater risk of hazard than a dirty floor. In other words, hazards must be prioritized, and the correction of critical concerns should take priority.

Note that the standards (or what some might call boundaries) applied in a formal HACCP system are no different from those that should be rigorously followed in any food service operation.

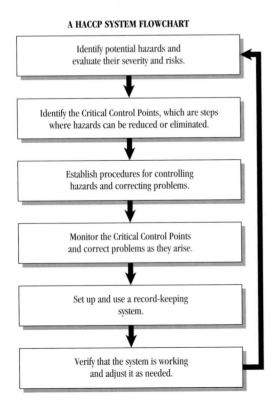

A HACCP SYSTEM FLOWCHART

Identify potential hazards and evaluate their severity and risks.

Identify the Critical Control Points, which are steps where hazards can be reduced or eliminated.

Establish procedures for controlling hazards and correcting problems.

Monitor the Critical Control Points and correct problems as they arise.

Set up and use a record-keeping system.

Verify that the system is working and adjust it as needed.

Table 2.3   HACCP ANALYSIS—THE FLOW OF FOOD

CONTROL POINT	HAZARDS	STANDARDS	CRITICAL ACTIONS
Selecting the menu and recipes	PHF; human hands involved in food preparation	Analyze menus and recipes for control points; wash hands frequently; use single-use gloves as appropriate	Plan physical work flow; train employees
Receiving	Contaminated or spoiled goods; PHF in the temperature danger zone	Do not accept torn bags, dented cans, broken glass containers or leaking or damaged packages; frozen food should be received at 0°F (−18°C) or below and refrigerated food at 40°F (4°C) or below	Inspect all deliveries and reject as necessary
Storing	Cross-contamination to and from other foods; bacterial growth; spoilage; improper holding temperatures	Avoid crowding and allow air to circulate in freezers and refrigerators; rotate stock and keep storage areas clean, dry and well lit; store frozen food at 0°F (−18°C) or below and refrigerated food at 40°F (4°C) or below	Maintain proper temperatures and other storage conditions; discard if necessary
Preparing	Cross-contamination; bacterial growth	Keep PHF at 40°F (4°C) or below or 140°F (60°C) or above; thaw frozen foods under refrigeration or under cold running water (70°F/21°C) for no more than 2 hours	Avoid the temperature danger zone; maintain good personal hygiene and use sanitary utensils
Cooking	Bacterial survival; physical or chemical contamination	Heat foods to the appropriate internal temperature; reheat leftover foods to at least 165°F (74°C)	Cook foods to their proper temperatures
Holding and service	Bacterial growth; contamination	Maintain hot holding temperatures at 140°F (60°C) or above and cold holding temperatures at 40°F (4°C) or below; do not mix new product with old and discard food after 2 hours of being held at room temperature	Maintain proper temperatures and use sanitary equipment
Cooling leftovers	Bacterial growth	Spread food into clean, shallow, metal containers; use an ice bath; stir periodically during cooling; cool to 70°F (21°C) within 2 hours, then cool to 40°F (4°C) or below within 4 hours; cover and refrigerate; store cooked food above raw	Cool foods quickly; label and store them properly
Reheating	Bacterial survival and growth	Use leftovers within 4 days; heat leftovers to 165°F (74°C) within 2 hours; do not mix old product with new and discard secondary leftovers	Reheat food quickly (do not use a steam table) and as close to serving time as possible; reheat smaller quantities as needed; discard if necessary

HACCP does not impose new or different food safety standards; it is merely a system for assuring that those standards are actually followed.

One way to assure compliance is to frequently check and record the temperature of PHF during cooking, cooling and holding. Maintaining written time-and-temperature logs allows management to evaluate and adjust procedures as necessary. Whatever system is followed, all personnel must be constantly aware of and responsive to risks and problems associated with the safety of the food they serve.

BEEF STROGANOFF

Yield: 8 Servings, 8 oz. (250 g) each   **Method:** Sautéing

Tenderloin tips, émincé	2 lb.	1 kg
Clarified butter	3 Tbsp.	45 ml
Onion, medium dice	4 oz.	120 g
Mushrooms, halved	1 lb.	450 g
Demi-glace	10 fl. oz.	300 ml
Heavy cream	10 fl. oz.	300 ml
Sour cream	8 oz.	250 g
Dijon mustard	1 Tbsp.	15 ml
Fresh dill, chopped	1 Tbsp.	15 ml
Fresh parsley, chopped	1 Tbsp.	15 ml
Salt and pepper	TT	TT
Egg noodles, cooked	24 oz.	700 g

PRE-PREPARATION

A. Wash hands before handling food, after handling raw foods and after any interruptions in work.

B. Cut the beef tenderloin using a clean, sanitized knife and cutting board. Place the émincé into a clean container, cover and refrigerate until ready to use. If work is interrupted, return the beef to refrigerated storage during the interruption.

C. Measure the demi-glace, cream and sour cream, cover and keep refrigerated until ready to use.

D. Chop the onions and herbs using a clean, sanitized knife and cutting board.

PREPARATION

CCP 1. Sauté the tenderloin tips in the butter, searing on all sides. Remove the meat **to a clean container and hold at 140°F (60°C) or higher for no more than 2 hours.**

2. Add the onions to the pan and sauté lightly. Add the mushrooms and sauté until dry.

3. Add the demi-glace. Bring to a boil, reduce to a simmer and cook for 10 minutes.

CCP 4. Add the cream, sour cream, mustard and any meat juices that accumulated while holding the meat. **Cook until an internal temperature of 145°F (63°C) is maintained for at least 15 seconds.**

CCP 5. Return the meat to the sauce. **Cook until the meat reaches an internal temperature of 145°F (63°C).** Stir in the dill and parsley. Adjust the seasonings and serve over hot egg noodles.

HOLDING

CCP   Transfer the sauce to a clean steam table pan and cover. Hold for service in a preheated steam table at **140°F (60°C) or higher. Use within 4 hours.**

LEFTOVERS

CCP   Place in shallow metal pans with a product depth of no more than 2 inches. **Cool from 140°F (60°C) to 70°F (21°C) within 2 hours and from 70°F (21°C) to 40°F (4°C) within 4 additional hours**, for a total cooling time of not more than 6 hours. Cover and store in a refrigerator so that the internal product temperature is 40°F (4°C) or less. Use leftovers within 4 days.

REHEATING

CCP   Reheat Stroganoff to an internal temperature of **165°F (74°C) or higher within 2 hours;** discard any product that is not consumed within 4 hours.

NOTES:

Measure all internal temperatures with a clean, sanitized thermocouple or thermometer.
Once cooked, egg noodles are a potentially hazardous food and should be held and stored accordingly.

FIGURE 2.6 ▶ A recipe showing critical control points (CCP).

One way that a food service operation can make workers aware of potential hazards and the critical actions that are necessary to avoid those hazards is by including detailed safety information in every recipe. Figure 2.6 shows the recipe for Beef Stroganoff from page 328, as it would appear with all critical control points (CCP) noted. When an operation writes this much detail into every one of its standardized recipes, it serves as a constant reminder to employees of both the specific actions necessary and the importance of food safety to the operation.

▶ THE SAFE WORKER

Kitchens are filled with objects that can cut, burn, break, crush or sprain the human body. The best ways to prevent work-related injuries are proper training, good work habits and careful supervision.

The federal government enacted legislation designed to reduce hazards in the work area, thereby reducing accidents. The Occupational Safety and Health Act (OSHA) covers a broad range of safety matters. Employers who fail to follow its rules can be severely fined. Unfortunately, human error is the leading cause of accidents, and no amount of legislation can protect someone who doesn't work in a safe manner.

Safe behavior on the job reflects pride, professionalism and consideration for fellow workers. The following list should alert you to conditions and activities aimed at preventing accidents and injuries:

▶ Clean up spills as soon as they occur.

▶ Learn to operate equipment properly; always use guards and safety devices.

▶ Wear clothing that fits properly; avoid wearing jewelry, which may get caught in equipment.

▶ Use knives and other equipment for their intended purposes only.

▶ Walk, do not run.

▶ Keep exits, aisles and stairs clear and unobstructed.

▶ Always assume pots and pans are hot; handle them with dry towels.

▶ Position pot and pan handles out of the aisles so that they do not get bumped.

▶ Get help or use a cart when lifting or moving heavy objects.

▶ Avoid back injury by lifting with your leg muscles; stoop, don't bend, when lifting.

▶ Use an appropriately placed ladder or stool for climbing; do not use a chair, box, drawer or shelf.

▶ Keep breakable items away from food storage or production areas.

▶ Warn people when you must walk behind them, especially when carrying a hot pan.

Some accidents will inevitably occur, and it is important to act appropriately in the event of an injury or emergency. This may mean calling for help or providing first aid. Every food service operation should be equipped with a complete first-aid kit. Municipal regulations may specify the exact contents of the kit. Be sure that the kit is conveniently located and well stocked at all times.

The American Red Cross and local public health departments offer training in first aid, cardiopulmonary resuscitation (CPR) and the Heimlich maneuver used for choking victims. All employees should be trained in basic emergency procedures. A list of emergency telephone numbers should be posted by each telephone.

CONCLUSION

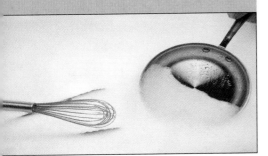

All food service workers are responsible for supplying food that is safe to eat. Microorganisms that cause food-borne illnesses can be destroyed or their growth severely limited by proper food-handling procedures. By learning about food contaminants, how they are spread and how they can be prevented or controlled, you can help ensure customer safety. You are also responsible for your own physical safety as well as that of your customers and fellow workers. Maintaining sanitary and safe facilities as well as high standards of personal hygiene are necessary parts of this responsibility.

QUESTIONS FOR DISCUSSION

1 Foods can be contaminated in several ways. Explain the differences between biological, chemical and physical contamination. Give an example of each.

2 Under what conditions will bacteria thrive? Explain what you can do to alter these conditions.

3 What is the temperature danger zone? What is its significance in food preparation?

4 Explain how improper or inadequate pest management can lead to food-borne illnesses.

5 Define HACCP. How is this system used in a typical food service facility?

6 Visit the Web sites of the U.S. Department of Agriculture and the Food and Drug Administration. What is the Model Food Code? What types of programs do these agencies offer for training consumers about food safety?

IF WE COULD GIVE EVERY INDIVIDUAL THE RIGHT
AMOUNT OF NOURISHMENT AND EXERCISE, NOT TOO
LITTLE AND NOT TOO MUCH, WE WOULD HAVE
FOUND THE SAFEST WAY TO HEALTH.
*—Hippocrates, Greek physician and father of
medicine (c. 460–377 B.C.E.)*

3

NUTRITION

AFTER STUDYING THIS
CHAPTER, YOU WILL BE
ABLE TO:

▶ identify categories of nutrients
and explain their importance in
a balanced diet

▶ understand the effects that
storage and preparation
techniques have on various
foods' nutritional values

▶ appreciate the use of ingredient
substitutes and alternatives

▶ provide diners with nutritious
foods

Since the days of prehistoric hunters and gatherers, people have understood that some animals and plants are good to eat and others are not. For thousands of years, cultures worldwide have attributed medicinal or beneficial effects to certain foods, particularly plants, and have recognized that foods that would otherwise be fine to eat may be unhealthy if improperly prepared or stored.

But not until the past few decades have people become increasingly concerned about understanding how all foods affect their health and what foods can and should be consumed in order to promote good health. These concerns compose the study of nutrition.

This chapter cannot provide an in-depth study of the nutritional sciences. Rather, it sets forth basic information about nutrients and guidelines for planning a healthy diet. The chapter also introduces the framework for understanding ingredient substitution and for preparing more nutritious meals.

Detailed nutritional information about many specific foods is found throughout the book. All recipes are accompanied by a nutritional analysis; recipes for dishes particularly low in calories, fat or sodium are marked with a ◢◣.

Nutrition is the science that studies nutrients—(chemical) substances found in food that nourish the body by promoting growth, maintenance and repair and by facilitating body functions. Some nutrients also provide energy.

The six categories of nutrients are carbohydrates, lipids (fats), proteins, vitamins, minerals and water. **Essential nutrients** are those that must be provided by food because the body does not produce them in sufficient quantities or cannot make them at all. See Table 3.1. Some nutritional components are consid-

Table 3.1 ESSENTIAL NUTRIENTS

Essential nutrients are those that must be provided because the human body does not produce them in sufficient quantities. They are the following:

Energy Nutrients
   Carbohydrates
   Fats (linoleic and linolenic acids)
   Proteins (the amino acids: histidine, isoleucine, leucine, lysine, methionine, phenylalanine, threonine, tryptophan and valine)

Vitamins (thiamine, riboflavin, niacin, pantothenic acid, biotin, vitamin B_6, vitamin B_{12}, folate, vitamin C, vitamin A, vitamin D, vitamin E and vitamin K)

Minerals (calcium, chloride, magnesium, phosphorous, potassium, sodium, sulfur, selenium, zinc, chromium, copper, fluoride, iodide, iron, manganese, and molybdenum)

Water

SHARON SALOMON, MS, RD

This chapter was researched and written by Sharon Salomon, a registered dietitian with a masters of science degree in clinical nutrition. As an undergraduate at Queens College in Flushing, New York, Ms. Salomon majored in cultural anthropology and traveled to Mexico, Turkey and Europe as part of her education. On these trips she enjoyed the benefits of living with local people in their homes, where she spent most of her free time in the families' kitchens learning authentic preparation of their native cuisines. Ms. Salomon has also studied at La Varenne Cooking School in Burgundy, France, and attended the Culinary Institute of America at Greystone for certification in nutritional cuisine.

Ms. Salomon has combined her love of food and cooking with her nutrition education in a variety of ways. She has taught nutrition and culinary nutrition courses and has worked as a caterer as well as a spokesperson for the Arizona Beef Council, the National Pork Producers Council and the California Kiwi Association. She appears regularly on Phoenix-area television and has written magazine and newspaper columns on sports nutrition and cooking with children.

ered nonessential because healthy, well-nourished bodies can make them in sufficient quantities to satisfy their needs.

Our bodies depend upon the various nutrients for different purposes and require different amounts of each depending on age, sex and health. In addition, some nutrients depend on one another for proper functioning. For example, calcium and vitamin D work together in the body: Vitamin D promotes the absorption of the calcium that the body utilizes for proper bone growth. Because foods differ with regard to their nutritional content, it is important to eat a variety of foods in order to achieve proper nutritional balance.

▶ ESSENTIAL NUTRIENTS

Three of the essential nutrients provide calories or energy. Sometimes referred to as **macronutrients** because they are needed in larger quantities than other nutrients, they are carbohydrates, lipids (fats) and proteins.

A **calorie** (abbreviated kcal) is the way we describe the amount of energy in food. The number of calories in a food is measured in a laboratory by a device called a calorimeter, which burns the food and measures the heat the food gives off. From that measurement, an estimate for how the food would be burned in the body is calculated. The results of that calculation are the calorie designations assigned to the energy nutrients.

One gram of pure fat supplies 9 kcal; one gram of pure carbohydrate supplies 4 kcal, as does one gram of pure protein. Most foods are a combination of carbohydrates, proteins and fats; their calorie content may not be easily determined unless we know how much of each nutrient the food contains.

Vitamins and minerals, sometimes referred to as **micronutrients** because they are needed in small quantities, are essential nutrients and must be provided through the diet because the body cannot manufacture them in quantities adequate to ensure good health. They provide no calories but are important to the body in generating energy from the foods we eat.

▶ **calorie** the unit of energy measured by the amount of heat required to raise 1000 grams of water one degree Celsius; it is also written as kilocalorie or kcal

CARBOHYDRATES

Carbohydrates comprise carbon, hydrogen and oxygen and are found exclusively in plant foods and milk sugars. Simple carbohydrates include monosaccharides (single sugars) and disaccharides (double sugars). See Table 3.2. **Simple carbohydrates** are found in the naturally occurring sugars in fruit, vegetables and milk, as well as sweeteners such as honey, corn syrup and table sugar. **Complex carbohydrates** are composed of long chains of the monosaccharide glucose. Starch is a complex carbohydrate. Complex carbohydrates are found in fruit, vegetables and cereal grains such as wheat, barley and oats. The

Table 3.2	**SUGARS**	
MONOSACCHARIDES		**DISACCHARIDES**
Glucose (blood sugar)		Lactose (milk sugar)
Fructose (fruit sugar)		Maltose (malt sugar)
Galactose (part of milk sugar)		Sucrose (table sugar)

body digests (or breaks down) these sugars and starches into glucose. Glucose, also known as blood sugar, is a very important source of energy for the body.

Another complex carbohydrate is fiber. Fiber is a unique carbohydrate because humans cannot digest it, so they do not derive calories from it. **Dietary fiber,** which generally comes from the seeds and cell walls of fruit, vegetables and cereal grains, plays an important role in health. There are two types of fiber: soluble and insoluble. Fiber-containing foods are usually composed of both kinds with one kind predominating. Because the body cannot digest dietary fiber, it passes through the digestive system almost completely unchanged. This helps keep the digestive tract running smoothly. Insoluble fiber, such as that found in whole wheat, increases fecal bulk, which encourages proper elimination of waste products from the large intestines and helps avoid some forms of gastrointestinal distress. Some forms of fiber also reduce serum cholesterol. In addition, because of its action in speeding up the passage of waste materials, it is believed that insoluble fiber may prevent colon cancer. Soluble fiber, found in oats and beans, reduces serum cholesterol, thereby lessening the risk for heart disease.

LIPIDS

Lipids, like carbohydrates, are composed of carbon, hydrogen and oxygen. The differences between carbohydrates and lipids are the number and arrangement of the carbon, hydrogen and oxygen atoms. Fats and cholesterol are considered lipids. Fats are found in both animal and plant foods, although fruits contain very little fat. Fats provide calories, help carry fat-soluble vitamins and give food a creamy, pleasant mouth-feel. A healthy diet contains a moderate amount of fat; in fact, some forms of fat are considered essential.

Cholesterol, also a lipid, is found only in foods of animal origin. Cholesterol is not considered an essential nutrient nor does it contribute calories. Cholesterol is, however, an important component of the body, although it is not necessary to eat foods containing cholesterol as the body can manufacture all it needs from the fat in the diet.

Depending upon their structure, the fats in foods can be classified as saturated, monounsaturated or polyunsaturated. Most foods contain a combination of the three kinds of fats, although one kind may predominate. If saturated fat is the most abundant kind (as in the fat surrounding muscle meats), the food is classified as being high in saturated fat even though it contains a mixture of all three kinds of fats.

Saturated fats are found mainly in animal products such as milk, eggs and meats, as well as in tropical oils such as coconut and palm. Monounsaturated fats come primarily from plants and plant foods such as avocados and olives and the oils made from them. Polyunsaturated fats come from plants (soy and corn, for example) and fish.

Vegetable oils such as rapeseed (canola) and olive are high in monounsaturated fat. Cottonseed, sunflower, corn and safflower oils are high in polyunsaturated fat. All oils, however, are a combination of the three kinds of fat. All vegetable oils are cholesterol-free, however, as cholesterol is not found in plants.

Saturated fats such as butter, lard and other animal fats are usually solid at room temperature. Monounsaturated and polyunsaturated fats are usually soft or liquid at room temperature. Hydrogenation is a process by which a liquid fat is made more solid (or saturated) by the addition of hydrogen atoms. Hydrogenation increases the percentage of saturated fatty acids, resulting in a more solid product (such as margarine made from a liquid polyunsaturated oil such as corn oil). Hydrogenation has positive effects as well; it reduces the tendency to rancidity, thus increasing shelf life. For this reason, it is a process used frequently in the food manufacturing industry.

Research suggests that high-fat diets, especially diets high in saturated fat, may be linked to heart disease, obesity and certain forms of cancer. Saturated fats are also linked to high levels of blood cholesterol, which are associated with arteriosclerosis (hardening of the arteries). Although the liver can produce all the cholesterol the body needs, additional cholesterol is often provided in the diet from meats, poultry, fish, eggs and dairy products. The combination of a diet high in saturated fat and a diet high in cholesterol can increase the risk of heart disease.

PROTEINS

Proteins are found in both animal and plant foods. They differ from carbohydrates and lipids in that they contain nitrogen as well as carbon, hydrogen and oxygen. Protein chains consist of amino acids, the building blocks of protein. There are 20 amino acids, 9 of which are essential. People who eat a varied diet with adequate calories and protein can easily get all the essential amino acids even if they do not eat any animal foods. The specific combination of amino acids gives each protein its unique characteristics and properties.

Proteins are necessary for manufacturing, maintaining and repairing body tissues. They are essential for the periodic replacement of the outer layer of skin as well as for blood clotting and scar tissue formation. Hair and nails, which provide a protective cover for the body, are composed of proteins.

Another important function of protein is the regulation of body processes. Proteins regulate the balance of water, acids and bases, and move nutrients in and out of cells. Proteins contribute to the immune system by producing antibodies, which are necessary for combating diseases. Proteins also form the enzymes that act as catalysts for body functions and the hormones that help direct body processes.

VITAMINS

Vitamins are vital dietary substances needed to regulate **metabolism** and for normal growth and body functions. They are essential and noncaloric, and are needed in the body in small amounts.

There are 13 vitamins. Table 3.3 lists them, their known functions in the human body, the foods that contain high concentrations of these nutrients and some of the preparation and storage techniques that help retain the maximum amount of the various vitamins in their food sources.

Vitamins are divided into two categories: fat-soluble and water-soluble. The fat-soluble vitamins are A, D, E and K and are found in foods containing fat. Excess supplies of these vitamins may be stored in fatty tissues and the liver. Water-soluble vitamins are vitamin C and the B-complex vitamins, including thiamin (B_1), riboflavin (B_2), niacin (B_3), cyano-cobalamin (B_{12}), pyridoxine (B_6), pantothenic acid, biotin and folate. Vitamins B_1 and B_2 are commonly referred to by their names (thiamin and riboflavin, respectively), whereas cobalamin and pyridoxine are commonly referred to by their letter designations (B_{12} and B_6, respectively). Water-soluble vitamins are not stored to the extent that fat-soluble vitamins are, and excesses may be excreted in the urine. Because of these differences, deficiencies in water-soluble vitamins usually develop more rapidly.

▶ **metabolism** all the chemical reactions and physical processes that occur continuously in living cells and organisms

Table 3.3   **VITAMINS: THEIR FUNCTIONS, SOURCES AND TECHNIQUES FOR RETAINING MAXIMUM NUTRIENT CONTENT**

VITAMIN	KNOWN FUNCTIONS IN THE HUMAN BODY	SOURCES	TECHNIQUES FOR NUTRIENT REACTION
Vitamin A	Keeps skin healthy; protects eyes; protects mouth and nose linings; supports immune functioning	Deep yellow and orange vegetables, leafy green vegetables, deep orange fruits, egg yolks, liver, fortified milk	Serve fruits and vegetables raw or lightly cooked; store vegetables covered and refrigerated; steam vegetables; roast or broil meats
Vitamin D	Helps body absorb calcium; regulates calcium and phosphorus in the bones; assists bone mineralization	Fortified milk, butter, some fish oils, egg yolks (exposure to sunlight produces vitamin D in the body)	Stable under heat and insoluble in water; therefore unaffected by cooking
Vitamin E	Antioxidant; protects membranes and cell walls	Vegetable oils, whole grains, dark leafy vegetables, wheat germ, nuts, seeds, whole grains	Use whole-grain flours, store foods in airtight containers; avoid exposing food to light and air
Vitamin K	Assists blood-clotting proteins	Liver, dark green leafy vegetables (bacteria in the intestinal tract also produce some vitamin K)	Steam or microwave vegetables; do not overcook meats
Vitamin C (ascorbic acid)	Supports immune system functioning; repairs connective tissues; promotes healing; assists amino acid metabolism	Citrus fruits, green vegetables, strawberries, cantaloupes, tomatoes, broccoli, potatoes	Serve fruits and vegetables raw; steam or microwave vegetables
Thiamin (vitamin B_1)	Assists energy metabolism; supports nervous system functioning	Meats (especially pork), legumes, whole grains	Use enriched or whole grain pasta or rice; do not wash whole grains before cooking or rinse afterward; steam or microwave vegetables; roast meats at moderate temperatures; cook meats only until done
Riboflavin (vitamin B_2)	Assists energy metabolism	Milk, cheese, yogurt, fish, enriched grain breads and cereals, dark green leafy vegetables	Store foods in opaque containers; roast or broil meats or poultry
Niacin (vitamin B_3)	Promotes normal digestion; supports nervous system functioning; assists energy metabolism	Meats, poultry, fish, dark green leafy vegetables, whole-grain or enriched breads and cereals, nuts	Steam or microwave vegetables; roast or broil beef, veal, lamb and poultry (pork retains about the same amount of niacin regardless of cooking method)
Vitamin B_6	Necessary for protein metabolism and red blood cell formation	Meats, fish, poultry, shellfish, whole grains, dark green vegetables, potatoes, liver	Serve vegetables raw; cook foods in a minimum amount of water and for the shortest possible time; roast or broil meats and fish
Vitamin B_{12}	Helps produce red blood cells; assists metabolism	Animal foods only, particularly milk, eggs, poultry and fish	Roast or broil meats, poultry and fish
Folate	Necessary for protein metabolism and red blood cell formation	Orange juice, dark green leafy vegetables, organ meats, legumes, seeds	Serve vegetables raw; steam or microwave vegetables; store vegetables covered and refrigerated
Biotin	Coenzyme in energy metabolism, glycogen synthesis and fat metabolism	Widespread in foods	
Pantothenic acid	Coenzyme in energy metabolism	Widespread in foods	

Virtually all foods contain some vitamins. Many factors contribute to a particular food's vitamin concentration. An animal's feed; the manner by which the produce is harvested, stored or processed; and even the type of soil, sunlight, rainfall and temperature have significant effects on a food's vitamin content. For example, tomatoes have a higher concentration of vitamin C when picked ripe from the vine than when picked green. Furthermore, different varieties of fruit and vegetables have different vitamin contents. A Wegener apple, for example, has 19 mg of vitamin C, whereas a Red Delicious has only 6 mg.

You can control vitamin concentration and retention through careful food preparation:

1 Try to prepare vegetables as close to service time as possible; vegetables cut long before service lose more vitamins than those cut immediately before cooking.

2 Whether a vegetable is boiled, steamed or microwaved also determines the amount of vitamins it retains. Because the B-complex vitamins and vitamin C are water-soluble, they are easily leached (washed out) or destroyed by food processing and preparation techniques involving high temperatures and water. Steaming and microwaving help retain nutrients (when steaming, keep the water level below the vegetables). But microwave cooking is best because it cooks vegetables with minimal water in less time.

3 In general, roasting and grilling meats, poultry, fish and shellfish preserve more vitamins than stewing and braising. The temperatures to which foods are cooked and the length of time they are cooked may affect vitamin retention as well.

4 Storage affects vitamin concentrations. For example, long exposure to air may destroy vitamin C. Using airtight containers prevents some of this loss. Riboflavin is sensitive to light, so milk products (which are good sources of riboflavin) should be stored in opaque containers.

MINERALS

Minerals cannot be manufactured by the body. They are obtained by eating plants that have drawn minerals from the ground or the flesh of animals that have eaten such plants.

Minerals are a critical component in hard and soft tissues (for example, the calcium, magnesium and phosphorus present in bones and teeth). Minerals also regulate certain necessary body functions. For example, nerve impulses are transmitted through an exchange of sodium and potassium ions in the nerve cells.

Minerals are divided into two categories: trace minerals and major minerals. Trace minerals such as iron are needed in only very small amounts. Major minerals such as calcium are needed in relatively larger quantities. Table 3.4 lists some minerals, their known functions in the human body and the foods that contain high concentrations of these nutrients.

As with vitamins, food processing and preparation can reduce a food's mineral content. Soaking or cooking in large amounts of water can leach out small quantities of water-soluble minerals. Processing or refining grains, such as the wheat used to make white flour, also removes minerals.

WATER

The human body is approximately 60 percent water. Water is necessary for transporting nutrients and wastes throughout the body. It cushions the cells, lubricates the joints, maintains stable body temperatures and assists waste elimination. It also promotes functioning of the nervous system and muscles.

Although the principal sources of water are beverages, water is also the predominant nutrient by weight in most foods. Some foods such as tomatoes,

▶ **acidulated water** a mildly acidic solution of water and lemon juice or vinegar used to prevent cut fruits and vegetables from darkening

▶ **artesian-well water** water obtained from an underground source; the water rises to the surface under pressure

▶ **bottled water** any water, either still or sparkling, that is bottled and sold

▶ **deionized water** water that has had the cations and anions removed by passing it over a bed of ion-exchange resins

▶ **demineralized water** water that has had all the minerals and impurities removed by passing it over a bed of ion-exchange resins

▶ **distilled water** water that has had all the minerals and impurities removed through distillation; it is generally used for pharmaceutical purposes

▶ **drinking water** water that comes from a government-approved source and has undergone some treatment and filtration; it can be bottled or available on tap and is used for drinking and general culinary purposes

▶ **fluoridated water** water, either naturally fluoridated or treated with a fluorine-containing compound, intended to promote healthy teeth by preventing tooth decay

▶ **hard water** water with relatively high calcium and magnesium concentrations

▶ **mineral water** drinking water that comes from a protected underground water source and contains at least 250 parts per million of total dissolved solids such as calcium

▶ **natural water** bottled drinking water not derived from a municipal water supply; it can be mineral, spring, well or artesian-well water

▶ **purified water** bottled water produced by distillation, reverse osmosis, deionization or suitable processes that meet governmental standards

▶ **seltzer water** a flavorless natural mineral water with carbonation, originally from the German town of Nieder Selters

Table 3.4   **MINERALS: THEIR FUNCTIONS AND SOURCES**

MINERAL	KNOWN FUNCTIONS IN THE HUMAN BODY	SOURCES
Major Minerals		
Calcium	Helps build bones and teeth; helps blood clot, promotes muscle and nerve functions	Dairy products, canned salmon and sardines, broccoli, kale, tofu, turnips
Magnesium	Muscle contraction; assists energy metabolism, bone formation	Green leafy vegetables, whole grains, legumes, fish, shellfish, cocoa
Phosphorus	Helps build bones and teeth; assists energy metabolism; formation of DNA	All animal tissues, milk, legumes, nuts
Potassium	Maintains electrolyte and fluid balance; promotes normal body functions; assists protein metabolism	Meats, poultry, fish, fruits (especially bananas, oranges, and cantaloupes), legumes, vegetables
Sodium	Maintains normal fluid balance; necessary for nerve impulse transmission	Salt, soy sauce, processed foods, MSG
Chloride	With sodium, involved in fluid balance; component of stomach acid	Salt, soy sauce, meats, milk, processed foods
Sulfur	A component of some proteins, insulin, and the vitamins biotin and thiamin	All protein-containing foods
Trace Minerals		
Iron	Part of hemoglobin (the red substance in blood that carries oxygen); prevents anemia	Liver, meats, shellfish, enriched breads and cereals, legumes
Zinc	A component of insulin, enhances healing, a component of many enzymes; involved in taste perception; bone formation	Protein foods, whole-grain breads and cereals, fish, shellfish, poultry, vegetables
Selenium	Antioxidant	Fish, shellfish, meats, eggs, grains (depends on soil conditions)
Iodine	Component of thyroid hormone	Iodized salt, fish, shellfish, bread, plants grown in iodide-rich soil
Copper	Facilitates iron absorption; part of enzymes	Meats, fish, shellfish, nuts, seeds
Fluoride	Necessary for bone and teeth formation; helps teeth resist tooth decay	Fluoridated drinking water, fish, shellfish
Chromium	Insulin cofactor	Liver, whole grains, brewer's yeast, nuts, oils
Molybdenum	Cofactor in metabolism	Legumes, cereals
Manganese	Cofactor in metabolism	Whole grains, nuts, organ meats
Cobalt	Component of vitamin B_{12} (cobalamin)	

▶ **soda water** a flavorless water with induced carbonation, consumed plain or used as a mixer for alcoholic drinks or soda fountain confections; also known as club soda and seltzer

▶ **soft water** water with a relatively high sodium concentration

▶ **spring water** water obtained from an underground source that flows naturally to the earth's surface

oranges, watermelon and iceberg lettuce are particularly high in water. Others such as dried fruits, nuts and seeds are lower. Even foods such as chicken and bread provide some water. The body also forms water when other nutrients are metabolized for energy.

The average adult should consume at least 8 to 10 glasses (64 fluid ounces or 2 liters) of water a day to ensure adequate intake. People who exercise, those who live in a warm climate and the elderly should replace body water lost through sweat by drinking even more.

PHYTOCHEMICALS

Recent scientific research has identified nonnutritive components of plant foods called phytochemicals, which may be important in preventing some forms of cancer and heart disease. More than nine hundred of these chemicals have been identified, including plant estrogens, carotenoids and flavonoids. The health benefits of these substances appear to depend on consumption of a varied diet

LIGHTEN UP!

On the night before their trials on the Colosseum floor, gladiators ate meat to make themselves strong. Until a few years ago, modern-day gladiators and coaches insisted that athletes needed meat the night before the game. Of course, being more scientific, they referred to their training-table steak as protein.

Times change, the pendulum swings, and whoever thought a brawny athlete would admit to being a vegetarian? The new message from the American Heart Association and the USDA's U.S. Dietary Goals is that we needn't stop eating meat entirely. Instead, we should reduce our consumption of beef, turning to alternative sources of protein such as fish, poultry, low-fat dairy products, nuts, beans and seeds, and increase our consumption of fresh fruit, vegetables, grains and other complex carbohydrates. The results: fewer fats, more fiber and lower cholesterol, helping to create a slimmer, energetic, longer-lasting body.

This new "fresh," "nutrient-dense," "light," "natural," "heart-healthy" approach to dining has gone from fad to fashion to fact of life.

From formal French to Mexican fast food, facilities offering portions of innovative, tasty, eye-catching healthy cuisine will surely win allegiance and accolades from patrons. So lighten up. Replace the deep-fat fryer with a griddle. Garnish with fresh fruit. Serve whole-grain bread, but take heed: Balance is paramount. An occasional indulgence is a joy. There will always be room for chocolate.

HARRIS GOLDEN, formerly executive chef of Elizabeth Arden's Maine Chance Health Resort, is the author of two cookbooks.

that includes plenty of grains, fruits and vegetables. The importance of phytochemicals to human health and well-being should not be minimized even though they do not constitute a nutrient category nor are there established recommendations for their intake.

► EATING FOR HEALTH

It is generally recognized that a balanced diet is an important component of a healthy lifestyle. Eating well and exercising, getting adequate sleep and living moderately all can contribute to a longer, healthier life.

HEALTH ORGANIZATION RECOMMENDATIONS

Planning a diet to enhance health is made simpler by diet and exercise recommendations from organizations such as the American Heart Association and the American Cancer Society. Both stress the importance of controlling the amount of fat in the diet and consuming plant foods such as vegetables, fruits and whole grains in greater quantities.

Another useful planning tool is *Dietary Guidelines for Americans,* jointly published by the USDA and the U.S. Department of Health and Human Services. The fifth edition (2000) presents health messages called the "ABCs of Good Health":

► *Aim for fitness* by maintaining a healthy weight and being physically active.
► *Build a healthy base* using the Food Guide Pyramid and keeping food safe to eat.
► *Choose sensibly* by eating a diet low in saturated fat, cholesterol, sugar and salt and drinking alcoholic beverages in moderation.

ESTABLISHING NUTRIENT REQUIREMENTS

In the past, the RDAs (Recommended Dietary Allowances), standards developed by the federal government, were used to establish guidelines for school lunch programs, food labeling regulations, government nutrition policies,

FOOD GROUPIES

For many years, nutritionists and others have attempted to define a healthy, balanced diet. Most plans divide foods into general categories and recommend that a certain number of servings or calories be consumed from each category for a balanced diet.

Before 1956, the USDA recognized seven food groups: (1) meats, eggs, dried peas and beans, (2) milk, cheese and ice cream, (3) potatoes and other vegetables and fruit, (4) green leafy and yellow vegetables, (5) citrus fruit, tomatoes and raw cabbage, (6) breads and flours and (7) butter and fortified margarine.

In 1956, the USDA reduced the seven groups to four: (1) milk and cheese, (2) meats and fish, (3) fruit and vegetables and (4) grains. An optional fifth category was sweets and fats. From these Four Basic Food Groups, the USDA recommended that the average adult eat a total of 12 servings daily. Two or more servings were to come from each of the meat and milk groups, and four or more servings from each of the other two groups.

In 1992, the USDA replaced the Four Basic Food Groups with the Food Guide Pyramid. The Food Guide Pyramid prioritizes and proportions the food choices among six food categories and gives a visual presentation of proper daily nutrition. The pyramid emphasizes flexibility and is designed to be used by people of all ages and backgrounds.

educational campaigns and the like. During the last decade, however, research regarding the nutrient needs of children, adults and the elderly has raised questions and concerns about the adequacy of the RDAs. Scientists are currently reviewing the pertinent literature to determine how the government can best revise these nutrient recommendations. An important criterion for making nutrient recommendations is the recognition that each person's body is unique and as health and growth status change, so do nutrient needs. The committee, therefore, has proposed different categories to include average needs, estimated needs and adequate needs to more fully meet the needs of different people. Some new recommendations have already been made. For the most up-to-date data, check with government nutrition Web sites.

THE FOOD GUIDE PYRAMID

The most useful diet planning tool available is the Food Guide Pyramid developed by the USDA. See Figure 3.1. It prioritizes and proportions food according to groupings that provide similar nutrients. The size of each section of the pyramid visually represents the number of daily servings recommended.

The base or foundation of the pyramid conveys the idea that a healthy diet is based on the consumption of adequate whole grains and cereals. As you move up the pyramid, fruit and vegetables are next in amount. Meats, poultry, fish, beans, eggs and nuts, as well as milk, yogurt and cheese are allotted smaller sections above the fruit and vegetables. Although they provide essential nutrients such as protein, vitamins and minerals, these foods may be high in fat and calories, and their intake should be moderated. The small tip of the pyramid includes fats, oils and sweets. The size and placement of these indicate that they can be a part of a healthy diet if used sparingly.

Pay careful attention to the serving sizes in Table 3.5. One of the principal complaints consumer health groups have about restaurant meals is the "supersizing" of portions. Often restaurant portions are two or more times what the Food Guide Pyramid recommends for a serving. Portion size represents a dilemma for the restaurateur because the public views larger portions as offering more value for their money. Health education messages, however, allow the dining public to eat out without guilt by teaching strategies such as eating only half of what is served and taking the other half home for another meal or sharing entrées to ensure more reasonable portion sizes.

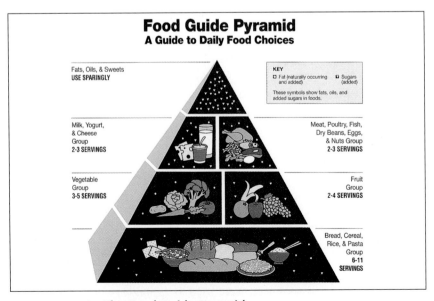

FIGURE 3.1 ▶ The Food Guide Pyramid

Table 3.5　SERVINGS AND SELECTIONS FROM THE FOOD GUIDE PYRAMID

FOOD GROUP AND SERVICE SIZE	NUTRIENTS PROVIDED	SELECTION TIPS
Bread, Cereal, Rice and Pasta Group (6–11 Servings)		
½ cup cooked cereal 1 ounce dry cereal 1 slice bread 2 cookies ½ medium doughnut	B vitamins, fiber, iron, magnesium, zinc	Choose whole-grain breads, cereals and grains such as whole-wheat or rye bread, oatmeal and brown rice. Moderate the intake of high-fat, high-sugar baked goods such as cakes, cookies and pastries. Limit fats and sugars added as spreads, sauces or toppings.
Vegetable Group (3–5 Servings)		
½ cup cooked or raw chopped vegetables 1 cup raw leafy vegetables ¾ cup vegetable juice 10 French fries	Vitamin A, vitamin C, folate, magnesium, iron, fiber	Eat a variety of vegetables, including dark green leafy vegetables (for example, spinach and broccoli), deep yellow vegetables (for example, carrots and sweet potatoes), starchy vegetables (for example, potatoes and corn), legumes (for example, kidney beans) and other vegetables such as green beans and tomatoes. Cook vegetables by steaming or baking. Avoid frying and limit high-fat spreads or dressings.
Fruit Group (2–4 Servings)		
1 medium apple, banana or orange ½ cup chopped, cooked or canned fruit ¾ cup fruit juice ¼ cup dried fruit	Vitamin A, vitamin C, potassium, fiber	Choose fresh fruit, fruit frozen without sugar, dried fruit or fruit canned in water or juice. If canned in heavy syrup, rinse with water before eating. Eat whole fruits more often than juices since they are higher in fiber. Regularly eat citrus fruits, melons or berries rich in vitamin C. Only 100 percent fruit juice should be counted as a fruit.
Milk, Yogurt and Cheese Group (2–3 Servings)		
1 cup milk or yogurt 1½ ounces natural cheese 2 ounces processed cheese 2 cups cottage cheese 1½ cups ice cream 1 cup frozen yogurt	Protein, calcium, riboflavin	Use skim or low-fat milk for healthy people older than two years of age. Choose low-fat and nonfat yogurt, part-skim and low-fat cheeses and lower-fat frozen desserts such as ice milk and frozen yogurt. Limit high-fat cheeses and ice cream.
Meat, Poultry, Fish, Dry Beans, Eggs and Nuts Group (2–3 Servings)		
2–3 ounces cooked lean meat, fish or poultry 2–3 eggs 4–6 tablespoons peanut butter 1½ cups cooked dry beans 1 cup nuts	Protein, niacin, vitamin B_{12}, iron, zinc	Select lean meat, poultry without skin, fish and dry beans. Trim fat and cook by broiling, roasting, grilling or boiling rather than frying. Limit egg yolks, which are high in cholesterol, and nuts and seeds, which are high in fat. Be aware of serving size; 3 ounces of meat is the size of an average hamburger.
Fats, Oils and Sweets (use sparingly)		
Butter, mayonnaise, salad dressing, cream cheese, sour cream, jam, jelly		These are high in energy and low in micronutrients. Substitute low-fat dressings and spreads.

Source: U.S. Department of Agriculture. *The Food Guide Pyramid. Home and Garden Bulletin No. 252.* Hyattsville, MD: Human Nutrition Information Service, 1992

THE FEDERAL GOVERNMENT GUARDS OUR LARDER

The federal government plays an important role in the way various foodstuffs are grown, raised, slaughtered, processed, marketed, stored and transported. The principal actors are the Food and Drug Administration of the U.S. Department of Health and Human Services (FDA) and the U.S. Department of Agriculture (USDA).

The FDA's activities are directed toward protecting the nation's health against impure and unsafe foods, as well as drugs, cosmetics, medical devices and other things. It develops and administers programs addressing food safety. For example, the FDA must approve any new food additive before a manufacturer markets it to food producers and processors. To gain FDA approval, the manufacturer must prove to the

FDA's satisfaction that the additive (1) is effective for the intended purpose, (2) can be detected and measured in the final product and (3) is safe. The FDA holds public hearings during which experts and consumers provide evidence and opinions before it decides to grant or deny approval. If it grants approval, the FDA issues regulations identifying the amount of the additive that can be used and the foods to which it can be added. The FDA also sets standards for labeling foods, including nutrition labels. Labeling regulations not only address the type of information that must be conveyed, but also the way it is presented.

The USDA's principal responsibility is to make sure that individual food items are safe,

wholesome and accurately labeled. It attempts to meet these responsibilities through inspection and grading procedures. The USDA also provides consumer services. It conducts and publishes research on nutrition and assists those producing our food to do so efficiently and effectively.

Other federal agencies that have a role in the nation's health and food supply include the U.S. Centers for Disease Control and Prevention (CDC), which tracks illnesses, including those caused by food-borne pathogens; the National Institutes of Health (NIH), which does basic biological and nutritional research; and the Department of the Interior, which sets environmental and land-use standards.

▶ INGREDIENT SUBSTITUTES AND ALTERNATIVES

More and more people are becoming health-conscious consumers. Many are trying to cut down on foods high in salt, fat, added sugar and cholesterol. To a degree, people can accomplish their goals—and chefs can assist them—by turning to ingredient substitutes and alternatives where possible.

Here we use the term **ingredient substitute** to mean the replacement of one ingredient with another of presumably similar—although not necessarily identical—flavor, texture, appearance and other sensory characteristics. The substitute may be more nutritious, however. So someone who is avoiding fats can use reduced-fat or nonfat sour cream in place of regular sour cream when baking quick breads. The differences in flavor, texture, appearance and baking quality should be minimal.

We use the term **ingredient alternative** to mean the replacement of one ingredient with another of different flavor, texture, appearance or other characteristic, but one that will not compromise—although it may change—the flavor of the dish. As with the ingredient substitute, the ingredient alternative may be more nutritious. Lemon juice and herbs, for instance, can be used as flavoring alternatives to salt; a salsa of fresh vegetables can replace a cream-based sauce. The dishes will not taste the same, but they will still taste good.

In attempting to modify a recipe, the chef should first identify the ingredient(s) or cooking method(s) that may need to be changed. He or she can then use the following principles—reduce, replace or eliminate—to make a dish healthier:

1 Reduce the amounts of the ingredient(s).
2 Replace the ingredient(s) with a substitute that will do the least to change the flavor and appearance of the dish.
3 Eliminate the ingredient(s).

SALT SUBSTITUTES AND ALTERNATIVES

A concern in the American diet is excessive sodium (salt). The average American consumes 3000 to 7000 mg of sodium per day, well in excess of daily needs. Research has linked excessive amounts of sodium to hypertension (high blood pressure), heart and kidney diseases and strokes.

Chefs are sometimes taught to use salt liberally to enhance flavors. Most salt substitutes (which are potassium chloride instead of sodium chloride), however, neither enhance flavors like salt nor are even palatable to many people. In trying to moderate the amount of salt in a dish, the chef should reduce the quantity of the sodium-containing ingredients or use a lower-sodium choice. Soy sauce is a good example; often the quantity can be reduced, and excellent low-sodium soy products are available. In addition, pepper, lemon, herbs, spices, fruit and flavored vinegars can be used as salt alternatives to heighten flavor.

ARTIFICIAL SWEETENERS

Saccharin, the oldest artificial sugar substitute, has been used for more than a century. It has no calories and tastes 300 times sweeter than table sugar. Saccharin has a bitter aftertaste, however, and many people find it unpalatable.

Aspartame (brand name NutraSweet), approved by the FDA in 1981, comprises the amino acids aspartic acid and phenylalanine. Unlike saccharin, aspartame does not have an aftertaste. It is 180 times sweeter than table sugar. It is now widely used in soft drinks, frozen yogurts, fruit spreads, candies and similar products. Aspartame breaks down when heated, so it cannot be used in cooked foods. According to the FDA, aspartame is a safe substitute for sugar, although it is a risk for those people with the rare disorder phenylketonuria (PKU), who cannot metabolize the phenylalanine in aspartame. Appropriate warnings are printed on all aspartame-sweetened foods.

Another sugar substitute is acesulfame-K (brand name Sunnette), which the FDA approved in 1988. The body cannot metabolize acesulfame-K, so it passes through the digestive system unchanged. Like aspartame, it has no aftertaste. Acesulfame-K is used in chewing gum, dry beverage mixes, instant coffees and teas, gelatins and nondairy creamers. It is more stable than aspartame, so it can be used in baking.

The latest alternative sweetener approved by the FDA, sucralose (brand name Splenda) was discovered in 1976. It is 600 times sweeter than sugar and can be used like sugar in some baked goods. Sucralose, a derivative of table sugar, is virtually calorie-free because its sweetness is so intense that only minute amounts are needed to replace the sweetness of sugar.

FAT SUBSTITUTES AND ALTERNATIVES

Several types of FDA-approved fat substitutes have been used with varying degrees of success in the food industry. They include olestra (brand name Olean), Simplesse, caprenin, salatrim (brand name Benefat) and oatrim (hydrolyzed oat flour; brand name Replace). Some are synthetic, others are derived from naturally occurring food substances.

Olestra is made of sucrose and vegetable oil. The two are bonded together, and the final product consists of molecules too large to be digested. Because it cannot be digested, olestra does not add any calories. Currently, olestra is used in snack foods such as potato chips. It may become a useful substitute for fats in baking or cooking, but health concerns have kept it from being widely available.

Simplesse is a fat substitute used in frozen desserts such as ice creams and yogurt. Simplesse, made from egg whites or milk proteins, has a rich, creamy texture similar to fat but is fat-free. Products made with Simplesse are not usually fat-free because other fat-containing ingredients are added.

Caprenin and salatrim are fat substitutes used in the candy industry and not available for home or restaurant use. Oatrim is used in baked goods and dairy products. It has also been found to have antioxidant properties and is available for home or restaurant use.

Table 3.6	INGREDIENT SUBSTITUTES
INSTEAD OF	**USE**
Bacon	Canadian bacon or well-cooked, drained bacon
Butter	Powdered butter granules plus liquid (either fat-free milk or water) or butter-flavored oil sprays
Chocolate	Cocoa (vegetable oil may be added as needed)
Cream cheese	Reduced-fat cream cheese or fat-free cream cheese
Emulsified salad dressing	Start with a base of reduced-fat or nonfat yogurt, sour cream or mayonnaise, then thin with fat-free milk; or use a slurry-thickened broth or juice as the oil and add vinegar and other seasonings; or blend silken tofu with other ingredients for a creamy dressing
Ground beef	Textured soy protein; tempeh; seitan, a form of wheat gluten
Light cream	Equal portions of low-fat milk and fat-free evaporated milk
Mayonnaise	Reduced-fat mayonnaise (it can be mixed with reduced-fat or nonfat sour cream)
Sour cream	Reduced-fat or nonfat sour cream; drained reduced-fat or nonfat plain yogurt without gelatin
Whipped cream	Whipped chilled evaporated fat-free milk; the milk and beaters need to be very cold (needs to be stabilized)

OTHER INGREDIENT SUBSTITUTES AND ALTERNATIVES

▶ **additives** substances added to many foods to prevent spoilage or improve appearance, texture, flavor or nutritional value; they may be synthetic materials copied from nature (for example, sugar substitutes) or naturally occurring substances (for example, lecithin). Some food additives may cause allergic reactions in sensitive people.

▶ **incidental food additives** those inadvertently or unintentionally added to foods during processing, such as pesticide residues on fruits

▶ **intentional food additives** those added to foods on purpose, such as the chemicals used to ensure longer shelf life or food colorings

There are many other ingredient substitutes, some of which are identified in Table 3.6. Often ingredient substitutes and alternatives will have a dramatic impact on the nutritional values of a completed dish. Compare, for example, Recipes 33.25 and 33.26 in Chapter 33; the former brownie recipe is made with traditional ingredients, while the latter uses ingredient substitutes. Note the differences, especially in the values for fat and cholesterol.

Ingredient substitutes and, especially, ingredient alternatives change the nutritional values of a dish; they may also change its flavor, texture or appearance. Sometimes these changes are acceptable; sometimes they are not. Because some changes result in unsatisfactory flavors, textures or appearance, many recipes are not suitable for substitution or alteration. Use your judgment.

▶ NUTRITION LABELING

In an effort to provide chefs and consumers with greater information about the nutritional values of foods they purchase, the FDA requires that most food products be clearly labeled. The FDA also closely regulates the language used on these labels. Terms such as "low fat" and "lite" have specific legal definitions. The FDA also closely monitors health claims on food labels. A cereal, for instance, may claim that its fiber content may reduce the incidence of heart disease only if it meets the criteria set forth by the FDA.

The FDA also sets standards for the nutrition claims that can be made on restaurant menus. The language for menus is the same as that for product labels. Restaurateurs, however, are required to supply nutrition information only if they make a claim about a specific dish. For example, if a menu selection is described as "low fat," the dish must have 3 grams or less of fat per serving and the nutrition information (nutrient analysis) should be available to anyone who requests it. Restaurateurs and chefs should consult the FDA and the National Restaurant Association for guidance in complying with these labeling regulations.

PRODUCT CLAIMS

The FDA requires that words such as "low fat" and "fat free" be used according to the following specific standards:

- *Free*–The food contains no or only "physiologically inconsequential" amounts of fat, saturated fat, cholesterol, sodium, sugars or calories.
- *Low, little, few* and *low source of*–The food can be eaten frequently without exceeding dietary guidelines for fat, saturated fat, cholesterol, sodium or calories.

Specific uses include the following:

- *Low fat*–The food has 3 grams or less of fat per serving.
- *Low saturated fat*–The food has 1 gram or less of saturated fat per serving; not more than 15 percent of a serving's calories are from saturated fat.
- *Low sodium*–The food has 140 mg or less of salt per serving.
- *Very low sodium*–The food has 35 mg or less of salt per serving.
- *Low cholesterol*–The food has 20 mg or less of cholesterol per serving.
- *Low calorie*–The food has 40 calories or fewer per serving.
- *Reduced, less* and *fewer*–The nutritionally altered product contains at least 25 percent fewer calories than the regular or reference (that is, FDA standard) food product.
- *Light* or *lite*–The nutritionally altered product contains at least one-third or 50 percent less fat than the reference product. *Light in sodium* means that the nutritionally altered product contains 50 percent or less sodium than the regular or reference product. *Light* may still be used to describe color, as in "light brown sugar."
- *High*–The food contains 20 percent or more of the daily value for a desirable nutrient per serving.
- *More*–The food contains at least 10 percent or more of the daily value for protein, vitamins, minerals, dietary fiber or potassium than the reference product.
- *Good source*–The food contains 10 to 19 percent of the daily value per serving for the specific nutrient such as calcium or dietary fiber.
- *Lean*–The meat, poultry, game, fish or shellfish item contains less than 10 grams of fat, less than 4 grams of saturated fat and less than 95 mg of cholesterol per serving and per 100 grams.
- *Extra lean*–The meat, poultry, game, fish or shellfish item contains less than 5 grams of fat, less than 2 grams of saturated fat and less than 95 mg of cholesterol per serving and per 100 grams.

▶ CONSUMER CONCERNS ABOUT FOOD AND NUTRITION

Many food ingredients have been linked to medical conditions. Some of the links are tenuous at best; others may be well supported by research. Nutrition is a science, and new information about the relationship of food to health and disease is always changing.

Americans have voiced concerns about the possible links of certain fats and dietary cholesterol to heart disease; they want to know if sugar intake is related to obesity, diabetes and heart disease. Some people are concerned that pesticide residues in produce may be dangerous, and they will seek out restaurants that serve organically grown produce. Some people are worried about the increasing prevalence of genetically modified organisms and other products of biotechnology in our food supply and would prefer not to consume foods made with these ingredients. Others are curious about the alleged medicinal or health benefits of foods. Others have metabolic or digestive conditions that make it difficult or even dangerous for them to eat specific ingredients. Because of these concerns, patrons may request that their meals be prepared in special ways or that ingredients be deleted from or added to a dish. Patrons who question the wait staff about ingredients expect complete and accurate information.

A food service operation must train its servers to accurately answer customers' questions about ingredients, especially those commonly known to cause allergic reactions. Some people are so dangerously allergic that even the smallest amount of a particular ingredient could cause a deadly reaction. Common allergens include peanuts, soy, eggs, wheat, shellfish, mushrooms and milk. When using prepared or packaged ingredients in the kitchen, be sure to study the ingredient list and learn to recognize disguised ingredients or ingredients that are not used in their common form. For example, miso and lecithin are soy derivatives. If a customer wants to know whether a dish contains soy, the well-trained server should be able to answer correctly.

The tremendous public interest in nutrition presents a special challenge to chefs. They should be able to prepare and serve food that meets the high standards for health demanded by some patrons, while maintaining the flavor and appearance important to everyone.

▶ NUTRITION, EATING OUT AND THE CHEF

On a typical day, almost half of all American adults eat at least one meal in a food service establishment. Yet even though eating out has become an integral part of everyday life, Americans still treat a restaurant meal as a special occasion. The quantity and choices of foods offered by many restaurants has wreaked havoc with the American diet. Restaurant meals typically have more calories, sodium, fat and cholesterol and less fiber, vitamins and minerals than meals prepared at home. A recent study found that people who eat out most often tend to weigh more than those who usually eat at home.

Ultimately, it is the consumer's responsibility to choose wisely and eat moderately. Nevertheless, restaurateurs complain that customers do not usually order heart-healthy or low-fat dishes, perhaps viewing such menu items as less-tasty options than the traditional fare.

Patrons concerned with calories and fat may choose to order appetizers in place of entrées to control quantity and thereby reduce calories and fat. They may request half-orders or split a full order with a companion. They can ask that dressings and sauces be served on the side or that a different cooking method be used—for instance, that a fish be broiled or baked instead of deep-fried or sautéed. Chefs and restaurateurs should be flexible and willing to accommodate these patrons.

The Food Guide Pyramid was designed to guide food consumption for a more healthful life. It presents a plan for a balanced diet. Chefs can use it to plan balanced menus as well. As the Food Guide Pyramid suggests, chefs do not need to use only meat as the center of the plate presentation. The pyramid demands that a variety of breads, pasta and grains be included on the menu along with an interesting selection of vegetable dishes. And it cautions against the use of too much fat and sugar.

Although not every food service operation can (or should) be devoted to "health food," to the extent appropriate you should offer healthful dining alternatives. Your ability to do so depends, of course, upon your facility. Chefs at hospitals, prisons and schools have much greater control over the foods their guests consume. Therefore, they have a far greater opportunity and responsibility to provide selections for a well-balanced diet. Chefs at most restaurants, however, do not have such captive audiences. But that does not mean that you can shirk your responsibilities. You assist customers when you do the following:

1 Use proper purchasing and storage techniques in order to preserve nutrients.
2 Offer a variety of foods from each tier of the Food Guide Pyramid so that customers have a choice.
3 Offer entrées that emphasize plant instead of animal foods.
4 Offer low-salt and low-fat dishes.
5 Use cooking procedures that preserve rather than destroy nutrients.
6 Use cooking procedures that minimize the use of added fat (for example, stocks, sauces and soups can be cooled and the congealed fats removed; foods can be browned in the oven instead of being sautéed in hot fat).
7 Use equipment that minimizes the use of added fat (e.g., nonstick pans).
8 Train the wait staff to respond properly to nutritional questions diners may have about menu items.
9 Use ingredient alternatives or substitutes where appropriate. If a dish does not lend itself to ingredient alternatives or substitutes, consider creating a new

dish that replaces less-nutritious traditional foods or preparations with more-nutritious ones. For example, instead of serving a sauce made with butter, flour and cream, you can reduce an appropriately seasoned wine, stock or juice and then thicken it with fruit or vegetable purées or cornstarch.

A registered dietician has analyzed all of the recipes in this book using nutritional analysis software that incorporates data from the USDA, research laboratories and food manufacturers. The nutrient information provided here should be used only as a reference, however. A margin of error of approximately 20 percent can be expected because of natural variations in ingredients; the federal government permits food manufacturers and other suppliers to use this same margin of error in their food labeling efforts. Preparation techniques and serving sizes may also significantly alter the values of many nutrients. For the nutritional analysis, if a recipe offers a choice of ingredients, the first-mentioned ingredient was the one used. Ingredients listed as "to taste" (TT) and "as needed" were omitted from the analysis. Corn oil and whole milk were used throughout for "vegetable oil" and "milk," respectively. When given a range of ingredient quantities or numbers of servings, the average was used.

Throughout this book various recipes are marked with the pyramid symbol illustrated in Figure 3.2. This symbol identifies dishes that are particularly low in calories, fat, saturated fat or sodium; if appropriate, they may also be a good source of vitamins, protein, fiber or calcium.

Vegetarian dishes are indicated with the symbol illustrated in Figure 3.3. These recipes do not contain any meat, fish, shellfish or poultry, but may contain dairy products and/or eggs. Vegetarian dishes are not necessarily low in calories, fat or sodium, nor are they automatically good sources of vitamins, protein, fiber or calcium, as defined by government standards.

FIGURE 3.2 ▶ Symbol for a healthy recipe

FIGURE 3.3 ▶ Symbol for a vegetarian recipe

CONCLUSION

A basic understanding and appreciation of nutrition are important for both the consumer and those who prepare the foods consumed.

What you serve is important. Carbohydrates, proteins, lipids (fats), vitamins, minerals, and water, in varying amounts, are all necessary for good health. The Food Guide Pyramid can guide selections to create and maintain a healthful diet.

How foods are prepared is also important. Remember that some cooking and storage techniques preserve nutrients; others do not. In addition, by substituting or modifying ingredients and preparation methods, many dishes can be made more nutritious.

QUESTIONS FOR DISCUSSION

1 Identify the six categories of nutrients and list two sources for each.

2 What are the differences between saturated fats and unsaturated fats? Identify two sources for each.

3 List four ways to reduce mineral and vitamin loss when storing or preparing foods.

4 Describe the Food Guide Pyramid. Explain how a chef can use it to plan well-balanced meals and how a consumer can use it to establish a healthful diet. What other diet-planning tools can be used along with the pyramid?

5 Locate the latest information on the U.S. government's standards for organic certification.

6 Find the address and contact information for your local extension service. Determine what nutritional guidance they offer consumers.

MY MOTHER'S [RECIPES] DON'T DO ME AS MUCH GOOD AS THEY MIGHT BECAUSE SHE NEVER INCLUDED DIRECTIONS. HER REASONING, OFTEN EXPRESSED, WAS THAT ANY COOK WORTH HER SALT WOULD KNOW, GIVEN A LIST OF INGREDIENTS, WHAT TO DO WITH THEM, AND IF SHE DID COME TO A MOMENTARY LOSS WHILE STIRRING UP A DISH—*TASTE* IT! COOKING WAS A MATTER OF BORN SENSE, ORDINARY GOOD JUDGMENT, ENOUGH EXPERIENCE, MATERIALS WORTH THE BOTHERING ABOUT, AND TASTING.

—Eudora Welty, American author (1909–2001) in her introduction to The Jackson Cookbook, *1971*

4

MENUS AND RECIPES

AFTER STUDYING THIS CHAPTER, YOU WILL BE ABLE TO:

▶ appreciate the different types and styles of menus

▶ understand the purpose of standardized recipes

▶ convert recipe yield amounts

▶ appreciate the need for cost controls in any food service operation

▶ **entrée** the main dish of an American meal, usually meat, poultry, fish or shellfish accompanied by a vegetable and starch; in France, the first course, served before the fish and meat courses

Today's professional chef must master more than the basics of béchamel, butchering and bread baking. You must be equally skilled in the business of food services. This means knowing what products cost and how to control and maintain food costs. It also means understanding how accurate measurements, portion control and proper food handling directly affect the food service operation's bottom line.

This chapter introduces you to various types and styles of menus. It then explains a standardized recipe format and presents information on measurements and techniques for changing or converting recipe yields. It then describes methods for determining unit and recipe costs and concludes with a discussion of methods for controlling food costs.

▶ THE MENU

Whether it lists Spanish dishes, hamburgers, just desserts or classic cuisine, and whether the prices range from inexpensive to exorbitant, the menu is the soul of every food service operation. Its purposes are to identify for the consumer the foods and beverages the operation offers, to create consumer enthusiasm and to increase sales. When combined with good food and good service, a good menu helps ensure success.

Most menus offer consumers sufficient selections to build an entire meal. A typical North American meal consists of three courses. The first course may be a hot or cold appetizer, soup or salad. The second course is the **entrée** or main dish, usually meat, poultry, fish or shellfish accompanied by a vegetable and starch. The third course is dessert, either a sweet preparation or fruit and cheese. For a more formal meal, there may be a progression of first courses, including a hot or cold appetizer and soup, as well as a fish course served before the main dish (which, in this case, would not be fish). For a meal served in the European tradition, the salad would be presented as a palate cleanser after the main dish and before the dessert.

TYPES OF MENUS

Menus are classified according to the regularity with which the foods are offered:

1 **Static menu**—All patrons are offered the same foods every day. Once a static menu is developed and established, it rarely changes. Static menus are typically found in fast-food operations, ethnic restaurants, steakhouses and the like. Static menus can also be used in institutional settings. For example, a static menu at an elementary school could offer students, along with a vegetable and dessert, the same luncheon choices every school day: a cheeseburger, fish sticks, chicken tacos, pizza wedges or a sandwich.

2 **Cycle menu**—A cycle menu is developed for a set period; at the end of that period it repeats itself (that is, on a seven-day cycle, the same menu is used every Monday). Some cycle menus are written on a seasonal basis, with a new menu for each season to take advantage of product availability. Cycle menus are used commonly in schools, hospitals and other institutions. Although cycle menus may be repetitious, the

FOOD IN FLICKS

Growing up in New York City afforded me a wide array of cultural experiences. East 86th Street had everything I needed: bookstores, record stores, pizza places, and my beloved movies. Ah, the movies. Remember that bygone era before the VCR when waiting on line at the cinema was a sociable experience?

A sojourn to the movies also meant a fine dining experience: a hot dog and a papaya drink at Papaya King. Laugh if you must, but Papaya King, just like Gramercy Tavern, is also listed in the Zagat guide. Even though I'm no longer a kid, I still occassionaly sneak in a contraband cheeseburger, as Woody Allen did at the now-defunct Bleecker Street Cinema in his 1989 film *Crimes and Misdemeanors.*

Movies have always embraced food as well; over the years, food has been celebrated, created, thrown, questionably digested and even animated. The combination of food and film could be considered, as Humphrey Bogart said to Claude Rains at the end of *Casablanca,* "the beginning of a beautiful friendship." Here's a list of some films and, if you'll allow, some editorial remarks to give you food for thought the next time you visit a video emporium.

Animal House (1978)—John Belushi at the cafeteria. His imitation of a zit, and ultimately the food fight.

Blazing Saddles (1974)—Mel Brooks. The campfire scene. Enough said.

Big Night (1996)—The creation of that amazing Timpano in hopes that Louis Prima would soon arrive to share in what would sadly be the restaurant's final night.

Diner (1982)—"You gonna finish that sandwich?"

Monty Python's The Meaning of Life (1983)—"One tiny wafer-thin mint?"

Italianamerican (1974)—Martin Scorsese's look at his parents' history from the old country and the secret to great sauce making.

Tom Jones (1963)—Food as seduction in Tony Richardson's Oscar winner.

My Dinner with André (1981)—The sharing of a meal and life lessons and philosophy between André Gregory and Wallace Shawn.

Fried Green Tomatoes (1991)—Secret-recipe barbecue and blackberry cobbler.

Tampopo (1986)—The quest of a truck driver to help a widow improve a noodle shop.

The Big Chill (1983)—Preparing dinner to the strains of the Temptations' "Ain't Too Proud to Beg."

Chocolat (2000)

The Godfather (1972)—Clemenza teaches the young Michael Corleone the secret to a good spaghetti sauce: "Ya might have to cook for twenty, thirty guys someday." Or Clemenza's instructions to one of his henchmen after dispatching a traitor: "Leave the gun . . . take the cannoli."

Like Water for Chocolate (1992)

Kramer vs. Kramer (1979)—Dustin Hoffman trying in vain to make French toast for his son the morning after his wife, Meryl Streep, has left them.

Eat Drink, Man Woman (1994)

Babe (1995)—Ferdinand the Duck's rant: "Christmas means dinner; dinner means death. Death means carnage; Christmas is carnage!"

Willy Wonka and the Chocolate Factory (1971)—Everlasting Gobstoppers, fizzy-lifting drink, a chocolate river . . . pure imagination.

Goodfellas (1990)—Paul Sorvino slicing garlic with a razor blade to enhance his jail cell cooking.

Soul Food (1997)

Five Easy Pieces (1970)—Jack Nicholson and the chicken salad sandwich.

The Silence of the Lambs (1991)—"A census taker once tried to test me. I ate his liver with some fava beans and a nice Chianti."

The Gold Rush (1925)—Charlie Chaplin's classic includes the dance of the dinner rolls and the preparation of a leather boot for dinner.

L.A. Story (1991)—"I'll have a half double decaffeinated half-caf, with a twist of lemon."

Babette's Feast (1987)—Oscar winner for Best Foreign Film in which the spoils of a lottery winning goes entirely towards a celebratory feast.

I would be remiss if I neglected Bugs Bunny, hence *French Rarebit* (1951). French chefs Louie and François argue over who will have Bugs on the menu. Bugs's suggestion: "Of course if you want something really good, you can't beat a Louisiana Back Bay Bayou Bunny Bordelaise . . . à la Antoine." Chef Louie: "À la Antoine? You mean Antoine of New Orleans?" Bugs: "I don't mean Antoine of Flatbush." That's all folks!

ROGER RAINES, an actor and writer who also works at Gramercy Tavern, New York, NY

repetition is not necessarily noticeable to diners because of the length of the cycles.

3 **Market menu**—A market menu is based upon product availability during a specific period; it is written to use foods when they are in peak season or readily available. Market menus are becoming increasingly popular with chefs (and consumers) since they challenge the chef's ingenuity in using fresh, seasonal products. Market menus are short-lived, however, because of limited product availability and perishability. In fact, they often change daily.

4 **Hybrid menu**—A hybrid menu combines a static menu with a cycle menu or a market menu of specials.

Food service operations may have separate menus for breakfast, lunch or dinner. If all three meals are available all day and are listed on the same menu, the menu is often called a **California menu;** California menus are typically found in 24-hour restaurants. Depending on the food service operation's objectives, separate specialty menus for drinks, hors d'oeuvres, desserts, brunch or afternoon tea, for example, are used.

Regardless of whether the menu is static, cycle, market or hybrid, it can offer consumers the opportunity to purchase their selections à la carte, semi à la carte, table d'hôte or some combination of the three.

1 **À la carte**—Every food and beverage item is priced and ordered separately.

2 **Semi à la carte**—With this popular menu style, some food items (particularly appetizers and desserts) are priced and ordered separately, while the entrée is accompanied by and priced to include other items, such as a salad, starch or vegetable.

3 **Table d'hôte** or **prix fixe**—This menu offers a complete meal at a set price. (The term *table d'hôte* is French for "host's table" and is derived from the innkeeper's practice of seating all guests at a large communal table and serving them all the same meal.) A table d'hôte meal can range from very elegant to a diner's blue-plate special.

Many menus combine à la carte, semi à la carte and table d'hôte choices. For example, appetizers, salads and desserts may be available à la carte; entrées may be offered semi à la carte (served with a salad, starch and vegetable), while the daily special is a complete (table d'hôte or prix fixe) meal.

MENU LANGUAGE

The menu is the principal way in which the food service operation, including the chef, communicates with the consumer. A well-designed menu often reflects the input of design, marketing, art and other consultants as well as the chef and management. The type of folds, cover, artwork, layout, typefaces, colors and paper are all important considerations. But the most important consideration is the language.

The menu should list the foods offered. It may include descriptions such as the preparation method, essential ingredients and service method as well as the quality, cut and quantity of product. For example, the menu can list "Porterhouse Steak" or "Mesquite Grilled 16-oz. Angus Beef Porterhouse Steak."

TRUTH IN ADVERTISING

Federal as well as some state and local laws require that certain menu language be accurate. Areas of particular concern include statements about quantity, quality, grade and freshness. Accurate references to an item's source are also important. If brand names are used, those brands must be served. If the restaurant claims to be serving "Fresh Dover Sole," it must be just that, not frozen sole from New England. (On the other hand, like French or Russian dressing, "English mint sauce" is a generic name for a style of food, so using that geographical adjective is appropriate even if the mint sauce is made in Arizona.) A reference to "our own fresh-baked" desserts means that the restaurant regularly bakes the desserts on premises, serves them soon after baking and does not substitute commercially prepared or frozen goods.

NUTRITIONAL STATEMENTS

As discussed in Chapter 3, Nutrition, the FDA carefully regulates the language used on packaged food labels. In 1997, the FDA extended its nutrition labeling regulations to restaurant menus. These regulations are intended to prevent restaurants from making misleading health or nutrition claims. For example, terms such as "light," "healthy" or "heart healthy" must be accurate and documented. The standards for calculating and presenting that information are far less stringent than the regulations for packaged foods, however. Restaurants may support their claims with data from any "reasonable" source, and may present that information in any format, including verbally. Nutritional data is not required for menu items that do not carry a nutritional content or health claim.

▶ STANDARDIZED RECIPES

Menu writing and **recipe** development are mutually dependent activities. Once the menu is created, standardized recipes should be prepared for each item. A **standardized recipe** is one that will produce a known quality and quantity of food for a specific operation. It specifies (1) the type and amount of each ingredient, (2) the preparation and cooking procedures and (3) the yield and portion size.

Standardized recipes are not found in books or provided by manufacturers; they are recipes customized to your operation—cooking time, temperature and utensils should be based on the equipment actually available. Yield should be adjusted to an amount appropriate for your operation. A recipe must be tested repeatedly and adjusted to fit your facility and your needs before it can be considered standardized.

Standardized recipes are a tool for the chef and management. The written forms assist with training cooks, educating service staff and controlling financial matters. They help ensure that customers receive a consistent quality and quantity of product. And they are essential for accurate recipe costing and menu pricing. Each recipe should be complete, consistent and simple to read and follow. These recipe forms should be stored in a readily accessible place. Index cards, notebook binders or a computerized database may be used, depending on the size and complexity of the operation.

▶ MEASUREMENTS AND CONVERSIONS

MEASUREMENT FORMATS

Accurate measurements are among the most important aspects of food production. Ingredients and portions must be measured correctly to ensure consistent product quality. In other words, the chef must be able to prepare a recipe the same way each time, and portion sizes must be the same from one order to the next. In a kitchen, measurements may be made in three ways: weight, volume and count.

Weight refers to the mass or heaviness of a substance. It is expressed in terms such as grams, ounces, pounds and tons. Weight may be used to measure liquid or dry ingredients (for example, 2 pounds of eggs for a bread recipe) and portions (for example, 4 ounces of sliced turkey for a sandwich). Since weight is generally the most accurate form of measurement, portion scales or balance scales are commonly used in kitchens.

Volume refers to the space occupied by a substance. This is mathematically expressed as *height × width × length*. It is expressed in terms such as cups, quarts, gallons, teaspoons, fluid ounces, bushels and liters. Volume is most commonly used to measure liquids. It may also be used for dry ingredients when the amount is too small to be weighed accurately (for example, ¼ teaspoon of salt). Although measuring by volume is somewhat less accurate than measuring by weight, volume measurements are generally quicker to do.

Frequently, mistakes are made in food preparation by chefs who assume wrongly that weight and volume are equal. Do not be fooled! One cup does not

▶ **recipe** a set of written instructions for producing a specific food or beverage; also known as a formula

▶ **standardized recipe** a recipe producing a known quality and quantity of food for a specific operation

Table 4.1 **COMMON ABBREVIATIONS**

teaspoon = tsp.
tablespoon = Tbsp.
cup = c.
pint = pt.
quart = qt.
gram = g
milliliter = ml
liter = lt
ounce = oz.
fluid ounce = fl. oz.
pound = lb.
kilogram = kg

always equal 8 ounces. Although it is true that 1 standard cup contains 8 *fluid* ounces, it is not true that the contents of that standard cup will *weigh* 8 ounces. For example, the weight of 1 cup of diced apples will vary depending on the size of the apple pieces. Errors are commonly made in the bakeshop by cooks who assume that 8 ounces of flour is the same as 1 cup of flour. In fact, 1 cup of flour weighs only about 4 ½ ounces.

It is not unusual to see both weight and volume measurements used in a single recipe. When a recipe ingredient is expressed in weight, weigh it. When it is expressed as a volume, measure it. Like most rules, however, this one has exceptions. The weight and volume of water, butter, eggs and milk are, in each case, the same. For these ingredients you may use whichever measurement is most convenient.

Count refers to the number of individual items. Count is used in recipes (for example, 4 eggs) and in portion control (for example, 2 fish fillets or 1 ear of corn). Count is also commonly used in purchasing to indicate the size of the individual items. For example, a "96 count" case of lemons means that a 40-pound case contains 96 individual lemons; a "115 count" case means that the same 40-pound case contains 115 individual lemons. So, each lemon in the 96-count case is larger than those in the 115-count case. Shrimp is another item commonly sold by count. One pound of shrimp may contain from eight to several hundred shrimp, depending on the size of the individual pieces. When placing an order, the chef must specify the desired count. For example, when ordering one pound of 21–25-count shrimp, the chef expects to receive not fewer than 21 nor more than 25 pieces.

MEASUREMENT SYSTEMS

The measurement formats of weight, volume and count are used in both the U.S. and metric measurement systems. Both of these systems are used in modern food service operations, so you should be able to prepare recipes written in either one.

The **U.S. system,** with which you are probably familiar, is actually the more difficult system to understand. It uses pounds for weight and cups for volume.

The **metric system** is the most commonly used system in the world. Developed in France during the late 18th century, it was intended to fill the need for a mathematically rational and uniform system of measurement. The metric system is a decimal system in which the gram, liter and meter are the basic units of weight, volume and length, respectively. Larger or smaller units of weight, volume and length are formed by adding a prefix to the words *gram, liter* or *meter.* Some of the more commonly used prefixes in food service operations are *deca-* (10), *kilo-* (1000), *deci-* ($\frac{1}{10}$) and *milli-* ($\frac{1}{1000}$). Thus, a kilogram is 1000 grams; a decameter is 10 meters; a milliliter is $\frac{1}{1000}$ of a liter. Because the metric system is based on multiples of 10, it is extremely easy to increase or decrease amounts.

The most important thing for a chef to know about the metric system is that *you do not need to convert between the metric system and the U.S. system in recipe preparation.* If a recipe is written in metric units, use metric measuring equipment; if it is written in U.S. units, use U.S. measuring equipment. Luckily, most modern measuring equipment is calibrated in both U.S. and metric increments. The need to convert amounts will arise only if the proper equipment is unavailable.

CONVERTING GRAMS AND OUNCES

As you can see from Table 4.2, 1 ounce equals 28.35 grams. Likewise, 1 fluid ounce equals 28.35 milliliters. So, to convert ounces/fluid ounces to grams/milliliters, multiply the number of ounces by 28 (rounded for convenience).

FANNIE MERRITT FARMER (1857–1915)

Fannie Farmer is more than the name on a cookbook. She was an early, vigorous and influential proponent of scientific cooking, nutrition and academic training for culinary professionals.

At age 30, Farmer enrolled in the Boston Cooking School. The school's curriculum was not designed to graduate chefs, but rather to produce cooking teachers. After graduating from the two-year course, Farmer stayed on, first as assistant principal and then as principal.

During her years there (and, indeed, for the rest of her career) she was obsessed with accurate measurements. She waged a campaign to eliminate measurements such as a "wine glass" of liquid, a "handful" of flour, a chunk of butter the "size of an egg" or a "heaping spoonful" of salt. For, as she once wrote, "correct measurements are absolutely necessary to insure the best results." Farmer also sought to replace the European system of measuring ingredients by weight with, for her, a more scientific measurement system based on volume and level measures (for example, a level tablespoon). To a great degree, she succeeded.

Her writings reflect her concern for accurate measurements. Her first book, *The Boston Cooking School Cookbook* (1896), includes clearly written recipes with precise measurements. Later editions add recipe yields, oven temperatures and baking times.

After leaving the Boston Cooking School, she opened Miss Farmer's School of Cookery.

The curriculum listed 60 lessons divided into six courses. The first course covered the basics: laying a fire and using a gas stove; making breads, eggs, soups, potatoes and coffee. The second and third courses emphasized more advanced cooking. Pastry, desserts and salads were taught during the fourth course; presentation and service were taught during the fifth course. Quite progressively for the time, her sixth course taught cooking for nurses and emphasized nutrition and the dietary needs of the sick and elderly. (This may have reflected Farmer's personal interests, for she was partially disabled and in poor health from time to time.)

Farmer wrote other cookbooks, including *Food and Cookery for the Sick and Convalescent* (1904) and *A New Book of Cookery* (first published in 1912 and republished in several revised versions). Her writings never address the joys of cooking and eating; rather, they reflect a scientific approach to cooking and rely on clearly written, accurately measured recipes for good, solid food.

$$8 \text{ oz.} \times 28 = 224 \text{ g}$$

$$8 \text{ fl. oz.} \times 28 = 224 \text{ ml}$$

To convert grams/milliliters to ounces/fluid ounces, divide the number of grams/milliliters by 28.

$$224 \text{ g} \div 28 = 8 \text{ oz.}$$

$$224 \text{ ml} \div 28 = 8 \text{ fl. oz.}$$

To help you develop a framework for judging conversions, remember that:

▷ A kilogram is about 2.2 pounds
▷ A gram is about $\frac{1}{30}$ ounce
▷ A pound is about 450 grams
▷ A liter is slightly more than a quart
▷ A centimeter is slightly less than $\frac{1}{2}$ inch
▷ 0°C (32°F) is the freezing point of water
▷ 100°C (212°F) is the boiling point of water

These approximations are not a substitute for accurate conversions, however. Appendix II contains additional information on equivalents and metric conversions. There is no substitute for knowing this information. In fact, it should become second nature to you.

Table 4.2	COMMON EQUIVALENTS
dash	= ⅛ teaspoon
3 teaspoons	= 1 tablespoon
2 tablespoons	= 1 fl. oz.
4 tablespoons	= ¼ cup (2 fl. oz.)
5⅓ tablespoons	= ⅓ cup (2⅔ fl. oz.)
16 tablespoons	= 1 cup (8 fl. oz.)
2 cups	= 1 pint (16 fl. oz.)
2 pints	= 1 quart (32 fl. oz.)
4 quarts	= 1 gallon (128 fl. oz.)
2 gallons	= 1 peck
4 pecks	= 1 bushel
1 gram	= 0.035 ounce (1/30 oz.)
1 ounce	= 28.35 grams
454 grams	= 1 pound
2.2 pounds	= 1 kilogram (1000 grams)
1 teaspoon	= 5 milliliters
1 tablespoon	= 15 milliliters
1 fluid ounce	= 28.35 milliliters
1 cup	= 0.24 liters
1 gallon	= 3.80 liters

▶ **yield** the total amount of a product made from a specific recipe; also, the amount of a food item remaining after cleaning or processing

▶ **conversion factor (C.F.)** the number used to increase or decrease ingredient quantities and recipe yields

$$\frac{New}{Old} = C.F.$$

$$\frac{Old\ Recipe \quad X \quad C.F.}{New\ Recipe}$$

▶ RECIPE CONVERSIONS

Whether 6 servings or 60, every recipe is designed to produce or **yield** a specific amount of product. A recipe's yield may be expressed in *volume, weight* or *servings* (for example, 1 quart of sauce; 8 pounds of bread dough; 8 half-cup servings). If the expected yield does not meet your needs, you must convert (that is, increase or decrease) the ingredient amounts. Recipe conversion is sometimes complicated by *portion size conversion*. For example, it may be necessary to convert a recipe that initially produces 24 8-ounce servings of soup into a recipe that produces 62 6-ounce servings.

It is just as easy to change yields by uneven amounts as it is to double or halve recipes. The mathematical principle is the same: *Each ingredient is multiplied by a* **conversion factor.** Do not take shortcuts by estimating recipe amounts or conversion factors. Inaccurate conversions lead to inedible foods, embarrassing shortages or wasteful excesses. Take the time to learn and apply proper conversion techniques.

CONVERTING TOTAL YIELD

When portion size is unimportant or remains the same, recipe yield is converted by a simple two-step process:

STEP 1 Divide the desired (new) yield by the recipe (old) yield to obtain the conversion factor (C.F.).

new yield ÷ old yield = conversion factor

STEP 2 Multiply each ingredient quantity by the conversion factor to obtain the new quantity.

old quantity × conversion factor = new quantity

EXAMPLE 4.1

You need to convert a recipe for cauliflower soup. The present recipe yields 1½ gallons. You need to make only ¾ gallon.

STEP 1 Determine the conversion factor:

0.75 gallon ÷ 1.5 gallons = 0.5

Note that any unit can be used, as long as the *same* unit is used with *both* the new and the old recipes. For example, the same conversion factor would be obtained if the recipe amounts were converted to fluid ounces:

96 fluid ounces ÷ 192 fluid ounces = 0.5

STEP 2 Apply the conversion factor to each ingredient in the soup recipe:

CAULIFLOWER SOUP

	old quantity	×	C.F.	=	new quantity
Cauliflower, chopped	5 lb.	×	0.5	=	2½ lb.
Celery stalks	4	×	0.5	=	2
Onion	1	×	0.5	=	½
Chicken stock	2 qt.	×	0.5	=	1 qt.
Heavy cream	3 pt.	×	0.5	=	1½ pt.

CONVERTING PORTION SIZE

Sometimes the amount of food served as a portion must be changed. For example, new soup cups may hold less than cups now being used, or a banquet menu may require a smaller entrée portion than is normally served à la carte. A few additional steps are necessary to convert recipes when portion sizes must also be changed. This is easy to understand if you think in terms of the total amount of a food item that is needed in relation to the total amount of that item (yield) produced by the current recipe. The key is to find a common denominator for the new and old recipes: ounces, grams, cups, servings and so on. Any unit can be used, as long as the *same* unit is used with *both* the new and the old recipes.

STEP 1 Determine the total yield of the existing recipe by multiplying the number of portions by the portion size.

original portions × original portion size = total (old) yield

STEP 2 Determine the total yield desired by multiplying the new number of portions by the new portion size.

desired portions × desired portion size = total (new) yield

STEP 3 Obtain the conversion factor as described earlier.

total (new) yield ÷ total (old) yield = conversion factor

STEP 4 Multiply each ingredient quantity by the conversion factor.

old quantity × conversion factor = new quantity

$$\frac{\text{No. of Portions} \times \text{Portion Size}}{\text{Yield}}$$

$$\frac{\text{New Yield}}{\text{Old Yield}} = \text{C.F.}$$

EXAMPLE 4.2

Returning to the cauliflower soup: The original recipe produced 1½ gallons or 48 4-ounce servings. Now you need 72 6-ounce servings.

STEP 1 Total original yield is 48 × 4 = 192 ounces.
STEP 2 Total desired yield is 72 × 6 = 432 ounces.
STEP 3 The conversion factor is calculated by dividing total new yield by total old yield:

432 ÷ 192 = 2.25

STEP 4 Old ingredient quantities are multiplied by the conversion factor to determine the new quantities:

CAULIFLOWER SOUP

	old quantity	×	C.F.	=	new quantity
Cauliflower, chopped	5 lb.	×	2.25	=	11.25 lb.
Celery stalks	4	×	2.25	=	9
Onion	1	×	2.25	=	2.25
Chicken stock	2 qt.	×	2.25	=	4.5 qt.
Heavy cream	3 pt.	×	2.25	=	6.75 pt.

ADDITIONAL CONVERSION PROBLEMS

When making large recipe changes—for example, from 5 to 25 portions or 600 to 300 portions—you may encounter additional problems. The mathematical conversions described here do not take into account changes in equipment, evaporation rates, unforeseen recipe errors or cooking times. Chefs learn to use their judgment, knowledge of cooking principles and skills to compensate for these factors.

EQUIPMENT

When you change the size of a recipe, you must often change the equipment used as well. Problems arise, however, when the production techniques previously used no longer work with the new quantity of ingredients. For example, if you normally make a muffin recipe in small quantities by hand and you increase the recipe size, it may be necessary to prepare the batter in a mixer. But if mixing time remains the same, the batter may become overmixed, resulting in poor-quality muffins. Trying to prepare a small amount of product in equipment that is too large for the task can also affect its quality.

EVAPORATION

Equipment changes can also affect product quality because of changes in evaporation rates. Increasing a soup recipe may require substituting a tilt skillet for a saucepan. But because a tilt skillet provides more surface area for evaporation than does a saucepan, reduction time must be decreased to prevent overthickening the soup. The increased evaporation caused by increased surface area may also alter the strength of the seasonings.

RECIPE ERRORS

A recipe may contain errors in ingredients or techniques that are not obvious when it is prepared in small quantities. When increased, however, small mistakes often become big (and obvious) ones, and the final product suffers. The only solution is to test recipes carefully and rely on your knowledge of cooking principles to compensate for unexpected problems.

TIME

Do not multiply time specifications given in a recipe by the conversion factor used with the recipe's ingredients. All things being equal, *cooking time* will not change when recipe size changes. For example, a muffin requires the same amount of baking time whether you prepare 1 dozen or 14 dozen. Cooking time will be affected, however, by changes in evaporation rate or heat conduction caused by equipment changes. *Mixing time* may change when recipe size is changed. Different equipment may perform mixing tasks more or less efficiently than previously used equipment. Again, rely on experience and good judgment.

▶ CALCULATING UNIT COSTS AND RECIPE COSTS

UNIT COSTS

Food service operations purchase most foods from suppliers in bulk or wholesale packages. For example, canned goods are purchased by the case; produce by the flat, case or lug; and flour and sugar by 25- or 50-pound bags. Even fish and meats are often purchased in large cuts, not individual serving-sized portions. The purchased amount is rarely used for a single recipe, however. It must be broken down into smaller units such as pounds, cups, quarts or ounces.

In order to allocate the proper ingredient costs to the recipe being prepared, it is necessary to convert **as-purchased (A.P.) costs or prices** to **unit costs or**

▶ **as purchased (A.P.)** the condition or cost of an item as it is purchased or received from the supplier

▶ **unit cost** the price paid to acquire one of the specified units

prices. To find the unit cost (that is, the cost of a particular unit, say, a single egg) in a package containing multiple units (for example, a 30-dozen case), divide the A.P. cost of the package by the number of units in the package.

A.P. cost ÷ number of units = cost per unit

$$\frac{\text{A.P. \$}}{\text{\# of Units}} = \text{\$ per Unit}$$

EXAMPLE 4.3

A case of #10 cans contains six individual cans. If a case of tomato paste costs $23.50, then each can costs $3.92.

$$\$23.50 \div 6 = \$3.92$$

If your recipe uses less than the total can, you must continue dividing the cost of the can until you arrive at the appropriate unit amount. Continuing with the tomato paste example, if you need only 1 cup of tomato paste, divide the can price ($3.92) by the total number of cups contained in the can to arrive at the cost per cup (unit). The list of canned-good sizes in Appendix II shows that a #10 can contains approximately 13 cups. Using the formula, each cup costs $0.30.

$$\$3.92 \div 13 = \$0.30$$

The cost of one cup can be reduced even further if necessary. If the recipe uses only 1 tablespoon of tomato paste, divide the cost per cup by the number of tablespoons in a cup. As you can see, the cost for 1 tablespoon of this tomato paste is $0.018.

$$\$0.30 \div 16 = \$.018$$

So when you are calculating the total cost of a recipe containing a tablespoon of tomato paste, the unit cost will be $.018 or 1.8¢.

Cost information is usually provided to the chef or manager from purchase invoices. It may also be necessary to examine a product's label or package to determine some information such as actual weight or size.

RECIPE COSTS

A standard recipe, listing the ingredients and their amounts, as well as the number and size of the portions, must be established in order to determine the cost of a completed menu item. Once an accurate recipe is written, the **total recipe cost** is calculated with the following two-step procedure:

STEP 1 Determine the cost for the given quantity of each recipe ingredient with the unit costing procedures described earlier.

STEP 2 Add all the ingredient costs together to obtain the total recipe cost.

The total recipe cost can then be broken down into the **cost per portion,** which is the most useful figure for food cost controls. To arrive at cost per portion, divide the total recipe cost by the total number of servings or portions produced by that recipe.

total recipe cost ÷ number of portions = cost per portion

The Recipe Costing Form shown in Figure 4.1 is useful for organizing recipe costing information. It provides space for listing each ingredient, the quantity of each ingredient needed, the cost of each unit (known as **edible portion** or **E.P**), and the total cost for the ingredient. Total yield, portion size and cost per portion are listed at the bottom of the form. Note that there is no space for recipe procedures, since these are generally irrelevant in recipe costing.

▶ **total recipe cost** the total cost of ingredients for a particular recipe; it does not reflect overhead, labor, fixed expenses or profit

▶ **cost per portion** the amount of the total recipe cost divided by the number of portions produced from that recipe; the cost of one serving

$$\frac{\text{Recipe \$}}{\text{\# of Portions}} = \text{\$ per Portion}$$

▶ **edible portion (E.P.)** the amount of a food item available for consumption or use after trimming or fabrication; a smaller, more convenient portion of a larger or bulk unit

RECIPE COSTING FORM

Menu Item _____Beef Stew_____ Date _____

Total Yield _____200 fl. oz._____ Portion Size _____4 fl. oz._____

| INGREDIENT | QUANTITY | COST | | | RECIPE COST |
		A.P. $	Yield %*	E.P. $	
Beef, cubes	6 lb.	1.60/lb.		1.60/lb.	9.60
Corn oil	3 Tbsp.	4.58/gal.		.29/c.	.05
Flour	1 1/2 oz.	11.20/50#		.22/lb.	.02
Beef stock	2 qt.	1.50/gal.		.375/qt.	.75
Carrots, diced	1 lb.	.26/lb.	82%	.32/lb.	.32
Potatoes, diced	2 lb.	.28/lb.	80%	.35/lb.	.70
Onions	2	.10 each		.10 each	.20
Salt	TT				-0-

TOTAL RECIPE COST $ _____11.64_____

Number of Portions _____25_____

Cost per Portion $ _____.465_____

*The yield percentage is used to calculate the amount of waste that naturally occurs when cleaning, peeling and processing certain foods. Calculating and applying yield factors is beyond the scope of this text.

FIGURE 4.1 ▶ Recipe costing form

▶ CONTROLLING FOOD COSTS

Many things affect food costs in any given operation; most can be controlled by the chef or manager. These controls do not require mathematical calculations or formulas, just basic management skills and a good dose of common sense. The following factors all have an impact on the operation's bottom line:

▶ Menu
▶ Purchasing/ordering
▶ Receiving
▶ Storing
▶ Issuing
▶ Kitchen procedures
  Establishing standard portions
  Waste
▶ Sales and service

Chefs tend to focus their control efforts in the area of kitchen preparation. Although this may seem logical, it is not adequate. A good chef will be involved in all aspects of the operation to help prevent problems from arising or to correct those that may occur.

MENU

A profitable menu is based upon many variables, including customer desires, physical space and equipment, ingredient availability, cost of goods sold, employee skills and competition. All management personnel, including the chef, should be consulted when planning the menu. Menu changes, though possibly desirable, must be executed with as much care as the original design.

PURCHASING/ORDERING

Purchasing techniques have a direct impact on cost controls. On the one hand, **parstock** must be adequate for efficient operations; on the other hand, too much inventory wastes space and resources and may spoil. Before any items are ordered, purchasing specifications should be established and communicated to potential purveyors. Specifications should precisely describe the item, including grade, quality, packaging and unit size. Each operation should design its own form to best meet its specific needs. A sample specification form is shown in Figure 4.2. This information can be used to obtain price quotes from several purveyors. Update these quotes periodically to ensure that you are getting the best value for your money.

▶ **parstock (par)** the amount of stock necessary to cover operating needs between deliveries

RECEIVING

Whether goods are received by a full-time clerk, as they are in a large hotel, or by the chef or kitchen manager, certain standards should be observed. The person signing for merchandise should first confirm that the items were actually ordered. Second, determine whether the items listed on the invoice are the ones being delivered and that the price and quantity listed are accurate. Third, the items, especially meats and produce, should be checked for quality, freshness and weight. The temperature of all perishable items should be carefully checked at the time of delivery to ensure compliance with food safety standards. Established purchase specifications should be readily available for anyone responsible for receiving goods.

STORING

Proper storage of foodstuffs is crucial in order to prevent spoilage, pilferage and waste. Stock must be rotated so that the older items are used first. Such a system for rotating stock is referred to as **FIFO:** first in, first out. Dry storage areas should be well ventilated and lit to prevent pest infestation and mold. Freezers and refrigerators should be easily accessible, operating properly, and kept clean and organized.

▶ **FIFO** first in, first out; a system of rotating inventory, particularly perishable and semiperishable goods, in which items are used in the order in which they are received

ISSUING

It may be necessary, particularly in larger operations, to limit storeroom access to specific personnel. Maintaining ongoing inventory records or parstock sheets helps the or-

MEAT PURCHASING SPECIFICATIONS	
Product:	
Menu Item:	
Grade/Quality:	NAMP/IMPS#:
Packaging:	
Pricing Unit:	
Delivery Conditions:	
Comments:	

FIGURE 4.2 ▶ Specification form

dering process. Controlling issuances eliminates waste caused by multiple opened containers and ensures proper stock rotation.

KITCHEN PROCEDURES: ESTABLISHING STANDARD PORTIONS

Standardizing portions is essential to controlling food costs. Unless portion quantity is uniform, it will be impossible to compute portion costs accurately. Portion discrepancies can also confuse or mislead customers.

Actual portion sizes depend on the food service operation itself, the menu, the prices and the customers' desires. Some items are generally purchased pre-portioned for convenience (for example, steaks are sold in uniform cuts, baking potatoes are available in uniform sizes, butter comes in preportioned pats and bread comes sliced for service). Other items must be portioned by the establishment prior to service. Special equipment makes consistent portioning easy. There are machines to slice meats, cutting guides for cakes and pies and portion scales for weighing quantities. Standardized portion scoops and ladles are indispensable for serving vegetables, soups, stews, salads and similar foods. Many of these items are discussed and illustrated in Chapter 5, Tools and Equipment.

Once acceptable portion sizes are established, employees must be properly trained to present them. If each employee of a sandwich shop prepared sandwiches the way he or she would like to eat them, customers would probably never receive the same sandwich twice. Customers may become confused and decide not to risk a repeat visit. Obviously, carelessness in portioning can also drastically affect food cost.

KITCHEN PROCEDURES: WASTE

The chef must also control waste from overproduction or failure to use leftovers. With an adequate sales history, the chef can accurately estimate the quantity of food to prepare for each week, day or meal. If the menu is designed properly, the chef can also use leftovers and trim from product fabrication. The less waste generated in food preparation, the lower the overall food cost will be.

SALES AND SERVICE

An improperly trained sales staff can undo even the most rigorous of food cost controls. Front-of-the-house personnel are, after all, ultimately responsible for the *sales* portion of the food cost equation. Prices charged must be accurate and complete. Poor service can lead to the need to "comp" (serve for free) an excessive amount of food. Dropped or spilled foods do not generate revenues. Proper training is once again critical. The dining room manager and the chef should work together to educate servers about menu items and sales techniques.

CONCLUSION

No food service operation becomes a success on the chef's cooking ability alone. A well-designed, enticing and accurately priced menu is also necessary. By following a standardized recipe, you should be able to repeatedly produce a known quality and quantity of food for your specific food service operation. Based upon the regularity with which you offer these foods, your menu can be classified as static, cycle, market or hybrid. You can offer your menu items either à la carte, semi à la carte or table d'hôte.

You must be able to understand and apply proper techniques for converting recipes, food costing and loss control. Although computers are useful and are becoming more common in kitchens, no machine can substitute for a chef's watchful eye and hands-on controls.

1 Describe the four types of menus. Can each type of menu offer foods à la carte, semi à la carte and/or table d'hôte? Explain your answer.

2 Discuss three factors in food preparation that affect successful recipe size changes.

3 Why is it important to calculate the portion cost of a recipe in professional food service operations? Why is the full recipe cost inadequate?

4 List several factors, other than kitchen procedures, that a chef should examine when looking for ways to control food costs.

5 Several recipe costing software programs are available online, or are sold through the Internet. Research two of these programs. What are their advantages and disadvantages? Why is it important for cooks to learn to calculate recipe costs without the aid of a computer?

And, indeed, is there not something holy about a great kitchen? . . . The scoured gleam of row upon row of metal vessels dangling from hooks or reposing on their shelves till needed with the air of so many chalices waiting for the celebration of the sacrament of food.

—Angela Carter, British novelist (1940–1992)

5

TOOLS
AND EQUIPMENT

AFTER STUDYING THIS
CHAPTER, YOU WILL BE
ABLE TO:

▶ recognize a variety of
professional kitchen tools and
equipment

▶ select and care for knives

▶ understand how a professional
kitchen is organized

Having the proper tools and equipment for a particular task may mean the difference between a job well done and one done carelessly, incorrectly or even dangerously. This chapter introduces most of the tools and equipment typically used in a professional kitchen. Items are divided into categories according to their function: hand tools, knives, measuring and portioning devices, cookware, strainers and sieves, processing equipment, storage containers, heavy equipment, buffet equipment and safety equipment.

A wide variety of specialized tools and equipment is available to today's chef. Breading machines, croissant shapers and doughnut glazers are designed to speed production by reducing handwork. Other devices —for instance, a duck press or a couscousière—are used only for unique tasks in preparing a few menu items. Much of this specialized equipment is quite expensive and found only in food manufacturing operations or specialized kitchens; a discussion of it is beyond the scope of this chapter. Brief descriptions of some of these specialized devices are, however, found in the Glossary. Baking pans and tools are discussed in Chapter 29, Principles of the Bakeshop.

Before using any equipment, study the operator's manual or have someone experienced with the particular item instruct you on proper procedures for its use and cleaning. And remember, always think safety first.

▶ STANDARDS FOR TOOLS AND EQUIPMENT

NSF International (NSF), previously known as the National Sanitation Foundation, promulgates consensus standards for the design, construction and installation of kitchen tools, cookware and equipment. Many states and municipalities require that food service operations use only NSF-certified equipment. Although NSF certification is voluntary, most manufacturers submit their designs to NSF for certification to show that they are suitable for use in professional food service operations. Certified equipment bears the NSF mark shown in Figure 5.1.

NSF standards reflect the following requirements:

1 Equipment must be easily cleaned.
2 All food contact surfaces must be nontoxic (under intended end-use conditions), nonabsorbent, corrosion resistant and nonreactive.
3 All food contact surfaces must be smooth—that is, free of pits, cracks, crevices, ledges, rivet heads and bolts.
4 Internal corners and edges must be rounded and smooth; external corners and angles must be smooth and sealed.
5 Coating materials must be nontoxic and easily cleaned; coatings must resist chipping and cracking.
6 Waste and waste liquids must be easily removed.

FIGURE 5.1 ▶ The NSF mark

► SELECTING TOOLS AND EQUIPMENT

In general, only commercial food service tools and equipment should be used in a professional kitchen. Household tools and appliances that are not NSF-certified may not withstand the rigors of a professional kitchen. Look for tools that are well constructed. For example, joints should be welded, not bonded with solder; handles should be comfortable, with rounded borders; plastic and rubber parts should be seamless.

Before purchasing or leasing any equipment, you should evaluate several factors:

1 Is this equipment necessary for producing menu items?
2 Will this equipment perform the job required in the space available?
3 Is this equipment the most economical for the operation's specific needs?
4 Is this equipment easy to clean, maintain and repair?

► HAND TOOLS

Hand tools are designed to aid in cutting, shaping, moving or combining foods. They have few, if any, moving parts. Knives, discussed separately later, are the most important hand tools. Others are metal or rubber spatulas, spoons, whisks, tongs and specialized cutters. In addition to the items shown here, many hand tools designed for specific tasks, such as pressing tortillas or pitting cherries, are available. Sturdiness, durability and safety are the watchwords when selecting hand tools. Choose tools that can withstand the heavy use of a professional kitchen and those that are easily cleaned.

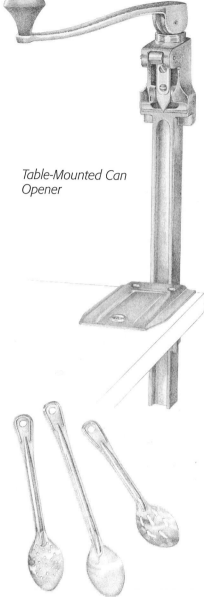

Table-Mounted Can Opener

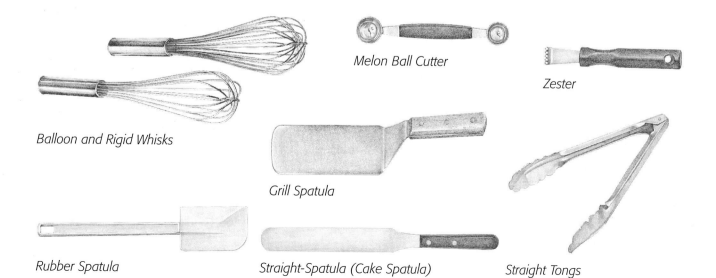

Chef's Fork

Meat Mallet

Vegetable Peeler

Perforated, Plain and Slotted Spoons

Balloon and Rigid Whisks

Melon Ball Cutter

Zester

Grill Spatula

Rubber Spatula

Straight-Spatula (Cake Spatula)

Straight Tongs

▶ KNIVES

Knives are the most important items in your tool kit. With a sharp knife, the skilled chef can accomplish a number of tasks more quickly and efficiently than any machine. Good-quality knives are expensive but will last for many years with proper care. Select easily sharpened, well-constructed knives that are comfortable and balanced in your hand. Knife construction and commonly used knives are discussed here; knife safety and care as well as cutting techniques are discussed in Chapter 6, Knife Skills.

KNIFE CONSTRUCTION

A good knife begins with a single piece of metal, stamped, cut or—best of all—forged and tempered into a blade of the desired shape. The metals generally used for knife blades are:

1 **Carbon steel**—An alloy of carbon and iron, carbon steel is traditionally used for blades because it is soft enough to be sharpened easily. It corrodes and discolors easily, however, especially when used with acidic foods.

2 **Stainless steel**—Stainless steel will not rust, corrode or discolor and is extremely durable. A stainless steel blade is much more difficult to sharpen than a carbon steel one, although once an edge is established, it lasts longer than the edge on a carbon steel blade.

3 **High-carbon stainless steel**—An alloy combining the best features of carbon steel and stainless steel, high-carbon stainless steel neither corrodes nor discolors and can be sharpened almost as easily as carbon steel. It is now the most frequently used metal for blades.

4 **Ceramic**—A ceramic called zirconium oxide is now used to make knife blades that are extremely sharp, very easy to clean, rustproof and nonreactive. With proper care, ceramic blades will remain sharp for years, but when sharpening is needed, it must be done professionally on special diamond wheels. Material costs and tariffs make ceramic-bladed knives very expensive. Although this ceramic is highly durable, it does not have the flexibility of metal, so never use a ceramic knife to pry anything, to strike a hard surface (for example, when crushing garlic or chopping through bones) or to cut against a china or ceramic surface.

A portion of the blade, known as the tang, fits inside the handle. The best knives are constructed with a full tang running the length of the handle; they also have a bolster where the blade meets the handle (the bolster is part of the blade, not a separate collar). Less expensive knives may have a ¾-length tang or a thin "rattail" tang. Neither provides as much support, durability or balance as a full tang.

Knife handles are often made of hard woods infused with plastic and riveted to the tang. Molded polypropylene handles are permanently bonded to a tang without seams or rivets. Stainless steel handles welded directly to the blade are durable but very lightweight. Any handle should be shaped for comfort and ground smooth to eliminate crevices where bacteria can grow.

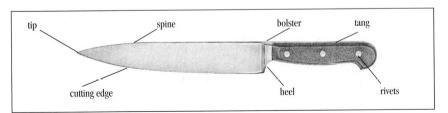

FIGURE 5.2 ▶ The parts of a chef's knife

KNIFE SHAPES AND SHARPENING EQUIPMENT

You will collect many knives during your career, many with specialized functions not described here. This list includes only the most basic knives and sharpening equipment.

French or Chef's Knife

FRENCH OR CHEF'S KNIFE

An all-purpose knife used for chopping, slicing and mincing. Its rigid 8- to 14-inch-long blade is wide at the heel and tapers to a point at the tip.

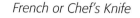

Utility Knife

UTILITY KNIFE

An all-purpose knife used for cutting fruits and vegetables and carving poultry. Its rigid 6- to 8-inch-long blade is shaped like a chef's knife but narrower.

Rigid Boning Knife

BONING KNIFE

A smaller knife with a thin blade used to separate meat from bone. The blade is usually 5 to 7 inches long and may be flexible or rigid.

Paring Knife

PARING KNIFE

A short knife used for detail work or cutting fruits and vegetables. The rigid blade is from 2 to 4 inches long. A tournée or **bird's-beak knife** is similar to a paring knife but with a curved blade; it is used to cut curved surfaces or tournée vegetables.

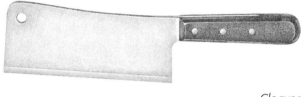

Cleaver

CLEAVER

A knife with a large, heavy rectangular blade used for chopping or cutting through bones.

Flexible Slicer

SLICER

A knife with a long, thin blade used primarily for slicing cooked meat. The tip may be round or pointed, and the blade may be flexible or rigid. A similar knife with a serrated edge is used for slicing bread or pastry items.

Serrated Slicer

Butcher Knive or Scimitar

BUTCHER KNIFE

Sometimes known as a **scimitar** because the rigid blade curves up in a 25-degree angle at the tip, it is used for fabricating raw meat and is available with 6- to 14-inch blades.

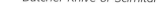

Oyster Knife

OYSTER AND CLAM KNIVES

The short, rigid blades of these knives are used to open oyster and clam shells. The tips are blunt; only the clam knife has a sharp edge.

Clam Knife

Three-Sided Sharpening or Whetstone

SHARPENING STONE

Also known as a **whetstone,** a flat brick of synthetic abrasives that is used to put an edge on a dull blade. Various grit sizes are available. The most practical sets include both coarse- and fine-grit stones.

STEEL

A scored, slightly abrasive steel rod used to hone or straighten a blade immediately after and between sharpenings.

Steel

▶ MEASURING AND PORTIONING DEVICES

Recipe ingredients must be measured precisely, especially in the bakeshop, and foods should be measured when served to control portion size and cost. The devices used to measure and portion foods are, for the most part, hand tools designed to make food preparation and service easier and more precise. The accuracy they afford prevents the cost of mistakes made when accurate measurements are ignored.

Measurements may be based upon weight (for example, grams, ounces, pounds) or volume (for example, teaspoons, cups, gallons). Therefore, it is necessary to have available several measuring devices, including liquid and dry measuring cups and a variety of scales. Thermometers and timers are also measuring devices and are discussed here. When purchasing measuring devices, look for quality construction and accurate markings.

SCALES

Scales are necessary to determine the weight of an ingredient or a portion of food (for example, the sliced meat for a sandwich). Portion scales use a spring mechanism, round dial and single flat tray. They are available calibrated in grams, ounces or pounds. Electronic scales also use a spring mechanism but provide digital readouts. They are often required where foods are priced for sale by weight. Balance scales (also known as baker's scales) use a two-tray, free-weight counterbalance system. A balance scale allows more weight to be measured at one time because it is not limited by spring capacity.

Any scale must be properly used and maintained to provide an accurate reading. Never pick up a scale by its platform as this can damage the balancing mechanism.

Portion Scale

Balance or Baker's Scale

VOLUME MEASURES

Ingredients may be measured by volume using measuring spoons and measuring cups. Measuring spoons sold as a set usually include ¼-teaspoon, ½-teaspoon, 1-teaspoon and 1-tablespoon units (or the metric equivalent). Liquid measuring cups are available in capacities from 1 cup to 1 gallon. They have a lip or pour spout above the top line of measurement to prevent spills. Measuring cups for dry ingredients are usually sold in sets of ¼-, ⅓-, ½-, and 1-cup units. They do not have pour spouts, so the top of the cup is level with the top measurement specified. Glass measuring cups are not recommended because they can break. Avoid using bent or dented measuring cups as the damage may distort the measurement capacity.

Measuring Spoons

Liquid Measuring Cup

Dry Measuring Cups

LADLES

Long-handled ladles are useful for portioning liquids such as stocks, sauces and soups. The capacity, in ounces or milliliters, is stamped on the handle.

PORTION SCOOPS

Portion scoops (also known as dishers) resemble ice cream scoops. They come in a range of standardized sizes and have a lever-operated blade for releasing their contents. Scoops are useful for portioning salads, vegetables, muffin batters or other soft foods. A number, stamped on either the handle or the release mechanism, indicates the number of level scoopfuls per quart. The higher the scoop number, the smaller the scoop's capacity. See Table 5.1.

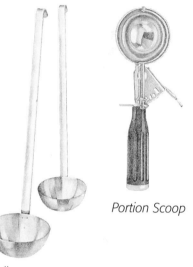

Portion Scoop

THERMOMETERS

Various types of thermometers are used in the kitchen.

Stem-type thermometers, including instant-read models, are inserted into foods to obtain temperature readings. Temperatures are shown on either a dial noted by an arrow or a digital readout. An instant-read thermometer is a small stem-type model, designed to be carried in a pocket and used to provide quick temperature readings. An instant-read thermometer should not be left in foods that are cooking because doing so damages the thermometer. Sanitize the stem of any thermometer before use in order to avoid cross-contamination.

Ladles

Candy and fat thermometers measure temperatures up to 400°F (204°C) using mercury in a column of glass. A back clip attaches the thermometer to the

Instant-Read Thermometer

Candy Thermometer

Table 5.1	PORTION SCOOP CAPACITIES			
SCOOP NUMBER	**VOLUME**		**APPROXIMATE WEIGHT***	
	U.S.	**METRIC**	**U.S.**	**METRIC**
6	⅔ c.	160 ml	5 oz.	160 g
8	½ c.	120 ml	4 oz.	120 g
10	3 fl. oz.	90 ml	3–3½ oz.	85–100 g
12	⅓ c.	80 ml	2½–3 oz.	75–85 g
16	¼ c.	60 ml	2 oz.	60 g
20	1½ fl. oz.	45 ml	1¾ oz.	50 g
24	1⅓ oz.	40 ml	1⅓ oz.	40 g
30	1 fl. oz.	30 ml	1 oz.	30 g
40	0.8 fl. oz.	24 ml	0.8 oz.	23 g
60	½ fl. oz.	15 ml	½ oz.	15 g

*Weights are approximate because they vary by food.

HOW TO CALIBRATE A STEM-TYPE THERMOMETER

All stem-type thermometers should be calibrated at least weekly as well as whenever they are dropped. To calibrate a stem-type thermometer, fill a glass with shaved ice, then add water. Place the thermometer in the ice slush and wait until the temperature reading stabilizes. Following the manufacturer's directions, adjust the thermometer's calibration nut until the temperature reads 32°F (0°C). Check the calibration by returning the thermometer to the slush. Then repeat the procedure, substituting boiling water for the ice slush, and calibrate the thermometer at 212°F (100°C).

pan, keeping the chef's hands free. Be careful not to subject glass thermometers to quick temperature changes as the glass may shatter.

Electronic probe thermometers are now reasonably priced and commonly used in food service facilities. These thermometers provide immediate, clear, digital readouts from a handheld unit attached to a metal probe (some are conveniently designed so that the probe is imbedded in the tines of a long-handled fork or the bowl of a ladle). A detachable probe is especially useful inside an oven and for deep-frying and grilling.

The latest advancement in thermometers relies on infrared sensors with laser sightings. Infrared thermometers can instantly monitor the surface temperature of foods during cooking or holding, and the temperature of goods at receiving and in storage. Units can respond to a wide range of temperatures in less than a second without actually touching the food, thus avoiding any risk of cross-contamination.

Because proper temperatures must be maintained for holding and storing foods, oven and refrigerator thermometers are also useful. Select thermometers with easy-to-read dials or column divisions.

TIMERS

Portable kitchen timers are useful for any busy chef. Small digital timers can be carried in a pocket; some even time three functions at once. Select a timer with a loud alarm signal and long timing capability.

▶ COOKWARE

Cookware includes the sauté pans and stockpots used on the stove top as well as the roasting pans, hotel pans and specialty molds used inside the oven. Cookware should be selected for its size, shape, ability to conduct heat evenly and overall quality of construction.

METALS AND HEAT CONDUCTION

Cookware that fails to distribute heat evenly may cause hot spots that burn foods. Because different metals conduct heat at different rates, and thicker layers of metal conduct heat more evenly than thinner ones, the most important considerations when choosing cookware are the type and thickness (known as the *gauge*) of the material used. No one cookware or material suits every process or need, however; always select the most appropriate material for the task at hand.

COPPER

Copper is an excellent conductor: It heats rapidly and evenly and cools quickly. Indeed, unlined copper pots are unsurpassed for cooking sugar and fruit mixtures. But copper cookware is extremely expensive. It also requires a great deal of care and is often quite heavy. Moreover, because copper may react with some foods, copper cookware usually has a tin lining, which is soft and easily scratched. Because of these problems, copper is now often sandwiched between layers of stainless steel or aluminum in the bottom of pots and pans.

ALUMINUM

Aluminum is the metal used most commonly in commercial utensils. It is lightweight and, after copper, conducts heat best. Aluminum is a soft metal, though, so it should be treated with care to avoid dents. Do not use aluminum containers for storage or for cooking acidic foods because the metal reacts chemically with many foods. Light-colored foods, such as soups or sauces, may be discolored when cooked in aluminum, especially if stirred with a metal whisk or spoon.

Anodized aluminum has a hard, dark, corrosion-resistant surface that helps prevent sticking and discoloration.

STAINLESS STEEL

Although stainless steel conducts and retains heat poorly, it is a hard, durable metal particularly useful for holding foods and for low-temperature cooking where hot spots and scorching are not problems. Stainless steel pots and pans are available with aluminum or copper bonded to the bottom or with an aluminum-layered core. Although expensive, such cookware combines the rapid, uniform heat conductivity of copper and aluminum with the strength, durability and non-reactivity of stainless steel. Stainless steel is also ideal for storage containers because it does not react with foods.

CAST IRON

Cast-iron cookware distributes heat evenly and holds high temperatures well. It is often used in griddles and large skillets. Although relatively inexpensive, cast iron is extremely heavy and brittle. It must be kept properly conditioned and dry to prevent rust and pitting.

GLASS

Glass retains heat well but conducts it poorly. It does not react with foods. Tempered glass is suitable for microwave cooking provided it does not have any metal band or decoration. Commercial operations rarely use glass cookware because of the danger of breakage.

CERAMICS

Ceramics, including earthenware, porcelain and stoneware, are used primarily for baking dishes, casseroles and baking stones because they conduct heat uniformly and retain temperatures well. Ceramics are nonreactive, inexpensive and generally suitable for use in a microwave oven (provided there is no metal in the glaze). Ceramics are easily chipped or cracked, however, and should not be used over a direct flame. Also, quick temperature changes may cause the cookware to crack or shatter.

PLASTIC

Plastic containers are frequently used in commercial kitchens for food storage or service, but they cannot be used for heating or cooking except in a microwave oven. Plastic microwave cookware is made of phenolic resin. It is easy to clean, relatively inexpensive and rigidly shaped, but its glasslike structure is brittle, and it can crack or shatter.

ENAMELWARE

Pans lined with enamel should not be used for cooking; in many areas, their use in commercial kitchens is prohibited by law. The enamel can chip or crack easily, providing good places for bacteria to grow. Also, the chemicals used to bond the enamel to the cookware can cause food poisoning if ingested.

NONSTICK COATINGS

Without affecting a metal's ability to conduct heat, a polymer (plastic) known as polytetrafluoroethylene (PTFE) and marketed under the trade names Teflon and Silverstone may be applied to many types of cookware. It provides a slippery, nonreactive finish that prevents food from sticking and allows the use of less fat in cooking. Cookware with nonstick coatings requires a great deal of care, however, since the coatings can scratch, chip and blister. Do not use metal spoons or spatulas in cookware with nonstick coatings.

ROMAN POTS, SOUTHERN STILLS AND CRAFT FAIRS

Lead is poisonous. Ingesting it can cause severe gastrointestinal pains, anemia and central nervous system disorders, including intelligence and memory deficits and behavioral changes.

The unwitting and dangerous consumption of lead is not limited to children eating peeling paint chips. Some historians suggest that the use of lead cookware and lead-lined storage vessels and water pipes may have caused pervasive lead poisoning among the elite of the Roman Empire and thus contributed to the empire's decline. There is also ample evidence that from ancient times until just a few hundred years ago, wine was heated in lead vessels to sweeten it. This had a disastrous effect on the drinker and, for several centuries in countries throughout Europe, on the wine purveyor as well. The former could be poisoned, and the latter could be punished by death for selling adulterated wine. More recently, it was found that much of the moonshine whiskey produced in the American South contained lead in potentially toxic ranges. The source was determined to be the lead solder used in homemade stills, some of which even included old lead-containing car radiators as condensers.

Although commercially available cookware does not contain lead, be careful of imported pottery and those lovely hand-thrown pots found at craft fairs—there could be lead in the glaze.

COMMON COOKWARE

POTS

Pots are large round vessels with straight sides and two loop handles. Available in a range of sizes based on volume, they are used on the stove top for making stocks or soups, or for boiling or simmering foods, particularly where rapid evaporation is not desired. Flat or fitted lids are available.

PANS

Pans are round vessels with one long handle and straight or sloped sides. They are usually smaller and shallower than pots. Pans are available in a range of diameters and are used for general stove top cooking, especially sautéing, frying or reducing liquids rapidly.

Stockpot with Spigot

Saucepan

Sautoir (Straight Sides)

Sauce pot

Cast-Iron Skillet (Griswold)

Rondeau/Brazier

Sauteuse (Sloped Sides)

WOKS

Originally used to prepare Asian foods, woks are now found in many professional kitchens. Their round bottoms and curved sides diffuse heat and make it easy to toss or stir contents. Their large domed lids retain heat for steaming vegetables. Woks are useful for quickly sautéing strips of meat, simmering a whole fish or deep-frying appetizers. Stove top woks range in diameter from 12 to 30 inches; larger built-in gas or electric models are also available.

Wok

HOTEL PANS

Hotel pans (also known as steam table pans) are rectangular stainless steel pans designed to hold food for service in steam tables. Hotel pans are also used for baking, roasting or poaching inside an oven. Perforated pans useful for draining, steaming or icing down foods are also available. The standard full-size pan is 12 by 20 inches, with pans one-half, one-third, one-sixth and other fractions of this size available. Hotel pan depth is standardized at 2 inches (referred to as a "200 pan"), 4, 6 and 8 inches.

MOLDS

Pâté molds are available in several shapes and sizes, and are usually made from tinned steel. Those with hinged sides, whether smooth or patterned, are more properly referred to as *pâté en croûte* molds. The hinged sides make it easier to remove the baked pâté. Terrine molds are traditionally lidded earthenware or enameled cast-iron containers used for baking ground meat mixtures. They may be round, oval or rectangular. Timbale molds are small (about 4 ounces) metal or ceramic containers used for molding aspic or baking individual portions of mousse, custard or vegetables. Their slightly flared sides allow the contents to release cleanly when inverted.

Hotel Pans

Timbales

Pâté en Croûte Mold

Colander

Round Mesh Strainer

▶ STRAINERS AND SIEVES

Strainers and sieves are used primarily to aerate and remove impurities from dry ingredients and drain or purée cooked foods. Strainers, colanders, drum sieves, china caps and chinois are nonmechanical devices with a stainless steel mesh or screen through which food passes. The size of the mesh or screen varies from extremely fine to several millimeters wide; select the fineness best suited for the task at hand.

Drum sieve (Tamis)

CHINOIS AND CHINA CAP

Both the chinois and china cap are cone-shaped metal strainers. The conical shape allows liquids to filter through small openings. The body of a chinois is made from a very fine mesh screen, while a china cap has a perforated metal body. Both are used for straining stocks and sauces, with the chinois being particularly useful for consommé. A china cap can also be used with a pestle to purée soft foods.

Chinois

China Cap

SKIMMER AND SPIDER

Both the skimmer and spider are long-handled tools used to remove foods or impurities from liquids. The flat, perforated disk of a skimmer is used for skimming stocks or removing foods from soups or stocks. The spider has a finer mesh disk, which makes it better for retrieving items from hot fat. Wooden-handled spiders are available but are less sturdy and harder to clean than all-metal designs.

CHEESECLOTH

Cheesecloth is a loosely woven cotton gauze used for straining stocks and sauces and wrapping poultry or fish for poaching. Cheesecloth is also indispensable for making sachets. Always rinse cheesecloth thoroughly before use; this removes lint and prevents the cheesecloth from absorbing other liquids.

Skimmer

FOOD MILL

A food mill purées and strains food at the same time. Food is placed in the hopper and a hand-crank mechanism turns a blade in the hopper against a perforated disk, forcing the food through the disk. Most models have interchangeable disks with various-sized holes. Choose a mill that can be taken apart easily for cleaning.

FLOUR SIFTER

A sifter is used for aerating, blending and removing impurities from dry ingredients such as flour, cocoa and leavening agents. The 8-cup hand-crank sifter shown here uses four curved rods to brush the contents through a curved mesh screen. The sifter should have a medium-fine screen and a comfortable handle.

Spider

Food Mill

Flour Sifter

▶ PROCESSING EQUIPMENT

Processing equipment includes both electrical and nonelectrical mechanical devices used to chop, purée, slice, grind or mix foods. Before using any such equipment, be sure to review its operating procedures and ask for assistance if necessary. Always turn the equipment off and disconnect the power before disassembling, cleaning or moving the appliance. Any problems or malfunctions should be reported immediately. *Never place your hand into any machinery when the power is on. Processing equipment is powerful and can cause serious injury.*

SLICER

An electric slicer is used to cut meat, bread, cheese or raw vegetables into uniform slices. It has a circular blade that rotates at high speed. Food is placed in a carrier, then passed (manually or by an electric motor) against the blade. Slice thickness is determined by the distance between the blade and the carrier. Because of the speed with which the blade rotates, foods can be cut into extremely thin slices very quickly. An electric slicer is convenient for preparing moderate to large quantities of food, but the time required to disassemble and clean the equipment makes it impractical when slicing only a few items.

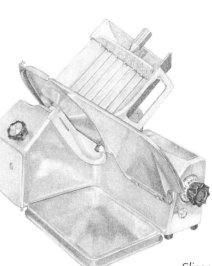

Slicer

MANDOLINE

A mandoline is a manually operated slicer made of stainless steel with adjustable slicing blades. It is also used to make julienne and waffle-cut slices. Its narrow, rectangular body sits on the work counter at a 45-degree angle. Foods are passed against a blade to obtain uniform slices. It is useful for slicing small quantities of fruits or vegetables when using a large electric slicer would be unwarranted. To avoid injury, always use a hand guard or steel glove when using a mandoline.

Mandoline

FOOD CHOPPER OR BUFFALO CHOPPER

This chopper is used to process moderate to large quantities of food to a uniform size, such as chopping onions or grinding bread for crumbs. The food is placed in a large bowl rotating beneath a hood where curved blades chop it. The size of the cut depends on how long the food is left in the machine. Buffalo choppers are available in floor or tabletop models. The motor can usually be fitted with a variety of other tools such as a meat grinder or a slicer/shredder, making it even more useful.

FOOD PROCESSOR

A food processor has a motor housing with a removable bowl and S-shaped blade. It is used, for example, to purée cooked foods, chop nuts, prepare compound butters and emulsify sauces. Special disks can be added that slice, shred or julienne foods. Bowl capacity and motor power vary; select a model large enough for your most common tasks.

Food Processor

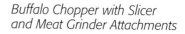

Buffalo Chopper with Slicer and Meat Grinder Attachments

BLENDER

Though similar in principle to a food processor, a blender has a tall, narrow food container and a four-pronged blade. Its design and whirlpool action is better for processing liquids or liquefying foods quickly. A blender is used to prepare smooth drinks, purée soups and sauces, blend batters and chop ice. A **vertical cutter/mixer (VCM)** operates like a very large, powerful blender. A VCM is usually floor-mounted and has a capacity of 15 to 80 quarts.

Heavy-Duty Blender

IMMERSION BLENDER

An immersion blender—as well as its household counterpart called a hand blender or wand—is a long shaft fitted with a rotating four-pronged blade at the bottom. Operated by pressing a button in the handle, an immersion blender is used to purée a soft food, soup or sauce directly in the container in which it was prepared, eliminating the need to transfer the food from one container to another. This is especially useful when working with hot foods. Small cordless, rechargeable models are convenient for puréeing or mixing small quantities or beverages, but larger heavy-duty electric models are more practical in commercial kitchens.

Immersion Blender

MIXER

A vertical mixer is indispensable in the bakeshop and most kitchens. The U-shaped arms hold a metal mixing bowl in place; the selected mixing attachment fits onto the rotating head. The three common mixing attachments are the whip (used for whipping eggs or cream), the paddle (used for general mixing) and the dough hook (used for kneading bread). Most mixers have several operating speeds. Bench models range in capacity from 4.5 to 20 quarts, while floor mixers can hold as much as 140 quarts. Some mixers can be fitted with shredder/slicers, meat grinders, juicers or power strainers, making the equipment more versatile.

Flat Paddle

Whip

Dough Hook

20-Quart Mixer and Attachments

JUICER

Two types of juicers are available: reamers and extractors. Reamers, also known as citrus juicers, remove juice from citrus fruits. They can be manual or electric. Manual models use a lever arm to squeeze the fruit with increased pressure. They are most often used to prepare small to moderate

Citrus Juicer

amounts of juice for cooking or beverages. Juice extractors are electrical devices that create juice by liquefying raw fruits, vegetables and herbs. They use centrifugal force to filter out fiber and pulp.

▶ STORAGE CONTAINERS

Proper storage containers are necessary for keeping leftovers and opened packages of food safe for consumption. Proper storage can also reduce the costs incurred by waste or spoilage.

Although stainless steel pans such as hotel pans are suitable and useful for some items, the expense of stainless steel and the lack of airtight lids makes these pans impractical for general storage purposes. Aluminum containers are not recommended because the metal can react with even mildly acidic items. Glass containers are generally not allowed in commercial kitchens because of the hazards of broken glass. The most useful storage containers are those made of high-density plastic such as polyethylene and polypropylene.

Storage containers must have well-fitting lids and should be available in a variety of sizes, including some that are small enough to hold even minimal quantities of food without allowing too much exposure to oxygen. Round and square plastic containers are widely available. Flat, snap-on lids allow containers to be stacked for more efficient storage. Containers may be clear or opaque white, which helps protect light-sensitive foods. Larger containers may be fitted with handles and spigots, making them especially suited for storing stock. Some storage containers are marked with graduated measurements so that content quantity can be determined at a glance.

Large quantities of dry ingredients, such as flour, sugar and rice, can be stored in rolling bins. The bins should be seamless with rounded corners for easy cleaning. They should have well-fitting but easy-to-open lids and should move easily on well-balanced casters.

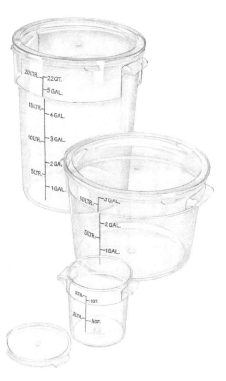

Storage Containers

▶ HEAVY EQUIPMENT

Heavy equipment includes the gas-, electric- or steam-operated appliances used for cooking, reheating or holding foods. It also includes dishwashers and refrigeration units. These items are usually installed in a fixed location determined by the kitchen's traffic flow and space limitations.

Heavy equipment may be purchased or leased new or used. Used equipment is most often purchased in an effort to save money. Although the initial cost is generally less for used equipment, the buyer should also consider the lack of a manufacturer's warranty or dealership guarantee and how the equipment was maintained by the prior owner. Functional used equipment is satisfactory for back-of-the-house areas, but it is usually better to purchase new equipment if it will be visible to the customer. Leasing equipment may be appropriate for some operations. The cost of leasing is less than purchasing and, if something goes wrong with the equipment, the operator is generally not responsible for repairs or service charges.

STOVE TOPS

Stove tops or ranges are often the most important cooking equipment in the kitchen. They have one or more burners powered by gas or electricity. The burners may be open or covered with a cast-iron or steel plate. Open burners supply quick, direct heat that is easy to regulate. A steel plate, known as a **flat top,** supplies even but less intense heat. Although it takes longer to heat than a burner, the flat top supports heavier weights and makes a larger area available for cooking. Many stoves include both flat tops and open burner arrangements.

INDUCTION—A NEW HEAT WAVE

Induction cooking uses special conductive coils called inductors placed below the stove top's surface in combination with cookware made of cast iron or magnetic stainless steel. The coil generates a magnetic current so that the cookware is heated rapidly with magnetic friction. Heat energy is then transferred from the cookware to the food by conduction. The cooking surface, which is made of a solid ceramic material, remains cool. Only the cookware and its contents get hot. This means that induction systems are extremely efficient with instant response time because power is directed into the cooking utensil, not the surrounding air.

Induction cooking is gaining acceptance in professional kitchens because of the speed with which foods can be heated and the ease of cleanup. Portable induction burners are useful on buffets, and cafeteria lines and for tableside cooking because they maintain a safer, cooler environment for both chefs and customers.

Induction Cooktop

Griddles are similar to flat tops except they are made of a thinner metal plate. Foods are usually cooked directly on the griddle's surface, not in pots or pans, which can nick or scratch the surface. The surface should be properly cleaned and conditioned after each use. Griddles are popular for short-order and fast-food-type operations.

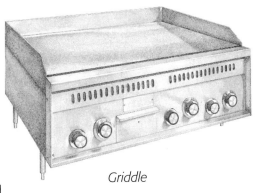

Griddle

OVENS

An oven is an enclosed space where food is cooked by being surrounded with hot, dry air. Conventional ovens are often located beneath the stove top. They have a heating element located at the unit's bottom or floor, and pans are placed on adjustable wire racks inside the oven's cavity. See Figure 5.3. Conventional ovens may also be separate, freestanding units or decks stacked one on top of the other. In stack ovens, pans are placed directly on the deck or floor and not on wire racks.

Convection ovens use internal fans to circulate the hot air. This tends to cook foods more quickly and evenly. Convection ovens are almost always freestanding units, powered either by gas or electricity. Because convection ovens cook foods more quickly, temperatures may need to be reduced by 25°F to 50°F (10°C to 20°C) from those recommended for conventional ovens.

Stack Oven

WOOD-BURNING OVENS

The ancient practice of baking in a retained-heat masonry oven has been revived in recent years, with many upscale restaurants and artesian bakeries installing brick or adobe ovens for baking pizzas and breads as well as for roasting fish, poultry and vegetables. These ovens have a curved interior chamber that is usually recessed into a wall. Although gas-fired models are available, wood-firing is more traditional and provides the aromas and flavors associated with brick ovens. A wood fire is built inside the oven to heat the brick chamber. The ashes are then swept out and the food is placed on the flat oven floor. The combination of high heat and wood smoke adds distinctive flavors to foods.

Wood-Burning Oven

MICROWAVE OVENS

Microwave ovens are electrically powered ovens used to cook or reheat foods. They are available in a range of sizes and power settings. Microwave ovens will not brown foods unless fitted with special browning elements. Microwave cooking is discussed in more detail in Chapter 10, Principles of Cooking.

Overhead Broiler

FIGURE 5.3 ▶ Gas burner and flat-top range with dual ovens and an overhead broiler (salamander).

BROILERS AND GRILLS

Broilers and grills are generally used to prepare meats, fish and poultry. For a grill, the heat source is beneath the rack on which the food is placed. For a broiler, the heat source is above the food. Most broilers are gas powered; grills may be gas or electric or may burn wood or charcoal. A **salamander** is a small overhead broiler primarily used to finish or top-brown foods. See Figure 5.3. A **rotisserie** is similar to a broiler except that the food is placed on a revolving spit in front of the heat source. The unit may be open or enclosed like an oven; it is most often used for cooking poultry or meats.

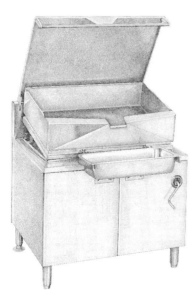

TILTING SKILLETS

Tilting skillets are large, freestanding, flat-bottomed pans about 6 inches deep with an internal heating element below the pan's bottom. They are usually made of stainless steel with a cover, and have a hand-crank mechanism that turns or tilts the pan to pour out the contents. Tilting

Tilting Skillet

Gas Grill

Rotisserie

Steam Kettle

Convection Steamer

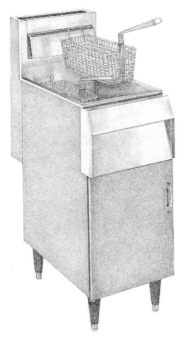

Deep-Fat Fryer

skillets can be used as stockpots, braziers, fry pans, griddles or steam tables, making them one of the most versatile of commercial appliances.

STEAM KETTLES

Steam kettles (also known as steam-jacketed kettles) are similar to stockpots except they are heated from the bottom and sides by steam circulating between layers of stainless steel. The steam may be generated internally or from an outside source. Because steam heats the kettle's sides, foods cook more quickly and evenly than they would in a pot sitting on the stove top. Steam kettles are most often used for making sauces, soups, custards or stocks. Steam kettles are available in a range of sizes, from a 2-gallon tabletop model to a 100-gallon floor model. Some models have a tilting mechanism that allows the contents to be poured out; others have a spigot near the bottom through which liquids can be drained.

STEAMERS

Pressure and convection steamers are used to cook foods rapidly and evenly, using direct contact with steam. Pressure steamers heat water above the boiling point in sealed compartments; the high temperature and sealed compartment increase the internal pressure in a range of 4 to 15 pounds per square inch. The increased pressure and temperature cook the foods rapidly. Convection steamers generate steam in an internal boiler, then release it over the foods in a cooking chamber. Both types of steamer are ideal for cooking vegetables with minimal loss of flavor or nutrients.

DEEP-FAT FRYERS

Deep-fat fryers are used to cook foods in a large amount of hot fat. Fryers are sized by the amount of fat they hold. Most commercial fryers range between 15 and 82 pounds. Fryers can be either gas or electric and are thermostatically controlled for temperatures between 200°F and 400°F (90°C and 200°C).

When choosing a fryer, look for a fry tank with curved, easy-to-clean sloping sides. Some fryers have a cold zone (an area of reduced temperature) at the bottom of the fry tank to trap particles. This prevents them from burning, creating off-flavors and shortening the life of the fryer fat.

Deep-fryers usually come with steel wire baskets to hold the food during cooking. Fryer baskets are usually lowered into the fat and raised manually, although some models have automatic basket mechanisms. The most important factor when choosing a deep-fryer is **recovery time.** Recovery time is the length of time it takes the fat to return to the desired cooking temperature after food is submerged in it. When food is submerged, heat is immediately transferred to the food from the fat. This heat transfer lowers the fat's temperature. The more food added at one time, the greater the drop in the fat's temperature. If the temperature drops too much or does not return quickly to the proper cooking temperature, the food may absorb excess fat and become greasy.

REFRIGERATORS

Proper refrigeration space is an essential component of any kitchen. Many foods must be stored at low temperatures to maintain quality and safety. Most commercial refrigeration is of two types: walk-in units and reach-in or upright units.

A walk-in is a large, room-sized box capable of holding hundreds of pounds of food on adjustable shelves. A separate freezer walk-in may be positioned nearby or even inside a refrigerated walk-in.

Reach-ins may be individual units or parts of a bank of units, each with shelves approximately the size of a full sheet pan. Reach-in refrigerators and freezers are usually located throughout the kitchen to provide quick access to foods. Small units may also be placed beneath the work counters. Freezers and refrigerators are available in a wide range of sizes and door designs to suit any operation.

Other forms of commercial refrigeration include chilled drawers located beneath a work area that are just large enough to accommodate a hotel pan, and display cases used to show foods to the customer.

DISHWASHERS

Mechanical dishwashers are available to wash, rinse and sanitize dishware, glassware, cookware and utensils. Small models clean one rack of items at a time, while larger models can handle several racks simultaneously on a conveyor belt system. Sanitation is accomplished either with extremely hot water (180°F/82°C) or with chemicals automatically dispensed during the final rinse cycle. Any dishwashing area should be carefully organized for efficient use of equipment and employees, and to prevent recontamination of clean items.

Insulated Carrier

► BUFFET EQUIPMENT

Food service operations that prepare buffets or cater off-premise events need a variety of specialized equipment to ensure that food is handled safely and efficiently and displayed appropriately. Proper temperatures must be maintained during transportation, display and service.

Insulated carriers hold food at its current temperature for a time. They are designed to hold hotel pans or sheet pans, and are available with wheels for easy movement. Some are available with a spigot for serving hot or cold beverages. Any carrier should be easy to clean and of a convenient size for the space available and the type of operation.

Temperature remains a concern when arranging food on a buffet table. **Chafing dishes** are commonly used for keeping hot foods hot during service. Chafing dishes are designed so that cans of solid fuel can be placed under a deep hotel pan of hot water. Like a double boiler or bain marie, the hot water then helps maintain the temperature of food placed in a second hotel pan suspended over the first. Chafing dishes, however, should never be used to heat food. Chafing dishes are available in several sizes and shapes, but the most convenient are those based on the size of a standard hotel pan. Round, deep chafing dishes are useful for serving soups or sauces. Exteriors can be plain or ornate, and made of silver, copper or stainless steel.

Roast beef, turkey, ham or other large cuts of meat are sometimes carved on a buffet in front of guests. **Heat lamps** can be used to keep these foods warm. Heat lamps are also useful for maintaining the temperature of pizza or fried foods, which might become soggy if held in a chafing dish.

Pastries, breads and cold foods can be arranged on a variety of platters, trays, baskets and serving pieces, depending on the size and style of the buffet. Some of the most elegant and traditional serving pieces are flat display mirrors. These may be plastic or glass and are available in a wide variety of shapes and sizes. The edges should be sealed in an easy-to-clean plastic to prevent chipping.

Although many of these items can be rented, operations that regularly serve buffets may prefer to invest in their own transportation and serving equipment.

Heat Lamp

Chafing Dish

► SAFETY EQUIPMENT

Safety devices, many of which are required by federal, state or local law, are critical to the well-being of a food service operation although they are not used in food preparation. Failing to include safety equipment in a kitchen or failing to maintain it properly endangers workers and customers.

Table 5.2	**FIRE EXTINGUISHERS**	
CLASS	**SYMBOL**	**USE**
Class A	▲	Fires involving wood, paper, cloth or plastic
Class B	■	Fires involving oil, grease or flammable chemicals
Class C	●	Fires involving electrical equipment or wiring

Combination extinguishers—AB, BC and ABC—are also available.

FIRE EXTINGUISHERS

Fire extinguishers are canisters of foam, dry chemicals (such as sodium bicarbonate or potassium bicarbonate) or pressurized water used to extinguish small fires. They must be placed within sight of and easily reached from the work areas in which fires are likely to occur. Different classes of extinguishers use different chemicals to fight different types of fires. The appropriate class must be used for the specific fire. See Table 5.2. Fire extinguishers must be recharged and checked from time to time. Be sure they have not been discharged, tampered with or otherwise damaged.

VENTILATION SYSTEMS

Ventilation systems (also called ventilation hoods) are commonly installed over cooking equipment to remove vapors, heat and smoke. Some systems include fire extinguishing agents or sprinklers. A properly operating hood makes the kitchen more comfortable for the staff and reduces the danger of fire. The system should be designed, installed and inspected by professionals, then cleaned and maintained regularly.

FIRST-AID KITS

First-aid supplies should be stored in a clearly marked box, conspicuously located near food preparation areas. State and local laws may specify the kit's exact contents. Generally, they should include a first-aid manual, bandages, gauze dressings, adhesive tape, antiseptics, scissors, cold packs and other supplies. The kit should be checked regularly and items replaced as needed. In addition, cards with emergency telephone numbers should be placed inside the first-aid kit and near a telephone.

▶ THE PROFESSIONAL KITCHEN

The kitchen is the heart of the food service operation. There, food and other items are received, stored, prepared and plated for service; dining room staff places orders, retrieves foods that are ready for service and returns dirty service items; dishes and other wares are cleaned and stored; and the chef conducts business. But commercial space is expensive, and most food service operators recognize that the greater number of customers served, the greater the revenues. Often this translates into a large dining area and small kitchen and storage facilities. Therefore, when designing a kitchen, it is important to use the space wisely so that each of its functions can be accomplished efficiently.

Kitchen design begins with a consideration of the tasks to be performed. Analyzing the menu identifies these tasks. A restaurant featuring steaks and chops, for example, will need areas to fabricate and grill meats. If it relies on commercially prepared desserts and breads, it will not need a bakeshop but will still need space to store and plate baked goods.

Once all food preparation tasks are identified, a work area for each particular task is designated. These work areas are called **work stations.** At a steak restaurant, an important work station is the broiler. If the restaurant serves fried foods, it will also need a fry station. The size and design of each work station is determined by the volume of food the operation intends to produce.

Usually work stations using the same or similar equipment for related tasks are grouped into **work sections.** See Table 5.3. (Note that work stations correspond to the kitchen brigade system discussed in Chapter 1, Professionalism.) For example, in a typical full-service restaurant, there will be a hot-foods section that includes broiler, fry, griddle, sauté and sauce stations. The principal cooking equipment (a range, broiler, deep-fat fryer, oven, griddle, and so on) will be arranged in a line under a ventilation hood. During service each work station within the hot-foods section may be staffed by a different line cook, but the proximity of the stations allows one line cook to cover more than one station if the kitchen is shorthanded or when business is slow.

When designing the work area, one must also consider what equipment and storage facilities can be placed beneath or on top of other equipment. For example, in a bakeshop, rolling storage bins for flour and sugar may be located beneath the work surface, while mixing bowls and dry ingredients are stored on shelves above. Ideally, each station should be designed so that the cook takes no more than three steps in any direction to perform all of his or her assigned station tasks.

In addition to the work sections where the menu items are produced, a typical restaurant kitchen includes areas dedicated to the following functions:

1 *Receiving and storing foods and other items.* Most kitchens will need freezer, refrigerator and dry-goods storage facilities. Each should have proper temperature, humidity and light controls in order to properly and safely maintain the stored items. Typically there is a combination of central and section storage. For example, up to 100 pounds of flour and sugar can be stored in rolling bins under a work table in the bakeshop, while several hundreds of pounds more remain in a central dry-goods area. Similarly, one box of salt can be stored near the hot line for immediate use, while the remainder of the case is stored in a central dry-goods area. Additional storage space will be needed for cleaning and paper supplies, dishes and other service ware.

2 *Washing dishes and other equipment.* These dish- and equipment-washing facilities should have their own sinks. Food-preparation and hand-washing sinks must be separate.

3 *Employee use.* Restrooms, locker facilities and an office are also found in most food service facilities.

The guiding principle behind a good kitchen design is to maximize the flow of goods and staff from one area to the next and within each area itself. Maximizing flow creates an efficient work environment and helps reduce preparation and service time.

Table 5.3	WORK SECTIONS AND THEIR STATIONS
SECTIONS	**STATIONS**
Hot-foods section	Broiler station Fry station Griddle station Sauté/sauce station Holding
Garde-manger section	Salad greens cleaning Salad preparation Cold foods preparation Sandwich station Showpiece preparation
Bakery section	Mixing station Dough holding and proofing Dough rolling and forming Baking and cooling Dessert preparation* Frozen desert preparation* Plating desserts*
Banquet section	Steam cooking Dry-heat cooking (roasting, broiling) Holding and plating
Short-order section	Griddle station Fry station Broiler station
Beverage section	Hot beverage station Cold beverage station Alcoholic beverage station

*These stations are sometimes found in the garde-manger section.

SAFETY ALERT

STORAGE

▶ Never store cleaning supplies or other chemicals with or near foods.

▶ Never store chemicals in a container that originally held food; never store food in a container that once held a chemical.

▶ Keep chemicals and cleaners in properly labeled containers.

ALEXIS SOYER (1809–1858)

The father of the contemporary celebrity chef was Alexis Soyer, a Frenchman whose tragically short working life was spent mostly in London. He was a flamboyant, talented and egocentric showman. He was also a renowned chef, restaurateur, social activist, author, purveyor of prepared foods and inventor.

In 1831, Soyer left his thriving catering business and restaurant in Paris for London. (A scandal was rumored to be behind his sudden departure.) There he quickly established a reputation as a talented chef in the latest French fashion. By

Alexis Soyer
Photo courtesy of Barbara Wheaton.

1838, he was employed at a gentlemen's club called the Reform. Able to assist in planning the club's new kitchen facility, Soyer installed the most modern equipment: gas ovens with temperature controls, a steam-driven mechanical spit and a storage locker cooled by running water. From this modern kitchen he produced his signature dish: lamb chops Reform.

The Reform was founded by members of the Liberal party, a political party interested in social reform. Their chef soon joined the party ranks. He developed recipes for inexpensive,

"The Kitchen Department of the Reform Club" (1841). "To show them at one glance," wrote the *Spectator,* "the partition walls are cut away, and a bird's eye view is given of the several kitchens, larders, sculleries, and batterie de cuisine; the different functionaries are at their posts, and the accomplished chef, Monsieur Soyer, is in the act of pointing out to a favoured visitor the various contrivances suggested by his ingenuity and experience."

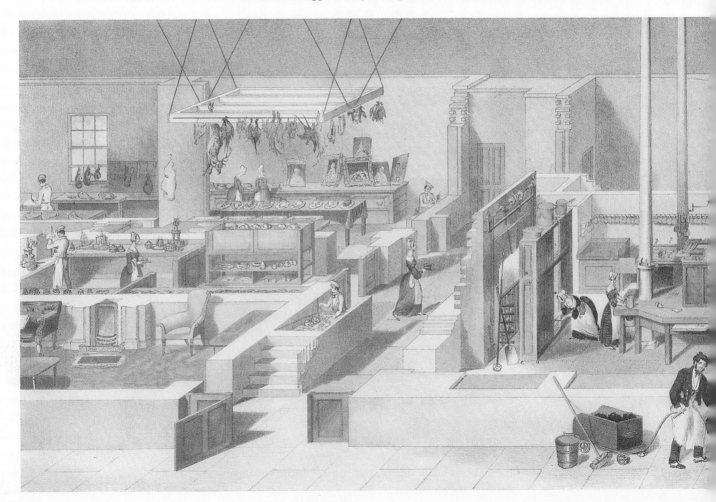

nutritious soups for the working class and in 1847 went to Ireland and opened soup kitchens to feed those who were starving as a result of the potato famine.

His most important writings reflect his interests in good food for the masses. The intended audience for *The Modern Housewife* (1849) was the middle class; the growing urban working class was the intended audience for his second book, *A Schilling Cookery for the People* (1855).

In 1851, Soyer opened his own lavishly decorated and expensively equipped restaurant called the Gastronomic Symposium of All Nations. It closed shortly thereafter, in part because of Soyer's debts, in part because he lost his operating license as a result of the rowdiness in the restaurant's American-style bar, at which customers were publicly served cocktails for the first time in London.

In addition to cooking and writing, Soyer created and marketed several prepared food items: Soyer's Sauce, Soyer's Nectar and Soyer's Relish. He was also fascinated with kitchen gadgets and invented several, including a sink stopper, jelly mold, egg cooker and coffeepot. The most notable, however, was a portable "Magic Stove" weighing less than 4 pounds, similar to a modern chafing dish. Soyer's final triumph was in the Crimean War (1854–1857). He developed army rations, reorganized field and hospital kitchens and introduced one of his last inventions, the campaign stove. Portable, efficient and requiring little fuel, it was used by the British army for the next 90 years.

Governmental building, health, fire and safety codes will dictate, to a degree, certain aspects of a professional kitchen's design. But to make the most of these spaces, the well-designed kitchen should reflect a sound understanding of the tasks to be performed and the equipment necessary to perform them efficiently.

CONCLUSION

Hundreds of tools and pieces of equipment can help you prepare, cook, store and present food. Every year, manufacturers offer new or improved items. Throughout your career, you will use many of them. Select those that are well constructed, durable and best suited for the task at hand. Then use them in a safe and efficient manner.

The way in which equipment is arranged and stored in a kitchen is also important. Good kitchen design emphasizes the efficient flow of goods and staff from one work section to another as well as within each work section or station.

QUESTIONS FOR DISCUSSION

1 What is NSF International? What is its significance with regard to commercial kitchen equipment?
2 List the parts of a chef's knife and describe the knife's construction.
3 List six materials used to make commercial cookware and describe the advantages and disadvantages of each.
4 Describe six pieces of equipment that can be used to slice or chop foods.
5 List three classes of fire extinguishers. For each one, describe its designating symbol and identify the type or types of fire it should be used to extinguish.
6 Explain the relationship between work sections and work stations and the kitchen brigade system discussed in Chapter 1, Professionalism.
7 Use the Internet to locate vendors, obtain specifications, and compare warranties and prices for a piece of commercial kitchen equipment.
8 Research information on selecting and installing a wood-burning oven in a commercial kitchen.

EVERY MORNING ONE MUST START FROM SCRATCH,
WITH NOTHING ON THE STOVES. THAT IS CUISINE.

*—Fernand Point, French restaurateur (1897–
1955)*

6

KNIFE SKILLS

Every professional must become skilled in the use of certain tools. The professional chef is no exception. One of the most important tools the student chef must master is the knife. Good knife skills are critical to a chef's success because the knife is the most commonly used tool in the kitchen. Every chef spends countless hours slicing, dicing, mincing and chopping. Learning to perform these tasks safely and efficiently is an essential part of your training.

At first, professional knives may feel large and awkward and the techniques discussed in this chapter may not seem all that efficient. But as you become familiar with knives and practice your knife skills, using knives correctly will become second nature.

Knives are identified in Chapter 5, Tools and Equipment. Here we show how they are used to cut vegetables. The techniques presented, however, can be used for most any food that holds its shape when cut. Knife skills for butchering and fabricating meat, poultry, fish and shellfish are discussed in Chapter 13, Principles of Meat Cookery, through Chapter 20, Fish and Shellfish.

A note about language: Many of the classic cuts are known by their French names: julienne, for example. Although these words are nouns and entered the English language as nouns (for example, a julienne of carrot), they are also used as verbs (to julienne a carrot) and adjectives (julienned carrots).

▶ USING YOUR KNIFE SAFELY

The first rule of knife safety is to think about what you are doing. Other basic rules of knife safety are as follows:

1 Use the correct knife for the task at hand.
2 Always cut away from yourself.
3 Always cut on a cutting board. Do not cut on glass, marble or metal.
4 Keep knives sharp; a dull knife is more dangerous than a sharp one.
5 When carrying a knife, hold it point down, parallel and close to your leg as you walk.
6 A falling knife has no handle. Do not attempt to catch a falling knife; step back and allow it to fall.
7 Never leave a knife in a sink of water; anyone reaching into the sink could be injured or the knife could be dented by pots or other utensils.

▶ Caring for Your Knife

KNIFE SHARPENING

A sharpening stone called a **whetstone** is used to put an edge on a dull knife blade. To use a whetstone, place the heel of the blade against the whetstone at a 20-degree angle. Keeping that angle, press down on the blade while pushing it away from you in one long arc, as if to slice off a thin piece of the stone. The entire length of the blade should come in contact with the stone during each sweep. Repeat the procedure on both sides of the blade until sufficiently sharp. With a triple-faced stone, such as that shown here, you progress from the coarsest to the finest surface. Any whetstone can be moistened with either water or mineral oil, but not both. Do not use vegetable oil on a whetstone since it will soon become rancid and gummy.

A **steel** does not sharpen a knife. Rather, it is used to hone or straighten the blade immediately after and between sharpenings. To use a steel, place the blade against the steel at a 20-degree angle. Then draw the blade along the entire length of the steel. Repeat the technique several times on each side of the blade.

A final note on knife care: Do not wash knives in commercial dishwashers. The heat and harsh chemicals can damage the edge and the handle. The blade can also be damaged if it knocks against cookware or utensils. In addition, the knife could injure an unsuspecting worker. Always wash and dry your knives by hand immediately after each use.

When sharpening a knife against a three-sided whetstone, go from the coarsest to the finest surface.

Honing a knife against a steel straightens the blade between sharpenings.

▶ Gripping Your Knife

There are several different ways to grip a knife. Use the grip that is most comfortable for you or the one dictated by the job at hand. Whichever grip you use should be firm but not so tight that your hand becomes tired. Gripping styles are shown here.

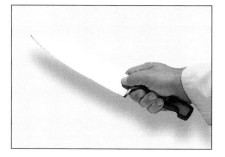

The most common grip: Hold the handle with three fingers while gripping the blade between the thumb and index finger.

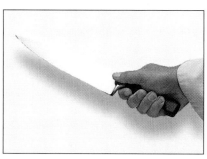

A variation on the most common grip: Grip the handle with four fingers and place the thumb on the front of the handle.

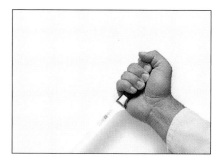

The underhand grip for a rigid boning knife: Grip the handle in a fist with four fingers and thumb. This grip allows you to use the knife tip to cut around joints and separate flesh from bone when boning meat and poultry.

▶ CONTROLLING YOUR KNIFE

To safely produce even cuts, you must control (or guide) your knife with one hand and hold the item being cut with the other. Always allow the blade's sharp edge to do the cutting. Never force the blade through the item being cut. Use smooth, even strokes. Using a dull knife or excessive force with any knife produces, at best, poor results and, at worst, a significant safety risk. Cutting without using your hand as a guide may also be dangerous. Two safe cutting methods that produce good results are shown here.

Method A

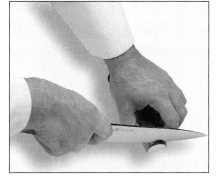

1 Keeping your fingertips curled back, grip the item being cut with three fingertips and your thumb. Hold the knife in the other hand. While keeping the knife's tip on the cutting board, lift the heel of the knife.

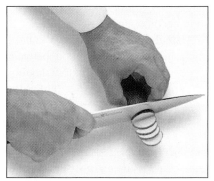

2 Using the second joint of your index finger as a guide, cut a slice using a smooth, even, downward stroke. Adjust the position of the guiding finger after each slice to produce slices of equal size. After a few cuts, slide your fingertips and thumb down the length of the item and continue slicing. For this slicing technique, the knife's tip acts as the fulcrum.

Method B

1 Grip the item as described above. Using the second joint of your index finger as a guide, lift the knife's tip and slice by drawing the knife slightly back toward you and down through the item, cutting the item to the desired thickness.

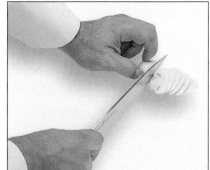

2 The motion of the knife should come almost entirely from the wrist, not the elbow. Allow the weight of the knife to do most of the work; very little downward pressure needs to be applied to the knife. For this slicing technique, your wrist should act as the fulcrum.

▶ CUTTING WITH YOUR KNIFE

A knife is used to shape and reduce an item's size. Uniformity of size and shape ensures even cooking and enhances the appearance of the finished product. Items are shaped by slicing, chopping, dicing, mincing and other special cutting techniques.

SLICING

To slice is to cut an item into relatively broad, thin pieces. Slices may be either the finished cut or the first step in producing other cuts. Slicing is typically used to create three specialty cuts: chiffonade, rondelle and diagonal. Slicing skills are also used to produce oblique or roll cuts and lozenges.

A **chiffonade** is a preparation of finely sliced or shredded leafy vegetables used as a garnish or a base under cold presentations. As shown here, slicing spinach en chiffonade is a relatively simple process.

▶ **chiffonade** (chef-fon-nahd) to finely slice or shred leafy vegetables or herbs

1 Wash and destem the leaves as necessary. Stack several leaves on top of each other and roll them tightly like a cigar.

2 Make fine slices across the leaves while holding the leaf roll tightly.

As seen here, **rondelles** or **rounds** are easily made disk-shaped slices of cylindrical vegetables or fruits.

▶ **rondelles** (ron-dellz) disk-shaped slices

Peel the item (if desired) and place it on a cutting board. Make even slices perpendicular to the item being cut.

Diagonals are elongated or oval-shaped slices of cylindrical vegetables or fruits. They are produced with a cut similar to that used to cut rondelles except that the knife is held at an angle to the item being cut.

▶ **diagonals** oval-shaped slices

Peel the item (if desired) and place it on a cutting board. Position the knife at the desired angle to the item being cut and slice it evenly.

▶ **oblique cuts** (oh-BLEEK) small pieces with two angle-cut sides

Oblique-cut or **roll-cut** items are small pieces with two angle-cut sides. It is a relatively simple cut most often used on carrots and parsnips.

Place the peeled item on a cutting board. Holding the knife at a 45-degree angle, make the first cut. Roll the item a half turn, keeping the knife at the same angle, and make another cut. The result is a wedge-shaped piece with two angled sides.

▶ **lozenges** diamond-shaped pieces, usually of firm vegetables

Lozenges are diamond-shaped cuts prepared from firm vegetables such as carrots, turnips, rutabagas and potatoes.

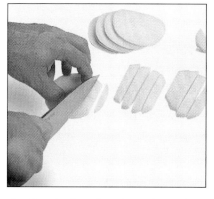

1 Slice the item into long slices of the desired thickness. Then cut the slices into strips of the desired width.

2 Cut the strips at an angle to produce diamond shapes.

HORIZONTAL SLICING

To horizontal slice is to **butterfly** or cut a pocket into meats, poultry or fish. It is also a method of cutting used to thinly slice soft vegetables.

▶ **butterfly** to slice boneless meat, poultry or fish nearly in half lengthwise so that it spreads open like a book

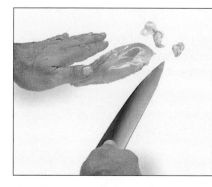

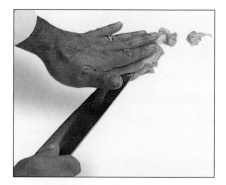

1 With your hand opened and your fingers arched upward, hold the item to be cut firmly in the center of your palm.

2 Holding the knife parallel to the table, slice a pocket to the desired depth, or cut through the item completely.

CHOPPING

To **chop** is to cut an item into small pieces where uniformity of size and shape is neither necessary (for example, coarsely chopped onions for a mirepoix that will be removed from the stock before service) nor feasible (for example, parsley).

▶ **chop** to cut into pieces where uniformity of size and shape is not important

COARSE CHOPPING

Coarse chopping does not mean carelessly hacking up food. Rather, the procedure is identical to that used for slicing but without the emphasis on uniformity. Coarsely chopped pieces should measure approximately ¾ inch × ¾ inch × ¾ inch (2 cm × 2 cm × 2 cm).

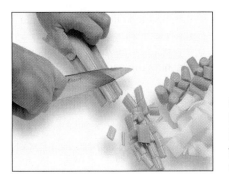

Grip the knife as for slicing. Hold the item being chopped with your other hand. It may not be necessary to use your finger as a guide because uniformity is not crucial.

CHOPPING PARSLEY AND SIMILAR FOODS

Parsley can be cut very coarsely or very finely. As shown here, it is easy to chop parsley and similar foods properly regardless of the desired fineness.

1 Wash the parsley in cold water; drain well. Remove the parsley sprigs from the stems.

2 Grip the knife in one hand. With the other hand spread flat, hold the knife's tip on the cutting board. Keeping the knife's tip on the board, chop the parsley sprigs by rocking the curved blade of the knife up and down while moving the knife back and forth over the parsley.

3 Place the chopped parsley in a clean kitchen towel or a double layer of cheesecloth. Rinse it under cold water and squeeze out as much water as possible. The chopped parsley should be dry and fluffy.

CHOPPING GARLIC

A daily chore in many food service facilities, peeling and chopping garlic is a simple job made easy with the procedure shown here.

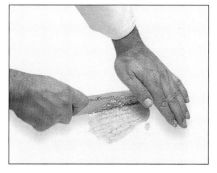

1 Break the head of garlic into individual cloves with your hands. Lightly crush the cloves using the flat edge of a chef's knife or a mallet. They will break open and the peel can be separated easily from the garlic flesh.

2 With a flat hand, hold the knife's tip on the cutting board. Using a rocking motion, chop the garlic cloves to the desired size. Garlic is usually chopped very finely.

3 Garlic paste can be made by first finely chopping the garlic and then turning the knife on an angle and repeatedly dragging the edge of the knife along the cutting board, mashing the garlic.

CUTTING STICKS AND DICING

▶ **dice** to cut into cubes with six equal-sized sides

To **dice** is to cut an item into cubes. The techniques described here are most often used when uniformity of size and shape is important (for example, julienned carrots for a salad or brunoised vegetables for a garnish).

Before an item can be diced, it must be cut into sticks such as juliennes and batonnets. These sticks are then reduced through dicing into the classic cuts known as brunoise, small dice, medium dice, large dice and paysanne. Although most cooks have some notion of what size and shape "small diced" potatoes or julienne carrots may be, there are specific sizes and shapes for these cuts. They are:

Julienne—(ju-lee-en) a stick-shaped item with dimensions of 1/8 inch × 1/8 inch × 2 inches (3 mm × 3 mm × 5 cm). When used with potatoes, this cut is sometimes referred to as an **allumette** (al-yoo-MEHT). A **fine julienne** has dimensions of 1/16 inch × 1/16 inch × 2 inches (1.5 mm × 1.5 mm × 5 cm).

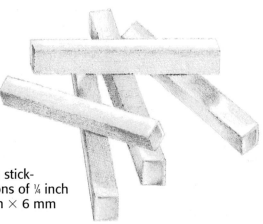

Batonnet—(bah-toh-nah) a stick-shaped item with dimensions of 1/4 inch × 1/4 inch × 2 inches (6 mm × 6 mm × 5 cm).

Brunoise—(broo-nwaz) a cube-shaped item with dimensions of ⅛ inch × ⅛ inch × ⅛ inch (3 mm × 3 mm × 3 mm). A ¹⁄₁₆-inch (1.5-mm) cube is referred to as a **fine brunoise.**

Small dice—a cube-shaped item with dimensions of ¼ inch × ¼ inch × ¼ inch (6 mm × 6 mm × 6 mm).

Medium dice—a cube-shaped item with dimensions of ½ inch × ½ inch × ½ inch (1.2 cm × 1.2 cm × 1.2 cm).

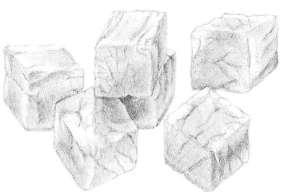

Large dice—a cube-shaped item with dimensions of ¾ inch × ¾ inch × ¾ inch (2 cm × 2 cm × 2 cm).

Paysanne—(pahy-sahn) a flat, square, round or triangular item with dimensions of ½ inch × ½ inch × ⅛ inch (1.2 cm × 1.2 cm × 3 mm).

CUTTING JULIENNE AND BATONNET

Julienne and batonnet are matchstick-shaped cuts prepared using the same procedure as cutting sticks for dicing.

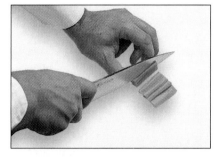

1 Peel the item (if desired) and square off the sides. Trim the item so that the slices cut from it will be the proper length. Cut even slices of the desired thickness, ⅛ inch (3 mm) for julienne or ¼ inch (6 mm) for batonnet.

2 Stack the slices and cut them evenly into sticks (also referred to as "planks") that are the same thickness as the slices.

CUTTING BRUNOISE AND SMALL, MEDIUM AND LARGE DICE

Brunoise as well as small, medium and large dice are made by first cutting the item into sticks following the procedure for cutting julienne or batonnet, then making cuts perpendicular to the length of the sticks to produce small cubes. Making a ⅛-inch (3-mm) cut perpendicular to the length of a julienne produces a brunoise. Similarly, a fine julienne (1/16 inch × 1/16 inch × 2 inches) is used to produce a fine brunoise. Making a ¼-inch (6-mm) cut perpendicular to the length of a batonnet produces a small dice. A ½-inch (1.2-cm) cut from a ½-inch (1.2-cm) stick produces a medium dice, and a ¾-inch (1.8-cm) cut from a ¾-inch (1.8-cm) stick produces a large dice.

Batonnet and julienne sticks and the large, medium, small and brunoise dices cut from them.

CUTTING PAYSANNE

Paysanne is a classic vegetable cut for garnishing soups and other dishes. It could be described as a very thin ½-inch cube. It is produced by following the procedures for dicing, but in the final step the ½-inch × ½-inch (1.2-cm × 1.2-cm) sticks are cut into slices ⅛ inch (3 mm) thick. The term *paysanne* is also used to refer to similarly sized round or triangular pieces.

Cutting paysanne from a ½-inch × ½-inch (6-mm × 6-mm) stick.

DICING AN ONION

Onions are easily peeled and diced to any size desired using the procedure shown here.

1 Using a paring knife, remove the stem end. Trim the root end but leave it nearly intact (this helps prevent the onion from falling apart while dicing). Peel away the outer skin; be careful not to remove and waste too much onion.

2 Cut the onion in half through the stem and root. Place the cut side down on the cutting board.

3 Cut parallel slices of the desired thickness vertically through the onion from the root toward the stem end without cutting completely through the root end.

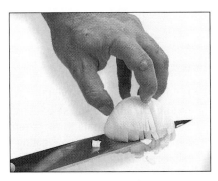

4 Make a single horizontal cut on a small onion or two horizontal cuts on a large onion through the width of the onion, again without cutting through the root end.

5 Turn the onion and cut slices perpendicular to the other slices to produce diced onion.

▶ **mince** to cut into very small pieces where uniformity of shape is not important

MINCING

To **mince** is to cut an item into very small pieces. The terms *finely chopped* and *minced* are often used interchangeably and are most often used when referring to garlic, shallots, herbs and other foods that do not have to be uniform in shape.

MINCING SHALLOTS

The procedure for mincing shallots is shown here.

1 Peel and dice the shallots, following the procedure for peeling and dicing an onion.

2 With a flat hand, hold the knife's tip on the cutting board. Using a rocking motion, mince the shallots with the heel of the knife.

TOURNER

▶ **tourner** (toor-nay) to cut into football-shaped pieces with seven equal sides and blunt ends

Tourner (toor-nay; "to turn" in French) is a cutting technique that results in a football-shaped finished product with seven equal sides and flat ends. The size of the finished product may vary, the most common being 2 inches (5 cm) long and 1 to 1½ inches in diameter. This is a more complicated procedure than other cuts and it takes considerable practice to produce good, consistent results.

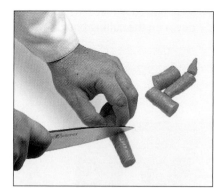

1 Cut the item being "turned" into pieces 2 inches (5 cm) × ¾ to 1 inch (2 to 2.5 cm). Each piece should have flat ends. (Potatoes, turnips and beets may be cut into as many as six or eight pieces; carrots can simply be cut into 2-inch lengths.) Peeling is optional because in most cases the item's entire surface area is trimmed away.

2 Holding the item between the thumb and forefinger, use a tourné knife or a paring knife to cut seven curved sides on the item, creating a flat-ended, football-shaped product.

PARISIENNES

A melon ball cutter or Parisienne scoop can be used to cut fruits and vegetables into uniform spheres, or **Parisiennes.** Small balls or spheres of fresh melon can be used in fruit salad, while tiny spheres of carrot, turnip, squash and so on can be used as a side dish or to garnish soup or an entrée. Melon ball cutters are available in a range of sizes, the smallest of which has an approximately ⅜-inch (9-mm) diameter and is known as a Parisienne (or Parisian) scoop.

▶ **parisienne** (pah-ree-zee-en) spheres of fruits or vegetables cut with a small melon ball cutter

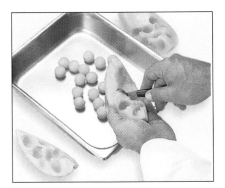

1 Cut each scoop with a pressing and twisting motion.

2 Make the cuts as close together as possible in order to minimize trim loss.

USING A MANDOLINE

The mandoline is a nonmechanical cutting tool. It does jobs that can be done with a chef's knife, such as very thinly sliced apples or large quantities of julienned vegetables, quickly, easily, and very accurately. It can also produce cuts such as a ridged slice or **gaufrette** that cannot be done with a conventional chef's knife.

When using the mandoline, always use the guard or a steel-mesh glove to protect your hand.

▶ **gaufrette** (goh-FREHT) a thin lattice or waffle-textured slice of vegetable cut on a mandoline

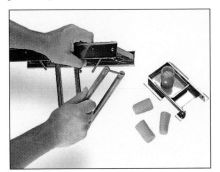

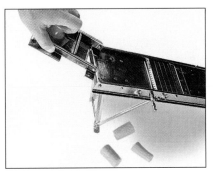

1 To use a mandoline, position the legs and set the blade to the desired shape and thickness.

2 Slide the guard into place.

3 To slice, slide the item against the blade with a single, smooth stroke.

4 To cut gaufrette, select the ridged blade and set it to the desired thickness. Make the first slice, turn the item 60° to 90° and make a second slice. Turn the item back to the original position and make another slice, and so on.

CONCLUSION

Although many slicing and dicing machines are available, none can ever completely replace a skilled chef with a sharp knife. As a student chef, you should make becoming efficient with your knives a high priority. Possessing good knife skills allows you to produce more attractive products in a safe and efficient manner. You will use the classic cuts and techniques outlined in this chapter throughout your career. You should memorize the procedures and practice them often. And remember, a dull or carelessly handled knife is dangerous.

QUESTIONS FOR DISCUSSION

1 Explain the step-by-step procedures for sharpening a knife using a three-sided whetstone.
2 What is the purpose of a steel? How is it used?
3 Why is it necessary to cut vegetables into uniform shapes and sizes?
4 Describe the following cutting procedures: slicing, chopping and dicing.
5 Identify the dimensions of the following cuts: julienne, batonnet, brunoise, small dice, medium dice, large dice and paysanne.
6 Describe the procedure for making tournéed vegetables.
7 Describe three preparations for which a mandoline would be useful.
8 A large number of vendors sell professional-quality knives through their Web sites. What are the advantages and disadvantages of buying knives from an online source?

SOME PEOPLE LIKE TO PAINT PICTURES, OR DO GARDENING, OR BUILD A BOAT IN THE BASEMENT. OTHER PEOPLE GET A TREMENDOUS PLEASURE OUT OF THE KITCHEN, BECAUSE COOKING IS JUST AS CREATIVE AND IMAGINATIVE AN ACTIVITY AS DRAWING, OR WOOD CARVING, OR MUSIC.
—*Julia Child, American cooking teacher and author (1912–)*

KITCHEN STAPLES

7

AFTER STUDYING THIS CHAPTER, YOU WILL BE ABLE TO:

▶ recognize and use a variety of herbs, spices, nuts, oils, vinegars and condiments

▶ prepare and serve quality coffees and teas

▶ **seasoning** an item added to enhance the natural flavors of a food without dramatically changing its taste; salt is the most common seasoning

▶ **flavoring** an item that adds a new taste to a food and alters its natural flavors; flavorings include herbs, spices, vinegars and condiments. The terms *seasoning* and *flavoring* are often used interchangeably.

▶ **herb** any of a large group of aromatic plants whose leaves, stems or flowers are used as a flavoring; used either dried or fresh

▶ **aromatic** a food added to enhance the natural aromas of another food; aromatics include most flavorings, such as herbs and spices, as well as some vegetables

▶ **spice** any of a large group of aromatic plants whose bark, roots, seeds, buds or berries are used as a flavoring; usually used in dried form, either whole or ground

▶ **condiment** traditionally, any item added to a dish for flavor, including herbs, spices and vinegars; now also refers to cooked or prepared flavorings such as prepared mustards, relishes, bottled sauces and pickles

Certain foods are used in almost all stations of the kitchen with such regularity that they have become known as staples. Included are many of the processed, packaged items we often take for granted: salt, pepper, flour, sugar, oil and flavorings. There is, however, no single list of staples. Each food service operation will have its own list, depending on the menu and the cooking methods used.

This chapter identifies and discusses selected herbs and spices, salt, nuts, oils, vinegars and condiments as well as two popular beverages, coffee and tea. We provide identifying characteristics for some of the more common staples and set forth standards of quality and usage. Other staples, such as flour and sugar, are covered in Chapter 29, Principles of the Bakeshop.

▶ HERBS AND SPICES

Herbs and spices are the kitchen staples used as **flavorings. Herbs** refer to the large group of **aromatic** plants whose leaves, stems or flowers are used to add flavors to other foods. Most herbs are available fresh or dried. Because drying alters their flavors and aromas, fresh herbs are generally preferred and should be used if possible. **Spices** are strongly flavored or aromatic portions of plants used as flavorings, **condiments** or aromatics. Spices are the bark, roots, seeds, buds or berries of plants, most of which grow naturally only in tropical climates. Spices are almost always used in their dried form, rarely fresh, and can usually be purchased whole or ground. Some plants—dill, for example—can be used as both an herb (its leaves) and a spice (its seeds).

HERBS

Basil (Fr. *basilique*) is considered one of the great culinary herbs. It is available in a variety of "flavors"— cinnamon, garlic, lemon, even chocolate—but the most common is sweet basil. **Sweet basil** has light green, tender leaves and small white flowers. Its flavor is strong, warm and slightly peppery, with a hint of cloves. Basil is used in Mediterranean cuisines and has a special affinity for garlic

Basil

and tomatoes. When purchasing fresh basil, look for bright green leaves; avoid flower buds and wilted or rust-colored leaves. Dried sweet basil is readily available but has a decidedly weaker flavor.

Opal basil is named for its vivid purple color. It has a tougher, crinkled leaf and a medium-strong flavor. Opal basil may be substituted for sweet basil in cooking, and its appearance makes it a distinctive garnish.

Opal Basil

Bay (Fr. *laurier*), also known as sweet laurel, is a small tree from Asia that produces tough, glossy leaves with a sweet balsamic aroma and peppery flavor. Bay symbolized wisdom and glory in ancient Rome; the leaves were used to form crowns or "laurels" worn by emperors and victorious athletes. In cooking, dried bay leaves are often preferred over the more bitter fresh leaves. Essential in French cuisine, bay leaves are part of the traditional bouquet garni and court bouillon. Whole dried leaves are usually added to a dish at the start of cooking, then removed when sufficient flavor has been extracted.

Bay Leaves

Chervil (Fr. *cerfeuil*), also known as sweet cicely, is native to Russia and the Middle East. Its lacy, fernlike leaves are similar to parsley and can be used as a garnish. Chervil's flavor is delicate, similar to parsley but with the distinctive aroma of anise. It should not be heated for long periods. Chervil is commonly used in French cuisine and is one of the traditional fines herbes.

Chervil

Chives (Fr. *ciboulette*) are perhaps the most delicate and sophisticated members of the onion family. Their hollow, thin grass-green stems grow in clumps and produce round, pale purple flowers, which are used as a garnish. Chives may be purchased dried, quick-frozen or fresh. They have a mild onion flavor and bright green color. Chives complement eggs, poultry, potatoes, fish and shellfish. They should not be cooked for long periods or at high temperatures. Chives make an excellent garnish when snipped with scissors or carefully chopped and sprinkled over finished soups or sauces.

Chives

Garlic chives, also known as Chinese chives, actually belong to another plant species. They have flat, solid (not hollow) stems and a mild garlic flavor. They may be used in place of regular chives if their garlic flavor is desired.

Garlic Chives

Cilantro (Fr. *coriander*) is the green leafy portion of the plant that yields seeds known as coriander. The flavors of the two portions of this plant are very different and cannot be substituted for each other.

Cilantro, also known as Chinese parsley, is sharp and tangy with a strong aroma and an almost citrus flavor. It is widely used in Asian, Mexican and South American cuisines, especially in salads and sauces. It should not be subjected to heat, and cilantro's flavor is completely destroyed by drying. Do not use yellow or discolored leaves or the tough stems.

Curry leaves (Hindi *karipatta; kitha neem*) are the distinctively flavored leaves of a small tree that grows wild in the Himalayan foothills, southern India and Sri Lanka. They look like small shiny bay leaves and have a strong currylike fragrance and a citrus-curry flavor. Often added to a preparation whole, then removed before serving, they can also be minced or finely chopped for marinades and sauces. Choose fresh bright green leaves, if possible, or frozen leaves; dried leaves have virtually no flavor. Although used in making southern Indian and Thai dishes, curry leaves (also known as neem leaves) must not be confused with curry powder, which is discussed later.

Cilantro

Dill (Fr. *aneth*), a member of the parsley family, has tiny, aromatic, yellow flowers and feathery, delicate blue-green leaves. The leaves taste like parsley, but sharper, with a touch of anise. Dill seeds are flat, oval and brown, with a bitter flavor similar to caraway. Both the seeds and the leaves of the dill plant are used in cooking. Dill is commonly used in Scandinavian and central European cuisines, particularly with fish and potatoes. Both leaves and seeds

Curry Leaves

Dill

Epazote

Lemongrass

Marjoram

Peppermint

are used in pickling and sour dishes. Dill leaves are available fresh or dried but lose their aroma and flavor during cooking, so add them only after the dish is removed from the heat. Dill seeds are available whole or ground and are used in fish dishes, pickles and breads.

Epazote, also known as wormseed or stinkweed, grows wild throughout the Americas. It has a strong aroma similar to kerosene and a wild flavor. Fresh epazote is used in salads and as a flavoring in Mexican and Southwestern cuisines. It is often cooked with beans to reduce their gaseousness. Dried epazote is brewed to make a beverage.

Lavender is an evergreen with thin leaves and tall stems bearing spikes of tiny purple flowers. Although lavender is known primarily for its aroma, which is widely used in perfumes, soaps and cosmetics, the flowers are also used as a flavoring, particularly in Middle Eastern and Provençal cuisines. These flowers have a sweet, lemony flavor and can be crystallized and used as a garnish. Lavender is also used in jams and preserves and to flavor teas and tisanes.

Lavender

Lemongrass (Fr. *herbe de citron*), also known as citronella grass, is a tropical grass with the strong aroma and flavor of a lemon. It is similar to scallions in appearance but with a woody texture. Only the lower base and white leaf stalks are used. Available fresh or quick-frozen, lemongrass is widely used in Southeast Asian cuisines.

Lovage (Fr. *celeri bâtard,* "false celery") has tall stalks and large dark green celery-like leaves. The leaves, stalks and seeds (which are commonly known as **celery seeds**) have a strong celery flavor. Also known as sea parsley and smallage, the leaves and stalks are used in salads and stews and the seeds are used for flavoring.

Marjoram (Fr. *marjolaine*), also known as sweet marjoram, is a flowering herb native to the Mediterranean and used since ancient times. Its flavor is similar to thyme but sweeter; it also has a stronger aroma. Marjoram is now used in many European cuisines. Although it is available fresh, marjoram is one of the few herbs whose flavor increases when dried. Wild marjoram is more commonly known as oregano.

Mint (Fr. *menthe*), a large family of herbs, includes many species and flavors (even chocolate). **Spearmint** is the most common garden and commercial variety. It has soft, bright green leaves and a tart aroma and flavor. Mint does not blend well with other herbs, so its use is confined to specific dishes, usually fruits or fatty meats such as lamb. Mint has an affinity for chocolate. It can also be brewed into a beverage or used as a garnish.

Spearmint

Peppermint has thin, stiff, pointed leaves and a sharper menthol flavor and aroma. Fresh peppermint is used less often in cooking or as a garnish than spearmint, but peppermint oil is a common flavoring in sweets and candies.

Oregano (Fr. *origan*), also known as wild marjoram, is a pungent, peppery herb used in Mediterranean cuisines, particularly Greek and Italian, as well as in Mexican cuisine. It is a classic complement to tomatoes. Oregano's thin, woody stalks bear clumps of tiny, dark green leaves, which are available dried and crushed.

Oregano

Parsley (Fr. *persil*) is probably the best known and most widely used herb in the world. It grows in almost all climates and is available in many varieties, all of which are rich in vitamins and minerals. The most common type in the United States and Northern Europe is **curly parsley.** It has small curly leaves and a bright green color. Its flavor is tangy and clean. Other cuisines use a variety sometimes known as **Italian parsley,** which has flat leaves, a darker color and coarser flavor. Curly parsley is a ubiquitous garnish; both types can be used in virtually any food except sweets. Parsley stalks have a stronger flavor than the leaves and are part of the standard bouquet garni. Chopped parsley forms the basis of any fine herb blend.

Parsley

Italian Parsley

Rosemary (Fr. *romarin*) is an evergreen bush that grows wild in warm, dry climates worldwide. It has stiff, needlelike leaves; some varieties bear pale blue flowers. It is highly aromatic, with a slight odor of camphor or pine. Rosemary is best used fresh. When dried, it loses flavor, and its leaves become very hard and unpleasant to chew. Whole rosemary stems may be added to a dish such as a stew and then removed when enough flavor has been imparted. They may also be added to a bouquet garni. Rosemary has a great affinity for roasted and grilled meats, especially lamb.

Rosemary

Sage (Fr. *sauge*) was used as a medicine for centuries before it entered the kitchen as a culinary herb. Culinary sage has narrow, fuzzy, gray-green leaves and blue flowers. Its flavor is strong and balsamic, with notes of camphor. Sage is used in poultry dishes, with fatty meats or brewed as a beverage. Sage's strong flavor does not blend well with other herbs. It dries well and is available in whole or chopped leaves or rubbed (coarsely ground).

Sage

Savory (Fr. *sariette*), also known as summer savory, has been used since ancient times. Its leaves are small and narrow, and it has a sharp, bitter flavor, vaguely like thyme. It dries well and is used in bean dishes, sausages and fine herb blends.

Tarragon (Fr. *estragon*), another of the great culinary herbs, is native to Siberia. It is a bushy plant with long, narrow, dark green leaves and tiny gray flowers. Tarragon goes well with fish and tomatoes and is essential in many French dishes such as béarnaise sauce and fine herb blends. Its flavor is strong and diffuses quickly through foods. It is available dried, but drying may cause haylike flavors to develop.

Savory

Tarragon

Thyme (Fr. *thym*) has been popular since 3500 B.C., when Egyptians used it as a medicine and for embalming. Thyme is a small, bushy plant with woody stems, tiny green-gray leaves and purple flowers. Its flavor is strong but refined, with notes of sage. Thyme dries well and complements virtually all types of meat, poultry, fish, shellfish and vegetables. It is often included in a bouquet garni or added to stocks.

Thyme

SPICES

Aleppo Pepper

Allspice

Star Anise

Capers

Aleppo pepper (ah-LEHP-oh) is made from bright red chiles grown in Turkey and northern Syria. The sun-dried Aleppo chiles are seeded and crushed, then used as a condiment. It has a sharp, but sweet, fruity flavor, with only mild heat (15,000 Scoville units). Although a member of the *Capsicum* family, Aleppo pepper is used more like ground peppercorns (*piper nigrum*) than a chile. Also known as Halaby pepper, it adds an authentic Mediterranean flavor and fragrance to foods.

Allspice (Fr. *toute-épice*), also known as Jamaican pepper, is the dried berry of a tree that flourishes in Jamaica, and one of the few spices still grown exclusively in the New World. Allspice is available whole; in berries that look like large, rough, brown peppercorns; or ground. Ground allspice is not a mixture of spices although it does taste like a blend of cinnamon, cloves and nutmeg. Allspice is now used throughout the world, in everything from cakes to curries, and is often included in peppercorn blends.

Anise (Fr. *anis*) is native to the eastern Mediterranean, where it was widely used by ancient civilizations. Today, it is grown commercially in warm climates throughout India, North Africa and southern Europe. The tiny, gray-green egg-shaped seeds have a distinctively strong, sweet flavor, similar to licorice and fennel. When anise seeds turn brown, they are stale and should be discarded. Anise is used in pastries as well as fish, shellfish and vegetable dishes, and is commonly used in alcoholic beverages (for example, Pernod and ouzo). The green leaves of the anise plant are occasionally used fresh as an herb or in salads.

Anise Seeds

Star anise, also known as Chinese anise, is the dried, star-shaped fruit of a Chinese magnolia tree. Although it is botanically unrelated, its flavor is similar to anise seeds but more bitter and pungent. It is an essential flavor in many Chinese dishes and one of the components of five-spice powder.

Annatto seeds (Fr. *roucou*) are the small, brick-red triangular seeds of a shrub from South America and the Caribbean. Annatto seeds add a mild, peppery flavor to rice, fish and shellfish dishes and are crushed to make Mexican achiote paste. Because they impart a bright yellow-orange color to foods, annatto seeds are commonly used as a natural food coloring, especially in cheeses and margarine.

Annatto Seeds

Asafetida (ah-sah-FEH-teh-dah; also spelled *asafoetida*) is a pale brown resin made from the sap of a giant fennel-like plant native to India and Iran. Also known as devil's dung, it has a garlicky flavor and a strong unpleasant fetid aroma (the aroma is not transferred to food being flavored). Available powdered or in lump form, it is used—very sparingly—as a flavoring in Indian and Middle Eastern cuisines.

Capers (Fr. *capres*) come from a small bush that grows wild throughout the Mediterranean basin. Its unopened flower buds have been pickled and used as a condiment for thousands of years. Fresh capers are not used, as the sharp, salty-sour flavor develops only after curing in strongly salted white vinegar. The finest capers are the smallest, known as nonpareils, which are produced in France's Provence region. Capers are used in a variety of sauces (tartare, rémoulade) and are excellent with fish and game. Capers will keep for long periods if moistened by their original liquid. Do not add or substitute vinegar, however, as this causes the capers to spoil.

A PINCH OF HISTORY

Spices have been used for many purposes for thousands of years. Egyptian papyri dating back to 2800 B.C. identify several spices native to the Middle and Far East that were used by the ruling and priestly classes for therapeutic, cosmetic, medicinal, ritualistic and culinary purposes.

By A.D. 300, the Romans were regularly importing spices for use as perfumes, medicines, preservatives and ingredients from China and India via long, difficult caravan journeys over sea and land. Spices were extremely expensive and unavailable to all but the wealthiest citizens.

After Rome fell in the second half of the 5th century A.D., much of the overland route through southern Europe became prey to bandits; and after Constantinople fell in 1453, the spice routes through the Middle East were controlled by the Ottoman Turks. Spice costs soared, and economies based upon the spice trade, such as that of Venice, were at risk.

By then highly spiced food had become common, especially in wealthier households. So, in part to maintain their culinary norm, the Europeans set out to break the Ottoman Turk monopoly. These efforts led to Columbus's exploration of the Americas and Vasco da Gama's discovery of a sea route to India. Although the New World contained none of the spices for which Columbus was searching, it provided many previously unknown foods and flavorings that subsequently changed European tables forever, including chiles, vanilla, tomatoes, potatoes and chocolate.

Formation of the Dutch East India Company in 1602 marked the start of the Dutch colonial empire and made spices widely available to the growing European middle classes. The transplantation and cultivation of spice plants eventually weakened the once-powerful trading empires until, by the 19th century, no European country could monopolize trade. Prices fell dramatically.

Caraway (Fr. *carvi*) is perhaps the world's oldest spice. Its use has been traced to the Stone Age, and seeds have been found in ancient Egyptian tombs. The caraway plant grows wild in Europe and temperate regions of Asia. It produces a small, crescent-shaped brown seed with the peppery flavor of rye. Seeds may be purchased whole or ground. (The leaves have a mild, bland flavor and are rarely used in cooking.) Caraway is a very European flavor, used extensively in German and Austrian dishes, particularly breads, meats and cabbage. It is also used in alcoholic beverages and cheeses.

Cardamom (Fr. *cardamome*) is one of the most expensive spices, second only to saffron in cost. Its seeds are encased in ¼-inch- (6-millimeter-) long light green or brown pods. Cardamom is highly aromatic. Its flavor, lemony with notes of camphor, is quite strong and is used in both sweet and savory dishes. Cardamom is widely used in Indian and Middle Eastern cuisines, where it is also used to flavor coffee. Scandinavians use cardamom to flavor breads and pastries. Ground cardamom loses its flavor rapidly and is easily adulterated, so it is best to purchase whole seeds and grind your own as needed.

Chiles, including paprika, chile peppers, bell peppers and cayenne, are members of the **capsicum** plant family. Although cultivated for thousands of years in the West Indies and Americas, capsicum peppers were unknown in the Old World prior to Spanish explorations during the 15th century. Capsicum peppers come in all shapes and sizes, with a wide range of flavors, from sweet to extremely hot. Some capsicums are used as a vegetable, while others are dried, ground and used as a spice. Fresh chiles and bell peppers are discussed in Chapter 22, Vegetables. Capsicums are botanically unrelated to **piper nigrum,** the black peppercorns discussed later.

Cayenne, sometimes simply labeled "red pepper," is ground from a blend of several particularly hot types of dried red chile peppers. Its flavor is extremely hot and pungent; it has a bright orange-red color and fine texture.

Paprika, also known as Hungarian pepper, is a bright red powder ground from specific varieties of red-ripened and dried chiles. Paprika's flavor ranges from sweet to pungent; its aroma is distinctive and strong. It is essential to many Spanish and eastern European dishes. Mild paprika is meant to be used in generous quantities and may be sprinkled on prepared foods as a garnish.

Caraway Seeds

Cardamom Seeds

► For our purposes, *chile* refers to the plant, *chili* refers to the stewlike dish containing chiles and *chilli* refers to the commercial spice powder

Cayenne Pepper

Paprika

Chilli Powder

Crushed Chiles

Cloves

Cumin

Fennel

Chile powders are made from a wide variety of dried chile peppers, ranging from sweet and mild to extremely hot and pungent. The finest pure chile powders come from dried chiles that are simply roasted, ground and sieved. Commercial chilli powder, an American invention, is actually a combination of spices—oregano, cumin, garlic and other flavorings—intended for use in Mexican dishes. Each brand is different and should be sampled before using.

Crushed chiles, also known as chile flakes, are blended from dried, coarsely crushed chiles. They are quite hot and are used in sauces and meat dishes.

Cinnamon (Fr. *cannelle*) and its cousin **cassia** are among the oldest known spices: Cinnamon's use is recorded in China as early as 2500 B.C., and the Far East still produces most of these products. Both cinnamon and cassia come from the bark of small evergreen trees, peeled from branches in thin layers and dried in the sun. High-quality cinnamon should be pale brown and thin, rolled up like paper into sticks known as quills. Cassia is coarser and has a stronger, less subtle flavor than cinnamon. Consequently, it is cheaper than true cinnamon. Cinnamon is usually purchased ground because it is difficult to grind. Cinnamon sticks are used when long cooking times allow for sufficient flavor to be extracted (for example, in stews or curries). Cinnamon's flavor is most often associated with pastries and sweets, but it has a great affinity for lamb and spicy dishes. Labeling laws do not require that packages distinguish between cassia and cinnamon, so most of what is sold as cinnamon in the United States is actually cassia, blended for consistent flavor and aroma.

Ground Cinnamon and Cinnamon Sticks

Cloves (Fr. *girofles*) are the unopened buds of evergreen trees that flourish in muggy tropical regions. When dried, whole cloves have hard, sharp prongs that can be used to push them into other foods, such as onions or fruit, in order to provide flavor. Cloves are extremely pungent, with a sweet, astringent aroma. A small amount provides a great deal of flavor. Cloves are used in desserts and meat dishes, preserves and liquors. They may be purchased whole or ground.

Coriander (Fr. *coriander*) seeds come from the cilantro plant. They are round and beige, with a distinctive sweet, spicy flavor and strong aroma. Unlike other plants in which the seeds and the leaves carry the same flavor and aroma, coriander and cilantro are very different. Coriander seeds are available whole or ground and are frequently used in Indian cuisine and pickling mixtures.

Coriander Seeds

Cumin is the seed of a small delicate plant of the parsley family that grows in North Africa and the Middle East. The small seeds are available whole or ground and look (but do not taste) like caraway seeds. Cumin has a strong earthy flavor and tends to dominate any dish in which it is included. It is used in Indian, Middle Eastern and Mexican cuisines, in sausages and a few cheeses.

Fennel (Fr. *fenouil*) is a perennial plant with feathery leaves and tiny flowers long cultivated in India and China as a medicine and cure for witchcraft. Its seeds are greenish brown with prominent ridges and short, hairlike fibers. Their taste and aroma are similar to anise, though not as sweet. Whole seeds are widely used in Italian stews and sausages; central European cuisines use fennel with fish, pork, pickles and vegetables. Ground seeds can also be used in breads, cakes and cookies. The same plant produces a bulbous stalk used as a vegetable.

Fenugreek (Fr. *fenugrec*), grown in Mediterranean countries since ancient times, is a small, beanlike plant with a tiny flower. The seeds, available whole or ground, are pebble shaped and transfer their pale orange color to the foods with which they are cooked. Their flavor is bittersweet, like burnt sugar with a bitter aftertaste. Fenugreek is a staple in Indian cuisines, especially curries and chutneys.

Filé powder (fee-LAY) is the dried, ground leaf of the sassafras plant. Long used by Choctaw Indians, it is now most commonly used as a thickener and flavoring in Cajun and Creole cuisines. Filé is also used as a table condiment to add a spicy note to stews, gumbo and the like. The powder forms strings if allowed to boil, so it should be added during the last minutes of cooking.

Galangal (guh-LANG-guhl) is the rhizome of a plant native to India and Southeast Asia. The rhizome has a reddish skin, an orange or whitish flesh and a peppery, gingerlike flavor and piny aroma. Also known as galanga root, Thai ginger and Laos ginger, it is peeled and crushed for used in Thai and Indonesian cuisines. Fresh ginger is an appropriate substitute.

Ginger (Fr. *gingembre*) is a well-known spice obtained from the root of a tall, flowering tropical plant. Fresh ginger root is known as a "hand" because it looks vaguely like a group of knobby fingers. It has grayish-tan skin and a pale yellow, fibrous interior. Fresh ginger should be plump and firm with smooth skin. It should keep for about a month under refrigeration. Its flavor is fiery but sweet, with notes of lemon and rosemary. Fresh ginger is widely available and is used in Indian and Asian cuisines. It has a special affinity for chicken, beef and curries. Ginger is also available peeled and pickled in vinegar, candied in sugar or preserved in alcohol or syrup. Dried, ground ginger is a fine yellow powder widely used in pastries. Its flavor is spicier and not as sweet as fresh ginger.

Grains of paradise are the seeds of a perennial reedlike plant indigenous to the West African coast. Related to cardamom, grains of paradise have a spicy, warm and slightly bitter flavor, similar to peppercorns. In fact, grains of paradise were traditionally used in place of black pepper and are also known as Guinea pepper or Melegueta pepper. Now enjoying a resurgence in popularity and increased availability, they are ground and used primarily in West African and Magreb dishes, and in the spice blend known as ras el hanout.

Horseradish (Fr. *cranson de Bretagne*) is the large off-white taproot of a hardy perennial (unrelated to radishes) that flourishes in cool climates. Fresh roots should be firm and plump; they will not have the distinctive horseradish aroma unless cut or bruised. The outer skin and inner core of a fresh horseradish root can have an unpleasant flavor and should be discarded. Typically used in Russian and Central European cuisines, especially as an accompaniment to roasted meats and fish and shellfish dishes, horseradish is usually served grated, creamed into a sauce or as part of a compound butter or mustard preparation. If horseradish is cooked, heat can destroy its flavor and pungency, so any horseradish should be added near the end of cooking.

Juniper (Fr. *genièvre*) is an evergreen bush grown throughout the northern hemisphere. It produces round purple berries with a sweet flavor similar to pine. Juniper berries are used for flavoring gin and other alcoholic beverages, and are crushed and incorporated in game dishes, particularly venison and wild boar.

Mustard seeds (Fr. *moutarde*), available in black, brown and yellow, come from three different plants in the cabbage family. Mustard seeds are small, hard spheres with a bitter flavor. The seeds have no aroma, but their flavor is sharp and fiery hot. Yellow seeds have the mildest and black seeds the strongest flavor. All are sold whole and can be crushed for cooking. Mustard seeds are a standard component of pickling spices and are processed and blended for prepared mustards, which we discuss later. Ground or dry mustard is a bright yellow powder made from a blend of ground seeds, wheat flour and turmeric.

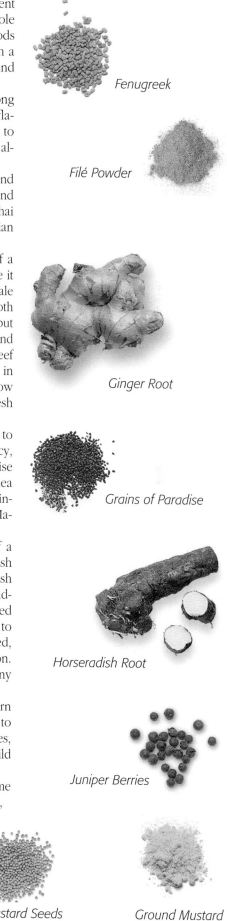

Fenugreek

Filé Powder

Ginger Root

Grains of Paradise

Horseradish Root

Juniper Berries

Mustard Seeds

Ground Mustard

Whole Nutmegs with Ground Mace (left) and Ground Nutmeg (right)

Mace

Green Peppercorns

Pink Peppercorns

Szechuan Pepper

Nutmeg (Fr. *muscade*) and **mace** come from the yellow plumlike fruit of a large tropical evergreen. These fruits are dried and opened to reveal the seed known as nutmeg. The seed is surrounded by a bright red lacy coating or *aril*; the aril is the spice mace. Whole nutmegs are oval and look rather like a piece of smooth wood. The flavor and aroma of nutmeg are strong and sweet, and a small quantity provides a great deal of flavor. Nutmeg should be grated directly into a dish as needed; once grated, flavor loss is rapid. Nutmeg is used in many European cuisines, mainly in pastries and sweets, but is also important in meat and savory dishes.

Mace is an expensive spice, with a flavor similar to nutmeg but more refined. It is almost always purchased ground and retains its flavor longer than other ground spices. Mace is used primarily in pastry items.

Peppercorns (Fr. *poivre*) are the berries of a vine plant (*piper nigrum*) native to tropical Asia. Peppercorns should not be confused with the chile (capsicum) peppers discussed earlier. Peppercorns vary in size, color, pungency and flavor. Many of these differences are the result of variations in climate and growing conditions. Good-quality pepper is expensive and should be purchased whole and ground fresh in a peppermill as needed. Whole peppercorns will last indefinitely if kept dry. They should be stored well covered in a cool, dark place.

Black and **white peppercorns** are produced from the same plant, but are picked and processed differently. For black peppercorns, the berries are picked when green and simply dried whole in the sun. Black pepper has a warm, pungent flavor and aroma. Tellicherry peppercorns from the southwest coast of India are generally considered the finest black peppercorns in the world and are priced accordingly.

Black Pepper (left) and White Pepper (right)

For white peppercorns, the berries are allowed to ripen until they turn red. The ripened berries are allowed to ferment, then the outer layer of skin is washed off. Nowadays, white pepper may be produced by mechanically removing the outer skin from black peppercorns. This is not true white pepper, and the resulting product should be labeled "decorticated." White pepper has less aroma than black pepper but is useful in white sauces or where the appearance of black speckles is undesirable.

Green peppercorns are unripened berries that are either freeze-dried or pickled in brine or vinegar. Pickled green peppercorns are soft, with a fresh, sour flavor similar to capers. They are excellent in spiced butters and sauces or with fish.

Pink peppercorns are actually the berries of a South American tree, not a vine pepper plant. Pink peppercorns are available dried or pickled in vinegar. Although they are attractive, their flavor is bitter and pinelike, with less spiciness than true pepper.

Szechuan pepper (also spelled Szechwan and Sichuan) is the dried red berries of the prickly ash tree native to China. Also known as anise pepper and Chinese pepper, the berries have an extremely hot, peppery, spicy flavor with citrus overtones and are used in Chinese cuisines and as part of Chinese five-spice powder.

Poppy seeds (Fr. *pavot*) are the ripened seeds of the opium poppy, which flourishes in the Middle East and India. (When ripe, the seeds do not contain any of the medicinal alkaloids found elsewhere in the plant.) The tiny blue-gray seeds are round and hard with a sweet, nutty flavor. Poppy seeds are used in pastries and breads.

Poppy Seeds

Saffron

Saffron (Fr. *safran*) comes from the dried stigmas of the saffron crocus. Each flower bears only three threadlike stigmas, and each must be picked by hand. It takes about 250,000 flowers to produce one pound of saffron, making it the most expensive spice in the world. Beware of bargains; there is no such thing as cheap saffron. Luckily, a tiny pinch is enough to color and flavor a large quantity of food. Good saffron should be a brilliant orange color, not yellow, with a strong aroma and a bitter, honeylike taste. Saffron produces a yellow dye that diffuses through any warm liquid. Valencia or Spanish saffron is considered the finest. It is commonly used with fish and shellfish (a necessity for bouillabaisse) and rice dishes such as paella and risotto. When using saffron threads, first crush them gently, then soak them in some hot liquid from the recipe. Powdered saffron is less expensive but more easily adulterated. It may be added directly to the other ingredients when cooking.

Sesame Seeds

Sesame seeds, also known as benne seeds, are native to India. They are small, flat ovals, with a creamy white color. Their taste is nutty and earthy, with a pronounced aroma when roasted or ground into a paste (known as tahini). Sesame seeds are the source of sesame oil, which has a mild, nutty flavor and does not go rancid easily. Sesame seeds are roasted and used in or as a garnish for breads and meat dishes. They are popular in Indian and Asian cuisines, with a black variety of seeds most popular as a Japanese condiment.

Tamarind (Fr. *tamarin;* Sp. and It. *tamarindo*), also known as an Indian date, is the brown, bean-shaped pod of the tamarind tree, which is native to Africa. Although naturally sweet, tamarind also contains 12% tartaric acid, which makes it extremely tart. It is commonly used in Indian curries and Mediterranean cooking as a souring agent and in the West Indies in fruit drinks. Tamarind is sold as a concentrate or in sticky blocks of crushed pods, pulp and seeds, which should be soaked in warm water for about five minutes, then squeezed through a sieve. Tamarind's high pectin content is useful in chutneys and jams, and it is often included in barbeque sauces and marinades. It is a key ingredient in Worcestershire sauce.

Tamarind Pods   *Tamarind Paste*

Turmeric (Fr. *curcuma*), also known as Indian saffron, is produced from the roots of a flowering tropical plant related to ginger. Unlike ginger, fresh turmeric is not used in cooking. It is only available dried and usually ground. Turmeric is renowned for its vibrant yellow color and is used as a food coloring and dye. Turmeric's flavor is distinctive and strong; it should not be substituted for saffron. Turmeric is a traditional ingredient in Indian curries, to which it imparts color as well as flavor.

Turmeric

Wasabi is a pale green root similar, but unrelated, to horseradish. It has a strong aroma and a sharp, cleansing flavor with herbal overtones that is a bit hotter than that of horseradish. Fresh wasabi is rarely found outside Japan, but tins of powder and tubes of paste are readily available. It is commonly served with sushi and sashimi and can be used to add a spicy Asian note to other dishes, such as mashed potatoes or a compound butter.

Wasabi

HERB AND SPICE BLENDS

Many cuisines have created recognizable combinations of flavors that are found in a variety of dishes. Although many of these blends are available ready-prepared for convenience, most can be mixed by the chef as needed. A few of the more common herb and spice blends are described here. In addition, a recipe for Cajun Spice Mix appears on page 541 and one for Creole Spice Mix appears on page 582.

Chinese five-spice powder is a combination of equal parts finely ground Szechuan pepper, star anise, cloves, cinnamon and fennel seeds. This blend is widely used in Chinese and some Vietnamese foods and is excellent with pork and in pâtés.

Curry powder is a European invention that probably took its name from the

Five-Spice Powder

Curry Powder

Herbes de Provence

Pickling Spice

Tamil word *kari,* meaning "sauce." Created by 19th-century Britons returning from colonial India, it was meant to be the complete spicing for a "curry" dish. There are as many different formulas for curry powder as there are manufacturers, some mild and sweet (Bombay or Chinese style), others hot and pungent (Madras style). Typical ingredients in curry powder are black pepper, cinnamon, cloves, coriander, cumin, ginger, mace and turmeric.

Fine herbs (Fr. *fines herbes*) are a combination of parsley, tarragon, chervil and chives widely used in French cuisine. The mixture is available dried, or you can create your own from fresh ingredients.

Masala (mah-SAH-lah) is a flavorful, aromatic blend of roasted and ground spices used in Indian cuisines. A **garam masala** (gah-RAHM) is a masala made with hot spices (*garam* means warm or hot). A dry garam masala usually contains peppercorns, cardamom, cinnamon, cloves, coriander, nutmeg, turmeric, bay leaves and fennel seeds and is added toward the end of cooking or sprinkled on the food just before service. A wet garam masala is made by adding coconut milk, oil or sometimes tamarind water to a dry garam masala. A wet garam masala is typically added at the start of cooking.

Herbes de Provence (airbs duh pro-VAWNS) is a blend of dried herbs commonly grown and used in southern France. Commercial blends usually include thyme, rosemary, bay leaf, basil, fennel seeds, savory and lavender. The herb blend is used with grilled or roasted meat, fish or chicken; in vegetable dishes; on pizza; and even in steamed rice and yeast breads.

Italian seasoning blend is a commercially prepared mixture of dried basil, oregano, sage, marjoram, rosemary, thyme, savory and other herbs associated with Italian cuisine.

Pickling spice, as with other blends, varies by manufacturer. Most pickling spice blends are based on black peppercorns and red chiles, with some or all of the following added: allspice, cloves, ginger, mustard seeds, coriander seeds, bay leaves and dill. These blends are useful in making cucumber or vegetable pickles as well as in stews and soups.

Quatre-épices (kah-tray-pees), literally "four spices" in French, is a peppery mixture of black peppercorns with lesser amounts of nutmeg, cloves and dried ginger. Sometimes cinnamon or allspice is included. Quatre-épices is used in charcuterie and long-simmered stews.

Ras el hanout (rass al ha-noot) is a common Moroccan spice blend varying greatly from supplier to supplier. It typically contains 20 or more spices, such as turmeric, cinnamon, cloves, grains of paradise, coriander, cumin, cardamom, peppercorns, dried chiles, dried flower petals and, allegedly, an aphrodisiac or two. It is sold whole and ground by the cook as necessary to flavor stews, rice, couscous and game dishes.

Seasoned salts are commercially blended products containing salt and one or more natural flavoring ingredients such as garlic, spices or celery seeds, and, often, monosodium glutamate.

STORING HERBS AND SPICES

Fresh herbs should be kept refrigerated at 34°F–40°F (2°C–4°C). Large bouquets can be stored upright, their leaves loosely covered with plastic wrap and their stems submerged in water. Smaller bunches should be stored loosely covered with a damp towel. Excess fresh herbs can be dried for later use in an electric dehydrator or spread out on baking sheets in a 100°F (38°C) oven.

Dried herbs and spices should be stored in airtight, opaque containers in a cool, dry place. Avoid light and heat, both of which destroy delicate flavors.

USING HERBS AND SPICES

Herbs and spices are a simple, inexpensive way to bring individuality and variety to foods. Their proper use leads to better-flavored and distinctively different dishes. They add neither fat nor sodium and virtually no calories to foods; most contain only 3 to 10 calories per teaspoon. Table 7.1 lists just a few uses for some of the more common herbs and spices.

Table 7.1	USES FOR SOME COMMON HERBS AND SPICES	
FLAVORING	**FORM**	**SUGGESTED USES**
Allspice	Whole or ground	Fruits, relishes, braised meats
Anise	Whole or ground	Asian cuisines, pastries, breads, cheeses
Basil	Fresh or dried	Tomatoes, salads, eggs, fish, chicken, lamb, cheeses
Caraway	Whole or ground	Rye bread, cabbage, beans, pork, beef, veal
Chervil	Fresh or dried	Chicken, fish, eggs, salads, soups, vegetables
Chives	Fresh or dried	Eggs, fish, chicken, soups, potatoes, cheeses
Cilantro	Fresh leaves	Salsa, salads, Mexican cuisine, fish, shellfish, chicken
Cloves	Whole or ground	Marinades, baked goods, braised meats, pickles, fruits, beverages, stocks
Cumin	Whole or ground	Chili, sausages, stews, eggs
Dill	Fresh or dried leaves; whole seeds	Leaves or seeds in soups, salads, fish, shellfish, vegetables, breads; seeds in pickles, potatoes, vegetables
Fennel	Whole seeds	Sausages, stews, sauces, pickling, lamb, eggs
Ginger	Fresh root or powder	Asian, Caribbean and Indian cuisines, pastries, curries, stews, meats
Marjoram	Fresh or dried	Sausages, pâtés, meats, poultry, stews, green vegetables, tomatoes, game
Nutmeg	Ground	Curries, relishes, rice, eggs, beverages
Rosemary	Fresh or dried	Lamb, veal, beef, poultry, game, marinades, stews
Saffron	Threads or ground	Rice, breads, potatoes, soups, stews, chicken, fish, shellfish
Sage	Fresh or dried	Poultry, charcuterie, pork, stuffings, pasta, beans, tomatoes
Tarragon	Fresh or dried	Chicken, fish, eggs, salad dressings, sauces, tomatoes
Thyme	Fresh or dried	Fish, chicken, meats, stews, charcuterie, soups, tomatoes
Turmeric	Ground	Curries, relishes, rice, eggs, breads

FLAVOR CONCEPTS

In *Ethnic Cuisine: The Flavor Principle Cookbook,* Elisabeth Rozin writes: "Every culture tends to combine a small number of flavoring ingredients so frequently and so consistently that they become definitive of that particular cuisine" (p. xiv). She calls these defining flavors "flavor principles" and notes that they are "designed to abstract what is absolutely fundamental about a cuisine and, thus, to serve as a guide in cooking and developing new recipes" (p. xvii). She identifies the following flavor principles:

Central Asia: cinnamon, fruit and nuts

China: generally—soy sauce, rice wine and ginger root

 Northern China (Mandarin/Peking)—miso and/or garlic and/or sesame

 Western China (Szechuan)—sweet, sour and hot

 Southern China (Canton)—black beans, garlic

Eastern Europe (Jewish): onion and chicken fat

Eastern and Northern Europe: sour cream and dill or paprika or allspice or caraway

France: generally—olive oil, garlic and basil or wine and herb or butter and/or sour cream and/or cheese plus wine and/or stock

 Provence—olive oil, thyme, rosemary, marjoram, sage plus tomato as a variation

 Normandy—apple, cider, Calvados

Greece: tomato, cinnamon or olive oil, lemon, oregano

India: Northern—cumin, ginger, garlic

 Southern—mustard seed, coconut, tamarind, chile

Italy: generally—olive oil, garlic, basil

 Northern Italy—wine vinegar, garlic

 Southern Italy—olive oil, garlic, parsley, anchovy, tomato

Japan: soy sauce, sake, sugar

Mexico: tomato and chile or lime and chile

North Africa: cumin, coriander, cinnamon, ginger, onion and/or tomato and/or fruit

Spain: olive oil, garlic, nut or olive oil, onion, pepper, tomato

Thailand: fish sauce, curry, chile

West Africa: tomato, peanut, chile

Although the flavors and aromas of fresh herbs are generally preferred, dried herbs are widely used because they are readily available and convenient. Purchase only the amount of dried herbs that can be used within a short time. If stored properly, dried herbs should last for two to three months.

Use less dried herbs than you would fresh herbs. The loss of moisture strengthens and concentrates the flavor in dried herbs. In general, you should use only one-half to one-third as much dried herb as fresh in any given recipe. For example, if a recipe calls for 1 tablespoon of fresh basil, you should substitute only 1 *teaspoon* of dried basil. You can usually add more later if necessary.

Spices are often available whole or ground. Once ground, they lose their flavors rapidly, however. Whole spices should keep their flavors for many months if stored properly. Stale spices lose their spicy aroma and develop a bitter or musty aftertaste. Discard them.

Because ground spices release their flavors quickly, they should be added to cooked dishes near the end of the cooking period. In uncooked dishes that call for ground spices (for example, salad dressings), the mixture should be allowed to stand for several hours to develop good flavor.

Although some combinations are timeless—rosemary with lamb, dill with salmon, nutmeg with spinach, caraway with rye bread—less common pairings can be equally delicious and far more exciting. A chef must be willing and able to experiment with new flavors. But first you must be familiar with the distinctive flavor and aroma of the herb or spice. Then you can experiment, always bearing in mind the following guidelines:

▷ Flavorings should not hide the taste or aroma of the primary ingredient.

▷ Flavorings should be combined in balance, so as not to overwhelm the palate.

▷ Flavorings should not be used to disguise poor quality or poorly prepared products.

Even in a well-tested recipe, the quantity of flavorings may need to be adjusted because of a change in brands or the condition of the ingredients. A chef should strive to develop his or her palate to recognize and correct subtle variances as necessary.

▶ SALT

Salt (Fr. *sel*) is the most basic seasoning, and its use is universal. It preserves foods, heightens their flavors and provides the distinctive taste of saltiness. The presence of salt can be tasted easily but not smelled. Salt suppresses bitter flavors, making the sweet and sour ones more prominent. The flavor of salt will not evaporate or dissipate during cooking so it should be added to foods carefully, according to taste. Remember, you can always add more salt, but you can neither remove nor mask it if you have added too much.

Culinary or **table salt** is sodium chloride (NaCl), one of the minerals essential to human life. Salt contains no calories, proteins, fats or carbohydrates. It is available from several sources, each with its own flavor and degree of saltiness.

Rock salt, mined from underground deposits, is available in both edible and nonedible forms. It is used in ice cream churns, for thawing frozen sidewalks and, in edible form, in salt mills.

Common kitchen or table salt is produced by pumping water through underground salt deposits, then bringing the brine to the surface to evaporate, leaving behind crystals. Chemicals are usually added to prevent table salt from absorbing moisture and thus keep it free-flowing. Iodized salt is commonly used in the United States. The iodine has no effect on the salt's flavor or use; it is simply added to provide an easily available source of iodine, an important nutrient, to a large number of people.

Rock Salt

ABOUT FLAVORS

Flavor is to food what hue is to color. It is what timbre is to music. Flavor is adjective; food is noun. Each ingredient has its own particular character, which is altered by every other ingredient it encounters. A secret ingredient is one that mysteriously improves the flavor of a dish without calling attention to itself. It is either undetectable or extremely subtle, but its presence is crucial because the dish would not be nearly as good without it.

Primary flavors are those that are obvious, such as the flavors of chicken and tarragon in a chicken tarragon, shrimp and garlic in a shrimp scampi, or beef and red wine in a beef à la Bourguignon. Secret ingredients belong to the realm of secondary flavors. However obvious it is that you need tarragon to prepare a chicken tarragon, you would not achieve the most interesting result using only tarragon. Tarragon, in this case, needs secondary ingredients—a hint of celery seed and anise—to make it taste more like quintessential tarragon and at the same

time more than tarragon. In this way, primary flavors often depend on secret ingredients to make them more interesting and complex. Using only one herb or spice to achieve a certain taste usually results in a lackluster dish—each mouthful tastes the same. Whether they function in a primary or secondary way, flavors combine in only three different ways: They marry, oppose, or juxtapose.

When flavors marry, they combine to form one taste. Some secondary flavors marry with primary ones to create a new flavor greater than the sum of its parts, and often two flavors can do the job better than one. It may sound like an eccentric combination, but vanilla marries with the flavor of lobster, making it taste more like the essence of lobster than lobster does on its own. And when ginger and molasses marry, they create a flavor superior to either alone.

Opposite flavors can highlight or cancel each other; they can cut or balance each other.

Sweet/sour, sweet/salty, sweet/hot, salty/sour, and salty/tart are all opposites. Salt and sugar are so opposed, in fact, that when used in equal amounts they cancel each other entirely. Sweet relish helps to cancel the salty flavor of hot dogs. Chinese sauces usually contain some sugar to help balance the saltiness of soy sauce.

Because flavors are sensed on different parts of the tongue and palate, and because they are tasted at different times, we can juxtapose them, using flavors side by side or in layers. The layering of flavors makes the food we taste more interesting because each mouthful is different.

Knowing how to combine many flavors and aromas to achieve a simple and pure result (and knowing when not to combine flavors) will make you a better, more confident cook. Good cooks over the centuries have known these things intuitively—but they've had neither the huge variety of ingredients nor the knowledge of world cuisines that we have today.

CHEF MICHAEL ROBERTS, *Secret Ingredients*

"Fleur de Sel" (Sea Salt)

Sea salt, also known as *fleur de sel* or *sel gris,* is obtained, not surprisingly, by evaporating seawater. Unlike other table salts, sea salt contains additional mineral salts such as magnesium, calcium and potassium, which give it a stronger, more complex flavor and a grayish-brown color. The region where it is produced can also affect its flavor. For example, salt from the Mediterranean Sea will taste different from salt obtained from the Indian Ocean or the English Channel. Sea salt is considerably more expensive than other table salts and is often reserved for finishing a dish or used as a condiment.

Kosher salt has large, irregular crystals and is used in the "koshering" or curing of meats. It is purified rock salt that contains no iodine or additives. It can be substituted for common kitchen salt.

Because it is nonorganic, salt keeps indefinitely. It will, however, absorb moisture from the atmosphere, which prevents it from flowing properly. Salt is a powerful preservative; its presence stops or greatly slows down the growth of many undesirable organisms. Salt is used to preserve meats, vegetables and fish. It is also used to develop desirable flavors in bacon, ham, cheeses and fish products as well as pickled vegetables

Kosher Salt

▶ NUTS

A **nut** (Fr. *noix*) is the edible single-seed kernel of a fruit surrounded by a hard shell. A hazelnut is an example of a true nut. The term is used more generally, however, to refer to any seed or fruit with an edible kernel in a hard shell. Walnuts and peanuts are examples of non-nut "nuts" (peanuts are legumes that grow underground; walnuts have two kernels). Nuts are a good source of protein and B vitamins but are high in fat. Their high fat content makes them especially susceptible to rancidity and odor absorption. Nuts should be stored in nonmetal, airtight containers in a cool, dark place. Most nuts may be kept frozen for up to one year.

Nuts are used in foods to provide texture and flavor. They are often roasted in a low (275°F/135°C) oven before being used in order to heighten their flavor. Allowing roasted nuts to cool to room temperature before grinding prevents them from releasing too much oil.

Almonds (Fr. *almande*) are the seeds of a plumlike fruit. Native to western India, the almond was first cultivated by the ancient Greeks. It is now a major commercial crop in California. Almonds are available whole, sliced, slivered or ground. Blanched almonds have had their brown, textured skins removed; natural almonds retain their skins. Unless the brown color of natural almond skin is undesirable, the two types can be used interchangeably in recipes. Almonds are frequently used in pastries and candies and are the main ingredient in marzipan.

Almonds

Brazil nuts (Fr. *noix du Brésil*), sometimes referred to as cream nuts, are the large, oval-shaped seeds of huge trees that grow wild in the rainforests of Central and South America. Their high oil content gives them a rich, buttery flavor and a tender texture. Brazil nuts are available both in-shell and shelled, and are eaten raw, roasted, salted and in ice creams and bakery and confectionery products.

Brazil Nuts

Cashews (Fr. *noix de caju*), native to the Amazon, are now cultivated in India and east Africa. The cashew nut is actually the seed of a plant related to poison ivy. Because of toxins in the shell, cashews are always sold shelled. They are expensive and have a strong flavor. Cashews are used in some Asian cuisines and make a wonderful addition to cookies and candies.

Cashews

Chestnuts (Fr. *marrons*) are true nuts that must be cooked before using. Available steamed, dried, boiled or roasted, they are often sold as a canned purée, with or without added sugar. Candied or glazed chestnuts are also available. Most chestnuts are grown in Europe, primarily Italy, but new varieties are beginning to flourish in North America. Their distinctive flavor is found in many sweet dishes and pastries. Because of their high starch content, chestnuts are also used in soups and sauces and may be served as a side dish.

Coconuts (Fr. *noix de coco*) are the seeds from one of the largest of all fruits. They grow on the tropical coconut palm tree. The nut is a dark brown oval, covered with coarse fibers. The shell is thick and hard; inside is a layer of white, moist flesh. The interior also contains a clear liquid known as **coconut water.**

Chestnuts

(This is not the same as **coconut milk** or **coconut cream,** both of which are prepared from the flesh.) Coconut has a mild aroma, a sweet, nutty flavor and a crunchy, chewy texture. Fresh coconuts are readily available but require some effort to use. Coconut flesh is available shredded or flaked, with or without added sugar. Coconut is most often used in pastries and candies and is also an important ingredient in Indian and Caribbean cuisines. A good fresh coconut should feel heavy; you should be able to hear the coconut water sloshing around inside. Avoid cracked, moist or moldy coconuts.

Coconuts

▶ **coconut water** the thin, slightly opaque liquid contained within a fresh coconut

▶ **coconut milk** a coconut-flavored liquid made by pouring boiling water over shredded coconut; may be sweetened or unsweetened. Do not substitute cream of coconut for coconut milk.

▶ **coconut cream** (1) a coconut-flavored liquid made like coconut milk but with less water; it is creamier and thicker than coconut milk; (2) the thick fatty portion that separates and rises to the top of canned or frozen coconut milk. Do not substitute cream of coconut for true coconut cream.

▶ **cream of coconut** a canned commercial product consisting of thick, sweetened coconut-flavored liquid; used for baking and in beverages

Hazelnuts (Fr. *noisette*) are true nuts that grow wild in the northeastern and upper midwestern states. The cultivated form, known as a **filbert,** is native to temperate regions throughout the Northern Hemisphere. A bit larger than the hazelnut, the filbert has a weaker flavor than its wild cousin. Both nuts look like smooth brown marbles. Filberts are more abundant, so are generally less expensive. Hazelnuts are often ground for use in cakes or pastries. Their distinctive flavor goes well with chocolate and coffee.

Hazelnuts

To remove the hazelnut's bitter skin, roast whole nuts in a 275°F (135°C) oven for 12 to 15 minutes. They should give off a good aroma and just begin to darken. While still hot, rub the nuts in a dry towel or against a mesh sifter to remove the skin.

Macadamias, although commercially significant in Hawaii, are actually native to Australia. This small round nut is creamy white with a sweet, rich flavor and high fat content. Its shell is extremely hard and must be removed by machine, so the macadamia is always sold out of the shell. Its flavor blends well with fruit, coconut and white and dark chocolate.

Macadamias

Peanuts (Fr. *arachide*), also known as groundnuts, are actually legumes that grow underground. The peanut is native to South America; it made its way into North America via Africa and the slave trade. Peanuts are a good source of protein and fat and became an important source of food and oil during World War II. They may be eaten raw or roasted and are available shelled or unshelled, with or without their thin red skins. Peanuts are used in Asian cuisines and are ubiquitous ground with a bit of oil into peanut butter.

Pecans

Pecans (Fr. *noix de pacane*), native to the Mississippi River Valley, are perhaps the most popular nuts in America. Their flavor is rich and mapley and appears most often in breads, sweets and pastries. They are available whole in the shell or in various standard sizes and grades of pieces.

Pine nuts (Fr. *pignon*), also known as piñon nuts and pignole, are the seeds of several species of pine tree. The small, creamy white, teardrop-shaped nuts are commonly used in dishes from Spain, Italy and the American Southwest. They are rarely chopped or ground because of their small size, and will need roasting only if being used in a dish that will not receive further cooking. Pine nuts are used in breads, pastries and salads and are essential to classic pesto sauce.

Peanuts

Pistachios

Pine Nuts

Pistachios (Fr. *pistaches*) are native to central Asia, where they have been cultivated for more than 3000 years. California now produces most of the pistachios marketed in this country. Pistachios are unique for the green color of their meat. When ripe, the shell opens naturally at one end, aptly referred to as "smiling," which makes shelling the nuts quite easy. Red pistachios are dyed, not natural. Pistachios are sold whole, shelled or unshelled, and are used in pastries and meat dishes, particularly pâtés.

Walnuts (Fr. *noix*), relatives of the pecan, are native to Asia, Europe and North America. The black walnut, native to Appalachia, has a dark brown meat and a strong flavor. The English walnut, now grown primarily in California, has a milder flavor, is easier to shell and is less expensive. Walnuts are more popular than pecans outside the United States. They are used in baked goods and are pressed for oil.

English Walnuts

▶ OILS

Oils (Fr. *huile*) are a type of fat that remains liquid at room temperature. Cooking oils are refined from various seeds, plants and vegetables. (Other fats, such as butter and margarine, are discussed in Chapter 8, Dairy Products; animal and solid fats are discussed in Chapter 29, Principles of the Bakeshop.)

When purchasing oils, you should consider their use, **smoke point,** flavor and cost. Fats, including oils and **shortenings,** are manufactured for specific purposes such as deep-frying, cake baking, salad dressings and sautéing. Most food service operations purchase different ones for each of these needs.

Fats break down at different temperatures. When fats break down, their chemical structure is altered; the triglyceride molecules that make up fat are converted into individual fatty acids. These acids add undesirable flavors to the

▶ **smoke point** the temperature at which a fat begins to break down and smoke

▶ **shortening** (1) a white, flavorless, solid fat formulated for baking or deep-frying; (2) any fat used in baking to tenderize the product by shortening gluten strands

fat and can ruin the flavor of the food being cooked. The temperature at which a given fat begins to break down and smoke is known as its smoke point. Choose fats with higher smoke points for high-temperature cooking such as deep-frying and sautéing.

The flavor and cost of each oil must also be considered. For example, both corn oil and walnut oil can be used in a salad dressing. Their selection may depend on balancing cost (corn oil is less expensive) against flavor (walnut oil has a stronger, more distinctive flavor).

When fats spoil, they are said to go **rancid.** Rancidity is a chemical change caused by exposure to air, light or heat. It results in objectionable flavors and odors. Different fats turn rancid at different rates, but all fats benefit from refrigerated storage away from moisture, light and air. (Some oils are packaged in colored glass containers because certain tints of green and yellow block the damaging light rays that can cause an oil to go rancid.) Although oils may become thick and cloudy under refrigeration, this is not a cause for concern. The oils will return to their clear, liquid states at room temperature. Stored fats should also be covered to prevent them from absorbing odors.

Vegetable oils are extracted from a variety of plants, including corn, cottonseed, peanuts, grape seeds, sesame seeds and soybeans, by pressure or chemical solvents. The oil is then refined and cleaned to remove unwanted colors, odors or flavors. Vegetable oils are virtually odorless and have a neutral flavor. Because they contain no animal products, they are cholesterol-free. If a commercial product contains only one type of oil, it is labeled "pure" (as in "pure corn oil"). Products labeled "vegetable oil" are blended from several sources. Products labeled "salad oil" are highly refined blends of vegetable oil.

Canola oil is processed from rapeseeds. Its popularity is growing rapidly because it contains no cholesterol and has a high percentage of monounsaturated fat. Canola oil is useful for frying and general cooking because it has no flavor and a high smoke point.

Canola Oil

Nut oils are extracted from a variety of nuts and are almost always packaged as a "pure" product, never blended. A nut oil should have the strong flavor and aroma of the nut from which it was processed. Popular examples are walnut and hazelnut oils. These oils are used to give flavor to salad dressings, marinades and other dishes. But heat diminishes their flavor, so nut oils are not recommended for frying or baking. Nut oils tend to go rancid quickly and therefore are usually packaged in small containers.

Hazelnut Oil

Olive oil (Fr. *huile díolive*) is the only oil that is extracted from a fruit rather than a seed, nut or grain. Olive oil is produced primarily in Spain, Italy, France, Greece and North Africa; California produces a relatively minor amount of olive oil. Like wine, olive oils vary in color and flavor according to the variety of tree, the ripeness of the olives, the type of soil, the climate and the producer's preferences. Colors range from dark green to almost clear, depending on the ripeness of the olives at the time of pressing and the amount of subsequent refining. Color is not a good indication of flavor, however. Flavor is ultimately a matter of personal preference. A stronger-flavored oil may be desired for some foods, while a milder oil is better for others. Good olive oil should be thicker than refined vegetable oils, but not so thick that it has a fatty texture.

The label designations—extra virgin, virgin and pure—refer to the acidity of the oil (a low acid content is preferable) and the extent of processing used to extract the oil. The first cold-pressing of the olives results in virgin oil. (The designation "virgin" is used only when the oil is 100% unadulterated olive oil, unheated and without any chemical processing.) Virgin oil may still vary in

Extra Virgin Olive Oil

THE OLIVE

Olives (*Olea europaea*) are the fruit of a tree native to the Mediterranean area. Green olives are those harvested unripened; black olives are fully ripened. The raw fruit is inedibly bitter and must be washed, soaked and cured or pickled before eating. Green olives should have a smooth, tight skin. Ripe olives will be glossy but softer, with a slightly wrinkled skin. Many varieties and flavors are available, from the tiny black French niçoise to the large purplish Greek Kalamata. Ripe black olives are packaged in a range of seven sizes, from small to super colossal. Unripe green olives are available in eleven sizes, from subpetite to supercolossal. Both black and green olives are available whole (with the pit), pitted, sliced, halved or in pieces. Pitted green olives are often stuffed with strips of pimento, jalapeño pepper, almonds or other foods for flavor and appearance.

Olives are used as a finger food for snacks or hors d'oeuvre, or added to salads or pasta. They may even be cooked in breads, soups, sauces, stews and casseroles. A paste made of minced ripe olives, known as tapenade, is used as a dip or condiment.

Jumbo Spanish Olives

Ripe California Olives

Kalamata Olives

Niçoise Olives

quality depending on the level of free acidity, expressed as oleic acid. Extra virgin oil is virgin oil with not more than 1% free acidity (oleic acid); virgin oil may have up to 3%. Pure olive oil is processed from the pulp left after the first pressing using heat and chemicals. Pure oil is lighter in flavor and less expensive than virgin oil.

Flavored oils, also known as **infused oils,** are an interesting and increasingly popular condiment. These oils may be used as a dip for breads, a cooking medium or a flavoring accent in marinades, dressings, sauces or other dishes. Flavors include basil and other herbs, garlic, citrus and spice. Flavored oils are generally prepared with olive oil for additional flavor or canola oil, both considered more healthful than other fats.

Top-quality commercially flavored oils are prepared by extracting aromatic oils from the flavoring ingredients and then emulsifying them with a high-grade oil; any impurities are then removed by placing the oil in a centrifuge. Using the aromatic oils of the flavoring ingredients yields a more intense flavor than merely steeping the same ingredients in the oil. Flavored oils should be stored as you would any other high-quality oil.

▶ FATS FOR DEEP FRYING

Many types of fats can be used for deep-frying. Although animal fats, such as rendered beef fat, are sometimes used to impart their specific flavors to deep-fried foods, their low smoke points generally make them unsuitable for deep-frying unless blended with vegetable fats. By far the most common fats used for deep-frying are vegetable oils such as soybean, peanut and canola oil, all of which have high smoke points and are relatively inexpensive. See Table 7.2.

Specially formulated deep-frying compounds are also available. These are usually composed of a vegetable oil or oils to which antifoaming agents, antioxidants and preservatives have been added. These additives increase the oil's usable life and raise its smoke point.

Table 7.2 REACTION TEMPERATURES OF FATS

FAT	MELT POINT	SMOKE POINT	FLASH POINT
Butter	92–98°F/33–36°C	260°F/127°C	Possible at any temperature above 300°F/150°C
Butter, clarified	92–98°F/33–36°C	335–380°F/168–193°C	Possible at any temperature above 300°F/150°C
Lard	89–98°F/32–36°C	370°F/188°C	n/a
Deep-fryer shortening, heavy-duty, premium	102°F/39°C	440°F/227°C	690°F/365°C
Canola oil	n/a	430–448°F/220–230°C	553–560°F/275–290°C
Corn oil	40–50°F/5–7°C	410°F/210°C	610°F/321°C
Cocoa butter	88–93°F/31–34°C	n/a	n/a
Cottonseed oil	55°F/13°C	450°F/232°C	650°F/343°C
Margarine	94–98°F/34–36°C	410–430°F/210–221°C	Possible at any temperature above 300°F/150°C
Olive oil, extra virgin	32°F/0°C	250°F/121°C	n/a
Olive oil, pure or pumice	32°F/0°C	410°F/210°C	437°F/225°C
Peanut oil	28°F/−2°C	450°F/232°C	540°F/283°C
Shortening, vegetable, all-purpose	120°F/49°C	410°F/210°C	625°F/329°C
Soybean oil	−5°F/−20°C	495°F/257°C	540°F/282°C
Walnut oil	n/a	450°F/232°C	620°F/326°C

This data was compiled from a variety of sources and is meant as a guideline only. Because reaction temperatures depend on the exact type and ratio of fatty acids present, the actual temperatures will vary depending on the brand or manufacturer of the fat in question. Temperatures are for clean, previously unused fats. Heating a fat, even one time, can lower the smoke and flash points dramatically.

n/a = not available

Deep-fryer fats may also be hydrogenated. **Hydrogenation** is a chemical process that adds hydrogen to oil, turning the liquid oil into a solid (margarine is hydrogenated vegetable oil). Hydrogenated fats are more resistant to oxidation and chemical breakdown.

To choose the right fat, consider flavor, smoke point and resistance to chemical breakdown. High-quality frying fat should have a clean or natural flavor and a high smoke point and, when properly maintained, should be resistant to chemical breakdown.

Properly maintaining deep-fryer fat will greatly extend its useful life. To do so:

1 Store the fat in tightly sealed containers away from strong light; cover the deep fryer when not in use. Prolonged exposure to air and light turns fat rancid.

2 Skim and remove food particles from the fat's surface during frying. Food particles cause fat to break down; if they are not removed, they will accumulate in the fryer and burn.

3 Do not salt food over the fat. Salt causes fat to break down chemically.

4 Prevent excessive water from coming into contact with the fat; pat-dry moist foods as much as possible before cooking and dry the fryer, baskets and utensils well after cleaning. Water, like salt, causes fat to break down.

5 Do not overheat the fat (turn the fryer down or off if not in use). High temperatures break down the fat.

6 Filter the fat each day or after each shift if the fryer is heavily used. Best results are obtained by using a filtering machine designed specifically for this purpose. Many large commercial fryers even have built-in filter systems. Less well-equipped operations can simply pour the hot fat through a paper filter.

Table 7.3

FRYER FAT CAN BE DAMAGED BY:

Salt

Water

Overheating

Food particles

Oxygen

CHANGE FRYER FAT WHEN IT:

Becomes dark

Smokes

Foams

Develops off-flavors

▶ VINEGARS

Vinegar (Fr. *vinaigre*) is a thin, sour liquid used for thousands of years as a preservative, cooking ingredient, condiment and cleaning solution. Vinegar is obtained through the fermentation of wine or other alcoholic liquid. Bacteria attacks the alcohol in the solution, turning it into acetic acid. No alcohol will remain when the transformation is complete. The quality of vinegar depends upon the quality of the wine or other liquid on which it is based. Vinegar flavors are as varied as the liquids from which they are made.

Vinegars should be clear and clean-looking, never cloudy or muddy. Commercial vinegars are pasteurized, so an unopened bottle should last indefinitely in a cool, dark place. Once opened, vinegars should last about three months if tightly capped. Any sediment that develops can be strained out; if mold develops, discard the vinegar.

Wine vinegars are as old as wine itself. They may be made from white or red wine, sherry or even champagne, and should bear the color and flavor hallmarks of the wine used. Wine vinegars are preferred in French and Mediterranean cuisines.

Malt vinegar is produced from malted barley. Its slightly sweet, mild flavor is used as a condiment, especially with fried foods.

Distilled vinegar, made from grain alcohol, is completely clear with a stronger vinegary flavor and higher acid content than other vinegars. It is preferred for pickling and preserving.

Cider vinegar is produced from unpasteurized apple juice or cider. It is pale brown in color with a mild acidity and fruity aroma. Cider vinegar is particularly popular in the United States.

Rice vinegar is a clear, slightly sweet product brewed from rice wine. Its flavor is clean and elegant, making it useful in a variety of dishes.

Flavored vinegars are simply traditional vinegars in which herbs, spices, fruits or other foods are steeped to infuse their flavors. They are easily produced from commercial wine or distilled vinegars, using any herb, spice or fruit desired. The use of flavored vinegars is extremely popular but definitely not new. Clove, raspberry and fennel vinegars were sold on the streets of Paris during the 13th century. Making fruit-flavored vinegars was also one of the responsibilities of American housewives during the 18th and 19th centuries.

Balsamic vinegar (It. *aceto Balsamico*) is newly popular in the United States, though it has been produced in Italy for more than 800 years. To produce balsamic vinegar, red wine vinegar is aged in a succession of wooden barrels made from a variety of woods—oak, cherry, locust, ash, mulberry and juniper—for at least 4, but sometimes up to 50, years. The resulting liquid is dark reddish-brown and sweet. Balsamic has a high acid level, but the sweetness covers the tart flavor, making it very mellow. True balsamic is extremely expensive because of the long aging process and the small quantities available. Most of the commercial products imported from Italy are now made by a quick carmelization and flavoring process. Balsamic is excellent as a condiment or seasoning and has a remarkable affinity for tomatoes and strawberries.

Balsamic Vinegar, Raspberry Vinegar and Cider Vinegar

▶ **relish** a cooked or pickled sauce usually made with vegetables or fruits and often used as a condiment; can be smooth or chunky, sweet or savory and hot or mild

▶ **pickle** (1) to preserve food in a brine or vinegar solution; (2) food that has been preserved in a seasoned brine or vinegar, especially cucumbers. Pickled cucumbers are available whole, sliced, in wedges, or chopped as a relish, and may be sweet, sour, dill-flavored or hot and spicy.

▶ CONDIMENTS

Strictly speaking, a condiment is any food added to a dish for flavor, including herbs, spices and vinegars. Today, however, condiments more often refer to cooked or prepared flavorings, such as prepared mustards, **relishes,** bottled sauces and **pickles.** We discuss several frequently used condiments here. These staples may be used to alter or enhance the flavor of a dish during cooking or added to a completed dish at the table by the consumer.

Fermented black bean sauce is a Chinese condiment and flavoring ingredient made from black soybeans that have been heavily salted, then fermented and either slightly mashed (whole bean sauce) or puréed (paste). Both versions are usually mixed with hoisin, chile sauce or minced garlic to produce a sauce that has an intense, pungent, salty flavor. Yellow bean sauces are similar, but milder and sweeter.

Fish sauce (Viet. *nuoc mam;* Thai *nam pla*), is the liquid drained from fermenting salted anchovy-like fish. It is a thin, golden to light brown liquid with a very pungent, rotting odor and salty flavor. There is no substitute for the savory richness that it adds to food and it is considered an essential flavoring and condiment throughout Southeast Asia, where it is used in and served with most every sort of dish.

Ketchup (also known as catsup or catchup) originally referred to any salty extract from fish, fruits or vegetables. Prepared tomato ketchup is really a sauce, created in America and used worldwide as a flavoring ingredient or condiment. It is bright red and thick, with a tangy, sweet-sour flavor. Ketchup can be stored either in the refrigerator or at room temperature; it should keep well for up to four months after opening. Ketchup does not turn rancid or develop mold, but it will darken and lose flavor as it ages.

Prepared mustard is a mixture of crushed mustard seeds, vinegar or wine and salt or spices. It can be flavored in many ways—with herbs, onions, peppers and even citrus zest. It can be a smooth paste or coarse and chunky, depending on how finely the seeds are ground and whether the skins are strained out. Prepared mustard gets its tangy flavor from an essential oil that forms only when the seeds are crushed and mixed with water. Prepared mustard can be used as a condiment, particularly with meat and charcuterie items, or as a flavoring ingredient in sauces, stews and marinades.

Dijon mustard takes its name from a town and the surrounding region in France that produces about half of the world's mustard. French mustard labeled

Fermented Black Bean Sauce

Fish Sauce

Yellow Mustard

Dijon Mustard

FROM YOUR GROCER'S SHELF

Even the most sophisticated food service operation occasionally uses prepared condiments or flavorings. The products described here are widely used and available from grocery stores or wholesale purveyors. Some are brand-name items that have become almost synonymous with the product itself; others are available from several manufacturers.

Barbecue sauce—Commercial barbecue sauce is a mixture of tomatoes, vinegar and spices used primarily for marinating or basting meat, poultry or fish. A tremendous variety of barbecue sauces are available, with various flavors, textures and aromas. Sample several before selecting the most appropriate for your specific needs.

Chile sauce—Asian chile sauce, or hot sauce, varies somewhat depending on the country of origin or style, but all are thick, reddish-orange and extremely pungent and spicy. They usually contain pieces of chiles and/or garlic and less vinegar than Louisiana-style hot sauce. Asian

cuisines incorporate these bottled sauces in curries and other dishes, and use them as table condiments. One of the most popular and readily available brands is the Vietnamese-style Tuong ót Srirachar with its rooster logo.

Hoisin sauce—Hoisin sauce is a dark, thick, salty-sweet sauce made from fermented soy beans, vinegar, garlic and caramel. It is used in Chinese dishes or served as a dipping sauce.

Old Bay brand seasoning—Old Bay is a dry spice blend containing celery salt, dry mustard, paprika and other flavorings. It is widely used in shellfish preparations, especially boiled shrimp and crab.

Oyster sauce—Oyster sauce is a thick, dark sauce made from oyster extract. It has a salty-sweet flavor and a rich aroma. Oyster sauce is often used with stir-fried meats and poultry.

Pickapeppa brand sauce—Pickapeppa sauce is a dark, thick, sweet-hot blend of tomatoes, onions, sugar, vinegar, mango, raisins, tamarinds and spices. Produced in Jamaica, West In-

dies, it is used as a condiment for meat, game or fish and as a seasoning in sauces, soups and dressings.

Tabasco brand sauce—Tabasco sauce is a thin, bright red liquid blended from vinegar, chiles and salt. Its fiery flavor is widely used in sauces, soups and prepared dishes; it is a popular condiment for Mexican, southern and southwestern cuisines. Tabasco sauce has been produced in Louisiana since 1868. Other "Louisiana-style" hot sauces (those containing only peppers, vinegar and salt) may be substituted.

Worcestershire sauce – Worcestershire sauce is a thin, dark brown liquid made from malt vinegar, tamarind, molasses and spices. It is used as a condiment for beef and as a seasoning in sauces, soups, stews and prepared dishes. Its flavor should be rich and full, but not salty.

Whole-Grain Mustard

Brown Mustard

"Dijon" must, by law, be produced only in that region. Dijon and Dijon-style mustards are smooth with a rich, complex flavor.

English and Chinese mustards are made from mustard flour and cool water. They are extremely hot and powerful. American or "ballpark" mustard is mild and vinegary with a bright yellow color.

Mustard never really spoils; its flavor just fades away. Because of its high acid content, mustard does not turn rancid, but it will oxidize and develop a dark surface crust. Once opened, mustard should be kept well-covered and refrigerated.

Soy sauce is a thin, dark brown liquid fermented from cooked soy beans, wheat and salt. Available in several flavors and strengths, it is ubiquitous in most Asian cuisines. Light soy sauce is thin, with a light brown color and a very salty flavor. Dark soy sauce is thicker and dark brown, with a sweet, less salty flavor. Necessary for preparing many Asian dishes, soy sauce is also used in marinades and sauces and as an all-purpose condiment. Other soy-based condiments include tamari, teriyaki sauce and fermented bean paste (miso).

Soy Sauce

▶ COFFEES AND TEAS

Coffee and tea are the staples of most beverage menus. Despite their relatively low price, a good cup of coffee or tea can be extremely important to a customer's impression of your food service operation. A cup of coffee is often either the very first or the very last item consumed by a customer. Tea, whether iced or hot, is often consumed throughout the meal. Consequently, it is important that you learn to prepare and serve these beverages properly.

COFFEE

Coffee (Fr. *café*) begins as the fruit of a small tree grown in tropical and subtropical regions throughout the world. The fruit, referred to as a cherry, is bright red with translucent flesh surrounding two flat-sided seeds. These seeds are the coffee beans. When ripe, the cherries are harvested by hand, then cleaned, fermented and hulled, leaving the green coffee beans. The beans are then roasted, blended, ground and brewed. Note that any coffee bean can be roasted to any degree of darkness, ground to any degree of fineness and brewed by any number of methods.

Only two species of coffee bean are routinely used: arabica and robusta. Arabica beans are the most important commercially and the ones from which the finest coffees are produced. Robusta beans do not produce as flavorful a drink as arabica. Nevertheless, robusta beans are becoming increasingly significant commercially, in part because robusta trees are heartier and more fertile than arabica trees.

The conditions in which the beans are grown have almost as much effect on the final product as subsequent roasting, grinding and brewing. Because coffee takes much of its flavor and character from the soil, sunlight and air, the beans' origin is critical to the product's final quality. Each valley and mountain produces coffee distinct from all others, so geographic names are used to identify the beans whether they are from arabica or robusta trees. Thus, purveyors may offer beans known as Columbian, Chanchamayo (from Peru), Kilimanjaro (from Tanzania), Blue Mountain (from Jamaica), Java, Sumatra or Kona (from Hawaii), to name a few.

Although many so-called gourmet coffees are made from a single type of bean, nearly all coffee sold in the United States is a blend of various qualities and types of bean.

ROASTING COFFEE

Roasting releases and enhances the flavors in coffee. It also darkens the beans and brings natural oils to the surface. Traditionally, almost everyone roasted their own coffee beans because all coffee beans were sold green. Today, however, roasting is left to experts who possess the necessary equipment.

It is important to recognize and understand some of the standard descriptions used for various types of roasting. No single international organization controls the naming of roasted coffee, however, so a coffee roaster may refer to products by any name. The following descriptions are based on the most common terminology:

▶ **City roast:** Also called American or brown roast, city roast is the most widely used coffee style in this country. City roast produces a beverage that may lack brilliance or be a bit flat, yet it is the roast most Americans assume they prefer because it is the roast most often used in grocery store blends.

▶ **Brazilian:** Somewhat darker than a city roast, Brazilian roast should begin to show a hint of dark-roast flavor. The beans should show a trace of oil. In this context, the word *Brazilian* has no relationship to coffee grown in Brazil.

▶ **Viennese:** Also called medium-dark roast, Viennese roast generally falls somewhere between a standard city roast and French roast.

▶ **French roast:** French roast, also called New Orleans or dark roast, approaches espresso in flavor without sacrificing smoothness. The beans should be the color of semisweet chocolate, with apparent oiliness on the surface.

▶ **Espresso roast:** Espresso roast, also called Italian roast, is the darkest of all. The beans are roasted until they are virtually burnt. The beans should be black with a shiny, oily surface.

Green Coffee Beans

City-Roast Beans

French-Roast Beans

GRINDING COFFEE

Unlike roasting, which is best left to the experts, the grinding of coffee beans is best left to the consumer or food service operation. Whole coffee beans stay fresh longer than ground coffee. Ground coffee kept in an airtight container away from heat and light will stay fresh for three or four days. Whole beans will stay fresh for a few weeks and may be kept frozen for several months, as long as they are dry and protected from other flavors. Frozen coffee beans do not need to be thawed before grinding and brewing. Do not refrigerate coffee.

The fineness of the grind depends entirely on the type of coffee maker being used. The grind determines the length of time it takes to achieve the optimum (19%) extraction from the beans. The proper grind is simply whatever grind allows this to happen in the time it takes a specific coffee maker to complete its brewing cycle. Follow the directions for your coffee maker, or ask your specialty coffee purveyor for guidance.

BREWING COFFEE

Coffee is brewed by one of two methods: decoction or infusion. **Decoction** means boiling a substance until its flavor is removed. Boiling is the oldest method of making coffee, but is no longer used except in preparing extremely strong Turkish coffee. Infusion refers to the extraction of flavors at temperatures below boiling. **Infusion** techniques include steeping (mixing hot water with ground coffee), filtering (slowly pouring hot water over ground coffee held in a disposable cloth or paper filter) and dripping (pouring hot water over ground coffee and allowing the liquid to run through a strainer). Percolating is undesirable, as the continuous boiling ruins the coffee's flavor.

The secrets to brewing a good cup of coffee are knowing the exact proportion of coffee to water as well as the length of time to maintain contact between

DON'T WRECK THE ENDING

Lots of time and thought are spent on selecting the wines to accompany the various savory courses of a meal, but too often at the sweet course the dessert wine finds itself up against its worst enemy: chocolate. A good sauterne, or a good-quality dessert wine of almost any kind, works best with a fruit tart or with noncitrus sorbets accompanied by "dry cookie-like things," to use Richard Olney's phrase. Chocolate, whether in the form of pastry or confection, belongs with coffee, whose aromatic bitterness is a perfect foil for it.

The late RICHARD H. GRAFF, Chairman
Chalone Wine Group

the two. The best results are nearly always achieved by using two level table-spoons of ground coffee per ¾ measuring cup (6 ounces) of water. (A standard cup of coffee is three-quarters the size of a standard measuring cup; one pound of coffee yields approximately 80 level tablespoons or enough for 40 "cups" of coffee.) An Approved Coffee Measure (ACM) was developed by the Coffee Brewing Institute to measure two level tablespoons accurately. ACM scoops are readily available and are often included with retail coffee packages.

Premeasured packages of ground coffee are generally used with commercial brewing equipment. These packages are available in a range of sizes for making single pots or large urns of coffee.

If stronger coffee is desired, use more coffee per cup of water, not a longer brewing time. For weaker coffee, prepare regular-strength coffee and dilute it with hot water. Never reuse coffee grounds.

Coffeepots and carafes should be cleaned well with hot water between each use; coffee makers should be disassembled and cleaned according to the man-ufacturer's directions. Unless equipment is properly cleaned, oils from coffee form an invisible film on the inside of the maker and pots, imparting a rancid or stale flavor to each subsequent batch.

Finally, coffee should be served as soon as it is brewed. Oxidation takes a toll on the aroma and flavor, which soon become flat and eventually bitter. Coffee may be held for a short time on the coffee maker's hot plate at temperatures of 185°F to 190°F (85°C to 88°C). A better holding method, however, is to im-mediately pour freshly brewed coffee into a thermal carafe. Never attempt to re-heat cold coffee, as drastic temperature shifts destroy flavor.

TASTING COFFEE

Coffee can be judged on four characteristics: aroma, acidity, body and flavor.

As a general rule, coffee will taste the way it smells. Some coffees, particu-larly Colombian, are more fragrant than others, however.

Acidity, also called wininess, refers to the tartness of the coffee. Acidity is a desirable characteristic that indicates snap, life or thinness. Kenyan and Guatemalan are examples of particularly acidic coffees.

Body refers to the feeling of heaviness or thickness that coffee provides on the palate. Sumatran is generally the heaviest, with Mexican and Venezuelan be-ing the lightest.

Flavor, of course, is the most ambiguous as well as the most important char-acteristic. Terms such as *mellow, harsh, grassy* or *earthy* are used to describe the rather subjective characteristics of flavor.

SERVING COFFEE

Coffee may be served unadorned, unsweetened and black (without milk or cream). The customer then adds the desired amount of sugar and milk. Other coffee beverages are made with specific additions and provide value-added menu alternatives. The most common ways of serving coffee are described here.

▶ *Espresso:* Espresso refers to a unique brewing method in which hot water is forced through finely ground and packed coffee under high pressure. Properly made, it will be strong, rich and smooth, not bitter or acidic. Espresso is usually made with beans that have been roasted very dark, but any type of bean may be used. A single serving of espresso uses about ¼ ounce (7 grams) of coffee to 1½ ounces (45 milliliters) of water. Americans tend to prefer a larger portion, known as espresso lungo, made with 2 to 3 ounces (60 to 90 grams) of water.

▶ *Espresso machiatto:* Espresso "marked" with a tiny portion of **steamed milk.**

Espresso

▶ **steamed milk** milk that is heated with steam generated by an espresso machine; it should be approximately 150°F to 170°F (65°C to 76°C)

▶ *Cappuccino:* One-third espresso, one-third steamed milk and one-third **foamed milk;** the total serving is still rather small, about 4 to 6 ounces (120 to 180 grams).

▶ *Caffè latte:* One-third espresso and two-thirds steamed milk without foam; usually served in a tall glass.

▶ *Café au lait:* The French version of the Italian caffè latte, café au lait (or café crème) is made with strong coffee instead of espresso and hot, not steamed, milk. It is traditionally served in a handleless bowl.

▶ *Caffè mocha:* One-third espresso and two-thirds steamed milk, flavored with chocolate syrup; usually topped with whipped cream and chocolate shavings or cocoa.

▶ *Flavored coffees:* Dried, ground chicory root has long been added to coffee, particularly by the French, who enjoy its bitter flavor. Toasted barley, dried figs and spices have also been used by various cultures for years. Coffees flavored with vanilla, chocolate, liquors, spices and nuts have recently become popular in the United States. These flavors are added to roasted coffee beans by tumbling the beans with special flavoring oils. The results are strongly aromatic flavors such as vanilla hazelnut, chocolate raspberry or maple walnut.

DECAFFEINATED COFFEE

Caffeine is an alkaloid found in coffee beans (as well as in tea leaves and cocoa beans). It is a stimulant that can improve alertness or reduce fatigue. In excess, however, caffeine can cause some people to suffer palpitations or insomnia. Regular filtered coffee contains from 85 to 100 milligrams of caffeine per cup. Robusta beans contain more caffeine than the better-quality arabica beans. Decaffeinated coffee (with 97 percent or more of the caffeine removed) is designed to meet consumer desires for a caffeine-free product.

OTHER USES

In addition to its use as a beverage, coffee is frequently an ingredient in mixed drinks such as Irish coffee (with whiskey and cream) or café brûlot (with

▶ **foamed milk** milk that is heated and frothed with air and steam generated by an espresso machine; it will be slightly cooler than steamed milk

Cappuccino

Caffè Latte

A CUP OF COFFEE HISTORY

Some anthropologists suggest that coffee was initially consumed by central African warriors in the form of a paste made from mashed coffee beans and animal fat rolled into balls. Eaten before battle, the animal fat and bean protein provided nourishment; the caffeine provided a stimulant.

A hot coffee drink may first have been consumed sometime during the 9th century A.D. in Persia. Made by a decoction of ripe beans, the drink was probably very thick and acrid. Nevertheless, by the year 1000, the elite of the Arab world were regularly drinking a decoction of dried coffee beans. The beans were harvested in Abyssinia (Ethiopia) and brought to market by Egyptian merchants. Within a century or so, *kahwa* became immensely popular with members of all strata of Arab society. Coffeehouses opened throughout the Levant, catering to cus-

tomers who sipped the thick, brown brew while discussing affairs of heart and state.

Although European travelers to the Ottoman Empire had tasted coffee, and a few Arab or Turkish merchants living in Marseilles offered their guests a chance to sample the rare drink, coffee did not become popular in Europe until the 17th century. Its popularity is due in great part to Suleiman Aga, the Grand Panjandrum of the Ottoman Empire. In 1669, he arrived at the court of King Louis XIV of France as ambassador, bringing with him many exotic treasures, including caffè. Offered at his opulent parties, caffè soon became the drink of choice for the French aristocracy.

Coffee became popular in Vienna as a fortune of war. By 1683, the Turks were at the gates of Vienna. A decisive battle was fought, and the Turks fled, leaving behind stores of

gold, equipment, supplies and a barely known provision—green coffee beans. One of the victorious leaders, Franz George Kolschitzky, recognized the treasure, took it as his own and soon opened the first coffeehouse in Vienna, The Blue Bottle.

Despite its growing popularity, coffee was exorbitantly expensive, in part, the result of the sultan's monopoly on coffee beans. His agents, principally in Marseilles, controlled the sale of beans. But the monopoly was not to survive. By the end of the 17th century, the Dutch had stolen coffee plants from Arabia and began cultivating them in Java. By the early 18th century, the French had transported seedlings to the West Indies; from there coffee plantations spread throughout the New World.

orange, cloves and brandy). Coffee is also used in stews, sauces and pan gravy. It may be added to breads, such as rye and pumpernickel, cakes, custards, ice creams, dessert sauces and frostings. The flavor of coffee has a strong affinity for chocolate, nuts and rum.

TEA

Tea (Fr. *thé*) is the name given to the leaves of *Camellia sinensis*, a tree or shrub that grows at high altitudes in damp tropical regions. Although tea comes from only one species of plant, there are three general types of tea—black, green and oolong. The differences among the three are the result of the manner in which the leaves are treated after picking.

Black tea is amber-brown and strongly flavored. Its color and flavor result from fermenting the leaves. Black tea leaves are named or graded by leaf size. Because larger leaves brew more slowly than smaller ones, teas are sorted by leaf size for efficient brewing. *Souchong* denotes large leaves, *pekoe* denotes medium-sized leaves and *orange pekoe* denotes the smallest whole leaves. (Note that *orange pekoe* does not refer to any type of orange flavor.) Broken tea, graded as either broken orange pekoe or broken pekoe, is smaller, resulting in a darker, stronger brew. Broken tea is most often used in tea bags. These grades apply to both Chinese and Indian black teas.

Green tea is yellowish-green in color with a bitter flavor. Leaves used for green tea are not fermented. Chinese green tea leaves are also graded according to leaf size and age. The finest green tea is Gunpowder, followed by Imperial and Hyson.

Oolong tea is partially fermented to combine the characteristics of black and green teas. Oolong is popular in China and Japan, often flavored with jasmine flowers. Oolong tea leaves are also graded by size and age.

As with coffee, tea takes much of its flavor from the geographic conditions in which it is grown. Teas are named for their place of origin—for example, Darjeeling, Ceylon (now Sri Lanka) or Assam. Many popular and commercially available teas are actually blends of leaves from various sources. Blended and unblended teas may also be flavored with oils, dried fruit, spices, flowers or herbs.

Fruit Tea

Gunpowder

Darjeeling

TEA FLAVORS

The following descriptions apply to some of the teas frequently available through wholesalers or gourmet suppliers. Taste several different ones to find the best for your purposes. Remember that the same tea from different blenders or distributors may taste different, and that different flavors will be more or less appropriate for different times of the day. You may wish to offer your patrons a selection of flavors.

Assam—a rich black tea with a reddish color from northeastern India. It is valued by connoisseurs, especially for breakfast.

Ceylon—a full-flavored black tea with a golden color and delicate fragrance. Ideal for serving iced, it does not become cloudy when cold.

Darjeeling—the champagne of teas, grown in the foothills of the Himalayas in northeastern India. It is a full-bodied, black tea with a muscat flavor.

Earl Grey—a blend of black teas, usually including Darjeeling, flavored with oil of bergamot. A popular choice for afternoon tea.

English Breakfast—an English blend of Indian and Sri Lankan black teas; it is full-bodied and robust, with a rich color.

Gunpowder—a green Chinese tea with a tightly curled leaf and gray-green color. It has a pungent flavor and a light straw color. It is often served after the evening meal.

Keemum—a mellow black Chinese tea with a strong aroma. It is less astringent than other teas and is delicious iced.

Lapsang Souchong—a large-leafed (souchong) tea from the Lapsang district of China. It has a distinctive tarry, smoky flavor and aroma, appropriate for afternoon tea or dinner.

Formosa Oolong—a unique and expensive large-leafed oolong tea with the flavor of ripe peaches. It is appropriate for breakfast or afternoon tea.

BREWING TEA

Tea may be brewed by the cup or the pot. In either case, it is important to use the following procedure:

1 Always begin with clean equipment and freshly drawn cold water. Water that has been sitting in a kettle or hot water tank contains less air and will taste flat or stale.

2 Warm the teapot by rinsing its interior with hot water. This begins to relax the tea leaves and ensures that the water will stay hot when it comes in contact with the tea.

3 Place 1 teaspoon (5 milliliters) of loose tea or one tea bag per ¾ cup (6 ounces/180 grams) of water capacity in the warmed teapot.

4 As soon as the water comes to a boil, pour the appropriate amount over the tea. Do not allow the water to continue boiling as this removes the oxygen, leaving a flat taste. The water should be at a full boil when it comes in contact with the tea so that the tea leaves will uncurl and release their flavor.

5 Replace the lid of the teapot and allow the tea to infuse for 3 to 5 minutes. Time the brew. Color is not a reliable indication of brewing time; tea leaves release color before flavor, and different types of tea will be different colors when properly brewed.

6 Remove the tea bags or loose tea from the water when brewing is complete. This can be accomplished easily if the teapot is fitted with a removable leaf basket or if a tea bag or a perforated tea ball is used. Otherwise, decant the tea through a strainer into a second warmed teapot.

7 Serve immediately, accompanied with sugar, lemon, milk (not cream) and honey as desired. Dilute the tea with hot water if necessary.

8 Do not reuse tea leaves. One pound of tea yields 200 cups, making it the most inexpensive beverage after tap water.

A CUP OF TEA HISTORY

Some believe that the Chinese Emperor Shen Nung discovered tea drinking in 2737 B.C. Legend holds that the emperor was boiling his drinking water beneath a tree when some leaves fell into the pot. Enchanted with the drink, he began to cultivate the plant. Whether this is myth or truth, it is known that a hot drink made from powdered dried tea leaves whipped into hot water was regularly consumed in China sometime after the 4th century. Later, decoctions of tea leaves (as well as rice, spices and nuts) became popular. But it was not until the Ming dynasty (A.D. 1368–1644) that infusions of tea leaves became commonplace.

By the 9th century, tea drinking had spread to Japan. In both Chinese and Japanese cultures, tea drinking developed into a ritual. For the Chinese, a cup of tea became the mirror of the soul. For the Japanese, it was the drink of immortality.

Tea was first transported from China to Europe by Dutch merchants during the early 1600s. By midcentury, it was introduced into England. In 1669, the British East India Company was granted a charter by Queen Elizabeth I to import tea, a monopoly it held until 1833. To ensure a steady supply, the English surreptitiously procured plants from China and started plantations throughout the Indian subcontinent, as did the Dutch.

Tea drinking became fashionable in England, at least in court circles, through Charles II (raised in exile at The Hague in Holland, he reigned from 1660 to 1685) and his Portuguese wife, Catherine of Braganza. Queen Anne of England (who reigned from 1702 to 1714) introduced several concepts that eventually became part of the English tea custom. For example, she substituted tea for ale at breakfast and began using large silver pots instead of tiny china pots.

The social custom of afternoon tea began in the late 1700s, thanks to Anna, Duchess of Bedford. Historians attribute to her the late-afternoon ritual of snacking on sandwiches and pastries accompanied by tea. She began the practice in order to quell her hunger pangs between breakfast and dinner (which was typically served at 9:30 or 10:00 P.M.).

Eventually, two distinct types of teatime evolved. Low tea was aristocratic in origin and consisted of a snack of pastries and sandwiches, with tea, served in the late afternoon as a prelude to the evening meal. High tea was bourgeois in origin, consisting of leftovers from the typically large middle-class lunch, such as cold meats, bread and cheeses. High tea became a substitute for the evening meal.

For iced tea, prepare regular brewed tea using 50 percent more tea. Then pour the tea into a pitcher or glass filled with ice. The stronger brew will hold its flavor better as the ice melts.

SERVING TEA

▶ **tisanes** herbal infusions that do not contain any "real" tea; examples include chamomile, ginseng and lemon balm. Tisanes are prepared in the same way as tea infusions.

Black and oolong tea may be served hot or cold, but green tea is best served hot. Black tea is served with milk or lemon and sugar; green and oolong tea are most often served plain. Adding milk to hot tea is a British preference (not normally followed in Europe or Asia) that reduces the astringency of the tea. Iced tea, an American invention, may be served plain or sweetened, and is often garnished with lemon, orange or fresh mint.

CONCLUSION

Kitchen staples include fresh and dried herbs, spices, salt, nuts, oils, vinegars, condiments, coffees and teas. You must be able to recognize, purchase, store and use many of these staples.

The only way to determine which brand or type of staple is best for your particular needs is to taste, smell, sample and use a variety of those available. Cost, convenience and storage factors must also be considered. By maintaining a supply of seasonings, flavorings, condiments and other staples, you will be able to create new dishes or enhance standard ones at a moment's notice.

QUESTIONS FOR DISCUSSION

1 What is a staple? Does every kitchen keep the same staples on hand? Explain your answer.
2 What are the differences between an herb and a spice? Give an example of a plant that is used as both an herb and a spice.
3 If a recipe calls for a fresh herb and you only have the herb dried, what do you do? Explain your answer.
4 How are condiments used by chefs and by customers?
5 What qualities should be considered when choosing a fat for deep-frying?
6 List three signs that fryer fat has broken down and should be replaced. What causes fryer fat to break down? What can you do to extend the life of fryer fat?
7 Discuss the importance of using proper preparation and service techniques for coffee and tea. How can these beverages be used to improve or enhance your food service operation?
8 Assume that you are interested in opening a coffeehouse in your local community. What resources are available to you on the Internet to assist in planning your new business? Research two potential vendors for the equipment and supplies that you will need.

FOOD HISTORY IS AS IMPORTANT AS A BAROQUE CHURCH. GOVERNMENTS SHOULD RECOGNIZE CULTURAL HERITAGE AND PROTECT TRADITIONAL FOODS. A CHEESE IS AS WORTHY OF PRESERVING AS A SIXTEENTH-CENTURY BUILDING.

—Carlo Petrini, Italian journalist (1950–)

DAIRY PRODUCTS

▶ identify, store and use a variety of milk-based products

▶ identify, store and serve a variety of fine cheeses

▶ **ewe's milk** milk produced by a female sheep; it has approximately 7.9% milkfat, 11.4% milk solids and 80.7% water

▶ **goat's milk** milk produced by a female goat; it has approximately 4.1% milkfat, 8.9% milk solids and 87% water

▶ **water buffalo's milk** milk produced by a female water buffalo; it has approximately 7.5% milkfat, 10.3% milk solids and 82.2% water

Dairy products include cow's milk and foods produced from cow's milk such as butter, yogurt, sour cream and cheese. The milk of other mammals, namely, goats, sheep (ewe) and buffaloes, is also made into cheeses that are used in commercial food service operations. Dairy products are extremely versatile and are used throughout the kitchen, served either as is or as ingredients in everything from soups and salads to breads and desserts.

▶ MILK

Milk is not only a popular beverage, it is also an ingredient in many dishes. It provides texture, flavor, color and nutritional value for cooked or baked items. Indeed, milk is one of the most nutritious foods available, providing proteins, vitamins and minerals (particularly calcium). But milk is also highly perishable and an excellent bacterial breeding ground. Care must be exercised when handling and storing milk and other dairy products.

Whole milk—that is, milk as it comes from the cow—consists of water primarily (about 88%). It contains approximately 3.5% milkfat and 8.5% other milk solids (proteins, milk sugar [lactose] and minerals).

Whole milk is graded A, B or C according to standards recommended by the U.S. Public Health Service. Grades are assigned based on bacterial count, with Grade A products having the lowest count. Grades B and C, though still safe and wholesome, are rarely available for retail or commercial use. Fresh whole milk is not available raw, but must be processed as we describe shortly.

PROCESSING TECHNIQUES

PASTEURIZATION

By law, all Grade A milk must be pasteurized prior to retail sale. Pasteurization is the process of heating milk to a sufficiently high temperature for a sufficient length of time to destroy pathogenic bacteria. This typically requires holding milk at a temperature of 161°F (72°C) for 15 seconds. Pasteurization also destroys enzymes that cause spoilage, thus increasing shelf life. Milk's nutritional value is not significantly affected by pasteurization.

ULTRA-PASTEURIZATION

Ultra-pasteurization is a process in which milk is heated to a very high temperature (275°F/135°C) for a very short time (2 to 4 seconds) in order to destroy virtually all bacteria. Ultra-pasteurization is most often used with whipping cream and individual creamers. Although the process may reduce cream's whipping properties, it extends its shelf life dramatically.

ULTRA-HIGH-TEMPERATURE PROCESSING

Ultra-high-temperature (UHT) processing is a form of ultra-pasteurization in which milk is held at a temperature of 280°F–300°F (138°C–150°C) for 2 to 6 seconds. It is then packed in sterile containers under sterile conditions and aseptically sealed to prevent bacteria from entering the container. Unopened UHT milk can be stored without refrigeration for at least three months. Although UHT milk can be stored unrefrigerated, it should be chilled before serving and stored like fresh milk once opened. UHT processing may give milk a slightly cooked taste, but it has no significant effect on milk's nutritional value. Long available in Europe, it is now gaining popularity in the United States.

HOMOGENIZATION

Homogenization is a process in which the fat globules in whole milk are reduced in size and permanently dispersed throughout the liquid. This prevents the fat from clumping together and rising to the surface as a layer of cream. Although homogenization is not required, milk sold commercially is generally homogenized because it ensures a uniform consistency, a whiter color and a richer taste.

MILKFAT REMOVAL

Whole milk can also be processed in a centrifuge to remove all or a portion of the milkfat, resulting in reduced-fat, low-fat and nonfat milks. All reduced-fat milks must still be nutritionally equivalent to full-fat milk and must provide at least the same amounts of the fat-soluble vitamins A and D as full-fat milk.

Reduced-fat or less-fat milk is whole milk from which sufficient milkfat has been removed to produce a liquid with 2% milkfat. **Low-fat** or little-fat milk contains 1% milkfat. **Nonfat** milk, also referred to as fat-free, no-fat or skim milk, has had as much milkfat removed as possible. The fat content must be less than 0.5%.

STORAGE

Fluid milk is a potentially hazardous food and should be kept refrigerated at or below 40°F (4°C). Its shelf life is reduced by half for every five-degree rise in temperature above 40°F (4°C). Keep milk containers closed to prevent absorption of odors and flavors. Freezing is not recommended.

CONCENTRATED MILKS

Concentrated or condensed milk products are produced by using a vacuum to remove all or part of the water from whole milk. The resulting products have a high concentration of milkfat and milk solids and an extended shelf life.

Evaporated milk is produced by removing approximately 60 percent of the water from whole, homogenized milk. The concentrated liquid is canned and heat-sterilized. This results in a cooked flavor and darker color. Evaporated skim milk, with a milkfat content of 0.5%, is also available. A can of evaporated milk requires no refrigeration until opened, although the can should be stored in a cool place. Evaporated milk can be reconstituted with an equal amount of water and used like whole milk for cooking or drinking.

Sweetened condensed milk is similar to evaporated milk in that 60 percent of the water has been removed. But unlike evaporated milk, sweetened condensed milk contains large amounts of sugar (40 to 45 percent). Sweetened condensed milk is also canned; the canning process darkens the color and adds a caramel flavor. Sweetened condensed milk cannot be substituted for whole milk or evaporated milk because of its sugar content. Its distinctive flavor is most often found in desserts and confections.

Dry milk powder is made by removing virtually all the moisture from pasteurized milk. Dry whole milk, nonfat milk and buttermilk are available. The lack of moisture prevents the growth of microorganisms and allows dry milk powders to be stored for extended periods without refrigeration. Powdered milks can be reconstituted with water and used like fresh milk. Milk powder may also be added to foods directly, with additional liquid included in the recipe. This procedure is typical in bread making and does not alter the function of the milk or the flavor in the finished product.

CREAM

Cream is a rich, liquid milk product containing at least 18% fat. It must be pasteurized or ultra-pasteurized and may be homogenized. Cream has a slight

SAFETY ALERT

MILK STORAGE
Canned milks, aseptically packaged milks and dry milk powders are shelf-stable products needing no refrigeration. After the can or box is opened or the powder is reconstituted with water, however, these become potentially hazardous foods and must be handled just as carefully as fresh milk. Do not store an open can of milk in its original container, and keep all milk products refrigerated at or below 40°F (4°C).

yellow or ivory color and is more viscous than milk. It is used throughout the kitchen to give flavor and body to sauces, soups and desserts. Whipping cream, containing not less than 30% milkfat, can be whipped into a stiff foam and used in pastries and desserts. Cream is marketed in several forms with different fat contents, as described here.

Half-and-half is a mixture of whole milk and cream containing between 10% and 18% milkfat. It is often served with cereal or coffee, but does not contain enough fat to whip into a foam.

Light cream, coffee cream and **table cream** are all products with more than 18% but less than 30% milkfat. These products are often used in baked goods or soups as well as with coffee, fruit and cereal.

Light whipping cream or, simply, **whipping cream,** contains between 30% and 36% milkfat. It is generally used for thickening and enriching sauces and making ice cream. It can be whipped into a foam and used as a dessert topping or folded into custards or mousses to add flavor and lightness.

Heavy whipping cream or, simply, **heavy cream,** contains not less than 36% milkfat. It whips easily and holds its whipped texture longer than other creams. It must be pasteurized, but is rarely homogenized. Heavy cream is used throughout the kitchen in the same ways as light whipping cream.

STORAGE

Ultra-pasteurized cream will keep for six to eight weeks if refrigerated at or below 40°F (4°C). Unwhipped cream should not be frozen. Keep cream away from strong odors and bright lights, as they can adversely affect its flavor.

CULTURED DAIRY PRODUCTS

Cultured dairy products such as yogurt, buttermilk and sour cream are produced by adding specific bacterial cultures to fluid dairy products. The bacteria convert the milk sugar **lactose** into lactic acid, giving these products their body and tangy, unique flavors. The acid content also retards the growth of undesirable microorganisms; thus cultured products have been used for centuries to preserve milk.

► **lactose** a disaccharide that occurs naturally in mammalian milk; milk sugar

Buttermilk originally referred to the liquid remaining after cream was churned into butter. Today, buttermilk is produced by adding a culture (*Streptococcus lactis*) to fresh, pasteurized skim or low-fat milk. This results in a tart milk with a thick texture. Buttermilk is most often used as a beverage or in baked goods.

Sour cream is produced by adding the same culture to pasteurized, homogenized light cream. The resulting product is a white, tangy gel used as a condiment or to give baked goods a distinctive flavor. Sour cream must have a milkfat content of not less than 18%.

Crème fraîche is a cultured cream popular in French cuisine. Although thinner and richer than sour cream, it has a similar tart, tangy flavor. It is used extensively in soups and sauces, especially with poultry, rabbit and lamb dishes. It is easily prepared from the following recipe.

Yogurt is a thick, tart, custardlike product made from milk (either whole, low-fat or nonfat) cultured with *Lactobacillus bulgaricus* and *Streptococcus thermophilus.* Though touted as a health or diet food, yogurt contains the same amount of milkfat as the milk from which it is made. Yogurt may also contain a variety of sweeteners, flavorings and fruits. Yogurt is generally eaten as is, but may be used in baked products, salad dressings and frozen desserts. It is used in many Middle Eastern cuisines.

STORAGE

Cultured products are potentially hazardous foods and should be kept refrigerated at or below 40°F (4°C). Under proper conditions, sour cream will last up to

CRÈME FRAÎCHE

Yield: 1 pint (500 ml)

Heavy cream	16 fl. oz.	500 g
Buttermilk, with active cultures	1 fl. oz.	30 g

1 Heat the cream (preferably not ultra-pasteurized) to approximately 100°F (43°C).
2 Remove the cream from the heat and stir in the buttermilk.
3 Allow the mixture to stand in a warm place, loosely covered, until it thickens, approximately 12 to 36 hours.
4 Chill thoroughly before using. Crème fraîche will keep for up to 10 days in the refrigerator.

Approximate values per 1-oz. (30-g) serving: **Calories** 90, **Total fat** 10 g, **Saturated fat** 6 g, **Cholesterol** 35 mg, **Sodium** 10 mg, **Total carbohydrates** 1 g, **Protein** 1 g, **Vitamin A** 10%, **Claims**— very low sodium

four weeks, yogurt up to three weeks and buttermilk up to two weeks. Freezing is not recommended for these products, but dishes prepared with cultured products generally can be frozen.

BUTTER

Butter is a fatty substance produced by agitating or churning cream. Its flavor is unequaled in sauces, breads and pastries. Butter contains at least 80% milkfat, not more than 16% water and 2–4% milk solids. It may or may not contain added salt. Butter is firm when chilled and soft at room temperature. It melts into a liquid at approximately 93°F (33°C) and reaches the smoke point at 260°F (127°C).

Government grading is not mandatory, but most processors submit their butters for testing. The USDA label on the package assures the buyer that the butter meets federal standards for the grade indicated:

► USDA Grade AA—butter of superior quality, with a fresh, sweet flavor and aroma, a smooth, creamy texture and good spreadability.
► USDA Grade A—butter of very good quality, with a pleasing flavor and fairly smooth texture.
► USDA Grade B—butter of standard quality, made from sour cream; has an acceptable flavor but lacks the flavor, texture and body of Grades AA and A. Grade B is most often used in the manufacturing of foods.

Salted butter is butter with up to 2.5% salt added. This not only changes the butter's flavor, it also extends its keeping qualities. When using salted butter in cooking or baking, the salt content must be considered in the total recipe.

European-style butter contains more milkfat than regular butter, usually from 82 to 86%, and very little or no added salt. It is often churned from cultured cream, giving it a more intense, buttery flavor. It may be used in lieu of any regular butter in cooking or baking.

Whipped butter is made by incorporating air into the butter. This increases its volume and spreadability, but also increases the speed with which the butter will become rancid. Because of the change in density, whipped butter should not be substituted in recipes calling for regular butter.

Clarified butter is butter that has had its water and milk solids removed by a process called clarification. Although **whole butter** can be used for cooking

► **whole butter** butter that is not clarified, whipped or reduced-fat

MARGARINE: FROM LABORATORY BENCH TO DINNER TABLE

Margarine was invented by a French chemist in 1869 after Napoleon III offered a prize for the development of a synthetic edible fat. Originally produced from animal fat and milk, margarine is now made almost exclusively from vegetable fats.

In *On Food and Cooking: The Science and Lore of the Kitchen,* Harold McGee recounts the history of margarine. He explains that margarine caught on quickly in Europe and America, with large-scale production underway by 1880. But the American dairy industry and the U.S. government put up fierce resistance. First, margarine was defined as a harmful drug and its sale restricted. Then it was heavily taxed; stores had to be licensed to sell it and, like alcohol and tobacco, it was bootlegged. The U.S. government refused to purchase it for use by the armed forces. And, in an attempt to hold it to its true colors, some states did not allow margarine to be dyed yellow (animal fats and vegetable oils are much paler than butter); the dye was sold separately and mixed in by the consumer. World War II, which brought butter rationing, probably did the most to establish margarine's respectability. But it was not until 1967 that yellow margarine could be sold in Wisconsin.

or sauce making, sometimes a more stable and consistent product will be achieved by using clarified butter. The clarification process is described in Chapter 9, Mise en Place.

STORAGE

Butter should be well wrapped and stored at temperatures between 32°F and 35°F (0°C and 2°C). Unsalted butter is best kept frozen until needed. If well wrapped, frozen butter will keep for up to nine months at a temperature of 0°F (18°C).

MARGARINE

Margarine is not a dairy product but is included in this section because it is so frequently substituted for butter in cooking, baking and table service. Margarine is manufactured from animal or vegetable fats or a combination of such fats. Flavorings, colorings, emulsifiers, preservatives and vitamins are added, and the mixture is firmed or solidified by exposure to hydrogen gas at very high temperatures, a process known as hydrogenation. Generally, the firmer the margarine, the greater the degree of hydrogenation and the longer its shelf life. Like butter, margarine is approximately 80% fat and 16% water. But even the finest margarine cannot match the flavor of butter.

Margarine packaged in tubs is softer and more spreadable than solid products and generally contains more water and air. Indeed, diet margarine is approximately 50% water. Because of their decreased density, these soft products should not be substituted for regular butter or margarine in cooking or baking.

Specially formulated and blended margarine is available for commercial use in making puff pastry, croissant doughs, frostings and the like.

▶ NUTRITION

Dairy products are naturally high in vitamins, minerals and protein. Often liquid products such as milk are fortified with additional vitamins and minerals, especially vitamins A and D. Because milk and butter are animal products, they do contain cholesterol. Their overall fat content varies depending upon the amount of milkfat left after processing.

► Natural Cheeses

Cheese (Fr. *fromage;* It. *fromaggio*) is one of the oldest and most widely used foods known to man. It is served alone or as a principal ingredient in or an accompaniment to countless dishes. Cheese is commonly used in commercial kitchens, appearing in everything from breakfast to snacks to desserts.

Literally hundreds of natural cheeses are produced worldwide. Although their shapes, ages and flavors vary according to local preferences and traditions, all natural cheeses are produced in the same basic fashion as has been used for centuries. Each starts with a mammal's milk; cows, goats and sheep are the most commonly used. The milk proteins (known as *casein*) are coagulated with the addition of an enzyme, usually rennet, which is found in calves' stomachs. As the milk coagulates, it separates into solid curds and liquid whey. After draining off the whey, either the curds are made into fresh cheese, such as ricotta or cottage cheese, or the curds are further processed by cutting, kneading and cooking. The resulting substance, known as "green cheese," is packed into molds to drain. Salt or special bacteria may be added to the molded cheeses, which are then allowed to age or ripen under controlled conditions to develop the desired texture, color and flavor.

Cheeses are a product of their environment, which is why most fine cheeses cannot be reproduced outside their native locale. The breed and feed of the milk animal, the wild spores and molds in the air and even the wind currents in a storage area can affect the manner in which a cheese develops. (Roquefort, for example, develops its distinctive flavor from aging in particular caves filled with crosscurrents of cool, moist air.)

Some cheeses develop a natural rind or surface because of the application of bacteria (bloomy rind) or by repeated washing with brine (washed rind). Most natural rinds may be eaten if desired. Other cheeses are coated with an inedible wax rind to prevent moisture loss. Fresh cheeses have no rind whatsoever.

Moisture and fat contents are good indicators of a cheese's texture and shelf life. The higher the moisture content, the softer the product and the more perishable it will be. Low-moisture cheeses may be used for grating and will keep for several weeks if properly stored. (Reduced water activity levels prohibit bacterial growth.) Fat content ranges from low fat (less than 20% fat) to double cream (at least 60% fat) and triple cream (at least 72% fat). Cheeses with a high fat content will be creamier and have a richer flavor and texture than low-fat products.

Most cheeses contain high percentages of fat and protein. Cheese is also rich in calcium, phosphorus and vitamin A. As animal products, natural cheeses contain cholesterol. Today, many low-fat and even nonfat processed cheeses are available. Sodium has also been reduced or eliminated from some modern products.

CHEESE VARIETIES

Cheeses can be classified by country of origin, ripening method, fat content or texture. Here we classify fine cheeses by texture and have adopted five categories: fresh or unripened, soft, semisoft, firm and hard. A separate section on goat's-milk cheeses is also included.

FRESH OR UNRIPENED CHEESES

Fresh cheeses are uncooked and unripened. Referred to as *fromage blanc* or *fromage frais* in French, they are generally mild and creamy with a tart tanginess. They should not taste acidic or bitter. Fresh cheeses have a moisture content of 40 to 80% and are highly perishable.

Cream cheese is a soft cow's-milk cheese from the United States containing approximately 35% fat. It is available in various-sized solid white blocks or

MAKING MOZZARELLA

In Italy, mozzarella is made every day; it is meant to be consumed just as often. Before there was refrigeration, the balls of mozzarella were stored in well water to keep them cool, which is where the tradition originated of storing fresh mozzarella in liquid.

Once the milk is coagulated and the curds are cut, the mass is slowly stirred to enhance the whey's expulsion. A few hours later, when the curds are mature, they are removed from the whey, chopped or shredded and then mixed with hot water.

To test the exact amount of maturity, a handful of curds is dipped into a bucket of hot water for 10 seconds. When the curds are removed, they should be kneaded briefly and then, holding the mass with two hands, it should be pulled and stretched out to determine its maturity. When it is exactly ready to be strung, it can be stretched as thin and opaque as tissue paper. At this point, small amounts of curd are dumped into a small vat and stirred with hot water using a paddle. This is known as "stringing" the cheese because as the curds are mixed with the water they begin to melt somewhat and become stringy. The more the cheese is stirred, the longer the strings are stretched. Eventually, all the strings come together to make a large mass of satiny-smooth cheese. In Italian, the word *filare* means "to string"; therefore, all cheeses that are strung are members of the *pasta filata* family.

When stringing is complete, the cheese is ready to be shaped and hand-formed into balls. The balls are tossed immediately into vats of cool water so they will maintain the desired shapes. When cool, the balls are immersed in brine solution and then wrapped in parchment paper.

PAULA LAMBERT, owner,
Mozzarella Company, Dallas, Texas

whipped and flavored. It is used throughout the kitchen in baking, dips, dressings and confections and is popular as a spread for bagels and toast.

Feta is a semisoft Greek or Italian product made from sheep's and/or goat's milk. It is a white, flaky cheese that is pickled (but not ripened) and stored in brine water, giving it a shelf life of four to six weeks. Its flavor becomes sharper and saltier with age. Feta is good for snacks and salads and melts easily for sauces and fillings.

Feta

Mascarpone (mas-cahr-POHN-ay) is a soft cow's-milk cheese originally from Italy's Lombard region. It contains 70 to 75% fat and is extremely smooth and creamy. Mascarpone is highly perishable and is available in bulk or in 8- or 16-ounce tubs. With its pale ivory color and rich, sweet flavor, it is useful in both sweet and savory sauces as well as desserts. It is also eaten plain, with fresh fruit or spread on bread and sprinkled with cocoa or sugar.

Mascarpone

Mozzarella (maht-suh-REHL-lah) is a firm Italian cheese traditionally made with water buffalo's milk (today, cow's milk is more common) and containing 40 to 45% fat. Mozzarella becomes elastic when melted and is well known as "pizza cheese." Fresh mozzarella is excellent in salads or topped simply with olive oil and herbs. It is a very mild white cheese best eaten within hours of production. Commercial mozzarella is rather bland and rubbery and is best reserved for cooking, for which it may be purchased already shredded.

Mozzarella

Queso Oaxaca (KEH-soh wah-HA-kaa), also known as Quesillo or Asadero, is one of the most popular cheeses of Mexico. It is a cow's-milk *pasta filata* or stretched-curd cheese that is kneaded and wound into balls, then soaked in brine for several minutes. It is pulled apart into thin strings before being used to fill tortillas or melted over cooked dishes. Queso Oaxaca is a good melting cheese with a smooth semisoft texture, white color and 45% fat content. It is invaluable in preparing Mexican and Mexican-American dishes such as quesadillas, nachos and tacos, and is also available blended with herbs, spices or chiles.

Queso Oaxaca

Ricotta (rih-COH-tah) is a soft Italian cheese, similar to American cottage cheese, made from the whey left when other cow's-milk cheeses are produced. It contains only 4 to 10% fat. It is white or ivory in color and fluffy, with a small grain and sweet flavor. Ricotta is an important ingredient in many pasta dishes and desserts. It can be made easily with the following recipe.

Ricotta

RICOTTA CHEESE

RECIPE 8.2

THE ART INSTITUTE OF WASHINGTON, ARLINGTON, VA
Chef John Harrison

Yield: 8 oz. (225 g)

Milk	1 qt.	950 ml
Fresh lime juice	3 fl. oz.	85 ml

1 Allow the milk to reach room temperature in a covered container.

2 In a stainless steel saucepan slowly heat the milk to 180°F (82°C), stirring often. Hold the heated milk at 180°F (82°C) for 5 minutes.

3 Remove the milk from the heat and gently stir it while adding the lime juice. Continue to stir until curds form.

4 Gently pour the curds into a strainer or china cap lined with new, rinsed cheesecloth. Allow the whey (liquid) to separate and drain away from the curds (solids). Discard the whey.

5 Allow the cheese to rest undisturbed for 1 hour. For a firm, dry ricotta, lift the corners of the cheesecloth and tie them together with twine. Suspend the bag in a tall, covered container, place it in the refrigerator and allow the cheese to drain for 4 hours or overnight.

6 Unwrap the cheese. Season it with salt if desired. Use the cheese as you would use commercially produced ricotta.

Approximate values per 1-oz. (30-g) serving: **Calories** 80, **Total fat** 4 g, **Saturated fat** 2.5 g, **Cholesterol** 15 mg, **Sodium** 60 mg, **Total carbohydrates** 7 g, **Protein** 4 g, **Calcium** 15%

1 Heat the milk to 180°F (82°C).

2 Gently stir in the lime juice.

3 Strain the mixture through cheesecloth.

4 The finished ricotta.

SOFT CHEESES

Soft cheeses are characterized by their thin skins and creamy centers. They are among the most delicious and popular of cheeses. They ripen quickly and are at their peak for only a few days, sometimes less. Moisture content ranges from 50 to 75%.

Bel Paese (bell pah-AYZ-eh) is a 20th-century Italian creation made from cow's milk and containing approximately 50% fat. It is mild and creamy with a fruity flavor. The inside is yellowish, and the outside is brown or gray. Bel Paese is excellent for snacking and melts easily.

Brie (bree) is a rind-ripened French cheese made with cow's milk and containing about 60% fat. Brie is made in round, flat disks weighing 2 or 4 pounds; it is coated with a bloomy white rind. At the peak of ripeness, it is creamy and rich, with a texture that oozes. Selecting a properly ripened Brie is a matter of judgment and experience. Select a cheese that is bulging a bit inside its rind; there should be just the beginning of a brown coloring on the rind. If underripe, Brie will be bland with a hard, chalky core. Once the cheese is cut, it will not ripen any further. If overripe, Brie will have a brownish rind that may be gummy or sagging and will smell strongly of ammonia. The rind is edible, but trim it off if preferred. The classic after-dinner cheese, Brie is also used in soups, sauces and hors d'oeuvres.

Brie

Boursin (boor-SAHN) is a triple-cream cow's-milk cheese from France containing approximately 75% fat. Boursin is usually flavored with peppers, herbs or garlic. It is rindless, with a smooth, creamy texture, and is packed in small, foil-wrapped cylinders. Boursin is a good breakfast cheese and a welcome addition to any cheese board. It is also a popular filling for baked chicken.

Boursin

Camembert (kam-uhm-BAIR) is a rind-ripened cheese from France containing approximately 45% fat. Bavaria also produces a Camembert, though of a somewhat lesser quality. Camembert is creamy, like Brie, but milder. It is shaped in small round or oval disks and is coated with a white bloomy rind. Selecting a properly ripened Camembert is similar to selecting a Brie, but Camembert will become overripe and ammoniated even more quickly than Brie. Camembert is an excellent dessert or after-dinner cheese and goes particularly well with fruit.

Taleggio (tahl-EH-zhee-oh) is a semisoft cheese that has been produced since the 10th century in a small town near Bergamo in the Lombardy region of Italy. Made with pasteurized or unpasteurized cow's milk, it contains 48% fat and is aged for one to two months. Taleggio has an orange-colored washed rind that is edible but pungent. It is molded in a distinctive 8-inch square, approximately 2 inches thick. Its nutty, salty flavor and strong aroma become softer, creamier and more piquant with age. Serve as a dessert cheese with a strong red wine, crusty bread and fruit, or with a salad at the end of a meal.

Taleggio

SEMISOFT CHEESES

Semisoft cheeses include many mild, buttery cheeses with smooth, sliceable textures. Some semisoft cheeses are also known as monastery or Trappist cheeses because their development is traced to monasteries, some recipes having originated during the Middle Ages. The moisture content of semisoft cheeses ranges from 40 to 50%.

Cabrales (kah-BRAH-layss) is a blue-veined Spanish cheese made primarily from a blend of raw goat's, ewe's and cow's milks and containing 45 to 48% fat. Its wrapper made from large maple, oak or sycamore leaves is easily recognized. The outer foil wrapper is marked with the *Denominación de Origen* (D.O.) logo, and each 5- to 9-pound (2.5- to 4.5-kg) wheel is stamped with a unique number. It is aged for three to six months under the cold, humid and breezy conditions in natural caves found in the Asturias region. Cabrales has a moist, crumbly interior with purple-blue veins and a rough, salt-cured rind. It has a thick, creamy texture, a strong aroma and a complex sour, piquant flavor. Cabrales is especially good with salami and a full-bodied red wine or for dessert with a sweet sherry such as Pedro Ximenex.

Cabrales

Doux de Montagne (doo duh mahn-tahn-yuh) is a cow's-milk cheese from France containing approximately 45% fat. Produced in the foothills of the Pyrenees, it is also referred to as **pain de Pyrenees.** Doux de Montagne is pale yellow with irregular holes and a mellow, sweet, nutty flavor. It is sometimes studded with green peppercorns, which provide a tangy flavor contrast. It is usually shaped in large, slightly squashed spheres and coated with brown wax. Doux de Montagne is good before dinner and for snacking.

Doux de Montagne

Fontina (fon-TEE-nah) is a cow's-milk cheese from Italy's Piedmont region containing approximately 45% fat. The original, known as **Fontina Val D'Aosta,** has a dark gold, crusty rind; the pale gold, dense interior has a few small holes. It is nutty and rich. The original must have a purple trademark stamped on the rind. Imitation Fontinas (properly known as **Fontal** or **Fontinella**) are produced in Denmark, France, Sweden, the United States and other regions of Italy. They tend to be softer, with less depth of flavor, and may have a rubbery texture. Real Fontina is a good after-dinner cheese; the imitations are often added to sauces, soups or sandwiches.

Gorgonzola (gohr-guhn-ZOH-lah) is a blue-veined cow's-milk cheese from Italy containing 48% fat. Gorgonzola has a white or ivory interior with bluish-green veins. It is creamier than other blues such as Stilton or Roquefort, with a somewhat more pungent, spicy, earthy flavor. White Gorgonzola has no veins but a similar flavor, while aged Gorgonzola is drier and crumbly with a very strong, sharp flavor. The milder Gorgonzolas are excellent with fresh peaches or pears or crumbled in a salad. Gorgonzola is also used in sauces and in torta con basilico, a cakelike cheese loaf composed of layers of cheese, fresh basil and pine nuts.

Gouda (GOO-dah) is a Dutch cheese containing approximately 48% fat. Gouda is sold in various-sized wheels covered with red or yellow wax. The cheese is yellow with a few small holes and a mild, buttery

LEFTOVER CHEESE

Never discard those little leftover bits and pieces of cheese lurking in your refrigerator. The tag ends of Brie, cheddar, farmer cheese, chevre, Roquefort, Mozzarella, and scores of other cheese can be quickly transformed into a tasty mixture that the thrifty French call *fromage fort* ("strong cheese"). Seasoned with fresh garlic and a few splashes of wine, it makes an assertively flavored topping for toast or thick slices of bread and tastes best when briefly melted under the broiler.

To make fromage fort, gather together 1 pound of leftover cheese (3 kinds is enough, 6 or 7 will be even better). Trim off any mold or very dried out parts from the surface. Toss 3 or 4 peeled cloves of garlic into a food processor and process for several seconds until coarsely chopped. Add the cheese to the garlic along with ½ cup dry white wine and at least 1 teaspoon of freshly ground black pepper. Process until the mixture becomes soft and creamy, about 30 seconds. Remove the mixture from the processor and transfer it to a crock or bowl. Cover tightly with plastic wrap and refrigerate.

STEVE JENKINS,
Steve Jenkins Cheese Primer

Gorgonzola

▶ **fondue** a Swiss specialty made with melted cheese, wine and flavorings; eaten by dipping pieces of bread into the hot mixture with long forks

▶ **blue cheese** (1) a generic term for any cheese containing visible blue-green molds that contribute a characteristic tart, sharp flavor and aroma; also known as a blue-veined cheese or bleu; (2) a group of Roquefort-style cheeses made in the United States and Canada from cow's or goat's milk rather than ewe's milk and injected with molds that form blue-green veins; also known as blue mold cheese or blue-veined cheese

flavor. Gouda may be sold soon after production, or it may be aged for several months, resulting in a firmer, more flavorful cheese. Gouda is widely popular for snacking and in **fondue.**

Havarti (hah-VAHR-tee) is a cow's-milk monastery-style cheese from Denmark containing 45 to 60% fat. Havarti is also known as **Danish Tilsit** or by the brand name **Dofino.** Pale yellow with many small, irregular holes, it is sold in small rounds, rectangular blocks or loaves. Havarti has a mild flavor and creamy texture. It is often flavored with dill, caraway seeds or peppers. Havarti is very popular for snacking and in sandwiches.

Port du Salut (por dah suh-LOO) is a monastery cow's-milk product from France containing approximately 50% fat. Port du Salut (also known as Port Salut) is smooth, rich and savory. It is shaped in thick wheels with a dense, pale yellow interior and an edible, bright orange rind. The Danish version is known as Esrom. One of the best and most authentic Port du Saluts has the initials S.A.F.R. stamped on the rind. Lesser-quality brands may be bland and rubbery. It is popular for breakfast and snacking, especially with fruit.

Havarti

Roquefort (ROHK-fuhr) is a blue-veined sheep's-milk cheese from France containing approximately 45% fat. It was first mentioned in a text dated to 79 A.D. and Roquefort producers have held a legal monopoly over making this cheese since 1411. Roquefort is intensely pungent with a rich, salty flavor and strong aroma. It is a white paste with veins of blue mold and a thin natural rind shaped into thick, foil-wrapped cylinders. Roquefort is always aged for at least three months in the limestone caves of Mount Combalou. Since 1926, no producer outside this region can legally use the name Roquefort or even "Roquefort-style." Roquefort is an excellent choice for serving before or after dinner and is, of course, essential for Roquefort dressing.

Roquefort

Stilton is a blue-veined cow's-milk cheese from Great Britain containing 45% fat. Stilton is one of the oldest and grandest cheeses in the world. It has a white or pale yellow interior with evenly spaced blue veins. Stilton's distinctive flavor is pungent, rich and tangy, combining the best of blues and cheddars. It is aged in cool ripening rooms for four to six months to develop the blue veining; it is then sold in tall cylinders with a crusty, edible rind. Stilton should be wrapped in a cloth dampened with salt water and stored at cool temperatures, but not refrigerated. It is best served alone, with plain crackers, dried fruit or vintage port.

FIRM CHEESES

Firm cheeses are not hard or brittle. Some are close-textured and flaky, like Cheddar; others are dense, holey cheeses like Emmenthaler. Most firm cheeses are actually imitators of these two classics. Their moisture content ranges from 30 to 40%.

Stilton

Cheddars are produced in both North America and Great Britain. **American Cheddar** is a cow's-milk cheese made primarily in New York, Wisconsin, Vermont and Oregon, containing from 45 to 50% fat. The best cheddars are made from raw milk and aged for several months. (Raw milk may be used in the United States provided the cheese is then aged at least 60 days.) They have a dense, crumbly texture. Cheddars may be white or colored orange with vegetable dyes, depending on local preference. Flavors range from mild to very sharp, depending on the age of the cheese. **Colby** and **Longhorn** are two well-known mild, soft-textured Wisconsin Cheddars. Cheddars are sold in a variety of shapes and sizes, often coated with wax. Good-quality Cheddars are welcome additions to any cheese board, while those of lesser quality are better reserved for cooking and sandwiches. **English Cheddar** is a variety of cow's-milk cheese produced in Great Britain containing approximately 45% fat. Perhaps the most imitated cheese in the world, true English Cheddar is rarely seen in the United States because of import restrictions. It is a moist yet sliceable cheese, aged at least six months.

American Cheddar—Wisconsin Sharp, Vermont Cabot, Canadian Black Diamond

Emmenthaler (EM-en-tah-ler) is a cow's-milk cheese from Switzerland containing approximately 45% fat. Emmenthaler is the original Swiss cheese; it accounts for more than half of Switzerland's cheese production. It is mellow, rich and nutty with a natural rind and a light yellow interior full of large holes. It is ripened in three stages with the aid of fermenting bacteria. The holes or "eyes" are caused by gases expanding inside the cheese during fermentation. Authentic Emmenthaler is sold in 200-pound wheels with the word *Switzerland* stamped on the rind like the spokes of a wheel. Emmenthaler, one of the basic fondue cheeses, is also popular for sandwiches, snacks and after dinner with fruit and nuts.

Emmenthaler (Swiss)

Gruyère (groo-YAIR) is a cow's-milk cheese made near Fribourg in the Swiss Alps and containing approximately 45 to 50% fat. Gruyère is often imitated, as the name is not legally protected. True Gruyère is moist and highly flavorful, with a sweet nuttiness similar to Emmenthaler. Gruyère is aged for up to 12 months and then sold in huge wheels. It should have small, well-spaced holes and a brown, wrinkled rind. Gruyère melts easily and is often used with meats and in sauces, but it is also appropriate before or after dinner.

Jarlsberg (YAHRLZ-behrg) is a Swiss-type cow's-milk cheese from Norway containing approximately 45% fat. Jarlsberg closely resembles Emmenthaler in both flavor and appearance. It is mild with a delicate, sweet flavor and large holes. Jarlsberg has a pale yellow interior; it is coated with yellow wax and sold in huge wheels. It has a long shelf life and is popular for sandwiches and snacks and in cooking.

Gruyère

Manchego

Manchego (mahn-CHAY-goh) is the best-known and most widely available Spanish sheep's-milk cheese. Its ivory to pale yellow interior is firm and compact with a few small air pockets. It has a buttery and slightly piquant flavor with an aftertaste of sheep's milk. The inedible rind is black, gray or beige with a very distinctive zigzag pattern imprinted by the traditional esparto grass molds.

There are two types of Manchego: farmhouse style, made with unpasteurized sheep's milk, and industrial, made with pasteurized milk. For both, only milk from Manchega sheep raised in the La Mancha region is used. Manchego is aged from two months (*fresco*) to one year (*curado*) to two years (*añejo* or *viejo*) and contains 45 to 57% fat. Its intense flavor and crumbly texture make it excellent for eating as is, with bread or fruit, or as the focal point of antipasto with a robust red wine or a dry sherry.

Monterey Jack is a cheddarlike cow's-milk cheese from California containing 50% fat. It is very mild and rich, with a pale ivory interior. It is sold in wheels or loaves coated with dark wax. "Jack" is often flavored with peppers or herbs and is good for snacking and sandwiches and in Mexican dishes. Dry-aged Jack develops a tough, wrinkled brown rind and a rich, firm yellow interior. It has a nutty, sharp flavor and is dry enough for grating.

Monterey Jack

Provolone (pro-voh-LOH-nee) is a cow's-milk cheese from southern Italy containing approximately 45% fat. Provolone *dolce,* aged only two months, is mild, with a smooth texture. Provolone *piccante,* aged up to six months, is stronger and somewhat flaky or stringy. Smoked provolone is also popular, especially for snacking. Provolone is shaped in various ways, from huge salamis to plump spheres to tiny piglets shaped by hand. It is excellent in sandwiches and for cooking, and is often used for melting and in pizza and pasta dishes.

HARD CHEESES

Hard cheeses are not simply cheeses that have been allowed to dry out. Rather, they are carefully aged for extended periods and have a moisture content of about 30%. Hard cheeses are most often used for grating; the best flavor will come from cheeses grated as needed. Even the finest hard cheeses begin to lose their flavor within hours of grating. The most famous and popular of the hard cheeses are those from Italy, where they are known as *grana.* Hard cheeses can also be served as a table cheese or with a salad.

Provolone

Asiago (ah-zee-AH-go) is a cow's-milk cheese from Italy containing approximately 30% fat. After only one year of aging, Asiago is sharp and nutty with a cheddarlike texture. If aged for two years or more, Asiago becomes dry, brittle and suitable for grating. Either version should be an even white to pale yellow in color with no dark spots, cracks or strong aromas. Asiago melts easily and is often used in cooking.

Asiago

Parmigiano-Reggiano (Parmesan) (pahr-me-ZHAN-no reg-gee-AH-no) is a cow's-milk cheese made exclusively in the region near Parma, Italy, containing from 32 to 35% fat. Parmigiano-Reggiano is one of the world's oldest and most widely copied cheeses. Used primarily for grating and cooking, it is rich, spicy and sharp with a golden interior and a hard oily rind. It should not be overly salty or bitter. Reggiano, as it is known, is produced only from mid-April to mid-November. It is shaped into huge wheels of about 80 pounds (36 kilos) each, with the name stenciled repeatedly around the rind. Imitation Parmesan is produced in the United States, Argentina and elsewhere, but none can match the distinctive flavor of freshly grated Reggiano.

Parmigiano-Reggiano (Parmesan)

Pecorino Romano (peh-coh-REE-no roh-MAH-no) is a sheep's-milk cheese from central and southern Italy containing approximately 35% fat. Romano is very brittle and sharper than other grating cheeses, with a "sheepy" tang. Its light, grainy interior is whiter than Parmesan or Asiago. It is packed in large cylinders with a yellow rind. Romano is often substituted for, or combined with, Parmesan in cooking, but it is also good eaten with olives, sausages and red wine.

GOAT'S-MILK CHEESES

Because of their increasing popularity, cheeses made from goat's milk deserve a few words of their own. Although goats give less milk than cows, their milk is higher in fat and protein and richer and more concentrated in flavor. Cheeses made with goat's milk have a sharp, tangy flavor. They may range in texture from very soft and fresh to very hard, depending on age.

Chèvre (shehv; French for "goat") refers to small, soft, creamy cheeses produced in a variety of shapes: cones, disks, pyramids or logs. Chèvres are often coated with ash, herbs or seasonings. They are excellent for cooking and complement a wide variety of flavors. Unfortunately, they have a short shelf life, perhaps only two weeks. Cheese labeled *pur chèvre* must be made with 100% goat's milk, while others may be a mixture of cow's and goat's milk.

The finest goat's-milk cheeses usually come from France. Preferred brands include Bucheron, exported from France in 5-pound (2-kilograms) logs; Chevrotin, one of the mildest; and Montrachet, a tangy soft cheese from the

Goat's Milk Cheeses

AMERICAN CHEESE PRODUCTION

The first cheese factory in the United States was built in 1851 in Oneida County, New York. Herkimer County, which adjoins Oneida County, soon became the center of the American cheese industry and remained so for the next 50 years. During this time, the largest cheese market in the world was at Little Falls, New York, where farm-produced cheeses and cheeses from more than 200 factories were sold. At the turn of the century, as New York's population increased, there was a corresponding increase in demand for fluid milk. Because dairies could receive more money for fluid milk than for cheese, cheese production declined.

Although New York still produces some outstanding cheddars, the bulk of the American cheese industry gradually moved westward, eventually settling in Wisconsin's rich farmlands. The United States is now the world's largest manufacturer of cheeses, producing nearly twice as many pounds per year as its nearest competitor, France.

Burgundy wine region. Spurred on by the increased popularity of chèvre, several American producers have developed excellent goat's-milk cheeses in a wide variety of shapes and styles.

▶ PROCESSED CHEESES

Pasteurized processed cheese is made from a combination of aged and green cheeses mixed with emulsifiers and flavorings, pasteurized and poured into molds to solidify. Manufacturers can thus produce cheeses with consistent textures and flavors. Processed cheeses are commonly used in food service operations because they are less expensive than natural cheeses. And, because they will not age or ripen, their shelf life is greatly extended. Nutritionally, processed cheeses generally contain less protein, calcium and vitamin A and more sodium than natural cheeses.

Processed cheese food contains less natural cheese (but at least 51 precent by weight) and more moisture than regular processed cheese. Often vegetable oils and milk solids are added, making cheese food soft and spreadable.

Imitation cheese is usually manufactured with dairy by-products and soy products mixed with emulsifiers, colorings and flavoring agents and enzymes. Although considerably less expensive than natural cheese, imitation cheese tends to be dense and rubbery, with little flavor other than that of salt.

▶ SERVING CHEESES

Cheeses may be served at any time of day. In Northern Europe, they are common for breakfast; in Great Britain, they are a staple at lunch. Cheeses are widely used for sandwiches, snacks and cooking in America, and they are often served following the entrée or instead of dessert at formal dinners.

The flavor and texture of natural cheeses are best at room temperature. So, except for fresh cheeses, all cheeses should be removed from the refrigerator 30 minutes to an hour before service to allow them to come to room temperature. Fresh cheeses, such as cottage and cream, should be eaten chilled.

CHEESE TERMINOLOGY

The following terms often appear on cheese labels and may help you identify or appreciate new or unfamiliar cheeses:

Affiné–French term for a washed-rind cheese.

Bleu–French for "blue."

Brique or *briquette*–refers to a group of French brick-shaped cheeses.

Brosse–French term for cheeses that are brushed during ripening.

Capra–Italian for goat's-milk cheese.

Carré–French term for square, flat cheeses.

Cendré–French term for cheeses ripened in ashes.

Coulant–French for "flowing," used to describe Brie, Camembert and other cheeses when their interiors ooze or flow.

Ferme or *fermier*–French adjective used to indicate farm-produced cheeses.

Kaas–Dutch for "cheese."

Käse–German for "cheese."

Lait cru–French term for raw milk.

Laiterie or *laitier*–French for "dairy"; appears on factory-made cheeses.

Matières grasses–French term for dry matter.

Mi chevre–a French product so labeled must contain at least 25 percent goat's milk.

Ost–Scandinavian for "cheese."

Pecorino–Italian term for all sheep's-milk cheeses.

Queso–Spanish for "cheese."

Râpé–French term applied to cheeses that are suitable for grating.

Tome or *tomme*–term used by the French, Italians and Swiss to refer to mountain cheeses, particularly from the Pyrenees or Savoie regions.

Tyrophile–one who loves cheese.

Vaccino–Italian term for cow's-milk cheese.

Vache–French term for cow's-milk cheese.

Cheeseboard Ready for Service

Any selection of fine cheeses should include a variety of flavors and textures: from mild to sharp, from soft to creamy to firm. Use a variety of shapes and colors for visual appeal. Do not precut the cheeses, as this only causes them to become dry. Provide an adequate supply of serving knives so that stronger-flavored cheeses will not combine with and overpower milder ones. Fine cheeses are best appreciated with plain bread and crackers, as salted or seasoned crackers can mask the cheese's flavor. Noncitrus fruits are also a nice accompaniment.

STORAGE

Most cheeses are best kept refrigerated, well wrapped to keep odors out and moisture in. Firm and hard cheeses can be kept for several weeks; fresh cheeses will spoil in 7 to 10 days because of their high moisture content. Some cheeses that have become hard or dry may still be grated for cooking or baking. Freezing is possible but not recommended because it changes the cheese's texture, making it mealy or tough.

WINE AND CHEESE: CLASSIC COMBINATIONS

Some cheeses are delicious with beers or ales. Others are best with strong coffee or apple cider, and nothing accompanies a Cheddar cheese sandwich as well as ice-cold milk. For most cheeses, however, the ultimate partner is wine. Wine and cheese bring out the best in each other. The proteins and fats in cheeses take the edge off harsh or acidic wines, while the tannins and acids in wines bring out the creamy richness of cheeses.

Because of their natural affinity, certain pairings are universal favorites: Stilton with port, Camembert with Bordeaux, Roquefort with Sauternes and English Cheddar with Burgundy. Although taste preferences are an individual matter, cheese-wine marriages follow two schools of thought: either pair likes or pair opposites.

Pairing like with like is simple: Cheeses are often best served with wines produced in the same region. For example, a white Burgundy such as Montrachet would be an excellent choice for cheeses from Burgundy; and goat cheeses from the Rhone Valley go well with wines of that region. Hearty Italian wines such as Chianti, Barolo and Valpolicella are delicious with Italian cheese—Gorgonzola, Provolone, Taleggio. And a dry, aged Monterey Jack is perhaps the perfect mate for California Zinfandel.

Opposites do attract, however. Sweet wines such as Sauternes and Gewürztraminer go well with sharp, tangy blues, especially Roquefort. And light, sparkling wines such as Champagne or Spanish Cava are a nice complement to rich, creamy cheeses such as Brie and Camembert.

CONCLUSION

Dairy products are versatile foods used throughout the kitchen. They may be served as is or incorporated into many dishes, including soups, sauces, entrées, breads and desserts. Fine natural cheeses are useful in prepared dishes but are most important for buffets, as the cheese course during a meal or whenever cheese is the primary ingredient or dominant flavor. Dairy products spoil easily and must be handled and stored properly.

QUESTIONS FOR DISCUSSION

1 What is milkfat, and how is it used in classifying milk-based products?
2 If a recipe calls for whole milk and you have only dried milk, what do you do? Explain your answer.
3 What is clarified butter, and when is it used? Describe the procedure for clarifying butter.
4 The texture and shelf life of cheese depend on what two factors?
5 Cheeses are categorized as fresh, soft, semisoft, firm and hard. Give two examples of each, and explain how they are generally used.
6 The FDA has proposed extending the mandatory aging period for cheeses made from raw (unpasteurized) milk beyond the 60 days currently required. The FDA has also proposed banning importation of raw-milk cheeses altogether on food safety grounds. Several groups, including the American Cheese Society and Oldways Preservation & Exchange Trust, are fighting these proposals. What is the current status of the FDA proposals? What arguments are used in support of and in opposition to these proposals?
7 Use the Internet to locate a U.S. producer of European-style goat cheeses. What varieties of goat cheeses do they market?

WHEN YOU BECOME A GOOD COOK,
YOU BECOME A GOOD CRAFTSMAN, FIRST. YOU
REPEAT AND REPEAT AND REPEAT UNTIL YOUR
HANDS KNOW HOW TO MOVE WITHOUT THINKING
ABOUT IT.
—*Jacques Pepin, French chef and teacher*
(1935–)

9

MISE EN PLACE

**AFTER STUDYING THIS
CHAPTER, YOU WILL BE
ABLE TO:**

▶ organize and plan your work
more efficiently

▶ understand basic flavoring
techniques

▶ prepare items needed prior to
actual cooking

▶ set up and use the standard
breading procedure

The French term *mise en place* (meez ahn plahs) literally means "to put in place" or "everything in its place." But in the culinary context, it means much more. Escoffier defined the phrase as "those elementary preparations that are constantly resorted to during the various steps of most culinary preparations." He meant, essentially, gathering and prepping the ingredients to be cooked as well as assembling the tools and equipment necessary to cook them.

In this chapter, we discuss many of the basics that must be in place before cooking begins: for example, creating bouquets garni, clarifying butter, making bread crumbs, toasting nuts and battering foods. Chopping, dicing, cutting and slicing—important techniques used to prepare foods as well—are discussed in Chapter 6, Knife Skills, while specific preparations, such as roasting peppers and trimming pineapples, are discussed elsewhere.

The concept of mise en place is simple: A chef should have at hand everything he or she needs to prepare and serve food in an organized and efficient manner.

Proper mise en place can consist of just a few items—for example, those needed to prepare a small quantity of chicken soup. Or it can be quite extensive—for example, when setting up the hot line for a busy restaurant with a large menu. A proper mise en place requires the chef to consider work patterns, ingredient lists and tool and equipment needs.

Mise en place will differ from one restaurant to another. A banquet chef's mise en place could include organizing large quantities of meats, vegetables, salad ingredients, breads, condiments and pastries for several dinners, all with different menus. Regardless of the specific menu, banquet mise en place may also include gathering hot boxes, plates, chafing dishes, tongs, spoons and ladles, and setting up the dish-up line. The mise en place for the broiler station at a steakhouse could include properly storing raw steaks and chops that will be cooked to order, as well as gathering the salt, pepper, pre-prepared sauces and accompaniments that are used during cooking or served with the finished items. The broiler cook could also be responsible for gathering plates, building a charcoal fire for the grill, and stocking his or her work area with hand tools, towels and sanitizing solution. In the restaurant situation, unlike in banquet work, the cook's mise en place is probably identical night after night. A waiter's mise en place could include brewing tea, cutting lemon wedges and refilling salt and pepper shakers—preparations that will make work go more smoothly during actual service. Regardless of the number of items used or the complexity of the recipes being prepared, completing a proper mise en place requires careful planning, efficient organization and attention to detail.

Coordination of multiple tasks is also important. An organized cook will think about everything that needs to be done and the most efficient way to complete those tasks before beginning the actual work. Taking the time to first plan the day's activities can eliminate unnecessary steps and conserve resources.

Proper mise en place also requires a good sense of timing. Knowing how long before service to begin a task, or how far in advance of service some preparations can be made, allows a cook to better plan for the efficient execution of his or her duties. In this type of planning, it is also important to consider food safety issues, such as those relating to time and temperature controls. See Chapter 2, Food Safety and Sanitation, for detailed information.

▶ SELECTING TOOLS AND EQUIPMENT

An important step in creating the proper mise en place is to identify and gather all of the tools and equipment that will be needed to prepare a recipe properly or to work a station efficiently. The tools and equipment used to prepare, cook and store foods are discussed in Chapter 5, Tools and Equipment. A few general rules to bear in mind:

▶ All tools, equipment and work surfaces must be clean and sanitized.
▶ Knives should be honed and sharpened.
▶ Measuring devices should be checked periodically for accuracy.
▶ Ovens and cooking surfaces should be preheated, as necessary.
▶ Mixing bowls, saucepans and storage containers should be the correct size for the task at hand.
▶ Serving plates, cookware, utensils, hand tools and other necessary smallwares should be gathered and stored nearby.
▶ Foods should be gathered and stored conveniently at the proper temperatures.
▶ Expiration dates on foods should be checked periodically for validity.
▶ Sanitizing solution, hand towels, disposable gloves and trash receptacles should be conveniently located.

▶ MEASURING INGREDIENTS

In order to reproduce foods consistently and for the same cost day after day, it is important that the ingredients be measured accurately each time. As explained in more detail in Chapter 4, Menus and Recipes, ingredients may be measured by weight, volume or count. Weight refers to the mass or heaviness of

1 To use a balance scale to weigh an ingredient, place an empty container on the left, then set a counterbalance to that container on the right. Use weights and the sliding beam weight to add an amount equal to the amount of the ingredient needed.

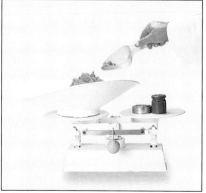

2 Place the ingredient on the left side of the scale until the two platforms are balanced.

Liquids should be measured in liquid measuring cups, which may be marked in U.S. and/or metric units.

Small amounts of dry ingredients are measured by overfilling the appropriate measuring spoon, then leveling the ingredient.

an item and is measured using a scale. Volume refers to the space occupied by a substance and is measured with graduated measuring cups and spoons. Count refers to the number of individual items. It is important to remember that foods do not weigh their volume. In other words, although 1 cup contains 8 *fluid ounces,* 1 cup of flour, honey, cinnamon, and so on does not *weigh* 8 ounces.

▶ PREPARING INGREDIENTS

Some ingredients that are used frequently throughout the kitchen are often prepared in large quantities so that they are ready when needed for a specific recipe. For example, dry bread crumbs can be made and stored whenever a supply of bread is available. Large quantities of butter can be clarified on a back burner while other operations proceed on the line. These chores may be simple, but they are time-consuming. As an entry-level cook, you may be assigned responsibility for this type of mise en place. Never feel that such chores are beneath you; consider, instead, how frustrating it would be for the chef to run out of a simple item just when it is needed during service.

CLARIFYING BUTTER

▶ **ghee** a form of clarified butter in which the milk solids remain with the fat and are allowed to brown; originating in India and now used worldwide as an ingredient and cooking medium, it has a long shelf life, a high smoke point and a nutty, caramel-like flavor

Unsalted whole butter is approximately 80% fat, 16% water and 4% milk solids. Although whole butter can be used for cooking or sauce making, sometimes a more stable and consistent product will be achieved by using butter that has had the water and milk solids removed by a process called **clarification.**

▶ PROCEDURE FOR CLARIFYING BUTTER

1 Slowly warm the butter in a saucepan over low heat without boiling or agitation. As the butter melts, the milk solids rise to the top as a foam and the water sinks to the bottom.

2 When the butter is completely melted, skim the milk solids from the top.

3 When all the milk solids have been removed, ladle the butterfat into a clean saucepan, being careful to leave the water in the bottom of the pan.

4 The clarified butter is now ready to use. One pound (454 grams) of whole butter will yield approximately 12 ounces (340 grams) of clarified butter—a yield of 75%.

Clarified butter will keep for extended periods in either the freezer or refrigerator.

Skimming milk solids from the surface of melted butter.

Ladling the butterfat into a clean pan.

TOASTING NUTS AND SPICES

Nuts are often toasted lightly before being used in baked goods, breadings, salads and sauces. Whole spices are sometimes toasted before being ground for a sauce or used as a garnish. Toasting not only browns the food, it brings out its flavor and makes it crispier and crunchier. Whether toasting nuts or spices in the oven or on the stove top, they should be watched closely as they can develop scorched flavors and burn easily.

MAKING BREAD CRUMBS

Most any bread can be used to make crumbs; the choice depends on how the crumbs will be used. **Fresh bread crumbs** are made from fresh bread that is slightly dried out, approximately two to four days old. If the bread is too fresh, the crumbs will be gummy and stick together; if the bread is too stale, the crumbs will taste stale as well. **Dry bread crumbs** are made from bread that has been lightly toasted in a warm oven. Do not make crumbs from stale or molding bread, as these undesirable flavors will be apparent when the crumbs are used.

To make crumbs, the bread is cubed or torn into pieces and ground in a food processor. Dried bread can be processed to a finer consistency than fresh bread. After processing, the crumbs should be passed through a tamis and stored in a tightly closed plastic container in a cool, dry place.

For additional flavors, dried herbs and spices can be mixed into the crumbs.

Toasting sesame seeds in a dry sauté pan on the stove top.

1 Grind chunks of bread in a food processor.

2 Pass the crumbs through a tamis or sieve so that they will be the same size.

CONVENIENCE PRODUCTS

Convenience products have now replaced many of the chores that were typically part of a cook's routine mise en place. For example, stock and sauce bases eliminate the time and labor necessary to make these products from scratch. Fresh onions and garlic can be purchased peeled, chopped and ready to use. Bread crumbs are available in bulk, and ready-to-use clarified butter is sold in refrigerated tubs. All this convenience comes at a price, of course. A chef must carefully consider whether the savings in employee time, along with the quality and consistency of available products, justify the higher cost of some of the convenience products now on the market.

▶ FLAVORING FOODS

Foods are often flavored with herbs or spices, marinades or rubs before they are actually cooked. This may require the chef to prepare various flavoring or seasoning mixtures and wait for a period of time between steps in a recipe.

BOUQUET GARNI AND SACHET

A bouquet garni and sachet are used to introduce flavorings, seasonings and aromatics into stocks, sauces, soups and stews.

A **bouquet garni** is a selection of herbs (usually fresh) and vegetables tied into a bundle with twine. A standard bouquet garni consists of parsley stems, celery, thyme, leeks and carrots.

A **sachet** (also known as a *sachet d'épices*) is made by tying seasonings together in cheesecloth. A standard sachet consists of peppercorns, bay leaves, parsley stems, thyme, cloves and, optionally, garlic. The exact quantity of these ingredients is determined by the amount of liquid the sachet is meant to flavor.

Bouquet Garni   *Sachet*

Oignon Piqué

Bouquets garni and sachets are used to add flavors in such a way that they can be easily removed from a dish when their flavors have been extracted. A similar technique, although less commonly used, is an **oignon piqué** (also known as an *onion piquet*). To prepare an oignon piqué, peel the onion and trim off the root end. Attach one or two dried bay leaves to the onion using whole cloves as pins. The oignon piqué is then simmered in milk or stock to extract flavors.

MARINADES

Marinating is the process of soaking meat or poultry in a seasoned liquid to flavor and tenderize it. Marinades can be a simple blend (herbs, seasonings and oil) or a complicated cooked recipe (red wine, fruit and other ingredients). Mild marinades should be used on more delicate meats, such as veal. Game and beef require strongly flavored marinades. In wine-based marinades, white wine is usually used for white meats and poultry, and red wine is used for red meats. Not only does the wine add a distinctive flavor, but the acids in it break down connective tissues and help tenderize the meat.

Poultry, veal and pork generally require less time to marinate than game, beef and lamb. Smaller pieces of meat take less time than larger pieces. When marinating, be sure to cover the meat or poultry completely and keep it refrigerated. Stir or turn it frequently so that the marinade can penetrate evenly.

Marinating chicken breasts

Some chefs prefer to marinate food in heavy-duty plastic food storage bags. These are useful for smaller quantities and allow for easy disposal of leftover marinades with less risk of cross-contamination. Label the bags properly and be sure to seal them tightly to prevent leaks.

RUBS AND PASTES

Additional flavors can be added to meat, fish and poultry by rubbing them with a mixture of fresh or dried herbs and spices ground together with a mortar and pestle or in a spice grinder. The flavoring blend, called a **rub,** can be used dried, or it can be mixed with a little oil, lemon juice, prepared mustard or ground fresh garlic or ginger to make a **paste** (also known as a **wet rub**). Rubs and pastes add flavor and, often, a bit of crispy crust. They do not, however, generally act as a tenderizer. They are most often used on foods that will be cooked with dry heat, especially by grilling, broiling, baking or roasting.

To apply a rub or paste, slather the mixture over the entire surface of the food to be flavored. Use enough pressure to make sure that the rub or paste adheres. (Pastes tend to adhere better than rubs.) The thicker the covering or the longer it remains on the food before cooking, the more pronounced the flavor. If the rubbed food is to be left for some time so that the flavors can be absorbed, it should be covered, refrigerated and turned from time to time.

It is best to wear disposable gloves when applying a rub or paste. Some spices can irritate or stain the skin, and cross-contamination can occur from handling raw meats.

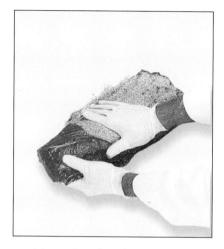

Applying a dry rub to beef

STEEPING

Steeping is the process of soaking dry ingredients in a liquid (usually hot) in order to either soften a food or to infuse its flavor into the liquid. Spices, coffee beans and nuts are often steeped in hot milk to extract their flavors. The milk is then used to flavor other foods during cooking. For example, coffee beans can be steeped in hot milk and then strained out, with the coffee-flavored milk being used to make a custard sauce.

Steeping is also used for rehydrating dried fruits and vegetables such as raisins and mushrooms. Typically, the softened fruits or vegetables will be used in a recipe and the liquid discarded. Additional flavors can be achieved by using wine, spirits, stock or other flavored liquids as the rehydrating medium.

Note that in both situations, the steeping mixture is generally covered and removed from the heat to avoid evaporation or reduction of the liquid.

Steeping a vanilla bean and cinnamon sticks in warm milk to extract their flavors.

Steeping raisins in hot water to rehydrate.

▶ PREPARING TO COOK

Some techniques are done very close to or almost as a part of the final preparation of a dish.

BREADING AND BATTERING FOODS

BREADING

▶ **meal** (1) the coarsely ground seeds of any edible grain such as corn or oats; (2) any dried, ground substance (such as bonemeal)

A breaded item is any food that is coated with bread crumbs, cracker meal, cornmeal or other dry **meal** to protect it during cooking. Breaded foods can be seasoned before the breading is applied, or seasonings may be added to the flour, bread crumbs or meal before the main item is coated. Breaded foods are generally cooked by deep-frying or pan-frying. The breading makes a solid coating that seals during cooking and prevents the fat from coming in direct contact with the food, which would make it greasy.

▶ STANDARD BREADING PROCEDURE

For breading meats, poultry, fish, shellfish or vegetables, a three-step process is typically used. Called the **standard breading procedure,** it gives foods a relatively thick, crisp coating.

1 Pat the food dry and dredge it in seasoned flour. The flour adds seasoning to the food, helps seal it, and allows the egg wash to adhere.

2 Dip the floured food in an egg wash. The egg wash should contain whole eggs whisked together with approximately 1 tablespoon (15 milliliters) milk or water per egg. The egg wash will cause the crumbs or meal to completely coat the item and form a tight seal when the food is cooked.

3 Coat the food with bread crumbs, cracker crumbs or other dry meal. Shake off excess crumbs and place the breaded item in a pan. As additional breaded items are added to the pan, align them in a single layer; do not stack them or the breadings will get soggy and the foods will stick together.

Figure 9.1 shows the proper setup for breading foods using the standard breading procedure. The following procedure helps to bread foods more efficiently:

1 Assemble the mise en place as shown in Figure 9.1.

2 With your left hand, place the food to be breaded in the flour and coat it evenly. With the same hand, remove the floured item, shake off the excess flour and place it in the egg wash.

3 With your right hand, remove the item from the egg wash and place it in the bread crumbs or meal.

4 With your left hand, cover the item with crumbs or meal and press lightly to make sure the item is completely and evenly coated. Shake off the excess crumbs or meal and place the breaded food in the empty pan for finished product.

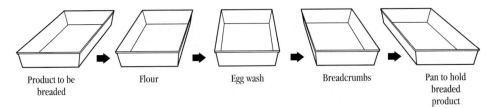

| Product to be breaded | Flour | Egg wash | Breadcrumbs | Pan to hold breaded product |

FIGURE 9.1 ▶ Setup for the standard breading procedure

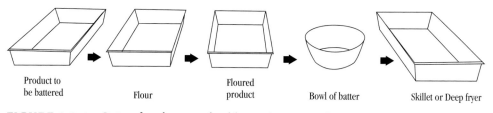

Product to be battered → Flour → Floured product → Bowl of batter → Skillet or Deep fryer

FIGURE 9.2 ▶ Setup for the standard battering procedure

The key is to use one hand for the liquid ingredients and the other hand for the dry ingredients. This prevents your fingers from becoming coated with layer after layer of breading.

BATTERING

Batters, like breading, coat the food being cooked, keeping it moist and preventing it from becoming excessively greasy. Batters consist of a liquid such as water, milk or beer, combined with a starch such as flour or cornstarch. Many batters also contain a leavening agent such as baking powder or whipped egg whites. Two common batters are beer batter, which uses the beer for leavening as well as for flavor and is illustrated in the recipe for Beer Battered Onion Rings, page 650, and tempura batter, which is used in Tempura Vegetables with Dipping Sauce, page 673. Items coated with a batter are cooked immediately, usually by deep-frying or pan-frying.

▶ PROCEDURE FOR BATTERING FOODS

1 Prepare the batter.
2 Pat the food dry and dredge in flour if desired.
3 Dip the item in the batter and place it directly in the hot fat.

BLANCHING AND PARBOILING

Some foods, especially vegetables, are **blanched** or **parboiled** before being used in a recipe. To do so, they are immersed in a large quantity of a boiling or simmering liquid—oil or water—and partially cooked. This **parcooking** assists preparation (for example, it loosens peels from vegetables), removes undesirable flavors, softens firm foods, sets colors and shortens final cooking times. The only difference between blanching and parboiling is cooking time. Blanching is done quickly, usually only a few seconds. Parboiling lasts longer, usually several minutes. Foods that are blanched or parboiled in water (rather than fat) are often **shocked** or **refreshed** in ice water to halt the cooking process.

▶ **blanching** very briefly and partially cooking a food in boiling water or hot fat; used to assist preparation (for example, to loosen peels from vegetables), as part of a combination cooking method or to remove undesirable flavors

▶ **parboiling** partially cooking a food in boiling or simmering liquid; similar to blanching but the cooking time is longer

▶ **parcooking** partially cooking a food by any cooking method

▶ **shocking** also called refreshing; the technique of quickly chilling blanched or parcooked foods in ice water; prevents further cooking and sets colors

1 Blanch or parboil the food as desired in boiling water.

2 Remove the food from the cooking liquid and submerge it in ice water to refresh.

MAKING AN ICE BATH

Because of the risk of food-borne illness, it is important to cool hot foods quickly to a temperature below 41°F (4°C) before storing them in the refrigerator. An ice bath is an easy, efficient way to do so. An ice bath is also necessary for shocking or refreshing blanched or parcooked vegetables and for stopping the cooking of delicate mixtures such as custards.

An ice bath is simply a container of ice cubes and cold water. The combination of ice and water will chill foods more rapidly than a container of only ice. The food being chilled will also cool faster if it is in a metal container, rather than one made of plastic or glass.

Chilling sauce in an ice bath

CONCLUSION

As with most endeavors, consistently good cooking requires careful planning, preparation and organization. With these skills, you should be able to create a proper mise en place for most any occasion.

QUESTIONS FOR DISCUSSION

1 Explain the differences between breading and battering foods.
2 Describe the correct mise en place for the standard breading procedure.
3 Choose a dessert recipe from the baking chapters of this book and describe the proper mise en place for preparing that dish.
4 How can the concepts of mise en place be applied to activities outside of the kitchen?

THE QUALITIES OF AN EXCEPTIONAL COOK ARE AKIN TO THOSE OF A SUCCESSFUL TIGHTROPE WALKER: AN ABIDING PASSION FOR THE TASK, COURAGE TO GO OUT ON A LIMB AND AN IMPECCABLE SENSE OF BALANCE.

—*Bryan Miller, American food writer*

PRINCIPLES
OF COOKING

AFTER STUDYING THIS
CHAPTER, YOU WILL BE
ABLE TO:

▶ understand how heat is
transferred to foods through
conduction, convection and
radiation

▶ understand how heat affects
foods

▶ understand the basic principles
of various cooking methods

Cooking can be defined as the transfer of energy from a heat source to a food. This energy alters the food's molecular structure, changing its texture, flavor, aroma and appearance. But why is food cooked at all? The obvious answer is that cooking makes food taste better. Cooking also destroys undesirable microorganisms and makes foods easier to ingest and digest.

To cook foods successfully, you must first understand the ways in which heat is transferred: conduction, convection and radiation. You should also understand what the application of heat does to the proteins, sugars, starches, water and fats in foods.

Perhaps most important, you must understand the cooking methods used to transfer heat: broiling, grilling, roasting and baking, sautéing, pan-frying, deep-frying, poaching, simmering, boiling, steaming, braising and stewing. Each method is used for many types of food, so you will be applying one or more of them every time you cook. The cooking method you select gives the finished product a specific texture, appearance, aroma and flavor. A thorough understanding of the basic procedures involved in each cooking method helps you produce consistent, high-quality products.

This chapter describes each of the cooking methods and uses photographs to outline their general procedures. Detailed procedures and recipes applying these methods to specific foods are found in subsequent chapters.

▶ HEAT TRANSFER

Heat is a type of energy. When a substance gets hot, its molecules have absorbed energy, which causes the molecules to vibrate rapidly, expand and bounce off one another. As the molecules move, they collide with nearby molecules, causing a transfer of heat energy. The faster the molecules within a substance move, the higher its temperature. This is true whether the substance is air, water, an aluminum pot or a sirloin steak.

Heat energy may be transferred *to* foods via conduction, convection or radiation. Heat then travels *through* foods by conduction. Only heat is transferred—cold is simply the absence of heat, so cold cannot be transferred from one substance to another.

CONDUCTION

Conduction is the most straightforward means of heat transfer. It is simply the movement of heat from one item to another through direct contact. For example, when the flame of a gas burner touches the bottom of a sauté pan, heat is conducted to the pan. The metal of the pan then conducts heat to the surface of the food lying in that pan.

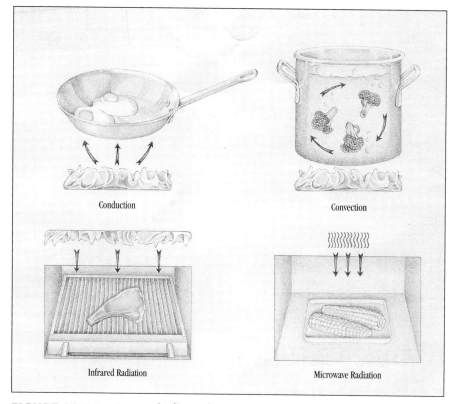

Conduction

Convection

Infrared Radiation

Microwave Radiation

FIGURE 10.1 ▶ Arrows indicate heat patterns during conduction, convection and radiation

Some materials conduct heat better than others. Water is a better conductor of heat than air. This explains why a potato cooks much faster in boiling water than in an oven, and why you cannot place your hand in boiling water at a temperature of 212°F (100°C), but can place your hand, at least very briefly, into a 400°F (200°C) oven. Generally, metals are good conductors (as discussed in Chapter 5, Tools and Equipment, copper and aluminum are the best conductors), while liquids and gases are poor conductors.

Conduction is a relatively slow method of heat transfer because there must be physical contact to transfer energy from one molecule to adjacent molecules. Consider what happens when a metal spoon is placed in a pot of simmering soup. At first the spoon handle remains cool. Gradually, however, heat travels up the handle, making it warmer and warmer, until it becomes too hot to touch.

Conduction is important in all cooking methods because it is responsible for the movement of heat from the surface of a food to its interior. As the molecules near the food's exterior gather energy, they move more and more rapidly. As they move, they conduct heat to the molecules nearby, thus transferring heat *through* the food (from the exterior of the item to the interior).

In conventional heating methods (nonmicrowave), the heat source causes food molecules to react largely from the surface inward so that layers of molecules heat in succession. This produces a range of temperatures within the food, which means that the outside can brown and form a crust long before the interior is noticeably warmer. That is why a steak can be fully cooked on the outside but still rare on the inside.

CONVECTION

Convection refers to the transfer of heat through a fluid, which may be liquid or gas. Convection is actually a combination of conduction and a mixing in which molecules in a fluid (whether air, water or fat) move from a warmer area to a cooler one. There are two types of convection: natural and mechanical.

Natural convection occurs because of the tendency of warm liquids and gases to rise while cooler ones fall. This causes a constant natural circulation of heat. For example, when a pot of stock is placed over a gas burner, the molecules at the bottom of the pot are warmed. These molecules rise while cooler, heavier molecules sink. Upon reaching the pot's bottom, the cooler molecules are warmed and begin to rise. This ongoing cycle creates currents within the stock, and these currents distribute the heat throughout the stock.

Mechanical convection relies on fans or stirring to circulate heat more quickly and evenly. This explains why foods heat faster and more evenly when stirred. Convection ovens are equipped with fans to increase the circulation of air currents, thus speeding up the cooking process. But even conventional ovens (that is, not convection ovens) rely on the natural circulation patterns of heated air to transfer heat energy to items being baked or roasted.

RADIATION

Unlike conduction and convection, **radiation** does not require physical contact between the heat source and the food being cooked. Instead, energy is transferred by waves of heat or light striking the food. Two kinds of radiant heat are used in the kitchen: infrared and microwave.

Infrared cooking uses an electric or ceramic element heated to such a high temperature that it gives off waves of radiant heat that cook the food. Radiant heat waves travel at the speed of light in any direction (unlike convection heat, which only rises) until they are absorbed by a food. Infrared cooking is commonly used with toasters and broilers. The glowing coals of a fire are another example of radiant heat.

Microwave cooking relies on radiation generated by a special oven to penetrate the food, where it agitates water molecules, creating friction and heat. This energy then spreads throughout the food by conduction (and by convection in liquids). Microwave cooking is much faster than other methods because energy penetrates the food up to a depth of several centimeters, setting all water molecules in motion at the same time. Heat is generated quickly and uniformly throughout the food. Microwave cooking does not brown foods, however, and often gives meats a dry, mushy texture, making microwave ovens an unacceptable replacement for traditional ovens.

Because microwave radiation affects only water molecules, a completely waterless material (such as a plate) will not get hot. Any warmth felt in a plate used when microwaving food results from heat being conducted from the food to the plate.

Microwave cooking requires the use of certain types of utensils, usually heat-resistant glass or microwavable plastic. But even heat-resistant glass can shatter and is not recommended for professional use. The aluminum and stainless steel utensils most common in professional kitchens cannot be used because metal deflects microwaves, and this can damage the oven.

▶ THE EFFECTS OF HEAT

Foods are composed of proteins, carbohydrates (starches and sugars), water and fats, plus small amounts of minerals and vitamins. Changes in the shape, texture, color and flavor of foods may occur when heat is applied to each of these nutrients. By understanding these changes and learning to control them, you will be able to prepare foods with the characteristics desired. Although volumes are written on these subjects, it is sufficient for you to know the following processes as you begin your study of cooking.

PROTEINS COAGULATE

The proper term for the cooking of proteins is **coagulation.** Proteins are large, complex molecules found in every living cell, plant as well as animal. Coagulation refers to the irreversible transformation of proteins from a liquid or semiliquid state to a solid state. As proteins cook, they lose moisture, shrink and become firm. Common examples of coagulation are the firming of meat fibers during cooking, egg whites changing from a clear liquid to a white solid when heated and the setting of the structure of wheat proteins (known as gluten) in bread during baking. Most proteins complete coagulation at 160°F to 185°F (71°C to 85°C).

STARCHES GELATINIZE

Gelatinization is the proper term for the cooking of starches. Starches are complex carbohydrates present in plants and grains such as potatoes, wheat, rice and corn. When a mixture of starch and liquid is heated, remarkable changes occur. The starch granules absorb water, causing them to swell, soften and clarify slightly. The liquid visibly thickens because of the water being absorbed into the starch granules and the granules themselves swelling to occupy more space.

Gelatinization occurs gradually over a range of temperatures—150°F to 212°F (66°C to 100°C)—depending on the type of starch used. Starch gelatinization affects not only sauces or liquids to which starches are added for the express purpose of thickening, but also any mixture of starch and liquid that is heated. For example, the flour (a starch) in cake batter gelatinizes by absorbing the water from eggs, milk or other ingredients as the batter bakes. This causes part of the firming and drying associated with baked goods.

SUGARS CARAMELIZE

The process of cooking sugars is properly known as **caramelization.** Sugars are simple carbohydrates used by all plants and animals to store energy. As sugars cook, they gradually turn brown and change flavor. Caramelized sugar is used in many sauces, candies and desserts. But caramelized sugar is also partly responsible for the flavor and color of bread crusts and the browning of meats and vegetables. In fact, the process of caramelization is responsible for most flavors we associate with cooking.

Sucrose (common table sugar) begins to brown at about 338°F (170°C). The naturally occurring sugars in other foods, such as maltose, lactose and fructose, also caramelize, but at varying temperatures. Because high temperatures are required for browning (that is, caramelizing), most foods will brown only on the outside and only through the application of dry heat. Because water cannot be heated above 212°F (100°C), foods cooked with moist-heat methods do not get hot enough to caramelize. Foods cooked with dry-heat methods, including those using fats, will reach the high temperatures at which browning occurs.

WATER EVAPORATES

All foods contain some water. Some foods, especially eggs, milk and leafy vegetables, are almost entirely water. Even as much as 75 percent of raw meat is water. As the internal temperature of a food increases, water molecules move faster and faster until the water turns to a gas (steam) and vaporizes. This **evaporation** of water is responsible for the drying of foods during cooking.

FATS MELT

Fat is an energy source for the plant or animal in which it is stored. Fats are smooth, greasy substances that do not dissolve in water. Their texture varies from very firm to liquid. Oils are simply fats that remain liquid at room temperature. Fats **melt** when heated; that is, they gradually soften, then liquefy. Fats will not evaporate. Most fats can be heated to very high temperatures without burning, so they can be used as a cooking medium to brown foods.

▶ COOKING METHODS

Foods can be cooked in air, fat, water or steam. These are collectively known as **cooking media.** There are two general types of cooking methods: dry heat and moist heat.

Dry-heat cooking methods are those using air or fat. They are broiling, grilling, roasting and baking, sautéing, pan-frying and deep-frying. Foods cooked using dry-heat cooking methods have a rich flavor caused by browning.

Moist-heat cooking methods are those using water or steam. They are poaching, simmering, boiling and steaming. Moist-heat cooking methods are used to tenderize and emphasize the natural flavors of food.

Other cooking methods employ a combination of dry- and moist-heat cooking methods. The two most significant of these **combination cooking methods** are braising and stewing.

Each of these cooking methods can be applied to a wide variety of foods—meats, fish, vegetables and even pastries. Here we describe each of the cooking methods and use photographs to outline their general procedures. Detailed procedures and recipes applying these methods to specific foods are found in subsequent chapters.

Table 10.1	COOKING METHODS	
METHOD	**MEDIUM**	**EQUIPMENT**
Dry-Heat Cooking Methods		
Broiling	Air	Overhead broiler, salamander, rotisserie
Grilling	Air	Grill
Roasting	Air	Oven
Baking	Air	Oven
Sautéing	Fat	Stove top
Pan-frying	Fat	Stove top, tilt skillet
Deep-frying	Fat	Deep-fat fryer
Moist-Heat Cooking Methods		
Poaching	Water or other liquid	Stove top, oven, steam-jacketed kettle, tilt skillet
Simmering	Water or other liquid	Stove top, steam-jacketed kettle, tilt skillet
Boiling	Water or other liquid	Stove top, steam-jacketed kettle, tilt skillet
Steaming	Steam	Stove top, convection steamer
Combination Cooking Methods		
Braising	Fat, then liquid	Stove top, oven, tilt skillet
Stewing	Fat, then liquid	Stove top, oven, tilt skillet

DRY-HEAT COOKING METHODS

Cooking by dry heat is the process of applying heat either directly, by subjecting the food to the heat of a flame, or indirectly, by surrounding the food with heated air or heated fat.

BROILING

Broiling uses radiant heat from an overhead source to cook foods. The temperature at the heat source can be as high as 2000°F (1093°C). The food to be broiled is placed on a preheated metal grate. Radiant heat from overhead cooks the food, while the hot grate below marks it with attractive crosshatch marks.

Delicate foods that may be damaged by being placed directly on a metal grate or foods on which crosshatch marks are not desirable may be placed on a preheated heatproof platter and then placed under the broiler. Cooking will take place through indirect heat from the preheated platter as well as by direct heat from the broiler's overhead heat source.

▶ PROCEDURE FOR BROILING FOODS

1 Heat the broiler.

2 If necessary, use a wire brush to remove any charred or burnt particles that may be stuck to the broiler grate. The grate can be wiped with a lightly oiled towel to remove any remaining particles and to help season it.

3 Cut, trim or otherwise prepare the food to be broiled. Marinate, rub or season it, as desired. Many foods can be brushed lightly with oil to keep them from sticking to the grate.

4 Place the food in the broiler, presentation side down. If necessary, use tongs to turn or flip the item without piercing its surface.

1 Preheat the grate under the broiler, then pull it out and place the food on the hot grate, presentation side down. If the item is oblong, place it at a 45-degree angle to the bars on the cooking grate. Slide the grate back under the broiler and cook long enough for the food to develop lines where it touches the grate. Pull the sliding grate out again and turn the food over at a 90-degree angle, working from left to right.

2 Pull the sliding grate out of the broiler to turn the food as necessary in order to cook it evenly. Note the handle visible on the right, which can be used to adjust the distance between the grate and the heat source.

3 Remove the cooked item from the broiler grate.

5 Cook the food to the desired degree of doneness while developing the proper surface color. To do so, adjust the position of the item on the broiler, or adjust the distance between the grate and heat source. Doneness is often determined by touch, internal temperature or specific visual cues (for example, clear juices running from poultry).

GRILLING

Although similar to broiling, grilling uses a heat source located beneath the cooking surface. Grills may be electric or gas, or they can burn wood or charcoal, which will add a smoky flavor to the food. Specific woods such as mesquite, hickory or vine clippings can be used to create special flavors. Grilled foods are often identified by crosshatch markings.

▶ PROCEDURE FOR GRILLING FOODS

1 Heat the grill.
2 If necessary, use a wire brush to remove any charred or burnt particles that may be stuck to the grill grate. The grate can be wiped with a lightly oiled towel to remove any remaining particles and to help season it.
3 Cut, trim or otherwise prepare the food to be grilled. Marinate, rub or season it, as desired. Many foods can be brushed lightly with oil to keep them from sticking to the grate.
4 Place the food on the grill, presentation side down. If practical, turn the food to produce the attractive crosshatch marks associated with grilling. Use tongs to turn or flip the item without piercing its surface.
5 Cook the food to the desired degree of doneness while developing the proper surface color. To do so, adjust the position of the item on the grill, or adjust the distance between the grate and heat source. Doneness is often determined by touch, internal temperature or specific visual cues (for example, clear juices running from poultry).

1 Decide which side of the grilled food will be presented face up to the customer. Place the food on the hot grill with this side facing down. If the item is oblong, place it at a 45-degree angle to the bars on the cooking grate. Cook long enough for the food to develop dark charred lines where it touches the grate.

2 Rotate the food 90 degrees and allow it to cook long enough for the grates to char it to the same extent as in Step 1.

3 Turn the food over and finish cooking it. It is usually unnecessary to create the crosshatch markings on the reverse side since the customer will not see this side.

ROASTING AND BAKING

Roasting and baking are the processes of surrounding a food with dry, heated air in a closed environment. The term roasting is usually applied to meats and poultry, while baking is used when referring to fish, fruits, vegetables, starches, breads or pastry items. Heat is transferred by convection to the food's surface, and then penetrates the food by conduction. The surface dehydrates, and the food browns from caramelization, completing the cooking process.

Poêléing (pwah-lay-ing) is a cooking method similar to both roasting and braising. The food is cooked in an oven, but in a covered pot with aromatic vegetables and bacon fat or butter, so that it steams in its own juices. Also known as butter roasting, the French poêlé technique is perhaps most similar to pot-roasting. Like a typical roasted dish (and unlike a typical braised dish), this method is used for tender cuts of meats and poultry that do not require long, slow cooking, and no additional liquid is added during cooking. The meat or poultry can first be browned in hot fat or it can be browned toward the end of cooking by removing the lid of the cooking vessel. Doneness is determined using the same techniques as those used for roasting. The meat or poultry is usually served with a sauce made from the pan juices mixed with a liquid and finished in the same way as a sauce for a braised dish. A recipe for Poêlé of Chicken with Pearl Onions and Mushrooms is given on page 429.

▶ PROCEDURE FOR ROASTING OR BAKING FOODS

1 Preheat the oven.

2 Cut, trim or otherwise prepare the food to be roasted or baked. Marinate or season as desired. Brush with oil or butter, as appropriate.

3 Place the food on a rack or directly in a roasting pan or baking dish.

4 Roast the food, generally uncovered, at the desired temperature. **Baste** as necessary.

5 Cook to the desired internal temperature or doneness, remembering that many foods will undergo **carryover cooking** after they are removed from the oven.

▶ **baste** to moisten foods during cooking (usually grilling, broiling or roasting) with melted fat, pan drippings, a sauce or other liquids to prevent drying and to add flavor

▶ **carryover cooking** the cooking that occurs after a food is removed from a heat source; it is accomplished by the residual heat remaining in the food

1 Season the item to be roasted, arrange it in an uncovered pan and place it in a preheated oven.

2 Use a thermometer to check the internal temperature of the item being roasted.

SAUTÉING

Sautéing is a dry-heat cooking method that uses conduction to transfer heat from a hot sauté pan to food with the aid of a small amount of fat. Heat then penetrates the food through conduction. High temperatures are used to sauté, and the foods are usually cut into small pieces to promote even cooking.

To sauté foods properly, begin by heating a sauté pan on the stove top, then add a small amount of fat. The fat should just cover the bottom of the pan. Heat the fat to the point where it just begins to smoke. The food to be cooked should be as dry as possible when it is added to the pan to promote browning and to prevent excessive spattering. Place the food in the pan in a single layer. (The pan should be just large enough to hold the food in a single layer; a pan that is too large may cause the fat to burn.) The heat should be adjusted so that the food cooks thoroughly; it should not be so hot that the outside of the food burns before the inside is cooked. The food should be turned or tossed periodically to develop the proper color. Larger items should be turned using tongs without piercing the surface. Smaller items are often turned by using the sauteuse's sloped sides to flip them back on top of themselves. When tossing sautéed foods, keep the pan in contact with the heat source as much as possible to prevent it from cooling. Sautéing sometimes includes the preparation of a sauce directly in the pan after the main item has been removed.

Stir-frying is a variation of sautéing. A wok is used instead of a sauté pan; the curved sides and rounded bottom of the wok diffuse heat efficiently and facilitate tossing and stirring. Otherwise, stir-frying procedures are the same as those outlined for sautéing and will not be discussed separately here.

▶ PROCEDURE FOR SAUTÉING FOODS

1 Cut, pound or otherwise prepare the food to be sautéed. Season and dredge it in flour, if desired.

2 Heat a sauté pan and add enough fat (typically, oil or clarified butter) to just cover the pan's bottom.

3 Add the food to the sauté pan in a single layer, presentation side down. Do not crowd the pan.

4 Adjust the temperature so that the food's exterior browns properly without burning and the interior cooks. The heat should be high enough to complete the cooking process before the food begins to stew in its own juices.

5 Turn or toss the food as needed. Avoid burns by not splashing hot fat.

6 Cook until done. Doneness is usually determined by timing or touch.

1 Heat a small amount of oil in the sauté pan before adding the food.

2 The sloped edge of the pan can be used to toss the food. The item being sautéed should be cooked quickly.

PAN-FRYING

Pan-frying shares similarities with both sautéing and deep-frying. It is a dry-heat cooking method in which heat is transferred by conduction from the pan to the food, using a moderate amount of fat. Heat is also transferred to the food from the hot fat by convection. Foods to be pan-fried are usually coated in breading. This forms a seal that keeps the food moist and prevents the hot fat from penetrating the food and causing it to become greasy. (Breading procedures are explained in Chapter 9, Mise en Place.)

To pan-fry foods properly, first heat the fat in a sauté pan. Use enough fat so that when the food to be cooked is added, the fat comes one-third to halfway up the item being cooked. The fat should be at a temperature somewhat lower than that used for sautéing; it should not smoke but should be hot enough so that when the food is added it crackles and spatters from the rapid vaporization of moisture. If the temperature is too low, the food will absorb excessive amounts of fat; if it is too high, the food will burn on the outside before the interior is fully cooked. When the food is properly browned on one side, use tongs to turn it without piercing. Always turn the food away from you to prevent being burned by any fat that may splash. When the food is fully cooked, remove it from the pan, drain it on absorbent paper and serve it immediately.

▶ PROCEDURE FOR PAN-FRYING FOODS

1 Cut, pound or otherwise prepare the food to be pan-fried; then bread, batter or flour it as desired.

2 Heat a moderate amount of fat or oil in a heavy pan—usually enough to cover the item one-third to halfway up its sides.

3 Add the food to the pan, being careful not to splash the hot fat.

4 Fry the food on one side until brown. Using tongs, turn and brown the other side. Generally, pan-fried foods are fully cooked when they are well browned on both sides.

5 Remove the food from the pan and drain it on absorbent paper before serving.

1 Use tongs to carefully place the item being pan-fried into a moderate amount of hot oil.

2 Turn the item to brown the other side.

3 Drain the cooked item on absorbent paper.

DEEP-FRYING

Deep-frying is a dry-heat cooking method that uses conduction and convection to transfer heat to food submerged in hot fat. Although conceptually similar to boiling, deep-frying is not a moist-heat cooking method because the liquid fat

▶ **recovery time** the length of time it takes a cooking medium such as fat or water to return to the desired cooking temperature after food is submerged in it

contains no water. A key difference between boiling and deep-frying is the temperature of the cooking medium. The boiling point, 212°F (100°C), is the hottest temperature at which food can be cooked in water. At this temperature, most foods require a long cooking period and surface sugars cannot caramelize. With deep-frying, temperatures up to 400°F (200°C) are used. These high temperatures cook food more quickly and allow the food's surface to brown.

Foods to be deep-fried are usually first coated in batter or breading. This preserves moisture and prevents the food from absorbing excessive quantities of fat. Foods to be deep-fried should be of a size and shape that allows them to float freely in the fat. Foods that are to be deep-fried together should be of uniform size and shape. Delicately flavored foods should not be deep-fried in the same fat used for more strongly flavored ones, as the former could develop an odd taste from residual flavors left in the fat. Deep-fried foods should cook thoroughly while developing an attractive deep golden-brown color.

Today, most deep-frying is done in specially designed commercial fryers. These deep-fat fryers have built-in thermostats, making temperature control more precise. Deep-frying foods in a saucepan on the stove top is discouraged because it is both difficult and dangerous. **Recovery time** is usually very slow, and temperatures are difficult to control. Also, the fat can spill easily, leading to injuries or creating a fire hazard.

To deep-fry food, first heat the fat or oil to a temperature between 325°F and 375°F (160°C and 190°C). The cooking medium's temperature can be adjusted within this range to allow the interior of thicker foods or frozen foods to cook before their surfaces become too dark. The fat must be hot enough to quickly seal the surface of the food so that it does not become excessively greasy, yet it should not be so hot that the food's surface burns before the interior is cooked.

The basket method of deep-frying.

There are two methods of deep-frying: the basket method and the swimming method. The **basket method** uses a basket to hold foods that are breaded, are individually quick-frozen or otherwise will not tend to stick together during cooking. The basket is removed from the fryer and filled as much as two-thirds full of product. (Do not fill the basket while it is hanging over the fat, as this allows unnecessary salt and food particles to fall into the fat, shortening its life.) The filled basket is then submerged in the hot fat. When cooking is completed, the basket is used to remove the foods from the fat and hold them while excess fat drains off.

A variation on this procedure is the **double-basket method.** It is used because many foods float as they deep-fry. This may produce undesirable results because the portion of the food not submerged may not cook. To prevent this and to promote even cooking, a second basket is placed over the food held in the first basket, keeping the food submerged in the fat.

The double-basket method of deep-frying.

Most battered foods initially sink to the bottom when placed in hot fat, then rise to the top as they cook. Because they would stick to a basket, the **swimming method** is used for these foods. With the swimming method, battered foods are carefully dropped directly into the hot fat. (Baskets are not used.) They will rise to the top as they cook. When the surface that is in contact with the fat is properly browned, the food is turned over with a spider or a pair of tongs so that it can cook evenly on both sides. When done, the product is removed and drained, again using a spider or tongs.

▶ PROCEDURE FOR DEEP-FRYING FOODS

1 Cut, trim or otherwise prepare the food to be deep-fried. Bread or batter it, as desired.

2 Heat the oil or fat to the desired temperature.

3 Using either the basket method or swimming method, carefully place the food in the hot fat.

4 Deep-fry the food until done. Doneness is usually determined by timing, surface color or sampling.

The swimming method of deep-frying

5 Remove the deep-fried food from the fryer and hold it over the cooking fat, allowing the excess fat to drain off.

6 Transfer the food to a hotel pan either lined with absorbent paper or fitted with a rack.

7 If the deep-fried items are to be held for later service, place them under a heat lamp; steam tables will not keep fried foods properly hot.

MOIST-HEAT COOKING METHODS

Cooking with moist heat is the process of applying heat to food by submerging it directly into a hot liquid or by exposing it to steam.

POACHING

Poaching is a moist-heat cooking method that uses convection to transfer heat from a liquid to a food. It is most often associated with delicately flavored foods that do not require lengthy cooking times to tenderize them, such as eggs, fruit or fish.

For poaching, the food is placed in a liquid held at temperatures between 160°F and 180°F (71°C and 82°C). The surface of the liquid should show only slight movement, but no bubbles. It is important to maintain the desired temperature throughout the cooking process. Do not allow the liquid to reach a boil, since the agitation will cause meats to become tough and stringy and will destroy tender foods such as fresh fruit or fish.

The flavor of the poaching liquid strongly affects the ultimate flavor of the finished product, so stock, court bouillon or broth is generally used. The liquid used to poach a food is sometimes used to make an accompanying sauce.

Poaching (160°F–180°F/71°C–82°C)

There are two methods of poaching: submersion poaching and shallow poaching. For **submersion poaching,** the food is completely covered with the cooking liquid. There should not be too much excess liquid, however, as this could leach away much of the food's flavor. Nor should there be too little, as that could leave a portion of the food exposed, preventing it from cooking.

For **shallow poaching,** the food is placed in just enough liquid to come approximately halfway up its sides. The liquid, called a **cuisson,** is brought to a simmer on the stove top. The pan is then covered with a piece of buttered parchment paper or a lid, and cooking is completed either on the stove top or in the oven. Shallow poaching combines aspects of poaching and steaming.

Simmering (185°F–205°F/85°C–96°C)

▶ PROCEDURE FOR POACHING FOODS

1 Cut, trim or otherwise prepare the food to be poached.

2 Bring an adequate amount of cooking liquid to the desired starting temperature. (For some items, the cooking liquid is first brought to a boil and then reduced to the poaching temperature.) Place the food in the liquid.

3 For submersion poaching, the liquid should completely cover the food.

4 For shallow poaching, the liquid should come approximately halfway up the side of the food. If shallow poaching, cover the pan with a piece of buttered parchment paper or a lid.

5 Maintaining the proper temperature, poach the food to the desired doneness in the oven or on the stove top. Doneness is generally determined by timing, internal temperature or tenderness.

6 Remove the food and hold it for service in a portion of the cooking liquid or, using an ice bath, cool it in the cooking liquid.

7 The cooking liquid can sometimes be used to prepare an accompanying sauce or reserved for use in other dishes.

Boiling (212°F/100°C)

1 Season the poaching liquid as desired and bring it to the correct temperature.

2 Carefully place the food item into the poaching liquid.

3 Remove the cooked food from the poaching liquid.

SIMMERING

Simmering is another moist-heat cooking method that uses convection to transfer heat from a liquid to a food. It is often associated with foods that need to be tenderized through long, slow, moist cooking, such as less tender cuts of meat. Properly simmered foods should be moist and very tender. For simmering, the food is submerged in a liquid held at temperatures between 185°F and 205°F (85°C and 96°C). Because simmering temperatures are slightly higher than those used for poaching, there should be more action on the liquid's surface, with a few air bubbles breaking through.

As with poaching, the liquid used for simmering has a great effect on the food's flavor. Be sure to use a well-flavored stock or broth and to add mirepoix, herbs and seasonings as needed.

▶ PROCEDURE FOR SIMMERING FOODS

1 Cut, trim or otherwise prepare the food to be simmered.
2 Bring an adequate amount of the cooking liquid to the appropriate temperature (some foods, especially smoked or cured items, are started in a cold liquid). There should be enough liquid to cover the food completely.
3 Add the food to the simmering liquid.

1 The item being simmered should be fully submerged in the seasoned liquid.

2 Remove the cooked item from the liquid.

4 Maintaining the proper cooking temperature throughout the process, simmer the food to the desired doneness. Doneness is generally determined by timing or tenderness.

5 Remove the item and hold it for service in a portion of the cooking liquid or, using an ice bath, cool the food in its cooking liquid.

BOILING

Boiling is another moist-heat cooking method that uses the process of convection to transfer heat from a liquid to a food. Boiling uses large amounts of rapidly bubbling liquid to cook foods. The turbulent waters and the relatively high temperatures cook foods more quickly than do poaching or simmering. Few foods, however, are cooked by true boiling. Most "boiled" meats are actually simmered. Even "hard-boiled" eggs are really only simmered. Starches such as pasta and potatoes are among the only types of food that are truly boiled.

Under normal atmospheric pressure at sea level, water boils at 212°F (100°C). The addition of other ingredients or a change in atmospheric pressure can change the boiling point, however. As altitude increases, the boiling point decreases because of the drop in atmospheric pressure. For every 1000 feet above sea level, the boiling point of water drops 2°F (1°C). In the mile-high city of Denver, for example, water boils at 203°F (95°C). Because the boiling temperature is lower, it will take longer to cook foods in Denver than in, for example, Miami.

The addition of alcohol also lowers the boiling point of water because alcohol boils at about 175°F (80°C). In contrast, the addition of salt, sugar or other substances raises the boiling point slightly. This means that foods cooked in salted water cook faster because the boiling point is one or two degrees higher than normal.

Use as much water as practical when boiling food. Whenever food is added to boiling water, it lowers the water's temperature. The greater the amount of water, however, the faster it will return to the boil.

1 Bring the cooking liquid to a full boil. When the item being cooked is added to the liquid, its temperature will fall.

▶ PROCEDURE FOR BOILING FOODS

1 Bring an appropriate amount of a liquid to a boil over high heat. Add oil or seasonings, if desired.

2 Add the food to be boiled to the rapidly boiling water. Bring the liquid back to a boil and adjust the temperature to maintain the boil.

3 Cook until done. Doneness is usually determined by timing or texture.

4 Remove the boiled food from the cooking liquid, draining any excess liquid.

5 Serve the boiled food immediately. Some boiled foods can be refreshed in cold water and held for later service.

2 After a boiled item such as pasta is cooked, it may be drained through a colander.

STEAMING

Steaming is a moist-heat cooking method that uses the process of convection to transfer heat from the steam to the food being cooked. It is most often associated with tender, delicately flavored foods, such as fish and vegetables, which do not require long cooking times. Steaming tends to enhance a food's natural flavor and helps to retain its nutrients. Properly steamed foods should be moist and tender. Additional flavor can be introduced by adding wine, stock, aromatics, spices or herbs to the liquid used as the steaming medium. The steaming liquid can also often be used to make a sauce to be served with the steamed food.

The food to be steamed is usually placed in a basket or rack above a boiling liquid. The food should not touch the liquid; it should be positioned so that the steam can circulate around it. (Some foods, such as shellfish and ears of corn,

Table 10.2		MOIST-HEAT COOKING METHODS	
METHOD	**LIQUID'S TEMPERATURE**	**LIQUID'S CONDITION**	**USES**
Poaching	160–180°F 71–82°C	Liquid moves slightly but no bubbles	Eggs, fish, fruits
Simmering	185–205°F 85–96°C	Small bubbles break through the liquid's surface	Meats, stews, chicken
Boiling	212°F 100°C	Large bubbles and rapid movement	Vegetables, pasta
Steaming	212°F or higher 100°C or higher	Food is in contact only with the steam generated by a boiling liquid	Vegetables, fish, shellfish

however, can be placed directly in a shallow pool of boiling water.) A lid should be placed on the steaming pot to trap the steam and also create a slight pressure within the pot, which speeds the cooking process.

Another type of steaming uses a convection steamer. Convection steamers use pressurized steam to cook food very quickly in an enclosed chamber. Convection steamer cooking does not result in a flavored liquid that can be used to make a sauce.

Steamed foods should be served immediately. If held for later service, they should be refreshed and refrigerated until used.

▶ PROCEDURE FOR STEAMING FOODS

1 Cut, trim or otherwise prepare the food to be steamed.

2 If a convection steamer is not being used, prepare a steaming liquid and bring it to a boil in a covered pan or double boiler.

3 Place the food to be steamed on a rack, in a basket or on a perforated pan in a single layer. Do not crowd the items. Place the rack, basket or pan over the boiling liquid.

4 Alternatively, place the food in a shallow pool of the cooking liquid.

5 Cover the cooking assemblage and cook to the desired doneness. Doneness is usually determined by timing, color or tenderness.

1 Trim items before steaming them so that they cook evenly.

2 A perforated hotel pan can be set over a deeper pan of water, covered and used as a steamer.

COMBINATION COOKING METHODS

Some cooking methods employ both dry-heat and moist-heat cooking techniques. The two principal combination methods are braising and stewing. In both methods, the first step is usually to brown the main item using dry heat. The second step is to complete cooking by simmering the food in a liquid. Combination methods are often used for less tender but flavorful cuts of meat as well as for poultry and some vegetables.

BRAISING

Braised foods benefit from the best qualities of both dry- and moist-heat cooking methods. Foods to be braised are usually large pieces that are first browned in a small amount of fat at high temperatures. As with sautéing, heat is transferred from the pan to the food mainly by the process of conduction. Vegetables and seasonings are added, and enough sauce or liquid is added to come one-third to halfway up the item being cooked. The pan is covered, and the heat is reduced. The food is then cooked at low heat, using a combination of simmering and steaming to transfer heat from the liquid (conduction) and the air (convection) to the food. This can be done on the stove top or in the oven. A long, slow cooking period helps tenderize the main item. Braised foods are usually served with a sauce made from the cooking liquid.

▶ PROCEDURE FOR BRAISING FOODS

1 Cut, trim or otherwise prepare the food to be braised. Dredge it in flour, if desired.

2 Heat a small amount of fat in a heavy pan.

3 Sear the food on all sides. Some foods—notably, meats—should be removed from the pan after they are seared.

4 Add any other ingredients and sauté.

5 Add flour or roux, if used.

6 Add the cooking liquid; it should partially cover the food being braised.

7 Add aromatics and seasonings.

8 If the principal item was removed, return it to the pan.

9 Cover the pan and bring the cooking liquid to a simmer. Cook slowly, either on the stove top or in an oven at 250°F–300°F (120°C–150°C). Baste and turn the food as needed.

10 When the principal item is cooked, remove it from the pan and hold it in a warm place.

11 Prepare a sauce from the braising liquid if desired. This may be done by reducing the liquid on the stove top to intensify its flavors. If the food was braised in an unthickened stock, the stock may now be thickened using a roux, arrowroot or cornstarch. Strain the sauce or, if desired, purée the mirepoix and other ingredients and return them to the sauce. Adjust the sauce's consistency as desired.

STEWING

Stewing also uses a combination of dry- and moist-heat cooking methods. Stewing is most often associated with smaller pieces of food that are first cooked either by browning them in a small amount of fat or oil or by blanching them in a liquid. Cooking is then finished in a liquid or sauce. Stewed foods have enough liquid added to cover them completely and are simmered at a constant temperature until tender. Cooking time is generally shorter for stewing than for braising because the main items are smaller.

1 The item being braised is first browned in fat.

2 Liquid is added to the pan.

3 The item can be basted with the liquid during cooking.

▶ PROCEDURE FOR STEWING FOODS

1 Trim and cut the food to be stewed into small, uniform-sized pieces. Dredge the pieces in flour, if desired.

2 Heat a small amount of fat in a heavy pan. Then sear the food on all sides developing color as desired.

3 Add any other ingredients and sauté.

4 Add flour or roux.

5 Gradually add the cooking liquid, stirring to prevent lumps. The liquid should completely cover the principal items.

6 Bring the stew to the appropriate temperature. Cover and place in the oven at 250°F–300°F (120°C–150°C) or continue to simmer on the stove top until the principal items are tender.

7 Remove the principal items and hold them in a warm place.

8 Thicken the sauce as desired.

9 Return the principal items to the stew. If not added during the cooking process, vegetables and other garnishes may be cooked separately and added to the finished stew.

1 The item being stewed is first browned in a small amount of fat.

2 Flour is added to make a roux.

3 Liquid is added to the pan.

4 Degrease the finished stew as necessary.

CONCLUSION

Cooking is the transfer of heat energy to foods by conduction, convection or radiation. Cooking changes the molecular structure of certain nutrients. When heat is applied, proteins coagulate, starches gelatinize, sugars caramelize, fats melt and water evaporates. Foods can be cooked using a variety of methods. Some use dry heat: broiling, grilling, roasting and baking, sautéing, pan-frying and deep-frying. Others use moist heat: poaching, simmering, boiling and steaming. Still others use a combination of the two: braising and stewing. The method used affects the texture, appearance and flavor of the cooked foods. You must understand these principles in order to ensure that foods are cooked properly.

1 Describe the differences between conduction and convection. Identify four cooking methods that rely on both conduction and convection to heat foods. Explain your choices.

2 Identify two cooking methods that rely on infrared heat. What is the principal difference between these methods?

3 At the same temperature, will a food cook faster in a convection oven or a conventional oven? Explain your answer.

4 Describe the process of caramelization and its significance in food preparation. Will a braised food have a caramelized surface? Explain your answer.

5 Describe the process of coagulation and its significance in food preparation. Will a pure fat coagulate if heated? Explain your answer.

6 Describe the process of gelatinization and its significance in food preparation. Will a pure fat gelatinize? Explain your answer.

7 Name and describe two styles of deep-frying.

WHAT I LOVE ABOUT COOKING IS THAT AFTER A HARD DAY, THERE IS SOMETHING COMFORTING ABOUT THE FACT THAT IF YOU MELT BUTTER AND ADD FLOUR, THEN HOT STOCK, IT WILL GET THICK! IT'S A SURE THING. IT'S A SURE THING IN A WORLD WHERE NOTHING IS SURE!

—Nora Ephron, American author and filmmaker (1941–)

STOCKS
AND SAUCES

PRIMITIVO WINE BAR, Colorado Springs, CO
John Broening, Executive Chef

AFTER STUDYING THIS
CHAPTER, YOU WILL BE
ABLE TO:

▶ prepare a variety of stocks
▶ recognize and classify sauces
▶ use thickening agents properly
▶ prepare a variety of classic and
  modern sauces

A **stock** is a flavored liquid. A good stock is the key to a great soup, sauce or braised dish. The French appropriately call a stock *fond* ("base"), as stocks are the basis for many classic and modern dishes.

A **sauce** is a thickened liquid used to flavor and enhance other foods. A good sauce adds flavor, moisture, richness and visual appeal. A sauce should complement food; it should never disguise it. A sauce can be hot or cold, sweet or savory, smooth or chunky.

Although the thought of preparing stocks and sauces may be intimidating, the procedures are really quite simple. Carefully follow the basic procedures outlined in this chapter, use high-quality ingredients and, with practice and experience, you will soon be producing fine stocks and sauces.

This chapter addresses classical hot sauces as well as coulis, contemporary broths, flavored oils, salsas and relishes. Cold sauces, generally based on mayonnaise, are discussed in Chapter 24, Salads and Salad Dressings; dessert sauces are discussed in Chapter 34, Custards, Creams, Frozen Desserts and Dessert Sauces.

▶ STOCKS

There are several types of stocks. Although they are all made from a combination of bones, vegetables, seasonings and liquids, each type uses specific procedures to give it distinctive characteristics.

A **white stock** is made by simmering chicken, veal or beef bones in water with vegetables and seasonings. The stock remains relatively colorless during the cooking process.

A **brown stock** is made from chicken, veal, beef or game bones and vegetables, all of which are caramelized before being simmered in water with seasonings. The stock has a rich, dark color.

Both a **fish stock** and a **fumet** are made by slowly cooking fish bones or crustacean shells and vegetables without coloring them, then simmering them in water with seasonings for a short time. For a fumet, wine and lemon juice are also added. The resulting stock or fumet is a strongly flavored, relatively colorless liquid.

A **court bouillon** is made by simmering vegetables and seasonings in water and an acidic liquid such as vinegar or wine. It is used to poach fish or vegetables.

INGREDIENTS

The basic ingredients of any stock are bones, a vegetable mixture known as a **mirepoix,** seasonings and water.

BONES

Bones are the most important ingredient; they add flavor, richness and color to the stock. Traditionally, the kitchen or butcher shop saved the day's bones to make stock. But because many meats and poultry items are now purchased precut or portioned, food service operations often purchase bones specifically for stock making.

Different bones release their flavor at different rates. Even though the bones are cut into 3- to 4-inch (8- to 10-centimeter) pieces, a stock made entirely of beef and/or veal bones requires six to eight hours of cooking time, while a stock made entirely from chicken bones requires only five to six hours.

Beef and Veal Bones

The best bones for beef and veal stock are from younger animals. They contain a higher percentage of **cartilage** and other **connective tissue** than do bones from more mature animals. Connective tissue has a high **collagen** content. Through the cooking process, the collagen is converted into **gelatin** and water. The gelatin adds richness and body to the finished stock.

The best beef and veal bones are back, neck and shank bones, as they have high collagen contents. Beef and veal bones should be cut with a meat saw into small pieces, approximately 3 to 4 inches (8 to 10 centimeters) long, so that they can release as much flavor as possible while the stock cooks.

Chicken Bones

The best bones for chicken stock are from the neck and back. If a whole chicken carcass is used, it can be cut up for easier handling.

Fish Bones

The best bones for fish stock are from lean fish such as sole, flounder, whiting or turbot. Bones from fatty fish (for example, salmon, tuna and swordfish) do not produce good stock because of their high fat content and distinctive flavors. The entire fish carcass can be used, but it should be cut up with a cleaver or heavy knife for easy handling and even extraction of flavors. After cutting, the pieces should be rinsed in cold water to remove blood, loose scales and other impurities.

Other Bones

Lamb, turkey, game and ham bones can also be used for white or brown stocks. Although mixing bones is generally acceptable, be careful of blending strongly flavored bones, such as those from lamb or game, with beef, veal or chicken bones. The former's strong flavors may not be appropriate or desirable in the finished product.

MIREPOIX

A mirepoix is a mixture of onions, carrots and celery added to a stock to enhance its flavor and aroma. Although chefs differ on the ratio of vegetables, generally a mixture of 50 percent onions, 25 percent carrots and 25 percent celery, by weight, is used. (Unless otherwise noted, any reference to mirepoix in this book refers to this ratio.) For a brown stock, onion skins may be used to add color. It is not necessary to peel the carrots or celery because flavor, not aesthetics, is important.

The size in which the mirepoix is chopped is determined by the stock's cooking time: The shorter the cooking time, the smaller the vegetables must be chopped to ensure that all possible flavor is extracted. For white or brown stocks made from beef or veal bones, the vegetables should be coarsely chopped into large, 1- to 2-inch (2½- to 5-centimeter) pieces. For chicken and fish stocks, the vegetables should be more finely chopped into ½-inch (1¼-centimeter) pieces.

A white mirepoix is made by replacing the carrots in a standard mirepoix with parsnips and adding mushrooms and leeks. Some chefs prefer to use a white mirepoix when making a white stock, as it produces a lighter product. Sometimes parsnips, mushrooms and leeks are added to a standard mirepoix for additional flavors.

▶ **cartilage** also known as gristle, a tough, elastic, whitish connective tissue that helps give structure to an animal's body

▶ **connective tissue** tissue found throughout an animal's body that binds together and supports other tissues such as muscles

▶ **collagen** a protein found in nearly all connective tissue; it dissolves when cooked with moisture

▶ **gelatin** a tasteless and odorless mixture of proteins (especially collagen) extracted from boiling bones, connective tissue and other animal parts; when dissolved in a hot liquid and then cooled, it forms a jellylike substance used as a thickener and stabilizer

▶ **matignon** a standard mirepoix plus diced smoked bacon or smoked ham and, depending on the dish, mushrooms and herbs; sometimes called an edible mirepoix, it is usually cut more uniformly than a standard mirepoix and left in the finished dish as a garnish

Mirepoix Ingredients

SEASONINGS

Principal stock seasonings are peppercorns, bay leaves, thyme, parsley stems and optionally, garlic. These seasonings generally can be left whole. A stock is cooked long enough for all of their flavors to be extracted, so there is no reason to chop or grind them. Seasonings generally are added to the stock at the start of cooking. Some chefs do not add seasonings to beef or veal stock until midway through the cooking process, however, because of the extended cooking times. Seasonings can be added as a sachet d'épices or a bouquet garni.

Salt, an otherwise important seasoning, is not added to stock. Because a stock has a variety of uses, it is impossible for the chef to know how much salt to add when preparing it. If, for example, the stock was seasoned to taste with salt, the chef could not reduce it later; salt is not lost through reduction, and the concentrated product would taste too salty. Similarly, seasoning the stock to taste with salt could prevent the chef from adding other ingredients that are high in salt when finishing a recipe. Unlike many seasonings whose flavors must be incorporated into a product through lengthy cooking periods, salt can be added at any time during the cooking process with the same effect.

PRINCIPLES OF STOCK MAKING

The following principles, outlined in Figure 11.1, apply to all stocks. You should follow them in order to achieve the highest-quality stocks possible.

A. START THE STOCK IN COLD WATER

The ingredients should always be covered with cold water. When bones are covered with cold water, blood and other impurities dissolve. As the water heats, the impurities coagulate and rise to the surface, where they can be removed easily by skimming. If the bones were covered with hot water, the impurities would coagulate more quickly and remain dispersed in the stock without rising to the top, making the stock cloudy.

If the water level falls below the bones during cooking, add water to cover them. Flavor cannot be extracted from bones not under water, and bones exposed to the air will darken and discolor a white stock.

B. SIMMER THE STOCK GENTLY

The stock should be brought to a boil and then reduced to a simmer, a temperature of approximately 185°F (85°C). While simmering, the ingredients release their flavors into the liquid. If kept at a simmer, the liquid will remain clear as it reduces and the stock develops.

Never boil a stock for any length of time. Rapid boiling of a stock, even for a few minutes, causes impurities and fats to blend with the liquid, making it cloudy.

C. SKIM THE STOCK FREQUENTLY

A stock should be skimmed often to remove the fat and impurities that rise to the surface during cooking. If they are not removed, they may make the stock cloudy.

D. STRAIN THE STOCK CAREFULLY

Once a stock finishes cooking, the liquid must be separated from the bones, vegetables and other solid ingredients. In order to keep the liquid clear, it is important not to disturb the solid ingredients when removing the liquid. This is easily accomplished if the stock is cooked in a steam kettle or stockpot with a spigot at the bottom.

If the stock is cooked in a standard stockpot, to strain it:

1 Skim as much fat and as many impurities from the surface as possible before removing the stockpot from the heat.

Start the stock in cold water.

Simmer the stock gently.

Skim the stock frequently.

Strain the stock carefully.

Cool the stock quickly.

Store the stock properly.

Degrease the stock.

FIGURE 11.1 ▶ Principles of stock making

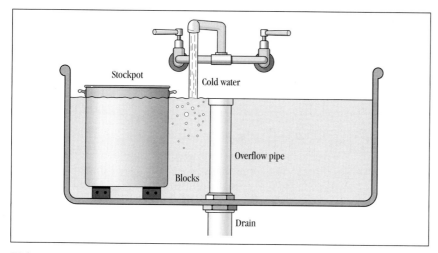

FIGURE 11.2 ▶ Venting a stockpot

2 After removing the pot from the heat, carefully ladle the stock from the pot without stirring it.

3 Strain the stock through a china cap lined with several layers of cheesecloth.

E. COOL THE STOCK QUICKLY

Most stocks are prepared in large quantities, cooled and held for later use. Great care must be taken when cooling a stock to prevent food-borne illnesses or souring. To cool a stock quickly and safely:

1 Keep the stock in a metal container. A plastic container insulates the stock and delays cooling.

2 Vent the stockpot in an empty sink by placing it on blocks or a rack. This allows water to circulate on all sides and below the pot when the sink is filled with water. See Figure 11.2.

3 Install an overflow pipe in the drain, and fill the sink with cold water or a combination of cold water and ice. Make sure that the weight of the stockpot is adequate to keep it from tipping over.

4 Let cold water run into the sink and drain out the overflow pipe. Stir the stock frequently to facilitate even, quick cooling.

In addition to this venting procedure, cooling wands can be used to speed the cooling of stocks, soups, sauces and other liquids. These wands (also known as ice paddles) are hollow plastic containers that can be filled with water or ice, sealed, frozen and then used to stir and cool liquids. Clean and sanitize the wand after each use to prevent cross-contamination.

F. STORE THE STOCK PROPERLY

Once the stock is cooled, transfer it to a sanitized covered container (either plastic or metal) and store it in the refrigerator. As the stock chills, fat rises to its surface and solidifies. If left intact, this layer of fat helps preserve the stock. Stocks can be stored for up to one week under refrigeration or frozen for several months.

G. DEGREASE THE STOCK

Degreasing a stock is simple: When a stock is refrigerated, fat rises to its surface, hardens and is easily lifted or scraped away before the stock is reheated.

Lifting fat from the surface of a cold stock.

▶ **degrease** to remove fat from the surface of a liquid such as a stock or sauce by skimming, scraping or lifting congealed fat

WHITE STOCK

A white or neutral stock may be made from beef, veal or chicken bones. The finished stock should have a good flavor, good clarity, high gelatin content and little or no color. Veal bones are most often used, but any combination of beef, veal or chicken bones may be used.

BLANCHING BONES

Chefs disagree on whether the bones for a white stock should be blanched to remove impurities. Some chefs argue that blanching keeps the stock as clear and colorless as possible; others argue that blanching removes nutrients and flavor.

▶ PROCEDURE FOR BLANCHING BONES

If you choose to blanch the bones:

1 Wash the cut-up bones, place them in a stockpot and cover them with cold water.
2 Bring the water to a boil over high heat.
3 As soon as the water boils, skim the rising impurities. Drain the water from the bones and discard it.
4 Refill the pot with cold water, and proceed with the stock recipe.

RECIPE 11.1   WHITE STOCK

Yield: 2 gal. (8 lt)

Bones, veal, chicken or beef	15 lb.	7 kg
Cold water	3 gal.	11 lt
Mirepoix	2 lb.	1 kg
Sachet:		
Bay leaves	2	2
Dried thyme	½ tsp.	2 ml
Peppercorns, crushed	½ tsp.	2 ml
Parsley stems	8	8

1 Cut the washed bones into pieces approximately 3–4 inches (8–10 centimeters) long.
2 Place the bones in a stockpot and cover them with cold water. If blanching, bring the water to a boil, skimming off the scum that rises to the surface. Drain off the water and the impurities. Then add the 3 gallons (11 liters) of cold water and bring to a boil. Reduce to a simmer.
3 If not blanching the bones, bring the cold water to a boil. Reduce to a simmer and skim the scum that forms.
4 Add the mirepoix and sachet to the simmering stock.
5 Continue simmering and skimming the stock for 6 to 8 hours. (If only chicken bones are used, simmer for 5 to 6 hours.)
6 Strain, cool and refrigerate.

Approximate values per 1-fl.-oz. (30-ml) serving: **Calories** 4, **Total fat** 0.1 g, **Saturated fat** 0.1 g, **Cholesterol** 0 mg, **Sodium** 5 mg, **Total carbohydrates** 0 g, **Protein** 0.2 g, **Claims**—fat free; very low sodium

BROWN STOCK

A brown stock is made from chicken, veal, beef or game bones. The finished stock should have a good flavor, rich dark brown color, good body and high gelatin content.

The primary differences between a brown stock and a white stock are that for a brown stock, the bones and mirepoix are caramelized before being simmered and a tomato product is added. These extra steps provide the finished stock with a rich dark color and a more intense flavor.

CARAMELIZING

Caramelization is the process of browning the sugars found on the surface of most foods. This gives the stock its characteristic flavor and color.

▶ PROCEDURE FOR CARAMELIZING BONES

For caramelizing, do not wash or blanch the bones as this retards browning. To caramelize:

1 Place the cut-up bones in a roasting pan one layer deep. It is better to roast several pans of bones than to overfill one pan.

2 Roast the bones for approximately 1 hour in a hot oven (375°F/190°C). Stirring occasionally, brown the bones thoroughly, but do not allow them to burn.

3 Transfer the roasted bones from the pan to the stockpot.

DEGLAZING THE PAN

After the bones are caramelized, the excess fat should be removed and reserved for future use. The caramelized and coagulated proteins remaining in the roasting pan are very flavorful. To utilize them, you **deglaze** the pan.

▶ PROCEDURE FOR DEGLAZING THE PAN

1 Place the pan on the stove top over medium heat, and add enough water to cover the bottom of the pan approximately ½ inch (12 millimeters) deep.

2 Stir and scrape the pan bottom to dissolve and remove all the caramelized materials while the water heats.

3 Pour the deglazing liquid (also known as the deglazing liquor) over the bones in the stockpot.

▶ PROCEDURE FOR CARAMELIZING MIREPOIX

1 Add a little of the reserved fat from the roasted bones to the roasting pan after it has been deglazed. (Or use a sautoir large enough to contain all the mirepoix comfortably.)

2 Sauté the mirepoix, browning all the vegetables well and evenly without burning them.

3 Add the caramelized mirepoix to the stockpot.

Most any tomato product can be used in a brown stock: fresh tomatoes, canned whole tomatoes, crushed tomatoes, tomato purée or paste. If using a concentrated tomato product such as paste or purée, use approximately half the amount by weight of fresh or canned tomatoes. The tomato product should be added to the stockpot when the mirepoix is added.

▶ **deglaze** to swirl or stir a liquid (usually wine or stock) in a sauté pan or other pan to dissolve cooked food particles remaining on the bottom; the resulting mixture often becomes the base for a sauce

▶ **remouillage** (rhur-moo-yahj) French for "rewetting"; a stock produced by reusing the bones left from making another stock. After draining the original stock from the stockpot, add fresh mirepoix, a new sachet and enough water to cover the bones and mirepoix, and a second stock can be made. A remouillage is treated like the original stock; allow it to simmer for four to five hours before straining. A remouillage will not be as clear or as flavorful as the original stock, however. It is often used to make glazes or in place of water when making stocks.

RECIPE 11.2   BROWN STOCK

Yield: 2 gal. (8 lt)

Bones, veal or beef, cut in 3- to 4-in. (8- to 10-cm) pieces	15 lb.	7 kg
Cold water	3 gal.	11 lt
Mirepoix	2 lb.	1 kg
Tomato paste	8 oz.	250 g
Sachet:		
Bay leaves	2	2
Dried thyme	½ tsp.	2 ml
Peppercorns, crushed	½ tsp.	2 ml
Garlic cloves, crushed	3	3
Parsley stems	12	12

1 Place the bones in a roasting pan, one layer deep, and brown in a 375°F (190°C) oven. Turn the bones occasionally to brown them evenly.

2 Remove the bones and place them in a stockpot. Pour off the fat from the roasting pan and reserve it.

3 Deglaze the roasting pan with part of the cold water.

4 Add the deglazing liquor and the rest of the cold water to the bones, covering them completely. Bring to a boil and reduce to a simmer.

5 Add a portion of the reserved fat to the roasting pan and sauté the mirepoix until evenly browned. Then add it to the simmering stock.

6 Add the tomato paste and sachet to the stock and continue to simmer for 6 to 8 hours, skimming as necessary.

7 Strain, cool and refrigerate.

Approximate values per 1-fl.-oz. (30-ml) serving: **Calories** 3, **Total fat** 0 g, **Saturated fat** 0 g, **Cholesterol** 0.3 mg, **Sodium** 105 mg, **Total carbohydrates** 0 g, **Protein** 0 g, **Claims**—fat free; low sodium

1 Caramelizing the bones.

2 Deglazing the pan with water.

3 Caramelizing the mirepoix.

4 Adding the proper amount of water.

FISH STOCK AND FISH FUMET

A fish stock and a fish fumet (foo-may) are similar and can be used interchangeably in most recipes. Both are clear with a pronounced fish flavor and very light body. A fumet, however, is more strongly flavored and aromatic and contains an acidic ingredient such as white wine and/or lemon juice.

The fish bones and crustacean shells used to make a fish stock or fumet should be washed but never blanched because blanching removes too much flavor. They may be **sweated** without browning if desired, however. Because of the size and structure of fish bones and crustacean shells, stocks and fumets made from them require much less cooking time than even a chicken stock; 30 to 45 minutes is usually sufficient to extract full flavor. Mirepoix or other vegetables should be cut small so that all of their flavors can be extracted during the short cooking time.

The procedure for making a fish stock is very similar to that for making a white stock.

▶ **sweat** to cook a food in a pan (usually covered), without browning, over low heat until the item softens and releases moisture; sweating allows the food to release its flavor more quickly when cooked with other foods

FISH STOCK

RECIPE 11.3

Yield: 1 gal. (4 lt)

Fish bones or crustacean shells	10 lb.	4.5 kg
Water	5 qts.	5 lt
Mirepoix, small dice	1 lb.	450 g
Mushroom trimmings	8 oz.	250 g
Sachet:		
Bay leaves	2	2
Dried thyme	½ tsp.	2 ml
Peppercorns, crushed	¼ tsp.	1 ml
Parsley stems	8	8

1 Combine all ingredients in a stockpot.
2 Bring to a simmer and skim impurities as necessary.
3 Simmer for 30 to 45 minutes.
4 Strain, cool and refrigerate.

Approximate values per 1-fl.-oz. (30-ml) serving: **Calories** 5, **Total fat** 0 g, **Saturated fat** 0 g, **Cholesterol** 0 mg, **Sodium** 100 mg, **Total carbohydrates** 0 g, **Protein** 1 g, **Claims**—fat free; low sodium

A fish stock is sometimes used to make a fish fumet; if so, the resulting product is very strongly flavored. A fish fumet is also flavored with white wine and lemon juice. When making a fumet, sweat the bones and vegetables before adding the cooking liquid and seasonings.

FISH FUMET

RECIPE 11.4

Yield: 2 gal. (8 lt)

Whole butter	2 oz.	60 g
Onion, small dice	1 lb.	500 g
Parsley stems	12	12
Fish bones	10 lb.	5 kg
Dry white wine	1½ pt.	750 ml
Lemon juice	2 fl. oz.	60 ml
Cold water or fish stock	7 qt.	7 lt
Mushroom trimmings	2 oz.	60 g
Fresh thyme	1 sprig	1 sprig
Lemon slices	10	10

1 Melt the butter in a stockpot.
2 Add the onion, parsley stems and fish bones. Cover the pot and sweat the bones over low heat.

3 Sprinkle the bones with the white wine and lemon juice.
4 Add the cold water or fish stock, mushroom trimmings, thyme and lemon slices. Bring to a boil, reduce to a simmer and cook approximately 30 minutes, skimming frequently.
5 Strain, cool and refrigerate.

Approximate values per 1-fl.-oz. (30-ml) serving: **Calories** 5, **Total fat** 0.7 g, **Saturated fat** 0.2 g, **Cholesterol** 0.5 mg, **Sodium** 90 g, **Total carbohydrates** 0 g, **Protein** 1 g, **Claims**—fat free; low sodium

1 Sweating the onions, parsley stems and fish bones.

2 Adding cold water and seasonings.

VEGETABLE STOCK

A good vegetable stock should be clear and light-colored. Because no animal products are used, it has no gelatin content. A vegetable stock can be used instead of a meat-based stock in most recipes. This substitution is useful when preparing vegetarian dishes or as a lighter, more healthful alternative when preparing sauces and soups. Although almost any combination of vegetables can be used for stock making, more variety is not always better. Sometimes a vegetable stock made with one or two vegetables that complement the finished dish particularly well will produce better results than a stock made with many vegetables.

RECIPE 11.5

VEGETABLE STOCK

Yield: 1 gal. (4 lt)

Vegetable oil	2 fl. oz.	60 ml
Mirepoix, small dice	2 lb.	900 g
Leek, whites and greens, chopped	8 oz.	250 g
Garlic cloves, chopped	4	4
Fennel, small dice	4 oz.	120 g
Turnip, diced	2 oz.	60 g
Tomato, diced	2 oz.	60 g
White wine	8 fl. oz.	250 ml
Water	1 gal.	4 lt
Sachet:		
Bay leaf	1	1
Dried thyme	½ tsp.	2 ml
Peppercorns, crushed	¼ tsp.	1 ml
Parsley stems	8	8

1 Heat the oil. Add the vegetables and sweat for 10 minutes.
2 Add the white wine, water and sachet.
3 Bring the mixture to a boil, reduce to a simmer and cook for 45 minutes.
4 Strain, cool and refrigerate.

Approximate values per 1-fl.-oz. (30-ml) serving: **Calories** 5, **Total fat** 0 g, **Saturated fat** 0 g, **Cholesterol** 0 mg, **Sodium** 0 mg, **Total carbohydrates** 0 g, **Protein** 0 g, **Claims**—fat free; low calorie

COURT BOUILLON

A court bouillon (bool-yawn), though not actually a stock, is prepared in much the same manner as stocks, so it is included here. A court bouillon (French for "short broth") is a flavored liquid, usually water and wine or vinegar, in which vegetables and seasonings have been simmered to impart their flavors and aromas.

Court bouillon is most commonly used to poach foods such as fish and shellfish. Recipes vary depending upon the foods to be poached. Although a court bouillon can be made in advance and refrigerated for later use, its simplicity lends itself to fresh preparation whenever needed.

COURT BOUILLON   RECIPE 11.6

Yield: 1 gal. (4 lt)

Water	1 gal.	4 lt
Vinegar	6 fl. oz.	180 ml
Lemon juice	2 fl. oz.	60 ml
Mirepoix	1 lb. 8 oz.	650 g
Peppercorns, crushed	1 tsp.	5 ml
Bay leaves	4	4
Dried thyme	pinch	pinch
Parsley stems	1 bunch	1 bunch

1 Combine all ingredients and bring to a boil.
2 Reduce to a simmer and cook for 45 minutes.
3 Strain and use immediately or cool and refrigerate.

Approximate values per 1-fl.-oz. (30-ml) serving: **Calories** 3, **Total fat** 0 g, **Saturated fat** 0 g, **Cholesterol** 0 mg, **Sodium** 0 mg, **Total carbohydrates** 0 g, **Protein** 0 g, **Claims**—fat free; low sodium

Note: This recipe can be used for poaching almost any fish, but it is particularly well suited to salmon, trout and shellfish. When poaching freshwater fish, replace the water and vinegar with equal parts white wine and water.

COMMERCIAL BASES

Commercially produced flavor (or convenience) bases are widely used in food service operations. They are powdered or paste flavorings added to water to create stocks or, when used in smaller amounts, to enhance the flavor of sauces and soups. These products are also sold as bouillon cubes or granules. Although inferior to well-made stocks, flavor bases do reduce the labor involved in the production of stocks, sauces and soups. Used properly, they also ensure a consistent product. Because bases do not contain gelatin, stocks and sauces made from them do not benefit from reduction.

Bases vary greatly in quality and price. Sodium (salt) is the main ingredient in many bases. Better bases are made primarily of meat, poultry or fish extracts. To judge the quality of a flavor base, prepare it according to package directions and compare the flavor to that of a well-made stock. The flavor base can be improved by adding a mirepoix, standard sachet and a few appropriate bones to the mixture, then simmering for one or two hours. It can then be strained, stored and used like a regular stock. Although convenience bases are widely used in the industry, it is important to remember that even the best base is a poor substitute for a well-made stock.

NAGE

An aromatic court bouillon is sometimes served as a light sauce or broth with fish or shellfish. This is known as a nage (nahj), and dishes served in this manner are described as *à la nage* (French for "swimming"). After the fish or shellfish is cooked, additional herbs and aromatic vegetables are added to the cooking liquid, which is then reduced slightly and strained.

Alternatively, the used court bouillon can be strained, chilled, and clarified with egg whites and aromatic vegetables in the same manner as a consommé. Finally, whole butter or cream may be added to a nage for richness.

GLAZE

A glaze is the dramatic reduction and concentration of a stock. One gallon (4 liters) of stock produces only 1 to 2 cups (2½ to 5 deciliters) of glaze. *Glace de viande* is made from brown stock, reduced until it becomes dark and syrupy. *Glace de volaille* is made from chicken stock, and *glace de poisson* from fish stock.

Glazes are added to soups or sauces to increase and intensify flavors. They are also used as a source of intense flavoring for several of the small sauces discussed next.

1 A properly thickened glaze made from brown stock.

2 Chilled glace de viande.

▶ PROCEDURE FOR REDUCING A STOCK TO A GLAZE

1 Simmer the stock over very low heat. Be careful not to let it burn, and skim it often.

2 As it reduces and the volume decreases, transfer the liquid into progressively smaller saucepans. Strain the liquid each time it is transferred into a smaller saucepan.

3 Strain it a final time, cool and refrigerate. A properly made glaze will keep for several months under refrigeration.

Table 11.1	TROUBLESHOOTING CHART FOR STOCKS	
PROBLEM	**REASON**	**SOLUTION**
Cloudy	Impurities Stock boiled during cooking	Start stock in cold water Strain through layers of cheesecloth
Lack of flavor	Not cooked long enough Inadequate seasoning Improper ratio of bones to water	Increase cooking time Add more flavoring ingredients Add more bones
Lack of color	Improperly caramelized bones and mirepoix Not cooked long enough	Caramelize bones and mirepoix until darker Cook longer
Lack of body	Wrong bones used Insufficient reduction Improper ratio of bones to water	Use bones with a higher content of connective tissue Cook longer Add more bones
Too salty	Commercial base used Salt added during cooking	Change base or make own stock; do not salt stock

► SAUCES

With a few exceptions, a sauce is a liquid plus thickening agent plus seasonings. Any chef can produce fine sauces by learning to do the following:

1 Make good stocks

2 Use thickening agents properly to achieve the desired texture, flavor and appearance

3 Use seasonings properly to achieve the desired flavors

Classic hot sauces are divided into two groups: **mother** or **leading sauces** (Fr. *sauce mère*) and **small** or **compound sauces.** The five classic mother sauces are béchamel, velouté, espagnole (brown), tomato and hollandaise. Except for hollandaise, leading sauces are rarely served as is; more often they are used to create the many small sauces.

Not all sauces fall into the traditional classifications, however. Some sauces use purées of fruits or vegetables as their base; they are known as **coulis.** Others, such as **beurre blanc** (French for "white butter") and **beurre rouge** ("red butter"), are based on an acidic reduction in which whole butter is incorporated. **Flavored butters, flavored oils, salsas, relishes** and **pan gravy** are also used as sauces in modern food service operations.

THICKENING AGENTS

One of the most traditional and commonly used methods for thickening sauces is through the gelatinization of starches. As discussed in Chapter 10, Principles of Cooking, gelatinization is the process by which starch granules absorb moisture when placed in a liquid and heated. As the moisture is absorbed, the product thickens. Starches generally used to thicken sauces are flour, cornstarch and arrowroot. Gelatinization may sound easy, but it takes practice to produce a good sauce that:

► Is lump-free

► Has a good clean flavor that is not pasty or floury

► Has a consistency that will coat the back of a spoon (the French call this *nappe*)

► Will not separate or break when the sauce is held or reduced

ROUX

Roux (roo) is the principal means used to thicken sauces. It is a combination of equal parts, by weight, of flour and fat, cooked together to form a paste. Cooking the flour in fat coats the starch granules with the fat and prevents them from lumping together or forming lumps when introduced into a liquid. In large production kitchens, large amounts of roux are prepared and held for use as needed. Smaller operations may make roux as required for each recipe.

There are three types of roux:

1 **White roux** is cooked only briefly and should be removed from the heat as soon as it develops a frothy, bubbly appearance. It is used in white sauces, such as béchamel, or in dishes where little or no color is desired.

2 **Blond roux** is cooked slightly longer than white roux, and should begin to take on a little color as the flour caramelizes. It is used in ivory-colored sauces, such as velouté, or where a richer flavor is desired.

3 **Brown roux** is cooked until it develops a darker color and a nutty aroma and flavor. Brown roux is used in brown sauces and dishes where a dark color is desired. It is important to remember that cooking a starch before

White, Blond and Brown Roux

adding a liquid breaks down the starch granules and prevents gelatinization from occurring. Therefore, because brown roux is cooked longer than white roux, more brown roux is required to thicken a given quantity of liquid.

▶ PROCEDURE FOR PREPARING ROUX

Whether it will be white, blond or brown, the procedure for making a roux is the same:

1 Using a heavy saucepan to prevent scorching, heat the clarified butter or other fat.
2 Add all the flour and stir to form a paste. Although all-purpose flour can be used, it is better to use cake or pastry flour because they contain a higher percentage of starch. Do not use high-gluten flour because of its greatly reduced starch content. (Flours are discussed in Chapter 29, Principles of the Bakeshop.)
3 Cook the paste over medium heat until the desired color is achieved. Stir the roux often to avoid burning. Burnt roux will not thicken a liquid; it will simply add dark specks and an undesirable flavor.

The temperature and amount of roux being prepared determine the exact length of cooking time. Generally, however, a white roux needs to cook for only a few minutes, long enough to minimize the raw flour taste. Blond roux is cooked longer, until the paste begins to change to a slightly darker color. Brown roux requires a much longer cooking time to develop its characteristic color and aroma. A good roux will be stiff, not runny or pourable.

Cooking the roux.

▶ INCORPORATING ROUX INTO A LIQUID

There are two ways to incorporate roux into a liquid without causing lumps:
1 Cold stock can be added to the hot roux while stirring vigorously with a whisk.
2 Room-temperature roux can be added to a hot stock while stirring vigorously with a whisk.

When the roux and the liquid are completely incorporated and the sauce begins to boil, it is necessary to cook the sauce for a time to remove any raw flour taste that may remain. Most chefs feel a minimum of 20 minutes is necessary.

(a)

Cold stock

Hot roux

(b)

Hot stock

Cold roux

When thickening stock with roux, either
(a) add cold stock to hot roux, or
(b) add cold roux to hot stock.

▶ GUIDELINES FOR USING ROUX

1 Avoid using aluminum pots. The scraping action of the whisk will turn light sauces gray and will impart a metallic flavor.
2 Use sufficiently heavy pots to prevent sauces from scorching or burning during extended cooking times.
3 Avoid extreme temperatures. Roux should be no colder than room temperature so that the fat is not fully solidified. Extremely hot roux is dangerous and can spatter when combined with a liquid. Stocks should not be ice cold when combined with roux; the roux will become very cold, and the solidified pieces may be very difficult to work out with a whisk.
4 Avoid overthickening. See Table 11.2. Roux does not begin to thicken a sauce until the sauce is almost at the boiling point; the thickening action continues for several minutes while the sauce simmers. If a sauce is to cook for a long time, it will also be thickened by reduction.

A SAUCY HISTORY

The word *sauce* is derived from the Latin word *salus,* meaning "salted." This derivation is appropriate. For millennia, salt has been the basic condiment for enhancing or disguising the flavor of many foods. Over the centuries, sauces have also been used for these purposes.

Cooks of ancient Rome flavored many dishes with *garum,* a golden-colored sauce made from fermented fish entrails combined with brine, condiments, water and wine or vinegar. They also used a sauce referred to as a "single" made from oil, wine and brine. When boiled with herbs and saffron, it became a "double" sauce. To this the Byzantines later added pepper, cloves, cinnamon, cardamom and coriander or spikenard (a fragrant ointment made from grains).

During the Middle Ages, chefs (and their employers) were fond of either very spicy or sweet-and-sour sauces. A typical sauce for roasted meat consisted of powdered cinnamon, mustard, red wine and a sweetener such as honey. It was thickened, if at all, with bits of stale or grilled bread. Other sauces were based on verjuice, an acidic stock prepared from the juice of unripe grapes. To it were added other fruit juices, honey, flower petals and herbs or spices. Indeed, most medieval sauces were heavily spiced. Perhaps this was done to hide the taste of salt-cured or less-than-fresh meats. More likely, however, these sauces were served to showcase the host's wealth.

Guillaume Tirel (c. 1312–1395), who called himself **Taillevent,** was the master chef for Charles V of France. Around 1375, Taillevent wrote *Le Viandier,* the oldest known French cookbook. The cooking style he describes relies heavily on pounding, puréeing and spicing most foods so that the finished dish bears little resemblance in shape, texture or flavor to the original ingredients. Included in his methods are 17 sauces. Among them is a recipe for a *cameline* sauce. It is made from grilled bread soaked in wine; the wine-soaked bread is then drained, squeeze-dried and ground with cinnamon, ginger, pepper, cloves and nutmeg; this mixture is then diluted with vinegar. There is also a recipe for a sauce called *taillemaslée,* made of fried onions, verjuice, vinegar and mustard. (Appropriately, on his grave marker, Taillevent is dressed as a sergeant-at-arms whose shield is decorated with three cooking pots.)

Recipes for some sauces of the Renaissance, such as poivrade or Robert, are recognizable today. Most sauces enjoyed in Renaissance-era Italy and France consisted of some combination of concentrated cooking juices, wines, herbs and spices (especially pepper), sometimes thickened with bread. Sweet, fruit-based sauces were also popular. Most important for the development of modern cuisine, however, was the growing use of sauces based on broths

thickened with cream, butter and egg yolks and flavored with herbs and spices.

Although he died in relative obscurity, many now consider **François Pierre de La Varenne** (1618–1678) to be one of the founding fathers of French cuisine. His treatises, especially *Le Cuisinier français* (1651), detail the early development, methods and manners of French cuisine. His analysis and recipes mark a departure from medieval cookery and a French cuisine heavily influenced by Italian traditions. His writings were uniquely modern in that he included recipes for new foods (especially fruits and vegetables native to the Americas or the Far East) and for indigenous foods (such as saltwater fish) that were gradually becoming more popular. La Varenne is credited with introducing roux as a thickening agent for sauces, especially velouté sauces. He emphasized the importance of properly prepared *fonds* and the reduction of cooking juices to concentrate flavors. He also popularized the use of bouquets garni to flavor stocks and sauces.

Sometime during the early 18th century, the chef to the French Duc de Levis-Mirepoix pioneered the use of onions, celery and carrots to enhance the flavor and aroma of stocks. The mixture, named for the chef's employer, soon became the standard way of enriching stocks. An enriched stock greatly improves the quality of the sauces derived from it.

During the early 19th century, **Antonin Carême** developed the modern system for classifying hundreds of sauces. It is unknown how many sauces Carême actually invented himself, but he wrote treatises containing the theories and recipes for many of the sauces still used today. Carême's extravagant lists of sauces were reduced and simplified by chefs later in the 19th century, most notably by **Auguste Escoffier.**

CORNSTARCH

Cornstarch, a very fine white powder, is a pure starch derived from corn. It is used widely as a thickening agent for hot and cold sauces and is especially popular in Asian cuisines for thickening sauces and soups. Liquids thickened with cornstarch have a glossy sheen that may or may not be desirable.

One unit of cornstarch thickens about twice as much liquid as an equal unit of flour. Sauces thickened with cornstarch are less stable than those thickened with roux because cornstarch can break down and lose its thickening power after prolonged heating. Products thickened with cornstarch should not be reheated.

Table 11.2		PROPORTIONS OF ROUX TO LIQUID						
FLOUR	+	**BUTTER**	=	**ROUX**	+	**LIQUID**	=	**SAUCE**
6 oz./190 g	+	6 oz./190 g	=	12 oz./375 g	+	1 gal./4 lt	=	light
8 oz./250 g	+	8 oz./250 g	=	1 lb./500 g	+	1 gal./4 lt	=	medium
12 oz./375 g	+	12 oz./375 g	=	24 oz./750 g	+	1 gal./4 lt	=	heavy

Variables: The starch content of a flour determines its thickening power. Cake flour, being lowest in protein and highest in starch, has more thickening power than bread flour, which is high in protein and low in starch. In addition, a dark roux has less thickening power than a lighter one, so more will be needed to thicken an equal amount of liquid.

▶ **slurry** a mixture of raw starch and cold liquid used for thickening

1 Kneading the butter and flour together.

2 Adding the beurre manié in small pieces to finish a sauce.

▶ **tempering** gradually raising the temperature of a cold liquid such as eggs by slowly stirring in a hot liquid

Incorporating Cornstarch

Cornstarch must be mixed with a cool liquid before it is introduced into a hot one. The cool liquid separates the grains of starch and allows them to begin absorbing liquid without lumping. A solution of a starch and a cool liquid is called a **slurry.**

The starch slurry may be added to either a hot or cold liquid. If added to a hot liquid, it must be stirred continuously during incorporation. Unlike roux, cornstarch begins to thicken almost immediately if the liquid is hot. Sauces thickened with cornstarch must be cooked gently until the raw starch flavor disappears, usually about five minutes.

ARROWROOT

Arrowroot, derived from the roots of several tropical plants, is similar in texture, appearance and thickening power to cornstarch and is used in exactly the same manner. Arrowroot does not break down as quickly as cornstarch, and it produces a slightly clearer finished product although it is much more expensive.

BEURRE MANIÉ

Beurre manié (burr mahn-yay) is a combination of equal amounts, by weight, of flour and soft whole butter. The flour and butter are kneaded together until smooth. The mixture is then formed into pea-sized balls and whisked into a simmering sauce. Beurre manié is used for quick thickening at the end of the cooking process. The butter also adds shine and flavor to the sauce as it melts.

LIAISON

Unlike the thickeners already described, a liaison (lee-yeh-zon) does not thicken a sauce through gelatinization. A liaison is a mixture of egg yolks and heavy cream; it adds richness and smoothness with minimal thickening. Special care must be taken to prevent the yolks from coagulating when they are added to a hot liquid because this could curdle the sauce.

▶ PROCEDURE FOR USING A LIAISON

1 Whisk together one part egg yolk and three parts whipping cream. Combining the yolk with cream raises the temperature at which the yolk's proteins coagulate, making it easier to incorporate them into a sauce without lumping or curdling.

2 **Temper** the egg yolk and cream mixture by slowly adding a small amount of the hot liquid while stirring continuously.

3 When enough of the hot liquid has been added to the liaison to warm it thoroughly, begin adding the warmed liaison to the remaining hot liquid.

Be sure to stir the mixture carefully to prevent the yolk from overcooking or lumping. Plain egg yolks coagulate at temperatures between 149°F and 158°F (65°C and 70°C). Mixing them with cream raises the temperatures at which they coagulate to approximately 180°F–185°F (82°C–85°C). Temperatures over 185°F (85°C) will cause the yolks to curdle. Great care must be taken to hold the sauce above 140°F (60°C) for food safety and sanitation reasons, yet below 185°F (85°C) to prevent curdling.

1 Adding hot liquid to the egg yolk and cream mixture.

FINISHING TECHNIQUES

REDUCTION

As sauces cook, moisture is released in the form of steam. As steam escapes, the remaining ingredients concentrate, thickening the sauce and strengthening the flavors. This process, known as **reduction,** is commonly used to thicken sauces because no starches or other flavor-altering ingredients are needed. Sauces are often finished by allowing them to reduce until the desired consistency is reached.

STRAINING

Smoothness is important to the success of most sauces. They can be strained through either a china cap lined with several layers of cheesecloth or a fine mesh chinois. As discussed later, often vegetables, herbs, spices and other seasonings are added to a sauce for flavor. Straining removes these ingredients as well as any lumps of roux or thickener remaining in the sauce after the desired flavor and consistency have been reached.

MONTER AU BEURRE

Monter au beurre (mohn-tay ah burr) is the process of swirling or whisking whole butter into a sauce to give it shine, flavor and richness. Compound or flavored butters, discussed later, can be used in place of whole butter to add specific flavors. Monter au beurre is widely used to enrich and finish small sauces.

SAUCE FAMILIES

Leading or **mother sauces** are the foundation for the entire classic repertoire of hot sauces. The five leading sauces—béchamel, velouté, espagnole (also known as brown), tomato and hollandaise—can be seasoned and garnished to create a wide variety of small or compound sauces. These five leading sauces are distinguished principally by the liquids and thickeners used to create them. See Table 11.3.

2 Adding the tempered egg yolk and cream liaison to the hot liquid.

▶ **reduction** cooking a liquid such as a sauce until its quantity decreases through evaporation. To reduce by one-half means that one-half of the original amount remains. To reduce by three-quarters means that only one-quarter of the original amount remains. To reduce au sec means that the liquid is cooked until nearly dry.

Table 11.3	SAUCE FAMILIES	
MOTHER SAUCE	**LIQUID**	**THICKENER**
Béchamel	Milk	Roux
Velouté	White Stock	Roux
Veal Velouté	Veal Stock	
Chicken Velouté	Chicken Stock	
Fish Velouté	Fish Stock	
Espagnole (Brown Sauce)	Brown Stock	Roux
Tomato Sauce	Tomato	Roux (optional)
Hollandaise	Butter	Egg yolks

Small or **compound sauces** are grouped into families based on their leading sauce. Some small sauces have a variety of uses; others are traditional accompaniments for specific foods. A small sauce may be named for its ingredients, place of origin or creator. Although there are numerous classic small sauces, we have included only a few of the more popular ones following each of the leading sauce recipes.

THE BÉCHAMEL FAMILY

Named for its creator, Louis de Béchameil (1630–1703), steward to Louis XIV of France, béchamel (bay-shah-mell) sauce is the easiest mother sauce to prepare. Traditionally, it is made by adding heavy cream to a thick veal velouté. Although some chefs still believe a béchamel should contain veal stock, today the sauce is almost always made by thickening scalded milk with a white roux and adding seasonings. Often used for vegetable, egg and gratin dishes, béchamel has fallen into relative disfavor recently because of its rich, heavy nature. It is nevertheless important to understand its production and its place in traditional sauce making.

A properly made béchamel is rich, creamy and absolutely smooth with no hint of graininess. The flavors of the onion and clove used to season it should be apparent but not overwhelm the sauce's clean, milky taste. The sauce should be the color of heavy cream and have a deep luster. It should be thick enough to coat foods lightly but should not taste like the roux used to thicken it.

RECIPE 11.7	BÉCHAMEL	

Béchamel

Yield: 1 gal. (4 lt)

Onion piquet	1	1
Milk	1 gal.	4 lt
Flour	8 oz.	250 g
Clarified butter	8 fl. oz.	250 ml
Salt and white pepper	TT	TT
Nutmeg	TT	TT

1 Add the onion piquet to the milk in a heavy saucepan and simmer for 20 minutes.
2 In a separate pot, make a white roux with the flour and butter.
3 Remove the onion piquet from the milk. Gradually add the hot milk to the roux while stirring constantly with a whisk to prevent lumps. Bring to a boil.
4 Reduce the sauce to a simmer, add the seasonings and continue cooking for 30 minutes.
5 Strain the sauce through a china cap lined with cheesecloth. Melted butter can be carefully ladled over the surface of the sauce to prevent a skin from forming. Hold for service or cool in a water bath.

Approximate values per 6-fl.-oz. (180-ml) serving: **Calories** 240, **Total fat** 15 g, **Saturated fat** 9 g, **Cholesterol** 50 mg, **Sodium** 180 mg, **Total carbohydrates** 18 g, **Protein** 7 g, **Vitamin A** 15%, **Calcium** 25%

Small Béchamel Sauces

With a good béchamel, producing the small sauces in its family is quite simple. The quantities given are for 1 quart (1 liter) of béchamel. The final step for each recipe is to season to taste with salt and pepper.

CREAM SAUCE   Add to béchamel 8–12 fluid ounces (250–360 milliliters) scalded cream and a few drops of lemon juice.

CHEESE   Add to béchamel 8 ounces (250 grams) grated Cheddar or American cheese, a dash of Worcestershire sauce and 1 tablespoon (15 milliliters) dry mustard.

MORNAY   Add to béchamel 4 ounces (120 grams) grated Gruyère and 1 ounce (30 grams) grated Parmesan. Thin as desired with scalded cream. Remove the sauce from the heat and swirl in 2 ounces (60 grams) whole butter.

NANTUA   Add to béchamel 4 fluid ounces (120 milliliters) heavy cream and 6 ounces (180 grams) crayfish butter (page 223). Add paprika to achieve the desired color. Garnish the finished sauce with diced crayfish meat.

SOUBISE (MODERN)   Sweat 1 pound (500 grams) diced onion in 1 ounce (30 grams) whole butter without browning. Add béchamel and simmer until the onions are fully cooked. Strain through a fine chinois.

THE VELOUTÉ FAMILY

Velouté (veh-loo-TAY) sauces are made by thickening a white stock or fish stock with roux. The white stock can be made from veal or chicken bones. A fish velouté sauce, made from fish stock, is used to create a few small sauces. A velouté sauce made from veal or chicken stock is usually used to make one of two intermediary sauces—allemande and suprême—from which many small sauces are derived. **Allemande** sauce is made by adding lemon juice and a liaison to either a veal or chicken velouté. (The stock used depends upon the dish with which the sauce will be served.) **Suprême** sauce is made by adding cream to a chicken velouté. See Table 11.4.

A properly made velouté should be rich, smooth and lump-free. If made from chicken or fish stock, it should taste of chicken or fish. A velouté made from veal stock should have a more neutral flavor. The sauce should be ivory-colored, with a deep luster. It should be thick enough to cling to foods without tasting like the roux used to thicken it.

▶ **allemande** (ah-leh-MAHND) an intermediary sauce made by adding lemon juice and a liaison to chicken or veal velouté

▶ **suprême** (soo-prem) an intermediary sauce made by adding cream to chicken velouté

Table 11.4	VELOUTÉ SAUCES				
Fish stock	+ Roux	= Velouté			
Chicken stock	+ Roux	= Velouté	+ Cream	=	Suprême
Chicken stock	+ Roux	= Velouté	+ Liaison and lemon	=	Allemande
Veal stock	+ Roux	= Velouté	+ Liaison and lemon	=	Allemande

VELOUTÉ   RECIPE 11.8

Yield: 1 gal. (4 lt)

Clarified butter	8 fl. oz.	250 ml
Flour	8 oz.	250 g
Chicken, veal or fish stock	5 qt.	5 lt
Salt and white pepper	TT	TT

1 Heat the butter in a heavy saucepan. Add the flour and cook to make a blond roux.

2 Gradually add the stock to the roux, stirring constantly with a whisk to prevent lumps. Bring to a boil and reduce to a simmer. (Seasonings are optional; their use depends upon the seasonings in the stock and the sauce's intended use.)

3 Simmer and reduce to 1 gallon (4 liters), approximately 30 minutes.

4 Strain through a china cap lined with cheesecloth.

5 Melted butter may be carefully ladled over the surface of the sauce to prevent a skin from forming. Hold for service or cool in a water bath.

Velouté

Approximate values per 1-fl.-oz. (30-ml) serving: **Calories** 25, **Total fat** 1.5 g, **Saturated fat** 1 g, **Cholesterol** 5 mg, **Sodium** 140 mg, **Total carbohydrates** 2 g, **Protein** 1 g

Small Fish Velouté Sauces

A few small sauces can be made from fish velouté. The quantities given are for 1 quart (1 liter) fish velouté sauce. The final step for each recipe is to season to taste with salt and pepper.

BERCY Sauté 2 ounces (60 grams) finely diced shallots in butter. Then add 8 fluid ounces (250 milliliters) dry white wine and 8 fluid ounces (250 milliliters) fish stock. Reduce this mixture by one-third and add the fish velouté. Finish with butter and garnish with chopped parsley.

CARDINAL Add 8 fluid ounces (250 milliliters) fish stock to 1 quart (1 liter) fish velouté. Reduce this mixture by half and add 1 pint (500 milliliters) heavy cream and a dash of cayenne pepper. Bring to a boil and swirl in 1½ ounces (45 grams) lobster butter (page 223). Garnish with chopped lobster coral at service time.

NORMANDY Add 4 ounces (120 grams) mushroom trimmings and 4 fluid ounces (120 milliliters) fish stock to 1 quart (1 liter) fish velouté. Reduce by one-third and finish with an egg yolk and cream liaison. Strain through a fine chinois.

RECIPE 11.9 **ALLEMANDE SAUCE**

Yield: 1 gal. (4 lt)

Veal or chicken velouté sauce	1 gal.	4 lt
Egg yolks	8	8
Heavy cream	24 fl. oz.	675 ml
Lemon juice	1 fl. oz.	30 ml
Salt and white pepper	TT	TT

1 Bring the velouté to a simmer.
2 In a stainless steel bowl, whip the egg yolks with the cream to create a liaison. Ladle approximately one-third of the hot velouté sauce into this mixture, while whisking, to temper the yolk and cream mixture.
3 When one-third of the velouté has been incorporated into the now-warmed yolk and cream mixture, gradually add the liaison to the remaining velouté sauce while whisking continuously.
4 Reheat the sauce. Do not let it boil.
5 Add the lemon juice; season with salt and white pepper to taste.
6 Strain through a china cap lined with cheesecloth.

Approximate values per 1-fl.-oz. (30-ml) serving: **Calories** 40, **Total fat** 3.5 g, **Saturated fat** 2 g, **Cholesterol** 25 mg, **Sodium** 95 mg, **Total carbohydrates** 1 g, **Protein** 1 g, **Vitamin A** 4%

Small Allemande Sauces

Several small sauces are easily produced from an allemande sauce made with either a chicken or veal velouté. The quantities given are for 1 quart (1 liter) allemande. The final step for each recipe is to season to taste with salt and pepper.

AURORA Add to allemande 2 ounces (60 grams) tomato paste and finish with 1 ounce (30 grams) butter.

HORSERADISH Add to allemande 4 fluid ounces (120 milliliters) heavy cream and 1 teaspoon (5 milliliters) dry mustard. Just before service add 2 ounces (60 grams) freshly grated horseradish. The horseradish should not be cooked with the sauce.

MUSHROOM Sauté 4 ounces (120 grams) sliced mushrooms in ½ ounce (15 grams) whole butter; add 2 teaspoons (10 milliliters) lemon juice. Then add the allemande to the mushrooms. Do not strain.

POULETTE   Sauté 8 ounces (250 grams) sliced mushrooms and ½ ounce (15 grams) diced shallots in 1 ounce (30 grams) whole butter. Add to the allemande; then add 2 fluid ounces (60 milliliters) heavy cream. Finish with lemon juice to taste and 1 tablespoon (15 milliliters) chopped parsley.

SUPRÊME SAUCE

RECIPE 11.10

Yield: 1 gal. (4 lt)

Chicken velouté sauce	1 gal.	4 lt
Mushroom trimmings	8 oz.	225 g
Heavy cream	1 qt.	1 lt
Salt and white pepper	TT	TT

1 Simmer the velouté sauce with the mushroom trimmings until reduced by one-fourth.
2 Gradually whisk in the heavy cream and return to a simmer.
3 Adjust the seasonings.
4 Strain through a china cap lined with cheesecloth.

Approximate values per 1-fl.-oz. (30-ml) serving: **Calories** 45, **Total fat** 4 g, **Saturated fat** 2.5 g, **Cholesterol** 15 mg, **Sodium** 95 mg, **Total carbohydrates** 1 g, **Protein** 1 g, **Vitamin A** 4%

Small Suprême Sauces

The following small sauces are easily made from a suprême sauce. The quantities given are for 1 quart (1 liter) suprême sauce. The final step for each recipe is to season to taste with salt and pepper.

ALBUFERA   Add to suprême 3 fluid ounces (90 milliliters) glace de volaille and 2 ounces (60 grams) red pepper butter (page 224).

HUNGARIAN   Sweat 2 ounces (60 grams) diced onion in 1 tablespoon (15 milliliters) whole butter. Add 1 tablespoon (15 milliliters) paprika. Stir in the suprême sauce. Cook for 2–3 minutes, strain and finish with whole butter.

IVORY   Add to suprême 3 fluid ounces (90 milliliters) glace de volaille.

THE ESPAGNOLE FAMILY

The mother sauce of the espagnole (ess-spah-nyol) or brown sauce family is full-bodied and rich. It is made from a brown stock to which brown roux, mirepoix and tomato purée have been added. Most often this sauce is used to produce demi-glace. Brown stock is also used to make jus lié. Demi-glace and jus lié are intermediary sauces used to create the small sauces of the espagnole family.

ESPAGNOLE (BROWN SAUCE)

RECIPE 11.11

Yield: 1 gal. (4 lt)

Mirepoix, medium dice	2 lb.	1 kg
Clarified butter	8 fl. oz.	250 ml
Flour	8 oz.	250 g
Brown stock	5 qt.	5 lt
Tomato purée	8 oz.	250 g
Sachet:		
Bay leaf	1	1
Dried thyme	½ tsp.	2 ml
Peppercorns, crushed	¼ tsp.	1 ml
Parsley stems	8	8
Salt and pepper	TT	TT

Espagnole

1 Sauté the mirepoix in butter until well caramelized.
2 Add the flour and cook to make a brown roux.
3 Add the brown stock and tomato purée. Stir to break up any lumps of roux. Bring to a boil; reduce to a simmer.
4 Add the sachet.
5 Simmer for approximately 1½ hours, allowing the sauce to reduce. Skim the surface as needed to remove impurities.
6 Strain the sauce through a china cap lined with several layers of cheesecloth. Adjust seasonings and cool in a water bath or hold for service.

Approximate values per 1-fl.-oz. (30-ml) serving: **Calories** 35, **Total fat** 2 g, **Saturated fat** 1 g, **Cholesterol** 5 mg, **Sodium** 150 mg, **Total carbohydrates** 4 g, **Protein** 1 g, **Vitamin A** 6%, **Claims**—low fat; low calorie

Demi-Glace

Brown stock is used to make the espagnole or brown sauce described earlier. Espagnole sauce can then be made into demi-glace, which in turn is used to make the small sauces of the espagnole family. Demi-glace is half brown sauce, half brown stock, reduced by half. It is usually finished with a small amount of Madeira or sherry wine. Because demi-glace creates a richer, more flavorful base, it produces finer small sauces than those made directly from a brown sauce.

A properly made demi-glace is rich, smooth and lump-free. Its prominent roasted flavor comes from the bones used for the brown stock. There should be no taste of roux. The caramelized bones and mirepoix as well as the tomato product contribute to its glossy dark brown, almost chocolate, color. It should be thick enough to cling to food without being pasty or heavy.

RECIPE 11.12   DEMI-GLACE

Demi-Glace

Yield: 1 qt. (1 lt)

Brown stock	1 qt.	1 lt
Brown sauce	1 qt.	1 lt

1 Combine the stock and sauce in a saucepan over medium heat.
2 Simmer until the mixture is reduced by half (a yield of 1 quart or 1 liter).
3 Strain and cool in a water bath.

Approximate values per 1-fl.-oz. (30-ml) serving: **Calories** 30, **Total fat** 1.5 g, **Saturated fat** 0.5 g, **Cholesterol** 5 mg, **Sodium** 200 mg, **Total carbohydrates** 4 g, **Protein** 1 g, **Vitamin A** 6%, **Claims**—low fat; low calorie

Jus Lié

Jus lié (zhoo lee-ay), also known as fond lié, is used like a demi-glace, especially to produce small sauces. Jus lié is lighter and easier to make than a demi-glace, however. It is made in one of two ways:

1 A rich brown stock is thickened with cornstarch or arrowroot and seasoned.
2 A rich brown stock is simmered and reduced so that it thickens naturally because of the concentrated amounts of gelatin and other proteins.

The starch-thickened method is a quick alternative to the long-simmering demi-glace. But because it is simply a brown stock thickened with cornstarch or arrowroot, it will only be as good as the stock with which it was begun. Sauces made from reduced stock usually have a better flavor but can be expensive to produce because of high food costs and lengthy reduction time.

A properly made jus lié is very rich and smooth. It shares many flavor characteristics with demi-glace. Its color should be dark brown and glossy from the concentrated gelatin content. Its consistency is somewhat lighter than demi-glace, but it should still cling lightly to foods.

Small Brown Sauces

Demi-glace and jus lié are used to produce many small sauces. The quantities given are for 1 quart (1 liter) demi-glace or jus lié. The final step for each recipe is to season to taste with salt and pepper.

BORDELAISE Combine 1 pint (250 milliliters) dry red wine, 2 ounces (60 grams) chopped shallots, 1 bay leaf, 1 sprig thyme and a pinch of black pepper in a saucepan. Reduce by three-fourths, then add demi-glace and simmer for 15 minutes. Strain through a fine chinois. Finish with 2 ounces (60 grams) whole butter and garnish with sliced, poached beef marrow.

CHASSEUR (HUNTER'S SAUCE) Sauté 4 ounces (120 grams) sliced mushrooms and 1 tablespoon (15 milliliters) diced shallots in whole butter. Add 8 fluid ounces (250 milliliters) white wine and reduce by three-fourths. Then add demi-glace and 6 ounces (170 grams) diced tomatoes; simmer for 5 minutes. Do not strain. Garnish with chopped parsley.

CHÂTEAUBRIAND Combine 1 pint (500 milliliters) dry white wine and 2 ounces (60 grams) diced shallots. Reduce the mixture by two-thirds. Add demi-glace and reduce by half. Season to taste with lemon juice and cayenne pepper. Do not strain. Swirl in 4 ounces (120 grams) whole butter to finish and garnish with chopped fresh tarragon.

CHEVREUIL Prepare a poivrade sauce but add 6 ounces (170 grams) bacon or game trimmings to the mirepoix. Finish with 4 fluid ounces (120 milliliters) red wine and a dash of cayenne pepper.

MADEIRA OR PORT Bring demi-glace to a boil, reduce slightly. Then add 4 fluid ounces (120 milliliters) madeira wine or ruby port.

MARCHAND DE VIN Reduce 8 fluid ounces (250 milliliters) dry red wine and 2 ounces (60 grams) diced shallots by two-thirds. Then add demi-glace, simmer and strain.

MUSHROOM Blanch 8 ounces (250 grams) mushroom caps in 8 fluid ounces (250 milliliters) boiling water seasoned with salt and lemon juice. Drain the mushrooms, saving the liquid. Reduce this liquid to 2 tablespoons (30 milliliters) and add it to the demi-glace. Just before service stir in 2 ounces (60 grams) whole butter and the mushroom caps.

PÉRIGUEUX Add finely diced truffles to Madeira sauce. **Périgourdine** sauce is the same, except that the truffles are cut into relatively thick slices.

PIQUANT Combine 1 ounce (30 grams) shallots, 4 fluid ounces (120 milliliters) white wine and 4 fluid ounces (120 milliliters) white wine vinegar. Reduce the mixture by two-thirds. Then add demi-glace and simmer for 10 minutes. Add 2 ounces (60 grams) diced cornichons, 1 tablespoon (15 milliliters) fresh tarragon, 1 tablespoon (15 milliliters) fresh parsley and 1 tablespoon (15 milliliters) fresh chervil. Do not strain.

POIVRADE Sweat 12 ounces (340 grams) mirepoix in 2 tablespoons (30 milliliters) oil. Add 1 bay leaf, 1 sprig thyme and 4 parsley stems. Then add 1 pint (500 milliliters) vinegar and 4 fluid ounces (120 milliliters) white wine. Reduce by half, add demi-glace and simmer for 40 minutes. Then add 20 crushed peppercorns and simmer for 5 more minutes. Strain through a fine chinois and finish with up to 2 ounces (60 grams) whole butter.

ROBERT Sauté 8 ounces (250 grams) chopped onion in 1 ounce (30 grams) whole butter. Add 8 fluid ounces (250 milliliters) dry white wine and reduce by two-thirds. Add demi-glace and simmer for 10 minutes. Strain and then add 2 teaspoons (10 milliliters) prepared Dijon mustard and 1 tablespoon (15 milliliters) granulated sugar. If the finished Robert sauce is garnished with sliced sour pickles, preferably cornichons, it is known as **Charcuterie.**

POIVRADE POUR GIBIER

Poivrade is also the name given a flavorful sauce traditionally made with game stock and seasoned with peppercorns. It is used for the wonderful *Sauce Grand Veneur*, one of the most complex small sauces in the classic repertoire. For *Grand Veneur*, game stock is flavored with demi-glace and finished with cream and currant jelly. The sweetness balances the strong flavor of the game meats.

THE TOMATO SAUCE FAMILY

Classic tomato sauce is made from tomatoes, vegetables, seasonings and white stock and thickened with a blond or brown roux. In today's kitchens, however, most tomato sauces are not thickened with roux. Rather, they are created from tomatoes, herbs, spices, vegetables and other flavoring ingredients simmered together and puréed.

▶ **gastrique** (gas-streek) caramelized sugar deglazed with vinegar; used to flavor tomato or savory fruit sauces

A **gastrique** is sometimes added to reduce the acidity of a tomato sauce. To prepare a gastrique, caramelize a small amount of sugar, then thin or deglaze with vinegar. This mixture is then used to finish the tomato sauce.

A properly made tomato sauce is thick, rich and full-flavored. Its texture should be grainier than most other classic sauces, but it should still be smooth. The vegetables and other seasonings should add flavor, but none should be pronounced. Tomato sauce should not be bitter, acidic or overly sweet. It should be deep red and thick enough to cling to foods.

RECIPE 11.13 — TOMATO SAUCE

1 Passing the sauce through a food mill.

2 The finished sauce.

Yield: 1 gal. (4 lt)

Salt pork, small dice	4 oz.	120 g
Mirepoix	1 lb. 8 oz.	750 g
Tomato, fresh or canned	3 qt.	3 lt
Tomato purée	2 qt.	2 lt
Sachet:		
Dried thyme	1 tsp.	5 ml
Bay leaves	3	3
Garlic cloves	3	3
Parsley stems	10	10
Peppercorns, crushed	½ tsp.	3 ml
Salt	1½ oz.	45 g
Granulated sugar	¾ oz.	20 g
White stock	3 qt.	3 lt
Pork bones	2 lb.	1 kg

1 Render the salt pork over medium heat.
2 Add the mirepoix and sauté, but do not brown.
3 Add the tomatoes and tomato purée, sachet, salt and sugar.
4 Add the white stock and bones.
5 Simmer slowly for ½ to 2 hours or until the desired consistency has been reached.
6 Remove the bones and sachet, and pass the sauce through a food mill. Cool in a water bath and refrigerate.

Approximate values per 1-fl.-oz. (30-ml) serving: **Calories** 30, **Total fat** 0.5 g, **Saturated fat** 0.2 g, **Cholesterol** 0.7 mg, **Sodium** 240 mg, **Total carbohydrates** 4 g, **Protein** 2 g, **Vitamin A** 6%, **Claims**—low fat; low calorie

Small Tomato Sauces

The following small sauces are made by adding the listed ingredients to 1 quart (1 liter) tomato sauce. The final step for each recipe is to season to taste with salt and pepper.

CREOLE Sauté 6 ounces (170 grams) finely diced onion, 4 ounces (120 grams) thinly sliced celery and 1 teaspoon (5 milliliters) garlic in 1 fluid ounce (30 milliliters) oil. Add tomato sauce, a bay leaf and a pinch of thyme; simmer for 15 minutes. Then add 4 ounces (120 grams) finely diced green pepper and a dash of hot pepper sauce; simmer for 15 minutes longer. Remove the bay leaf.

SPANISH   Prepare creole sauce as directed, adding 4 ounces (120 grams) sliced mushrooms to the sautéed onions. Garnish with sliced black or green olives.

MILANAISE   Sauté 5 ounces (140 grams) sliced mushrooms in ½ ounce (15 grams) whole butter. Add tomato sauce and then stir in 5 ounces (140 grams) cooked ham (julienne) and 5 ounces (140 grams) cooked tongue (julienne). Bring to a simmer.

THE HOLLANDAISE FAMILY

Hollandaise and the small sauces derived from it are **emulsified** sauces. Egg yolks, which contain large amounts of lecithin, a natural emulsifier, are used to emulsify warm butter and a small amount of water, lemon juice or vinegar. When the egg yolks are vigorously whipped with the liquid while the warm butter is slowly added, the lecithin coats the individual fat droplets and holds them in suspension in the liquid.

A properly made hollandaise is smooth, buttery, pale lemon-yellow-colored and very rich. It is lump-free and should not exhibit any signs of separation. The buttery flavor should dominate but not mask the flavors of the egg, lemon and vinegar. The sauce should be frothy and light, not heavy like a mayonnaise.

Temperatures and Sanitation Concerns

Temperatures play an important role in the proper production of a hollandaise sauce. As the egg yolks and liquid are whisked together, they are cooked over a bain marie until they thicken to the consistency of slightly whipped cream. Do not overheat this mixture, because even slightly cooked eggs lose their ability to emulsify. The clarified butter used to make the sauce should be warm but not so hot as to further cook the egg yolks. Although hollandaise sauce can be made from whole butter, a more stable and consistent product will be achieved by using clarified butter. (Clarification is described in Chapter 9, Mise en Place.)

Rescuing a Broken Hollandaise

Occasionally, a hollandaise will break or separate and appear thin, grainy or even lumpy. A sauce breaks when the emulsion has not formed or the emulsified butter, eggs and liquid have separated. This may happen for several reasons: The temperature of the eggs or butter may have been too high or too low; the butter may have been added too quickly; the egg yolks may have been overcooked; too much butter may have been added or the sauce may not have been whipped vigorously enough.

To rescue and re-emulsify broken hollandaise you must first determine if it is too hot or too cold. If it is too hot, allow the sauce to cool. If it is too cold, re-heat the sauce over a double boiler before attempting to rescue it.

For 1 quart (1 liter) of broken sauce, place 1 tablespoon (15 milliliters) of water in a clean stainless steel bowl and slowly beat in the broken sauce. If the problem seems to be that the eggs were overcooked or too much butter was added, add a yolk to the water before incorporating the broken sauce.

▶ **emulsification** the process by which generally unmixable liquids, such as oil and water, are forced into a uniform distribution

HOLLANDAISE

RECIPE 11.14

Yield: 1½ qt. (1.5 lt)

White peppercorns, crushed	½ tsp.	2 ml
White wine vinegar	6 fl. oz.	180 ml
Water	4 fl. oz.	120 ml
Egg yolks	10	10
Lemon juice	2½ fl. oz.	75 ml
Clarified butter, warm	1 qt.	1 lt
Salt and white pepper	TT	TT
Cayenne pepper	TT	TT

1 Combining the egg yolks with the vinegar and pepper reduction in a stainless steel bowl.

2 Whipping the mixture over a double boiler until it is thick enough to leave a trail when the whip is removed.

3 Using a kitchen towel and saucepot to firmly hold the bowl containing the yolks, add the butter slowly while whipping continuously.

4 Hollandaise at the proper consistency.

1 Combine the peppercorns, vinegar and water in a small saucepan and reduce by one-half.

2 Place the egg yolks in a stainless steel bowl. Strain the vinegar and pepper reduction through a chinois, into the yolks.

3 Place the bowl over a double boiler, whipping the mixture continuously with a wire whip. As the yolks cook, the mixture will thicken. When the mixture is thick enough to leave a trail across the surface when the whip is drawn away, remove the bowl from the double boiler. Do not overcook the egg yolks.

4 Whip in 1 fluid ounce (30 milliliters) lemon juice to stop the yolks from cooking.

5 Begin to add the warm clarified butter to the egg yolk mixture a drop at a time, while constantly whipping the mixture to form an emulsion. Once the emulsion is started, the butter may be added more quickly. Continue until all the butter is incorporated.

6 Whip in the remaining lemon juice. Adjust the seasonings with salt, white pepper and cayenne pepper.

7 Strain the sauce through cheesecloth if necessary and hold for service in a warm (not simmering) bain marie.

Approximate values per 1-fl.-oz. (30-ml) serving: **Calories** 170, **Total fat** 18 g, **Saturated fat** 11 g, **Cholesterol** 90 mg, **Sodium** 180 mg, **Total carbohydrates** 0 g, **Protein** 1 g, **Vitamin A** 20%

RECIPE 11.15   HOLLANDAISE, BLENDER METHOD

Yield: 1 qt. (1 lt)

Egg yolks	9	9
Water, warm	3 fl. oz.	90 ml
Lemon juice	1 fl. oz.	30 ml
Cayenne pepper	TT	TT
Salt	1 tsp.	5 ml
White pepper	¼ tsp.	1 ml
Tabasco sauce	TT	TT
Whole butter	24 oz.	750 g

1 Place the egg yolks, water, lemon juice, cayenne pepper, salt, white pepper and Tabasco sauce in the bowl of the blender. Cover and blend on high speed for approximately 5 seconds.

2 Heat the butter to approximately 175°F (80°C). This allows the butter to cook the yolks as it is added to them.

3 Turn the blender on and immediately begin to add the butter in a steady stream. Incorporate all the butter in 20 to 30 seconds. Adjust the seasonings.

4 If any lumps are present, strain the sauce through a mesh strainer. Transfer the sauce to a stainless steel container and adjust the seasonings. Hold for service in a bain marie, remembering the sanitation precautions discussed earlier.

Approximate values per 1-fl.-oz. (30-ml) serving: **Calories** 120, **Total fat** 12 g, **Saturated fat** 7 g, **Cholesterol** 70 mg, **Sodium** 170 mg, **Total carbohydrates** 0 g, **Protein** 1 g, **Vitamin A** 15%

Small Hollandaise Sauces

The following small sauces are easily made by adding the listed ingredients to 1 quart (1 liter) of hollandaise. The final step for each recipe is to season to taste with salt and pepper. Béarnaise is presented here as a small sauce although some chefs consider it a leading sauce.

BÉARNAISE (bair-NAYZ) Combine 2 ounces (60 grams) chopped shallots, 5 tablespoons (75 milliliters) chopped fresh tarragon, 3 tablespoons (45 milliliters) chopped fresh chervil and 1 teaspoon (5 milliliters) crushed peppercorns with 8 fluid ounces (250 milliliters) white wine vinegar. Reduce to 2 fluid ounces (60 milliliters). Add this reduction to the egg yolks and proceed with the hollandaise recipe. Strain the finished sauce and season to taste with salt and cayenne pepper. Garnish with additional chopped fresh tarragon.

CHORON Combine 2 ounces (60 grams) tomato paste and 2 fluid ounces (60 milliliters) heavy cream; add the mixture to a béarnaise.

FOYOT Add to béarnaise 3 fluid ounces (90 milliliters) melted glace de viande.

GRIMROD Infuse a hollandaise sauce with saffron.

MALTAISE Add to hollandaise 2 fluid ounces (60 milliliters) orange juice and 2 teaspoons (10 milliliters) finely grated orange zest. Blood oranges are traditionally used for this sauce.

MOUSSELINE (CHANTILLY SAUCE) Whip 8 fluid ounces (250 milliliters) heavy cream until stiff. Fold it into the hollandaise just before service. Mousseline sauce is also used as a **glaçage** coating.

▶ **glaçage** (glah-sahge) browning or glazing a food, usually under a salamander or broiler

BEURRE BLANC AND BEURRE ROUGE

Beurre blanc (burr blahnk) and beurre rouge (burr rooge) are emulsified butter sauces made without egg yolks. The small amounts of lecithin and other emulsifiers naturally found in butter are used to form an oil-in-water emulsion. Although similar to hollandaise in concept, they are not considered either classic leading or compound sauces. Beurre blancs are thinner and lighter than hollandaise and béarnaise. They should be smooth and slightly thicker than heavy cream.

Beurre blanc and beurre rouge are made from three main ingredients: shallots, white (Fr. *blanc*) wine or red (Fr. *rouge*) wine and whole butter (not clarified). The shallots and wine provide flavor, while the butter becomes the sauce. A good beurre blanc or beurre rouge is rich and buttery, with a neutral flavor that responds well to other seasonings and flavorings, thereby lending itself to the addition of herbs, spices and vegetable purées to complement the dish with which it is served. Its pale color changes depending upon the flavorings added. It should be light and airy yet still liquid, while thick enough to cling to food.

▶ **beurre noir** (burr NWAR) French for "black butter"; used to describe whole butter cooked until dark brown (not black); sometimes flavored with vinegar or lemon juice, capers and parsley and served over fish, eggs and vegetables

▶ **beurre noisette** (burr nwah-ZEHT) French for "brown butter"; used to describe butter cooked until it is a light brown color; it is flavored and used in much the same manner as beurre noir

▶ PROCEDURE FOR PREPARING BEURRE BLANC OR BEURRE ROUGE

1 Use a nonaluminum pan to prevent discoloring the sauce. Do not use a thin-walled or nonstick pan, as heat is not evenly distributed in a thin-walled pan and a nonstick pan makes it difficult for an emulsion to set.

2 Over medium heat, reduce the wine, shallots and herbs or other seasonings, if used, until *au sec* (that is, nearly dry). Some chefs add a small amount of heavy cream at this point and reduce the mixture. Although not necessary, the added cream helps stabilize the finished sauce.

3 Whisk in cold butter a small amount at a time. The butter should be well chilled, as this allows the butterfat, water and milk solids to be gradually incorporated into the sauce as the butter melts and the mixture is whisked.

4 When all the butter is incorporated, strain and hold the sauce in a bain marie.

TEMPERATURE

Do not let the sauce become too hot. At 136°F (58°C) some of the emulsifying proteins begin to break down and release the butterfat they hold in emulsion. Extended periods at temperatures over 136°F (58°C) will cause the sauce to separate. If the sauce separates, it can be corrected by cooling to approximately 110°F–120°F (43°C–49°C) and whisking to reincorporate the butterfat.

If the sauce is allowed to cool below 85°F (30°C), the butterfat will solidify. If the sauce is reheated it will separate into butterfat and water; whisking will not re-emulsify it. Cold beurre blanc can be used as a soft, flavored butter, however, simply by whisking it at room temperature until it smoothes out to the consistency of mayonnaise.

RECIPE 11.16   **BEURRE BLANC**

Yield: 1 qt. (1 lt)

White wine	1 fl. oz.	30 ml
White wine vinegar	4 fl. oz.	120 ml
Salt	1½ tsp.	7 ml
White pepper	½ tsp.	2 ml
Shallot, minced	3 Tbsp.	45 ml
Whole butter, chilled	2 lb.	1 kg

1 Reducing the shallots and wine au sec.

2 Whisking in the cold butter a little at a time.

3 Straining the sauce.

1 Combine the white wine, white wine vinegar, salt, white pepper and shallot in a small saucepan. Reduce the mixture until approximately 2 tablespoons (30 milliliters) of liquid remain. If more than 2 tablespoons of liquid are allowed to remain, the resulting sauce will be too thin. For a thicker sauce, reduce the mixture au sec.

2 Cut the butter into pieces approximately 1 ounce (30 grams) in weight. Over low heat, whisk in the butter a few pieces at a time, using the chilled butter to keep the sauce between 100°F and 120°F (43°C and 49°C).

3 Once all the butter has been incorporated, remove the saucepan from the heat. Strain through a chinois and hold the sauce at a temperature between 100°F and 130°F (38°C and 54°C) for service.

Variations: *Beurre Rouge*—Substitute a dry red wine for the white wine and red wine vinegar for the white wine vinegar.

Lemon-Dill—Heat 2 tablespoons (30 milliliters) lemon juice and whisk it into the beurre blanc. Stir in 4 tablespoons (60 milliliters) chopped fresh dill.

Pink Peppercorn—Add 2 tablespoons (30 milliliters) coarsely crushed pink peppercorns to the shallot-wine reduction when making beurre rouge. Garnish the finished sauce with whole pink peppercorns.

Approximate values per 1-fl.-oz. (30-ml) serving: **Calories** 210, **Total fat** 23 g, **Saturated fat** 14 g, **Cholesterol** 60 mg, **Sodium** 340 mg, **Total carbohydrates** 0 g, **Protein** 0 g, **Vitamin A** 20%

COMPOUND BUTTERS

A compound butter is made by incorporating various seasonings into softened whole butter. These butters, also known as *beurres composés,* give flavor and color to small sauces or may be served as sauces in their own right. For example, a slice of maître d'hôtel butter (parsley butter) is often placed on a grilled steak or piece of fish at the time of service. The butter quickly melts, creating a sauce for the beef or fish.

Butter and flavoring ingredients can be combined with a blender, food processor or mixer. Using parchment paper or plastic wrap, the butter is then rolled into a cylinder, chilled and sliced as needed. Or it can be piped into rosettes and refrigerated until firm. Most compound butters will keep for two to three days in the refrigerator, or they can be frozen for longer storage.

1 Placing the butter on the plastic wrap.

RECIPES FOR COMPOUND BUTTERS

For each of the following butters, add the listed ingredients to 1 pound (500 grams) of softened, unsalted butter. The compound butter should then be seasoned with salt and pepper to taste.

BASIL BUTTER   Mince 2 ounces (60 grams) basil and 2 ounces (60 grams) shallots; add to the butter with 2 teaspoons (10 milliliters) lemon juice.

HERB BUTTER   Add to the butter up to 1 cup (250 milliliters) of mixed chopped fresh herbs such as parsley, dill, chives, tarragon or chervil.

LOBSTER OR CRAYFISH BUTTER   Grind 8 ounces (250 grams) cooked lobster or crayfish meat, shells and/or coral with 1 pound (500 grams) butter. Place in a saucepan and clarify. Strain the butter through a fine chinois lined with cheesecloth. Refrigerate, then remove the butterfat when firm.

MAÎTRE D'HÔTEL BUTTER   Mix into the butter 4 tablespoons (60 milliliters) finely chopped parsley, 3 tablespoons (45 milliliters) lemon juice and a dash of white pepper.

MONTPELIER BUTTER   Blanch 1 ounce (30 grams) parsley, 1 ounce (30 grams) chervil, 1 ounce (30 grams) watercress and 1 ounce (30 grams)

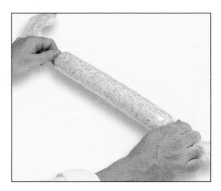

2 Rolling the butter in the plastic wrap to form a cylinder.

tarragon in boiling water. Drain thoroughly. Mince 2 hard-boiled egg yolks, 2 garlic cloves and 2 gherkin pickles. Blend everything into the butter.

RED PEPPER BUTTER   Purée 8 ounces (250 grams) roasted, peeled red bell peppers until liquid, then add to the butter.

SHALLOT BUTTER   Blanch 8 ounces (250 grams) of peeled shallots in boiling water. Dry and finely dice them and mix with the butter.

PAN GRAVY

▶ **gravy** a sauce made from meat or poultry juices combined with a liquid and thickening agent; usually made in the pan in which the meat or poultry was cooked

Pan gravy is aptly named: It is made directly in the pan used to roast the poultry, beef, lamb or pork that the gravy will accompany. Pan gravy is actually a sauce; it is a liquid thickened with a roux. Pan gravy gains additional flavors from the drippings left in the roasting pan and by using a portion of the fat rendered during the roasting process to make the roux. This technique is used in the recipe for Roast Turkey with Chestnut Dressing and Giblet Gravy (page 425).

A properly made pan gravy should have all the characteristics of any brown sauce except that it has a meatier flavor as a result of the pan drippings.

▶ PROCEDURE FOR PREPARING PAN GRAVY

1 Remove the cooked meat or poultry from the roasting pan.
2 If mirepoix was not added during the roasting process, add it to the pan containing the drippings and fat.
3 Place the roasting pan on the stove top and clarify the fat by cooking off any remaining moisture.
4 Pour off the fat, reserving it to make the roux.
5 Deglaze the pan using an appropriate stock. The deglazing liquid may be transferred to a saucepan for easier handling, or the gravy may be finished directly in the roasting pan.
6 Add enough stock or water to the deglazing liquid to yield the proper amount of finished gravy.
7 Determine the amount of roux needed to thicken the liquid and prepare it in a separate pan, using a portion of the reserved fat.
8 Add the roux to the liquid and bring the mixture to a simmer. Simmer until the mirepoix is well cooked, the flavor is extracted and the flour taste is cooked out.
9 Strain the gravy and adjust the seasonings.

COULIS

▶ **coulis** (koo-lee) a sauce made from a purée of vegetables and/or fruit; may be served hot or cold

The term *coulis* most often refers to a sauce made from a purée of vegetables and/or fruit. A vegetable coulis can be served as either a hot or a cold accompaniment to other vegetables, starches, meat, poultry, fish or shellfish. It is often made from a single vegetable base (popular examples include broccoli, tomatoes and sweet red peppers) cooked with flavoring ingredients such as onions, garlic, shallots, herbs and spices and then puréed. An appropriate liquid (stock, water or cream) may be added to thin the purée if necessary. Vegetable coulis are often prepared with very little fat and served as a healthy alternative to a heavier, classic sauce.

A fruit coulis, often made from fresh or frozen berries, is generally used as a dessert sauce. It is usually as simple as puréed fruit thinned to the desired consistency with sugar syrup.

Typically, both vegetable and fruit coulis have a texture similar to that of a thin tomato sauce. But their textures can range from slightly grainy to almost lumpy, depending on their intended use. The flavor and color of a coulis should be that of the main ingredient. The flavors of herbs, spices and other flavoring ingredients should only complement and not dominate the coulis.

▶ PROCEDURE FOR PREPARING A COULIS

Here we include a procedure for making a vegetable coulis. Procedures for making fruit coulis are included as recipes in Chapter 34, Custards, Creams, Frozen Desserts and Dessert Sauces.

1 Cook the main ingredient and any additional flavoring ingredients with an appropriate liquid.
2 Purée the main ingredient and flavoring ingredients in a food mill, blender or food processor.
3 Combine the purée with the appropriate liquid and simmer to blend the flavors.
4 Thin and season the coulis as desired.

RED PEPPER COULIS

RECIPE 11.17

Yield: 1 qt. (1 lt)

Vegetable oil	1 fl. oz.	30 ml
Garlic, chopped	2 tsp.	10 ml
Onion, small dice	3 oz.	90 g
Red bell pepper, medium dice	3 lb.	1.25 kg
White wine	8 fl. oz.	250 ml
Chicken stock	1 pt.	450 ml
Salt and pepper	TT	TT

1 Heat the oil and sauté the garlic and onion until translucent, without browning.
2 Add the bell pepper and sauté until tender.
3 Deglaze the pan with the white wine.
4 Add the chicken stock, bring to a simmer and cook for 15 minutes. Season with salt and pepper.
5 Purée in a blender or food processor and strain through a china cap.
6 Adjust the consistency and seasonings and hold for service.

Approximate values per 1-fl.-oz. (30-ml) serving: **Calories** 20, **Total fat** 1 g, **Saturated fat** 0 g, **Cholesterol** 0 mg, **Sodium** 45 mg, **Total carbohydrates** 2 g, **Protein** 1 g, **Vitamin C** 50%, **Claims**—low fat; low sodium; low calorie

1 Sautéing the red peppers.

2 Puréeing the cooked peppers.

3 Straining the coulis.

CONTEMPORARY SAUCES

Modern chefs and menu writers are relying less on traditional sauces and more on salsas, relishes, juices, broths, essences and infused oils in their work. Unlike classic sauces, these modern accompaniments do not rely on meat-based stocks and starch thickeners, but rather on fresh vegetables, vegetable juices, aromatic broths and intensely flavored oils. The names for these sauces are not codified, as are those in the classic sauce repertoire. Chefs apply various terms freely, using whatever name best fits the dish and the overall menu. Most of these contemporary sauces can be prepared more quickly than their classic counterparts, and the use of fresh fruits and vegetables enhances the healthfulness of the dish. These so-called contemporary or modern sauces may have a lighter body and less fat than classic sauces, but they are still derived from classical culinary techniques and principles. The sauces should be appropriate in flavor, texture and appearance and should complement, not overwhelm, the food they accompany.

SALSA AND RELISH

Many people think of salsa (Spanish for "sauce") as a chunky mixture of raw vegetables and chiles eaten with chips or ladled over Mexican food; they think

▶ **chutney** a sweet-and-sour condiment made of fruits and/or vegetables cooked in vinegar with sugar and spices; some chutneys are reduced to a purée; others retain recognizable pieces of their ingredients.

of relish as a sweet green condiment spooned on a hot dog. But salsas and relishes—generally, cold chunky mixtures of herbs, spices, fruits and/or vegetables—can be used as sauces for many meat, poultry, fish and shellfish items. They can include ingredients such as oranges, pineapple, papaya, black beans, jicama, tomatillos and an array of other vegetables.

Although not members of any classic sauce family, salsas and relishes are currently enjoying great popularity because of their intense fresh flavors, ease of preparation and low fat and calorie content. Salsas and relishes are often a riot of colors, textures and flavors, simultaneously cool and hot, spicy and sweet.

▶ PROCEDURE FOR PREPARING A SALSA OR RELISH

1 Cut or chop the ingredients.

2 Precook and chill items as directed in the recipe.

3 Toss all ingredients together and refrigerate, allowing the flavors to combine for at least 30 minutes before service.

RECIPE 11.18

TOMATO SALSA (PICO DE GALLO)

Mixing tomato salsa.

Yield: 1 qt. (1 lt)

Tomatoes, seeded, small dice	5	5
Green onions, sliced	1 bunch	1 bunch
Garlic cloves, minced	3	3
Cilantro, chopped	½ bunch	½ bunch
Jalapeño, chopped fine	3	3
Lemon juice	2 fl. oz.	60 ml
Cumin, ground	½ tsp.	2 ml
Salt and pepper	TT	TT

1 Combine all ingredients and gently toss. Adjust seasonings and refrigerate.

Approximate values per 1-fl.-oz. (30-ml) serving: **Calories** 5, **Total fat** 0 g, **Saturated fat** 0 g, **Cholesterol** 0 mg, **Sodium** 30 mg, **Total carbohydrates** 1 g, **Protein** 0 g, **Claims**—fat free; very low sodium; low calorie

VEGETABLE JUICE SAUCES

Juice extractors make it possible to prepare juice from fresh, uncooked vegetables such as carrots, beets and spinach. Thinner and smoother than a purée, vegetable juice can be heated, reduced, flavored and enriched with butter to create colorful, intensely flavored sauces. Cream or stock can be added to finish the sauce. Sauces made from vegetable juices are sometimes referred to as an **essence** or **tea** on menus.

▶ **essence** a sauce made from a concentrated vegetable juice

Juice from a single type of vegetable provides the purest, most pronounced flavor, but two or more vegetables sometimes can be combined successfully. Be careful of mixing too many flavors and colors in the juice, however. Juiced vegetable sauces are particularly appropriate with pasta, fish, shellfish and poultry, and can be useful in vegetarian cuisine or as a healthier alternative to classic sauces.

▶ PROCEDURE FOR PREPARING A VEGETABLE JUICE SAUCE

1 Wash and peel vegetables as needed.

2 Process the vegetables through a juice extractor.

3 Place the juice in a saucepan and add stock, lemon juice, herbs or other flavorings as desired.

4 Bring the sauce to a simmer and reduce as necessary.

5 Strain the sauce through a fine chinois.

6 Adjust the seasonings and whisk in whole butter to finish.

THYME-SCENTED CELERY ESSENCE   RECIPE 11.19

STOUFFER STANFORD COURT HOTEL, SAN FRANCISCO, CA
Former Executive Chef Ercolino Crugnale

Yield: 1 qt. (1 lt)

Celery juice	1 qt.	1 lt
Tomato juice	1 pt.	500 ml
Fresh thyme, chopped	½ oz.	15 g
Whole butter	6 oz.	180 g
Salt	TT	TT
Tabasco sauce	TT	TT

1 Combine the celery juice, tomato juice and thyme. Bring to a simmer and reduce to 1½ pints (750 milliliters).

2 Whisk in the butter and adjust the seasonings with salt and Tabasco sauce.

3 Strain through a chinois.

Approximate values per 1-fl.-oz. (30-ml) serving: **Calories** 50, **Total fat** 4.5 g, **Saturated fat** 2.4 g, **Cholesterol** 10 mg, **Sodium** 200 mg, **Total carbohydrates** 2 g, **Protein** 0 g

BROTH

Broth, which also appears on menus as a **tea, au jus, essence** or **nage,** is a thin, flavorful liquid served in a pool beneath the main food. The broth should not be so abundant as to turn an entrée into a soup, but it should provide moisture and flavor. The essence, broth or nage is often made by simply reducing and straining the liquid in which the main food was cooked. Alternatively, a specifically flavored stock—tomato, for example—can be prepared, then clarified like consommé to create a broth or essence to accompany an appetizer or entrée.

▶ **essence** a sauce made from a concentrated vegetable juice

FLAVORED OIL

Small amounts of intensely flavored oils can be used to dress or garnish a variety of dishes. Salads, soups, vegetable and starch dishes and entrées can be enhanced with a drizzle of colorful, appropriately flavored oil. Because such small quantities are used, these oils provide flavor and moisture without adding too many calories or fat.

Unless the flavoring ingredient goes especially well with olive oil (for example, basil), select a high-quality but neutral oil such as peanut, safflower or canola. Although flavoring ingredients can be simply steeped in oil for a time, a better way to flavor oil is to crush, purée or cook the flavoring ingredients first.

▶ PROCEDURE FOR PREPARING A FLAVORED OIL

1 Purée or chop fresh herbs, fruits or vegetables. Sweat dry spices or seeds in a small amount of oil to form a paste.

2 Place the selected oil and the flavoring ingredients in a jar or other tightly lidded container.

Table 11.5 USING SAUCES

SAUCE	QUALITIES	SMALL SAUCE OR FLAVORINGS	USE
Béchamel	Smooth, rich and creamy; no graininess; cream-colored with rich sheen	Cream	Vegetables, pasta, eggs, fish
		Cheese	Vegetables, pasta
		Mornay	Fish, shellfish, poultry, vegetables
		Nantua	Fish, shellfish
		Soubise	Veal, pork, eggs
Velouté	Smooth and rich; ivory-colored; good flavor of the stock used; not pasty or heavy	Fish Velouté	
		Bercy	Poached fish
		Cardinal	Lobster, white fish, crab, eggs
		Normandy	Delicate white fish, oysters
		Allemande (veal or chicken)	
		Aurora	Eggs, chicken, sweetbreads
		Horseradish	Roast beef, corned beef, baked ham
		Mushroom	Sautéed poultry, white meats
		Poulette	Vegetables, sweetbreads
		Suprême (chicken)	
		Albufera	Braised poultry, sweetbreads
		Hungarian	Eggs, chicken, chops, sweetbreads
		Ivory	Eggs, braised poultry
Espagnole	Smooth and rich; dark brown color; good meat flavor	Bordelaise	Sautéed or grilled meats
		Chasseur	Sautéed or grilled meats and poultry
		Châteaubriand	Broiled meats
		Chevreuil	Roasted meats and game
		Madeira/Port	Grilled or roasted meats and game, ham
		Marchand de Vin	Grilled or roasted meats
		Mushroom	Sautéed or grilled meats and poultry
		Périgueux/Périgourdine	Sautéed poultry, grilled meats and game, sweetbreads
		Piquant	Pork
		Poivrade	Grilled or roasted meats, game
		Robert	Pork
Tomato	Thick and rich; slightly grainy; full-flavored	Tomato	Meats, poultry, vegetables, pasta and for making small sauces
		Creole	Fish, eggs, chicken
		Spanish	Eggs, fish
		Milanaise	Pasta, grilled or sautéed poultry and white meats
Hollandaise	Smooth and rich; buttery flavor; light and slightly frothy; pale yellow color; no signs of separating	Béarnaise	Grilled or sautéed meats and fish
		Choron	Grilled meats and fish
		Foyot	Grilled meats and fish
		Grimrod	Eggs, poached fish
		Maltaise	Poached fish
		Mousseline	Poached fish, eggs, vegetables
Beurre blanc and beurre rouge	Rich and buttery; thinner than hollandaise; light and airy; pale-colored	Wide variety of seasonings and flavorings may be used	Steamed, grilled or poached fish, chicken or vegetables
Compound butter	Flavor ingredients should be evenly distributed	Wide variety of seasonings and flavorings may be used	Grilled meats, poultry and fish; finishing sauces
Pan gravy	Smooth; deep rich color; meaty flavor	Made from pan drippings	Roasted meats and poultry
Coulis	Rich color; moderately thin, grainy texture; strongly flavored	Made with a wide variety of vegetables or fruits	Vegetables, grilled or poached meats, poultry and fish
Salsa and relish	Chunky; bright colors; not watery	Made with a wide variety of vegetables, fruits and seasonings	Meats, fish, vegetables and poultry; used as a sauce or condiment
Flavored oil	Smooth; bright colors; intense flavors	Made with a variety of herbs, spices and seasonings	Used as a garnish

3 Allow the mixture to stand at room temperature until sufficient flavor is extracted. This may take from 1 to 24 hours. Shake the jar periodically. Do not allow the flavoring ingredients to remain in the oil indefinitely, as it may become harsh or bitter.

4 Strain the oil through a chinois lined with a coffee filter.

5 Store the flavored oil in a covered container in the refrigerator.

SHALLOT CURRY OIL

RECIPE 11. 20

Yield: 8 fl. oz. (225 ml)

Canola oil	8 fl. oz.	225 ml
Shallot, minced	1	1
Curry powder	4 Tbsp.	60 ml
Water	2 fl. oz.	60 ml

1 In a small saucepan, heat 1 tablespoon (15 milliliters) of oil over medium heat. Add the shallot and sauté until softened and translucent. Do not allow the shallot to brown.

2 Add the curry powder and sauté for 1 to 2 minutes.

3 Stir in the water and bring the mixture to a boil. Reduce the heat and simmer until most of the water evaporates, leaving a paste of curry and shallots.

4 Remove from the heat and stir in the remaining oil.

5 Place the mixture in a lidded jar and set aside at room temperature for 6 to 8 hours. Shake the jar occasionally.

6 Strain the oil through a chinois lined with a coffee filter. Place the flavored oil in a covered container and refrigerate until ready to use.

Approximate values per 1-fl.-oz. (30-ml) serving: **Calories** 208, **Total fat** 23 g, **Saturated fat** 2 g, **Cholesterol** 0 mg, **Sodium** 1 mg, **Total carbohydrates** 1 g, **Protein** 0 g, **Claims**—no cholesterol; no sodium

CONCLUSION

In *Le Guide culinaire,* Auguste Escoffier wrote "Indeed, stock is everything in cooking . . . without it, nothing can be done. If one's stock is good, what remains of the work is easy; if, on the other hand, it is bad or merely mediocre, it is quite hopeless to expect anything approaching a satisfactory result." Because stocks and the sauces made from them are still the basis for much of contemporary cuisine, Escoffier's words are as true today as when he wrote them.

Both the classic mother sauces and the small sauces derived from them as well as sauces such as beurre blanc and beurre rouge, coulis, flavored oils, salsas and relishes that are not based on classic recipes all share two goals: to complement the foods with which they are served and neither mask nor disguise poorly prepared foods. With practice and care (and the right ingredients), you will be able to make great sauces.

QUESTIONS FOR DISCUSSION

1 Why are the bones of younger animals preferred for making stocks?

2 Why should a stock made from beef or veal bones cook longer than a stock made from fish bones? What is the result if a stock does not cook long enough?

3 What can cause a stock to become cloudy? How can you prevent this from happening?

4 List three differences in the production of a white stock and a brown stock.

5 List the five classic mother sauces, and explain how they are used to prepare small sauces.

6 Why is demi-glace preferred when making brown sauces? Is jus lié different from classic demi-glace? Can they be used interchangeably?

7 Why are temperatures important when making hollandaise sauce? What precautions must be taken when holding hollandaise for service?

8 Compare a beurre blanc and a hollandaise sauce. How are they similar? How are they different?

9 How are compound butters used in making sauces? What are the ingredients for a traditional maître d'hôtel butter?

10 What are the differences between a salsa, a chutney and a relish? Can these items be used in place of classic sauces? Explain your answer.

11 What are the differences between a vegetable juice sauce and a broth?

SEARED DIVER SCALLOPS WITH TOMATILLO SAUCE, AVOCADO RELISH AND TOMATO SYRUP

RECIPE 11.21

Note: This dish appears in the chapter opening photograph.

PRIMITIVO WINE BAR, COLORADO SPRINGS, CO

John Broening, Executive Chef

Yield: 8 Servings   **Method:** Sautéing

Scallops, 1 oz. (30 g) each	24	24
Salt and white pepper	TT	TT
Clarified butter	4 fl. oz.	120 ml
Tomatillo Sauce (recipe follows)	as needed	as needed
Tomato Syrup (recipe follows)	as needed	as needed
Avocado Relish (recipe follows)	as needed	as needed
Cilantro	24 sprigs	24 sprigs
Black and white sesame seeds, toasted	3 Tbsp.	45 ml
Curried Chickpea Crisps (recipe follows)	as needed	as needed

1 Season the scallops with salt and white pepper. Heat the clarified butter in a sauté pan until very hot. Sear the scallops until golden brown, approximately 2 minutes on each side. Remove the scallops when they are done and drain on paper towels.

2 Spoon three pools of Tomatillo Sauce on each of 8 plates. Place a pool of Tomato Syrup next to each pool of Tomatillo Sauce. Place a scallop in the center of each pool of Tomatillo Sauce. Top each scallop with a quenelle-shaped dollop of Avocado Relish. Top the relish with a sprig of cilantro. Sprinkle each plate with sesame seeds and garnish with Curried Chickpea Crisps.

Approximate values per serving: **Calories** 360, **Total fat** 27 g, **Saturated fat** 10 g, **Cholesterol** 60 mg, **Sodium** 370 mg, **Total carbohydrates** 17 g, **Protein** 17 g, **Vitamin A** 45%, **Vitamin C** 80%, **Iron** 15%

CHEF JOHN BROENING

A graduate of Peter Kump's New York Cooking School, John Broening is executive chef of Primitivo Wine Bar in Colorado Springs. He is also a writer and the book reviewer for the Colorado Springs *Independent.*

Starting with a job at the Hit N Run Club in Baltimore's Memorial Stadium, Chef Broening moved on to such internationally known restaurants as Chef Patrick Clark's Metro in New York, Bistrot de l'Etoile and Le Grenadin in Paris and Bix, Roti, Grand Café and Obelisque in the San Francisco Bay area. He joined Primitivo Wine Bar in 1999 and has represented the restaurant at several James Beard House functions.

He advises students that "if you're in this profession for the long haul, take care of your health."

TOMATILLO SAUCE

Yield: 20 fl. oz. (570 ml)

Tomatillos, small	8	8
Olive oil	1 Tbsp.	15 ml
Lime	1	1
Cilantro leaves	2 c.	450 ml
Jalapeños, seeded, chopped fine	2	2
Garlic, minced	1 tsp.	5 ml
Cumin, ground, toasted	1 tsp.	5 ml
Honey	1 Tbsp.	15 ml
Salt and pepper	TT	TT

1 Remove the husks from the tomatillos. Soak them in warm water for 30 seconds. Drain and toss the tomatillos in the olive oil. Place the tomatillos on a half sheet pan and roast in a 300°F (150°C) oven until soft but not colored. Cool completely.

2 Juice the lime.

3 Combine the tomatillos with the other ingredients in the bowl of a blender and blend for a few seconds or until smooth.

Approximate values per 1-fl.-oz. (30-ml) serving: **Calories** 15, **Total fat** 1 g, **Saturated fat** 0 g, **Cholesterol** 0 mg, **Sodium** 0 mg, **Total carbohydrates** 2 g, **Protein** 0 g, **Vitamin C** 15%

TOMATO SYRUP

Yield: 6 fl. oz. (180 ml)

Tomato juice	1 pt.	450 ml
Chipotle powder	1 pinch	1 pinch
Cumin, ground, toasted	1 pinch	1 pinch
Salt and pepper	TT	TT

1 In a nonreactive sauce pan, reduce the tomato juice by two-thirds. Add the remaining ingredients, stir well and strain through a chinois.

Approximate values per 1-fl.-oz. (30-ml) serving: **Calories** 15, **Total fat** 0 g, **Saturated fat** 0 g, **Cholesterol** 0 mg, **Sodium** 290 mg, **Total carbohydrates** 3 g, **Protein** 1 g, **Vitamin A** 10%, **Vitamin C** 25%

AVOCADO RELISH

Yield: 16 fl. oz. (450 ml)

Lime	1	1
Ripe avocados, peeled and chopped fine	2	2
Jalapeño, seeded, chopped fine	1	1
Cilantro leaves, chopped coarse	2 Tbsp.	30 ml
Cumin, ground, toasted	½ tsp.	3 ml
Olive oil	1 Tbsp.	15 ml
Tomato concassée	4 Tbsp.	60 ml
Salt and pepper	TT	TT
Onion, minced	3 Tbsp.	45 ml

1 Juice the lime.
2 Combine the lime juice with all of the ingredients and mix well.

Approximate values per 1-fl.-oz. (30-ml) serving: **Calories** 50, **Total fat** 4.5 g, **Saturated fat** 0.5 g, **Cholesterol** 0 mg, **Sodium** 0 mg, **Total carbohydrates** 3 g, **Protein** 1 g, **Vitamin C** 10%

CURRIED CHICKPEA CRISPS

Yield: 2 qt. (2 lt)

All-purpose flour	1½ c.	350 ml
Chickpea flour	1 c.	240 ml
Turmeric	1 Tbsp.	15 ml
Cumin, ground	1 Tbsp.	15 ml
Coriander, ground	1 Tbsp.	15 ml
Cinnamon, ground	1 tsp.	5 ml
Cayenne pepper	½ tsp.	3 ml
Black pepper, ground	1 tsp.	5 ml
Salt	1 Tbsp.	15 ml
Granulated sugar	1 Tbsp.	15 ml
Water	¾ c.	180 ml
Extra virgin olive oil	2 Tbsp.	30 ml

1 In a stainless steel bowl, stir together the dry ingredients. Form a pool in the middle of the mixture and add the liquid ingredients. Mix together by hand, adding additional flour if necessary. Knead until smooth and elastic, approximately 5 minutes.
2 Roll out the dough using a pasta machine to thickness number 6. Using a ravioli cutter, cut the dough into 2-inch × ¼-inch (5-centimeter × 6-millimeter) strips.
3 Using the swimming method, deep-fry the strips at 275°F (135°C) for 3 minutes. Season with salt and hold warm.

MARCHAND DE VIN (RED-WINE SAUCE)

RECIPE 11.22

BRENNAN'S RESTAURANT, New Orleans, LA
Chef Michael Roussel

Yield: 24 fl. oz. (680 ml)   **Method:** Roux-thickened

Unsalted butter	3 oz.	90 g
Onion, chopped fine	2 oz.	60 g
Garlic, chopped fine	1½ tsp.	7 ml
Green onion, chopped fine	2 oz.	60 g
Boiled ham, chopped fine	2 oz.	60 g
Mushrooms, chopped fine	2 oz.	60 g
All-purpose flour	⅓ c.	75 ml
Worcestershire sauce	2 Tbsp.	30 ml
Beef stock	1 pt.	450 ml
Red wine	4 fl. oz.	120 ml
Thyme, dried leaves	1½ tsp.	7 ml
Bay leaf	1	1
Fresh parsley, chopped fine	1½ oz.	45 g
Salt and pepper	TT	TT

1 Melt the butter in a large saucepan and sauté the onion, garlic, green onions and ham for 5 minutes.

2 Add the mushrooms, reduce the heat to medium and cook for 2 minutes.

3 Blend in the flour and cook, stirring, for 4 minutes. Then add the Worcestershire sauce, stock, wine, thyme and bay leaf. Simmer until the sauce thickens, approximately 1 hour.

4 At service, remove the bay leaf and add the parsley. Season to taste with salt and pepper.

5 For a smoother texture, pass the sauce through a fine mesh strainer before adding the parsley.

Approximate values per 1½-fl.-oz. (45-ml) serving: **Calories** 45, **Total fat** 3 g, **Saturated fat** 2 g, **Cholesterol** 10 mg, **Sodium** 100 mg, **Total carbohydrates** 3 g, **Protein** 1 g, **Vitamin A** 15%

BRENNAN'S RED-WINE AND MUSHROOM SAUCE

RECIPE 11.23

BRENNAN'S RESTAURANT, New Orleans, LA
Chef Michael Roussel

Yield: 24 fl. oz. (680 ml)

Whole butter	4 oz.	120 g
Onion, diced	4 oz.	120 g
Tomato paste	4 oz.	120 g
Mushrooms, sliced	1 pt.	450 ml
Paprika	1½ Tbsp.	22 ml
All-purpose flour	1 oz.	30 g
Beef stock	24 fl. oz.	680 ml
Green onion, sliced	8 oz.	225 g
Worcestershire sauce	1 Tbsp.	15 ml
Burgundy wine	6 fl. oz.	180 ml
Garlic, minced	1 Tbsp.	15 ml
Salt and pepper	TT	TT

1 Melt the butter in a large saucepan. Add the onion and sauté until tender, approximately 3 minutes.

2 Stir in the tomato paste, mushrooms and paprika. Cook until the mushroom is tender, then add the flour. Stir until well blended.

3 Using a whisk, incorporate the stock. When the sauce is smooth, add the green onion, Worcestershire sauce, wine and garlic. Simmer until reduced and thickened, approximately 25 minutes. Season to taste with salt and pepper and hold for service.

Approximate values per 2-fl.-oz. (60-ml) serving: **Calories** 60, **Total fat** 4 g, **Saturated fat** 2.5 g, **Cholesterol** 10 mg, **Sodium** 95 mg, **Total carbohydrates** 5 g, **Protein** 1 g, **Vitamin A** 25%, **Vitamin C** 10%

RECIPE 11.24   RED-WINE THYME SAUCE

VINCENT ON CAMELBACK, Phoenix, AZ
Chef Vincent Guerithault

Yield: 1½ qt. (1.5 lt)   **Method:** Reduction

Red wine	8 fl. oz.	250 ml
Garlic, chopped	1 Tbsp.	15 ml
Shallot, chopped	2 oz.	60 g
Veal stock	1 qt.	1 lt
Fresh rosemary	1 sprig	1 sprig
Fresh thyme	1 sprig	1 sprig
Bay leaves	2	2
Unsalted butter	1 oz.	30 g

1 Reduce the red wine, garlic and shallot by one-quarter.

2 Add the veal stock, rosemary, thyme and bay leaves and reduce by one-quarter.

3 Remove from the heat and strain. Monter au beurre.

Approximate values per 1-fl.-oz. (30-ml) serving: **Calories** 40, **Total fat** 2 g, **Saturated fat** 1 g, **Cholesterol** 5 mg, **Sodium** 210 mg, **Total carbohydrates** 4 g, **Protein** 1 g, **Vitamin A** 10%, **Claims**—low fat; low calorie; no sugar

---

RECIPE 11.25   ROASTED GARLIC SAUCE

CHEF LELAND ATKINSON, Washington, DC

Yield: 12 fl. oz. (340 ml)

Shallot, minced	4 Tbsp.	60 ml
Clarified butter	1 Tbsp.	15 ml
Madeira	4 fl. oz.	120 ml
Fresh thyme	1 sprig	1 sprig
Bay leaf	1	1
Garlic head, trimmed and roasted	1	1
Demi-glace	1 pt.	450 ml
Roux	as needed	as needed
Salt and pepper	TT	TT

1 Sauté the shallot lightly in the clarified butter until slightly caramelized.

2 Add the Madeira, thyme and bay leaf and reduce by one-third.

3 Squeeze in the garlic, discarding the skins and root.

4 Add the demi-glace and reduce by one third.

5 Thicken slightly with roux if desired, adjust the seasonings and force through a fine strainer.

Approximate values per 1-fl.-oz. (30-ml) serving: **Calories** 15, **Total fat** 1 g, **Saturated fat** 0.5 g, **Cholesterol** 5 mg, **Sodium** 240 mg, **Total carbohydrates** 0 g, **Protein** 0 g

HORSERADISH CREAM SAUCE

RECIPE 11.26

BRENNAN'S RESTAURANT, New Orleans, LA
Chef Michael Roussel

Yield: 24 fl. oz. (680 ml)

Heavy cream	1 qt.	950 ml
Salt	½ tsp.	3 ml
White pepper	½ tsp.	3 ml
Whole butter	½ tsp.	3 ml
All-purpose flour	4 Tbsp.	60 ml
Horseradish, grated	4 Tbsp.	60 ml

1 Combine the cream, salt and pepper in a saucepan. Heat over medium heat. Do not allow the cream to boil.

2 Rub the butter and flour together to form small balls (beurre manié).

3 Add the beurre manié to the simmering cream. Cook until the sauce is smooth, then add the horseradish. Serve warm.

Approximate values per 1-fl.-oz. (30-ml) serving: **Calories** 140, **Total fat** 15 g, **Saturated fat** 9 g, **Cholesterol** 55 mg, **Sodium** 65 mg, **Total carbohydrates** 2 g, **Protein** 1 g, **Vitamin A** 10%

DUXELLES SAUCE

RECIPE 11.27

Yield: 1½ pt. (750 ml)

Mushroom, chopped fine	8 oz.	250 g
Shallot, chopped fine	3 oz.	90 g
Clarified butter	1 fl. oz.	30 ml
Olive oil	1 fl. oz.	30 ml
Dry white wine	12 fl. oz.	700 ml
Demi-glace	1 pt.	500 ml
Heavy cream	2 fl. oz.	60 ml
Salt and pepper	TT	TT
Parsley, chopped fine	1 Tbsp.	15 ml

1 Sauté the mushroom and shallot in the butter and oil. The mushrooms will release their liquid and darken. Cook until completely dry.

2 Deglaze with the white wine and reduce by two-thirds.

3 Add the demi-glace. Bring to a boil, then simmer for 5 minutes.

4 Stir in the cream. Adjust the seasonings. Garnish with parsley.

Approximate values per 1-fl.-oz. (30-ml) serving: **Calories** 100, **Total fat** 10 g, **Saturated fat** 6 g, **Cholesterol** 30 mg, **Sodium** 40 g, **Total carbohydrates** 2 g, **Protein** 1 g, **Vitamin A** 15%

FRESH TOMATO SAUCE FOR PASTA

RECIPE 11.28

Yield: 2½ qt. (2.5 lt)

Onion, small dice	8 oz.	250 g
Carrot, small dice	4 oz.	120 g
Garlic, minced	1 Tbsp.	15 ml
Olive oil	2 fl. oz.	60 ml
Tomato concassée	7 lb.	3.1 kg
Fresh oregano	1 Tbsp.	15 ml
Fresh thyme	2 tsp.	10 ml
Salt	1 tsp.	5 ml
Pepper	½ tsp.	2 ml
Fresh basil, chopped	½ oz.	15 g

1 Sweat the onion, carrot and garlic in the olive oil until tender.

2 Add the tomato concassée, oregano and thyme. Simmer for approximately 1 hour or until the desired consistency is reached.

3 Pass the sauce through a food mill if a smooth consistency is desired. Do not purée if a chunkier sauce is desired.

4 Adjust the seasonings and add the chopped basil.

Approximate values per 1-fl.-oz. (30-ml) serving: **Calories** 20, **Total fat** 1 g, **Saturated fat** 0 g, **Cholesterol** 0 mg, **Sodium** 35 mg, **Total carbohydrates** 2 g, **Protein** 0 g, **Vitamin** C 15%, **Claims**—low fat; low sodium; low calorie

RECIPE 11.29	BOLOGNESE SAUCE	

Yield: 1 qt. (1 lt)

Mirepoix, fine dice	8 oz.	250 g
Olive oil	2 fl. oz.	60 ml
Whole butter	1 oz.	30 g
Ground beef	1 lb.	500 g
White wine	8 fl. oz.	250 ml
Milk	6 fl. oz.	180 ml
Nutmeg	TT	TT
Tomato concassée	2 lb.	1 kg
White stock	approx. 8 fl. oz.	approx. 250 ml
Salt and pepper	TT	TT

1 Sauté the mirepoix in the olive oil and butter until tender. Add the beef and cook until no pink remains. Drain fat if necessary.

2 Add the wine. Cook and reduce the wine until nearly dry.

3 Add the milk and season with nutmeg. Cook and reduce the milk until nearly dry.

4 Add the tomato concassée and 8 fluid ounces (250 milliliters) of stock; season with salt and pepper. Simmer for 3 to 4 hours, adding stock as needed to prevent scorching. Adjust the seasonings.

Approximate values per 1-fl.-oz. (30-ml) serving: **Calories** 50, **Total fat** 4 g, **Saturated fat** 1.5 g, **Cholesterol** 10 mg, **Sodium** 115 mg, **Total carbohydrates** 2 g, **Protein** 2 g, **Vitamin C** 10%

RECIPE 11.30	MOLE	

Yield: 1 qt. (1 lt)

Cinnamon stick	1	1
Allspice	1/2 tsp.	3 ml
Guajillo chiles	2	2
Pasilla chiles	2	2
Sesame seeds	4 oz.	120 g
Pumpkin seeds	6 oz.	180 g
Cumin seeds	1 tsp.	5 ml
Onion, small	1	1
Olive oil	as needed	as needed
Plum tomatoes	4	4
Garlic cloves	4	4
Fresh thyme	1 sprig	1 sprig
Oregano, dried	1 tsp.	5 ml
Chicken stock	1 qt.	1 lt
Salt	TT	TT
Semisweet chocolate, chopped	2 oz.	60 g

1 Grind the cinnamon and allspice in a spice grinder.

2 Stem and seed the guajillo and pasilla chiles. Break them into small pieces and simmer them in water for 15 minutes. Drain well.

3 Combine the sesame seeds, pumpkin seeds and cumin seeds and fry them in a dry sauté pan until well toasted.

4 Slice the onion approximately ½ inch (1.2 centimeters) thick. Brush it with olive oil and grill it until well colored.

5 Roast the tomatoes in the flame of a gas burner until they are evenly charred and blistered. Remove the cores, peel the tomatoes and chop them coarsely.

6 Combine the cinnamon and allspice with the chiles, toasted seeds, onion, tomatoes, garlic, thyme, oregano and chicken stock in a saucepan. Season with salt and bring to a boil. Reduce to a simmer and cook for 15 minutes. Remove from the heat, cool and remove the sprig of thyme.

7 Blend the mixture in a blender until smooth. Strain through a china cap and stir in the chocolate until melted. Adjust the seasonings.

8 Serve the mole over grilled chicken, turkey, duck, quail or a meat such as pork or rabbit. Or, reheat cooked turkey or chicken pieces in the sauce until hot and serve with a portion of the sauce.

Approximate values per 1-fl.-oz. (30-ml) serving: **Calories** 70, **Total fat** 5 g, **Saturated fat** 1 g, **Cholesterol** 0 mg, **Sodium** 90 mg, **Total carbohydrates** 4 g, **Protein** 2 g, **Iron** 10%

FRESH TOMATO VINAIGRETTE FOR PASTA

RECIPE 11.31

Yield: 2 qt. (2 lt)

Tomato concassée	8 oz.	250 g
Fresh basil, thyme or marjoram	1 oz.	30 g
Balsamic vinegar	3 fl. oz.	90 ml
Shallot, minced	2 Tbsp.	30 ml
Olive oil	8 fl. oz.	250 ml
Salt and pepper	TT	TT

1 Combine all ingredients. Season to taste with salt and pepper. Set aside for 20 to 30 minutes to allow the flavors to blend.

2 Adjust the seasonings. Serve immediately or refrigerate and serve chilled.

Approximate values per 8-fl.-oz. (240-ml) serving: **Calories** 700, **Total fat** 58 g, **Saturated fat** 8 g, **Cholesterol** 35 mg, **Sodium** 600 mg, **Total carbohydrates** 38 g, **Protein** 7 g, **Vitamin C** 20%

PESTO SAUCE

RECIPE 11.32

Yield: 1½ pt. (750 ml)   **Method:** Puréeing

Olive oil	12 fl. oz.	360 ml
Pine nuts	3 oz.	90 g
Fresh basil leaves	6 oz.	180 g
Garlic, chopped	1 Tbsp.	15 ml
Parmesan, grated	4 oz.	120 g
Romano, grated	4 oz.	120 g
Salt and pepper	TT	TT

1 Place one-third of the olive oil in a blender or food processor and add all the remaining ingredients.

2 Blend or process until smooth. Add the remaining olive oil and blend a few seconds to incorporate.

1 Combining the pesto ingredients.

2 The finished pesto sauce.

Variations: *Walnut Pesto*—Substitute walnuts for pine nuts in the recipe.

Sun-Dried Tomato Pesto—Add 1 ounce (30 grams) of sun-dried tomatoes that have been softened in oil or water. Add additional olive oil as necessary.

Approximate values per 1-fl.-oz. (30-ml) serving: **Calories** 200, **Total fat** 19 g, **Saturated fat** 4 g, **Cholesterol** 10 mg, **Sodium** 250 mg, **Total carbohydrates** 1 g, **Protein** 4 g, **Calcium** 15%

RECIPE 11.33 | BRENNAN'S LEMON BUTTER SAUCE

BRENNAN'S RESTAURANT, NEW ORLEANS, LA
Chef Michael Roussel

Yield: 1 qt. (1 lt)

Brown Sauce (page 215)	4 fl. oz.	120 ml
Fresh lemon juice	2 fl. oz.	60 ml
Whole butter, room temperature	2 lb.	900 g

1 Combine the brown sauce and lemon juice in a large saucepan.
2 Working the pan on and off the direct heat, add the butter a bit at a time, whisking the sauce smooth between additions.
3 Adjust the flavor with additional lemon juice if necessary. Transfer the sauce to a clean container and hold at room temperature for service. Use the sauce within 2 hours or discard it.

Approximate values per 1-fl.-oz. (30-ml) serving: **Calories** 210, **Total fat** 23 g, **Saturated fat** 14 g, **Cholesterol** 65 g, **Sodium** 20 mg, **Total carbohydrates** 1 g, **Protein** 0 g, **Vitamin A** 15%

RECIPE 11.34 | CITRUS BEURRE BLANC

VINCENT ON CAMELBACK, PHOENIX, AZ
Chef Vincent Guerithault

Yield: 4 Servings, 5 fl. oz. (150 ml) each

Orange juice	8 fl. oz.	225 ml
Lime juice	1 Tbsp.	15 ml
Lemon juice	1 Tbsp.	15 ml
White wine	8 fl. oz.	225 ml
White wine vinegar	8 fl. oz.	225 ml
Shallot, chopped fine	1 Tbsp.	15 ml
Heavy cream	1 Tbsp.	15 ml
Unsalted butter	1 lb.	450 g
Salt and pepper	TT	TT
Orange rind, grated and blanched	1 Tbsp.	15 ml
Lime rind, grated and blanched	1 Tbsp.	15 ml
Lemon rind, grated and blanched	1 Tbsp.	15 ml

1 Combine the citrus juices, wine, vinegar and shallot and reduce au sec over moderate heat.
2 Whisk in the cream, then whisk in the butter 2 ounces (60 grams) at a time.

3 Strain the sauce, season with salt and pepper and stir in the citrus rinds. Keep hot for service.

Approximate values per 5-fl.-oz. (150-ml) serving: **Calories** 890, **Total fat** 94 g, **Saturated fat** 58 g, **Cholesterol** 255 mg, **Sodium** 600 mg, **Total carbohydrates** 9 g, **Protein** 2 g, **Vitamin A** 90%

CREAM BEURRE BLANC   RECIPE 11.35

THE ART INSTITUTE OF WASHINGTON, ARLINGTON, VA
Chef John Harrison

This version of beurre blanc is easier to master than a traditional beurre blanc. It is also less temperature-sensitive.

Yield: 12 fl. oz. (360 ml)

Shallot, chopped fine	1 Tbsp.	15 ml
Clarified butter	2 tsp.	10 ml
White wine	6 fl. oz.	180 ml
Heavy cream	8 fl. oz.	240 ml
Unsalted butter, softened	8 oz.	240 g
Salt and white pepper	TT	TT

1 Sauté the shallot in the clarified butter until translucent but not brown. Add the white wine and reduce by half.
2 Add the heavy cream, bring to a boil and reduce by two-thirds.
3 Remove from the heat and keep warm. Whisk the softened butter into the sauce in several batches. Move the pan back and forth over the heat to keep the sauce from becoming too hot or too cold.
4 Season the sauce with salt and white pepper. Strain if desired. Hold in a warm place for service.

Note: Like a traditional beurre blanc, this sauce can be flavored by adding any of a wide variety of herbs and spices. Beurre rouge may be prepared by substituting red wine for the white wine.

Approximate values per 2-fl.-oz. (60-ml) serving: **Calories** 220, **Total fat** 23 g, **Saturated fat** 15 g, **Cholesterol** 70 mg, **Sodium** 10 mg, **Total carbohydrates** 1 g, **Protein** 1 g, **Vitamin A** 20%

BEER BEURRE BLANC SAUCE   RECIPE 11.36

MISSISSIPPI UNIVERSITY FOR WOMEN, COLUMBUS, MS
Chef Jim Fitzgerald, Ph.D., CCP

Yield: 1½ qt. (1.4 lt)

Shallots, minced	4	4
Unsalted butter	1 Tbsp.	15 ml
Salt and pepper	TT	TT
White wine vinegar	3 fl. oz.	90 ml
Bay leaf	1	1
Fresh thyme	1 sprig	1 sprig
Beer	10 fl. oz.	300 ml
Unsalted butter, cold	1½ lb.	720 g

1 Sweat the shallots in the 1 tablespoon of butter over medium heat for approximately 2 minutes. Add the salt and pepper, vinegar, bay leaf, thyme and beer.
2 Reduce by two-thirds.

3 Whisk in the cold butter in pieces, moving the pan on and off the heat as necessary. Do not allow the sauce to boil. Adjust the seasonings, strain and hold in a bain marie for up to 2 hours. Serve with fried or grilled meat or poultry.

Approximate values per 1-fl.-oz. (30-ml) serving: **Calories** 110, **Total fat** 12 g, **Saturated fat** 7 g, **Cholesterol** 30 mg, **Sodium** 0, **Total carbohydrates** 0, **Protein** 0, **Vitamin A** 10%

RECIPE 11.37 — TOMATO BUTTER SAUCE WITH THYME

NEWBURY COLLEGE, Brookline, MA
Senior Instructor Scott Doughty

Yield: 1 pt. (480 ml)

Plum tomato concassée, minced	2½ lb.	1.1 kg
Olive oil	1 fl. oz.	30 ml
White wine	2 fl. oz.	60 ml
Vermouth, dry, red or white	2 fl. oz.	60 ml
Wine vinegar, red or white	2 fl. oz.	60 ml
Shallot, minced	2 Tbsp.	30 ml
Heavy cream	2 fl. oz.	60 ml
Fresh thyme, chopped	1 Tbsp.	15 ml
Salt	¾ tsp.	4 ml
Black pepper	¼ tsp.	1 ml
Whole butter, cut into pieces	4 oz.	120 g
Fresh parsley, chopped	½ c.	180 ml

1 Sauté the tomato concassée in the olive oil for approximately 2 minutes. Lower the heat to a simmer and reduce the tomato until thick but not dry.

2 In a saucepan, combine the wine, vermouth, vinegar and shallot. Bring to a boil and reduce au sec. Add the cream and reduce by half.

3 Add the thyme, salt and pepper to the tomatoes. Stir in the wine, cream and shallot reduction.

4 Bring the sauce to a simmer. Add the butter pieces and stir until incorporated. Do not allow the sauce to boil or the butter will separate. Adjust the seasonings and stir in the parsley.

Approximate values per 3-fl.-oz. (90-ml) serving: **Calories** 100, **Total fat** 9 g, **Saturated fat** 4.5 g, **Cholesterol** 20 mg, **Sodium** 120 mg, **Total carbohydrates** 4 g, **Protein** 1 g, **Vitamin A** 15%, **Vitamin C** 25%

RECIPE 11.38 — SORREL SAUCE

Yield: 1 qt. (1 lt)   **Method:** Puréeing

Shallot, coarsely chopped	1 Tbsp.	15 ml
Whole butter	1 oz.	30 g
White wine	8 fl. oz.	250 ml
Heavy cream	1 pt.	500 ml
Sorrel, stemmed	8 oz.	250 g
Spinach, stemmed	8 oz.	250 g
Salt and white pepper	TT	TT
Lemon juice	1 fl. oz.	30 ml

1 Sauté the shallot in the butter until tender.

2 Add the white wine and reduce by half.

3 Add the cream and reduce until it begins to thicken.

4 Add the sorrel and spinach to the cream and cook just until the leaves are wilted.

5 Purée the sauce in a blender or food processor and season with salt, white pepper and lemon juice. Serve the sauce with egg, chicken, veal or rich fish dishes.

Approximate values per 1-fl.-oz. (30-ml) serving: **Calories** 70, **Total fat** 7 g, **Saturated fat** 4 g, **Cholesterol** 25 mg, **Sodium** 90 mg, **Total carbohydrates** 1 g, **Protein** 1 g, **Vitamin A** 10%

BARBECUE SAUCE

RECIPE 11.39

Yield: 1½ qt. (1.5 lt)

Onion, small dice	8 oz.	250 g
Garlic, chopped	1 oz.	30 g
Vegetable oil	1 fl. oz.	30 ml
Red wine vinegar	6 fl. oz.	180 ml
Brown sugar	1 oz.	30 g
Honey	2 fl. oz.	60 ml
Beef stock	8 fl. oz.	250 ml
Ketchup	10 oz.	300 g
Dry mustard	1 oz.	30 g
Worcestershire sauce	2 Tbsp.	30 ml
Salt and pepper	TT	TT
Cayenne pepper	TT	TT

1 Sweat the onions and garlic in the oil until tender.

2 Combine the remaining ingredients and simmer for 30 minutes.

Approximate values per 1-fl.-oz. (30-ml) serving: **Calories** 25, **Total fat** 1 g, **Saturated fat** 0 g, **Cholesterol** 0 mg, **Sodium** 80 mg, **Total carbohydrates** 4 g, **Protein** 0 g, **Claims**–low fat; low sodium; low calorie

PEANUT SAUCE

RECIPE 11.40

Yield: 28 fl. oz. (800 ml)

Garlic, chopped	1 tsp.	5 ml
Onion, small dice	6 oz.	180 g
Red pepper flakes, crushed	1 tsp.	5 ml
Kaffir lime leaves (optional)	4	4
Curry powder	2 tsp.	10 ml
Lemongrass, minced	1 oz.	30 g
Vegetable oil	1 fl. oz.	30 ml
Coconut milk	8 fl. oz.	250 ml
Cinnamon sticks	2	2
Bay leaves	4	4
Lime juice	1 fl. oz.	30 ml
Rice wine vinegar	4 fl. oz.	120 ml
Chicken stock	10 fl. oz.	300 ml
Peanut butter	10 oz.	300 g

1 Sauté the garlic, onion, red pepper flakes, lime leaves, curry powder and lemongrass in the vegetable oil for 5 minutes.

2 Add the remaining ingredients and simmer for 30 minutes. Stir often, as the sauce can burn easily. Serve warm.

Approximate values per 1-fl.-oz. (30-ml) serving: **Calories** 100, **Total fat** 8 g, **Saturated fat** 3 g, **Cholesterol** 0 mg, **Sodium** 115 mg, **Total carbohydrates** 5 g, **Protein** 3 g

RECIPE 11.41   THAI MELON SALSA

Yield: 1 qt. (1 lt)

Assorted melons such as honeydew, cantaloupe, crenshaw	1 qt.	1 lt
Garlic, chopped	1 tsp.	5 ml
Brown sugar	2 Tbsp.	30 ml
Thai fish sauce	2 Tbsp.	30 ml
Serrano chiles, minced	1 Tbsp.	15 ml
Lime juice	2 fl. oz.	60 ml
Unsalted peanuts, roasted, chopped fine	4 Tbsp.	60 ml
Fresh mint	4 Tbsp.	60 ml

1 Cut the melons into small dice or shape into small balls using a parisienne scoop.

2 Combine remaining ingredients and toss with the melon pieces. Chill thoroughly. Serve with fish, shellfish or chicken.

Approximate values per 1-fl.-oz. (30-ml) serving: **Calories** 20, **Total fat** 0.5 g, **Saturated fat** 0 g, **Cholesterol** 0 mg, **Sodium** 70 mg, **Total carbohydrates** 4 g, **Protein** 0 g, **Vitamin C** 10%, **Claims**—low fat; low sodium; low calorie

RECIPE 11.42   AVOCADO SALSA

THE BOULDER'S RESORT, CAREFREE, AZ

Former Corporate Executive Chef Charles Wiley

Yield: 1½ pt. (750 ml)

Red bell pepper, diced fine	2 oz.	60 g
Green bell pepper, diced fine	2 oz.	60 g
Small red onion, diced fine	2 oz.	60 g
Green onion, sliced fine	1	1
Garlic, roasted and puréed	1½ tsp.	8 ml
Fresh lemon juice	1 fl. oz.	30 ml
Serrano chile, minced	1	1
Cilantro, chopped	TT	TT
Plum tomatoes, seeded and diced	4	4
Avocado, diced	1	1
Salt and pepper	TT	TT

1 In a mixing bowl, combine the bell peppers, onions, garlic, lemon juice, chile and cilantro. Mix well.

2 Carefully fold in the tomatoes, then the avocado. Season to taste.

Approximate values per 1-fl.-oz. (30-ml) serving: **Calories** 15, **Total fat** 1.5 g, **Saturated fat** 0 g, **Cholesterol** 0 mg, **Sodium** 0 mg, **Total carbohydrates** 1 g, **Protein** 0 g, **Vitamin C** 15%, **Claims**—low fat; no cholesterol; low calorie

RECIPE 11.43   TOMATILLO SALSA

Yield: 2 qt. (2 lt)

Tomatillo	5 lb.	2 kg
Water	8 fl. oz.	250 ml
Jalapeños	3	3
Salt	1 Tbsp.	15 ml
Pepper	½ tsp.	2 ml
Garlic	2 Tbsp.	30 ml
Onion, chopped	4 oz.	120 g
Cilantro, chopped	2 oz.	60 g

1 Remove the husks from the tomatillos.

2 Combine the tomatillos with the water, jalapeños, salt, pepper, garlic and onion. Bring to a boil and simmer until tender, approximately 20 minutes.

3 Chop all ingredients in a food chopper or purée them in a blender for a smoother sauce.

4 Add the cilantro and adjust the seasonings. The sauce may be served warm or cold.

Approximate values per 1-fl.-oz. (30-ml) serving: **Calories** 20, **Total fat** 0 g, **Saturated fat** 0 g, **Cholesterol** 0 mg, **Sodium** 120 mg, **Total carbohydrates** 3 g, **Protein** 1 g, **Claims**—fat free; low sodium; low calorie

 ## APPLE HORSERADISH SAUCE

RECIPE 11.44

Yield: 1 pt. (500 ml)

Granny Smith apples	4	4
Cider vinegar	2 fl. oz.	60 ml
Fresh horseradish, grated	2 oz.	60 g
Paprika	1 tsp.	5 ml
White wine	1 fl. oz.	30 ml

1 Grate the apples and moisten them with vinegar.

2 Add the horseradish and paprika.

3 Thin to the desired consistency with the wine.

Approximate values per 1-fl.-oz. (30-ml) serving: **Calories** 25, **Total fat** 0 g, **Saturated fat** 0 g, **Cholesterol** 0 mg, **Sodium** 0 mg, **Total carbohydrates** 6 g, **Protein** 0 g, **Claims**—fat free; no sodium; low calorie

MIGNONETTE SAUCE

RECIPE 11.45

Yield: 1 pt. (500 ml)

White pepper	2 tsp.	10 ml
Red wine vinegar	16 fl. oz.	500 ml
Shallot, minced	4 oz.	120 g
Salt	TT	TT

1 Combine all ingredients.

Approximate values per 1-fl.-oz. (30-ml) serving: **Calories** 5, **Total fat** 0 g, **Saturated fat** 0 g, **Cholesterol** 0 mg, **Sodium** 0.8 mg, **Total carbohydrates** 1 g, **Protein** 0 g, **Claims**—fat free; very low sodium; low calorie

NUOC CHAM (VIETNAMESE DIPPING SAUCE)

RECIPE 11.46

Yield: 10 fl. oz. (300 ml)

Granulated sugar	5 Tbsp.	75 ml
Water	3 Tbsp.	50 ml
Fish sauce (nuoc mam)	5 Tbsp.	75 ml
Fresh lemon juice	4 fl. oz.	120 ml
Garlic clove, minced	1	1
Thai chile, seeded and minced	1	1
Shallot, minced	1	1

1 Whisk all the ingredients together in a nonreactive bowl and allow to stand for at least 30 minutes at room temperature before serving.

Approximate values per 1-fl.-oz. (30-ml) serving: **Calories** 0, **Total fat** 0 g, **Saturated fat** 0 g, **Cholesterol** 0 mg, **Sodium** 700 mg, **Total carbohydrates** 8 g, **Protein** 1 g, **Vitamin C** 20%, **Claims**—no calories; fat free; good source of Vitamin C

RECIPE 11.47   HERB OIL

STOUFFER STANFORD COURT HOTEL, San Francisco, CA

Former Executive Chef Ercolino Crugnale

Yield: 4 fl. oz. (120 ml)

Fresh parsley	2 oz.	60 g
Fresh tarragon	1 oz.	30 g
Fresh thyme	1 oz.	30 g
Olive oil	approx. 4 fl. oz.	approx. 120 ml

1 Blanch the herbs in hot water for 10 seconds. Cool and dry thoroughly.
2 Measure the volume of the herbs and put them in a blender. Add an equal volume of olive oil.
3 Purée and strain through a mesh strainer.

Approximate values per 1-fl.-oz. (30-ml) serving: **Calories** 110, **Total fat** 8 g, **Saturated fat** 1 g, **Cholesterol** 0 mg, **Sodium** 35 mg, **Total carbohydrates** 8 g, **Protein** 3 g, **Vitamin A** 20%, **Iron** 70%, **Claims**—no cholesterol; low sodium

RECIPE 11.48   PERSILLADE

Although not a liquid sauce, persillade (payr-se-yad) is a classic parsley topping used to finish a dish in much the same way as a sauce. Persillade adds flavor and texture to grilled or roasted meats, especially beef and lamb, or vegetables.

Yield: 1 lb. (450 g)

Garlic, minced	1 oz.	30 g
Fresh parsley, chopped	3 oz.	90 g
Fresh bread crumbs	6 oz.	180 g
Whole butter, melted	6 fl. oz.	180 ml

1 Combine the garlic, parsley and bread crumbs. Drizzle on the butter and toss to blend.
2 Sprinkle the persillade over cooked meats or vegetables as a topping, then place the dish under a broiler until lightly browned.

Approximate values per ½-oz. (15-g) serving: **Calories** 50, **Total fat** 4.5 g, **Saturated fat** 3 g, **Cholesterol** 10 mg, **Sodium** 30 mg, **Total carbohydrates** 3 g, **Protein** 1 g

A WEEKEND PROJECT BOOK

GARDEN PROJECTS
YOU CAN BUILD

David & Jeanie Stiles

WITH ILLUSTRATIONS BY DAVID STILES

CHAPTERS PUBLISHING LTD., SHELBURNE, VERMONT 05482

Published by Chapters Publishing Ltd.
2031 Shelburne Road
Shelburne, Vermont 05482

Library of Congress Cataloging-in-Publication Data

Stiles, David R.
    Garden Projects you can build / David and Jeanie Stiles.
            p.   cm — (The weekend project book series)
    Includes bibliographical references (p.) .
    ISBN 1-881527-64-6 : $17.95
    1. Garden structures—Design and construction—Amateurs' manuals.
I. Stiles, Jeanie. II. Title. III. Series.
TH4961.S75 1995
684.1'8—dc20   94-25240

Trade distribution by Firefly Books Ltd.
250 Sparks Avenue
Willowdale, Ontario
Canada M2H 2S4

Printed and bound in Canada by Metropole Litho, Inc.
St. Bruno de Montarville, Quebec

Book design by Eugenie Seidenberg Delaney
Photography by Skip Hine

All designs by the author, unless otherwise noted.

To David's mother,

Ellen Fillebrown Stiles,

an inspired gardener.

ACKNOWLEDGMENTS

We wish to thank Virginia Conklin of Gardenscapes for her technical information on gardening, Warren and Inez Whipple for their inspired "folly," Alan and Catherine Manson for their constant moral support, Bayberry Nurseries in East Hampton for allowing us to use their beautiful plants and surroundings, and Alan and Susan Patricof, Abbie Zabar, William and Kate Cameron, Estelle McGowen and Helen Jacobs, for allowing us to photograph their glorious gardens. The quality of these photographs is due to Skip Hine, whose talent and good nature contributed greatly to the beauty of the book.

We also would like to thank Tom Martin at Firefly for his helpful advice. Above all, we are most grateful to Sandy Taylor, our editor, Clayton DeKorne, our copy editor, Eugenie Delaney, the book designer, and Barry Estabrook, our publisher. Together, they supplied us with a supportive team effort that proved invaluable.

CONTENTS

INTRODUCTION

Our goal in writing *Garden Projects You Can Build* was to give the reader clear, simple, easy-to-follow directions for constructing useful, long-lasting and well designed objects for the garden. The book contains 20 "how-to" projects (the majority of which are built from wood) that range from simple and practical (window box, garden toolbox) to more involved and unusual (garden cart, covered garden seat) and finally to the most complex (complete plans for two very different garden houses). Many of them can be built in less than a day and the majority require only basic hand tools. The advantages of constructing your own garden projects are numerous. You not only save money but also create something that fits your particular specifications and garden environment. And there's the obvious satisfaction that comes from building a project yourself.

This book is aimed at woodworkers with an interest in gardening and gardeners who have some carpentry skills. Each project includes a materials list and step-by-step instructions accompanied by detailed shop drawings and illustrations of the finished projects. Color photographs are also included for many of the projects. You will not only be able to understand the construction process through reading the text, but also be able to visualize how to build each project by referring to the clear step-by-step illustrations.

One of us being a designer, the other a writer, we often approach direction-giving in very different ways. The designer tends to ignore the written instructions and rely solely on the diagrams, while the writer carefully reads each step of the directions in sequence. Having acknowledged the difference in the way we perceive things, we have tried to use it to our advantage while writing this book. In other words, we have attempted to appeal to both right- and left-brain types!

GETTING STARTED

PLANNING

Any garden project, especially any permanent structure like a garden house or large pergola, should be carefully thought out before it is constructed. This can be either an exciting or a frustrating experience, depending upon how you approach it. To facilitate the planning stage, and make it a more enjoyable experience, we offer the following suggestions:

Permits: If you are planning to build a structure of any significant size, check with your local building department before beginning construction to see if you need a building permit.

Good Neighbors: If your building project will be visible from your neighbors', it is a good idea to show them a sketch of your design and get their blessing before you start construction.

Appearance: You will never know exactly how a particular design will look until you have built it. There are, however, three things you can do to help you visualize how an object will look in your garden:

1) Take a photograph of the location where the project is to be built and, using a pen with waterproof ink, sketch your design right onto the photograph. If it is difficult to visualize your project on the site, place stakes in the ground to correspond with the measurements of the project and then take your photograph. Before building the rose arbor we describe in this book, we photographed our client on the site, to give the photograph more scale.

2) If you are even slightly artistic, make an overlay, by taking a piece of clear prepared acetate and taping it over a photograph of your building site. Outline your garden design in waterproof ink, and using acrylics or opaque watercolors,

paint the proposed project onto the back of the acetate.

3) Another useful visual aid is to construct a scale model of the garden project that you are planning to build. Draw your design to scale (1 inch = 1 foot) on cardboard, cut it out using an Exacto knife and glue the pieces together with white glue. Three dimensional models take very little time to make and can be extremely helpful, often pointing out potential problems. We always make models for any major building project, both for our own edification and for our client's. Have someone hold the model in front of the proposed site while you look through the camera lens, making adjustments until the model is in focus and in the correct position. You'll be amazed at how true to life the project looks in the developed photo.

WOOD TO USE OUTDOORS

Redwood is probably the most well known of all the rot-resistant woods grown in the United States, and it is readily available in various dimensions in all lumberyards. It is with some misgivings that we recommend it for so many of the projects in this book, since the trees from which it comes are so magnificent! But it is hard to beat for beauty and lasting ability. We once built a deck out of spruce, which was decayed in less than five years. Unhappy with the prospect of re-doing the same job after such a short time, we invested in redwood for our second deck, carefully picking out, cutting and nailing each expensive piece of lumber ourselves. That was in 1979 and with a little maintenance every spring, our deck looks like new again each summer. We sand it lightly with a palm sander to remove the dirt and apply a water sealer which, after a couple of days, turns the color of the wood back into a rich shade of reddish brown. This is one annual chore we actually look forward to since the results are so satisfying.

Another alternative is pressure-treated (P.T.), or CCA, lumber. This is usually southern pine, which has been treated with chemicals so that it can come in contact with the ground without rotting. When buying P.T. lumber, avoid pieces with a white crust, which is evidence of excess chemicals that have not bonded to the wood. It is advisable to wear gloves and a mask when working with chemically treated wood. Since pressure-treated lumber is much less expensive than redwood, it has become quite popular. Although southern pine is beautiful in its natural state, when treated with chemicals, it turns a not so desirable shade of green. Lately, some attractive stains have become available that are made expressly for pressure-treated lumber. Osmose makes a semi-transparent stain that makes pressure-treated wood look like teak! Another option, and one we have used with great success, is to cover the wood with a gray stain, which immediately gives it a weathered look.

Some of the most rot-resistant woods grown in the United State are cypress, which originates along the Gulf Coast, and locust, which grows in the Northeast. We found a quantity of cypress in our local lumberyard in Long Island almost 20 years ago, and fortunately bought as much as we could lay our hands on. Having been over-cut, it has not been harvested much over the last decade and is difficult to find except where it is grown and milled locally. Clear cypress has a beautiful honey-colored grain and is slightly harder than pine. We used a few pieces of cypress to build a garden bench 15 years ago, and although some lichen has grown on it, the wood is in fine shape. Cypress is so impervious to water that fallen trees that have been submerged in Florida swamps for years are pulled out and sawn up to make beautiful lumber. After ten years of searching, we have finally located a good source for this wonderful wood (see Sources).

Locust has been used for hundreds of years to make posts to hold up houses. When freshly cut, it has a greenish yellow cast to it and is slightly heavier than pine. Locust is a fast-growing, long-lasting wood. We have yet to locate anyone who has milled it into lumber, probably because it is best used for posts. We once built an "Irish" garden house using locust log ends, mortared into the wall. Our supply of locust came from a wood lot 150 miles away, where we made periodic trips, loading our car as heavily as we dared with fallen locust logs. Fortunately for us, a hurricane struck that summer, near where we were building the garden house, and downed several locust trees. (Locust trees suffer from a weak root system.) Our neighbors were happy to have us remove their fallen trees, giving us more than enough wood to finish building the garden house.

Cedar is the last on the list of weather-resistant woods. Both cedar and pressure-treated southern pine are comparable in price, but we generally choose cedar. It has an appealing color, and is lightweight and easy to work with. Cedar will last longer outside than any of the other softwoods, but we feel its longevity is slightly overrated, based on the condition of the cedar shake roof on our barn!

Other types of wood should be avoided for outdoor use unless painted, given a coat of solid stain or oiled regularly. Pine, for example, is not rot resistant, but it can be periodically coated with generous amounts of wood preservative to keep it from turning gray and to extend its life.

Only "exterior" plywood, which is made with waterproof glues to keep it from delaminating, should be used outside.

Generally, it is a good idea not to varnish or paint outdoor structures, as they begin to blister and peel after a few years and become a nuisance to maintain. Stain is a better choice, and solid stains can give the appearance of paint without the problems of peeling.

SPECIALTY WOODS

The longest lasting, specialty hard wood for outdoor projects that we have discovered is "greenheart." It is so rot and insect proof that it is often used to make footings in the Virgin Islands, where termites can consume an entire house in no time at all. Greenheart logs were used to build several of the New York Harbor piers 150 years ago, and they remain solid even today. It is so dense that it will immediately sink when placed in water. It has a beautiful reddish color, somewhere between mahogany and teak, and needs only a light oiling once a year to retain its color.

There are some disadvantages to this extreme density and hardness, however. It is impossible to drive a nail into the wood, and when using screws, you must first drill an oversize pilot hole, so that the screw threads barely catch the wood. Make sure you position the screw correctly, since you will not be able to remove it, once it is imbedded in the wood. Some wood shops refuse to use it, since it dulls their saws. Oddly enough, when cut through, it gives off green sawdust, hence the name "greenheart." It is expensive and must be special ordered from a supplier, but is a good wood to use sparingly for a special project. We used greenheart to make a planter outside our kitchen window and its mellow color made a warm backdrop for the lush green herbs.

Two other specialty woods that can be ordered from a lumberyard are Honduras mahogany and teak. They are imported from South America and Burma, respectively. Because of their ability to withstand harsh weather, they are used extensively on boats. Both woods are expensive, but can show off small projects beautifully. Let the wood weather to a silvery gray, or periodically finish it off with a brightener and sealer. Teak has the advantage of having its own self-lubricating oil and a distinctive aroma.

People who are reluctant to use these specialty woods can substitute pressure-treated southern pine.

TOOLS AND SUPPLIES

We have tried to avoid projects that require expensive, high-tech woodworking machines. Instead, most of them can be constructed using basic hand tools, such as a hammer, pliers, screwdrivers, electric hand drill and a portable electric saw. A few projects require a drill press or a table saw, a good investment if you enjoy carpentry. Here are the most useful power tools that we recommend you invest in, if you don't already own them:

CIRCULAR SAW

A portable electric circular saw is an indispensable tool for making quick rough crosscuts on the site, especially if you are considering building any of the larger projects. We prefer the relatively small (6-inch) light-weight saws that have the blade on the left side, where you can see it. One that we particularly like is the Porter-Cable Saw Boss, which costs around $110 (see Sources).

TABLE SAW

A 10-inch table saw is an essential tool for making accurate miter cuts, bevel cuts, fine cuts and rip cuts along the length of a board. It is light-weight enough to be transported easily, yet strong enough to last a lifetime. It is not cheap ($180 and up), but is the workhorse of any wood-shop.

JIG SAW

An electric jig saw allows you to make curved cuts, scrolls or notches and is easy and safe to use. Our favorite is the variable-speed Bosch model 1587VS, which costs approximately $165.

CORDLESS DRILL

A cordless electric drill also comes in handy. Makita makes a good one that costs about $45.

SANDERS

If you have a lot of sanding to do, consider buying a palm orbital sander (approximately $60). It is generally considered to be a finishing sander and is used in the last stages of a carpentry project, right before painting.

If you want to shape, as well as remove a lot of material, a belt sander ($150 and up) is the best choice. It is a serious machine and must be used with caution, otherwise it can gouge your work. You can turn the belt sander upside down and use it as a table sander to sand small pieces of wood. We have even seen carpenters sharpen chisels on a belt sander.

Rotary or disc sanders, or grinders, are strictly for heavy-duty work and are useful for sanding quantities of wood in seconds. However, these sanders will leave large swirls in the wood, which must be removed by using a belt sander with a coarse-grit sanding belt (see Sources).

One of the best presents you can give yourself is a 6-x36-inch table belt sander (see Sources). Everytime we use it, we are amazed at how effortlessly it cleans up our carpentry, leaving a clean, crisp look. It makes the difference between an average job and a highly professional-looking piece of work.

SANDPAPER

Sandpaper comes in 9-x11-inch sheets or belts and is available in several grits, ranging from coarse to medium to fine. It is calibrated in numbers, with 24 referring to very coarse and 150 and higher referring to extra fine. The smaller the number, the larger the grit size.

There are various types of grit, the most common being aluminum oxide, which is brown or reddish-brown in color. Garnet sandpaper, which is orange in color, is also a good choice to use. If you can't find it in hardware stores, order it from The Woodworkers' Store (see Sources).

If you are sanding by hand, it is useful to make a sanding block from a piece of scrap lumber. Cover it with half a sheet of sandpaper, cut lengthwise. (An easy way to cut sandpaper is to score it on the back, fold it over a table edge and rip it along the fold.)

To sand in tight corners, fold a full sheet of sandpaper into eighths, and to sand round holes, curl sandpaper into a tight roll. A good way to sand curved edges is shown in the "Rose Arbor" on page 40.

Sanding is perhaps the most boring part of carpentry, but it is also the step that makes your work look the most professional. To keep this job from becoming too labor intensive, don't use only fine-grit sandpaper, but instead use a range of grits, beginning with the coarsest and graduating into the finest grit for the final smooth finish. A good selection of sandpaper to have on hand is 60 (coarse), 80 (medium) and 120 (fine).

GLUES

There are only two types of glue that we recommend using on outdoor projects, and both are considered "weather resistant." The first is an improved yellow glue called Titebond II. This is a "one part" water-resistant glue, which bonds in a few minutes, and should be used in areas that will be covered up with paint and not exposed to constant water. Use clamps to keep the pieces together while the glue dries, which takes approximately one hour if the temperature is above 55 degrees F. It has a limited shelf life and should never be allowed to freeze.

The second (and our favorite) type of glue is epoxy (see Sources), which is waterproof and consists of two parts—resin and hardener. It is expensive but well worth the price, considering how effective it is. The beauty of it is its versatility. Its consistency allows it to penetrate into the fibers of the wood, especially the end grain. It can also be mixed with a filler or a thickener, such as Micro Fiber Powder, and made into a paste to fill large gaps or dents. The drawback is that epoxy sets too fast in hot weather (10 to 15 minutes) and too slowly in cold weather (2 to 6 hours). Clamping is not always necessary for this "superglue." The epoxy is mixed in a 5-to-1 ratio with the hardener, which is difficult to do unless you buy two hand-pump dispensers, sold expressly for this purpose. One stroke of each pump is all you need for a perfect mix.

We always keep a supply of 4-ounce paper cups and ¼-inch disposable brushes on hand for mixing epoxy glue in small quantities. Acetone is a good solvent to use for cleaning up your hands and any spills after gluing is completed. This glue generates its own heat, and if a large quantity is mixed in a small, confined container on a hot day, it will harden up too quickly. When you need to use alot of the glue, the perfect container is a disposable aluminum chicken pot pie plate!

The best way to get the maximum bonding power from your glue is to carefully coat both pieces with a thin layer of glue. Spread the glue out, using a flat stick, and keep it away from the edges so that it won't ooze out from the sides. If you are gluing the end grain of a piece of wood, and it has soaked up the glue, make sure to recoat the wood before you put the pieces together. Press the pieces of wood together and shift them slightly. You should feel the pieces pull together. When gluing joints, put pressure on the pieces by clamping them together while the glue is drying. If you don't have a large supply of clamps, you can use rope or cord, or even tape, to temporarily hold the pieces together. Clean up any spills immediately or they may be difficult to stain later on.

SHOP TIPS

- As you cut the materials to size, label each piece on an end that won't show.
- If available, use two electric drills, so you don't have to keep changing the bits back and forth.
- When using an electric drill, use high speeds for boring wood and slower speeds for drilling holes in metal.
- For a more professional-looking job, always countersink your screws.
- A good investment is a #6 HSS (high-speed steel) countersink drill with a stop-collar combination. This little tool drills a tapered pilot hole with a countersink hole at the top. It can be adjusted with an Allen wrench to suit your specific project.
- It is easier and more accurate to join pieces of wood by gluing them first and then screwing them together after the glue is partially dry. By using glue, the pieces tend to slip less during assembly, and the joints will be stronger.
- If you are going to paint your project, use auto body filler to fill gaps quickly. It "sets up" hard in ten minutes, and is easy to sand.

POSTS AND GATES

The construction and installation of posts should not be taken lightly, as they are the main supporting structure for pergolas, arbors and gates. The strength and life of the structure depends on how well you prepare the posts.

Great care should be taken in the selection of wood. Check to make sure that the pieces you choose are free from warping. Locust is one of the best types of wood for posts, but it is seldom seen in lumberyards except as a companion for split-rail fences. As mentioned earlier, redwood and pressure-treated southern pine are the next most desirable, followed by red cedar. Although red cedar is a strong wood, it has a limited life unless steps are taken to protect it against dry rot

and insects, especially termites. At the very least, the butt (bottom) ends of the posts should be soaked overnight in wood preservative. The easiest way of doing this is to stand the posts up in a shallow pan or a trench lined with heavy plastic sheeting (see Fig. 1-1).

In Colonial times, farmers would sometimes burn the ends of posts which would provide a charcoal surface that was unsavory for bugs. To keep the posts from being affected by frost heave, they would sometimes sharpen the bottom ends before burying them.

Another good way to ensure that the post you plant will outlive you is to coat the end of the post with wax. Place the post bottom end up and heat it with a propane torch. When the end grain of the wood is very hot and begins to smolder, rub a candle against it, covering it with wax. You will notice how the pores of the wood open up under heat and practically suck the wax inside. Once the wood cools, the pores close, encapsulating the wax and making the wood impervious to moisture and termites (see Fig. 1-2).

The most vulnerable part of any post is directly above where it emerges from the ground, where wet conditions encourage deterioration and rot. To protect this area, cover the surface of the wood with a generous coating of roofing tar, continuing 6 inches above where the post emerges from the ground. We use a piece of shingle for this messy job, dabbing the tar on liberally, and disposing of the shingle when we are finished (see Fig. 1-3).

Posts should always be buried with a large stone or brick at the bottom of the posthole, to facilitate drainage of ground water and make a strong foundation for the post. Don't be too anxious to backfill the posthole immediately after the post is in place. Instead, use a temporary brace

Fig. 1-1

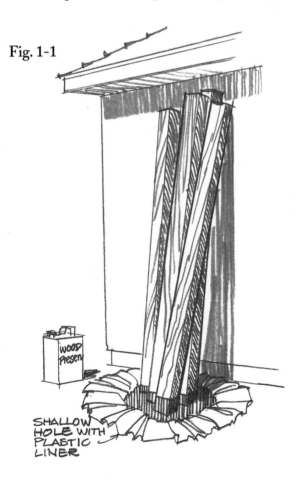

SHALLOW HOLE WITH PLASTIC LINER

WOOD Preserv

Fig. 1-2

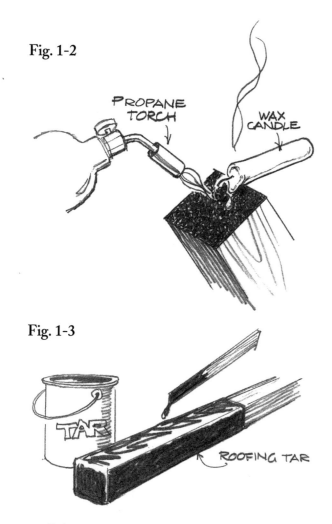

PROPANE TORCH

WAX CANDLE

Fig. 1-3

ROOFING TAR

TAR

until the structure is completed, allowing you to make last minute adjustments. Nothing is more frustrating than digging up a post after you have finished burying it.

When backfilling, it is important to gradually add small amounts of soil, tamping down the area well with a 2x4. Bear in mind that a post gets most of its strength from the friction caused by the earth pressing against its sides. Ideally, a post should have one-third of its length buried in the ground. However, if you are using a manual post-hole digger, the maximum you can bury it is about 30 inches.

Larger posts (especially pedestals) are generally built hollow and secured to a 4x4 pressure-treated post, pre-installed in the ground. If you

are using this method, position the outer post 1 inch above the ground (see Fig. 1-4). This will allow air to reach inside the post and keep the finished trim lumber off the damp ground.

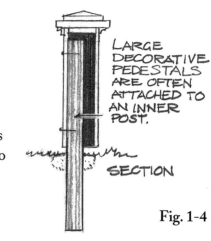

LARGE DECORATIVE PEDESTALS ARE OFTEN ATTACHED TO AN INNER POST.

SECTION

Fig. 1-4

Most posts are topped off with a wooden cap to help keep rain from entering the end grain of the wood. A typical cap is made from clear redwood and has a conical shape to help deflect water. Since this shape is difficult to make without sophisticated tools, lumberyards generally carry a line of redwood caps to fit most posts. They come

Fig. 1-5

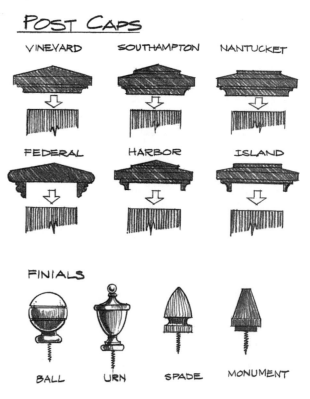

POST CAPS

VINEYARD   SOUTHAMPTON   NANTUCKET

FEDERAL   HARBOR   ISLAND

FINIALS

BALL   URN   SPADE   MONUMENT

Fig. 1-6

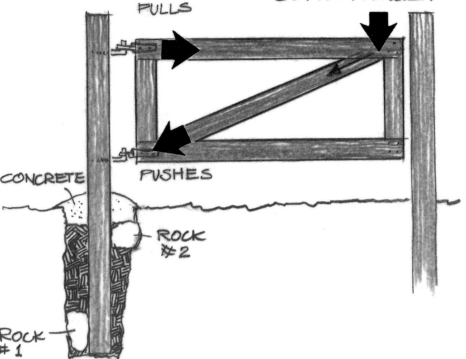

WEIGHT OF GATE
IS TRANSFERRED
DIAGONALLY TOWARD
BOTTOM HINGE.

PULLS

PUSHES

CONCRETE

ROCK #2

ROCK #1

in two basic styles, those that slip over the end of a post and those that are glued and nailed directly to the top of a post (see Fig. 1-5).

When building a gate, it is essential to have two strong posts supporting it. It is also important to understand the dynamic forces acting on the gate when it is swinging. When a gate is swung open, all the weight of the gate is pushing down and toward the bottom hinge and, at the same time, pulling away from the top hinge. To help transfer this force, it is advisable to attach a brace, extending diagonally from the top inside edge of the gate to the bottom hinge side (see Fig. 1-6). When you are setting the gatepost in the ground, another way to help stabilize it is to place two rocks in the ground, one against the bottom outside edge of the post, and a second one wedged against the inside of the post right below ground level (see Fig. 1-6).

Although it is not generally necessary to use concrete to set fence posts, it is always a good idea to use it when setting a gatepost, in addition to wedging rocks in the sides of the posthole. Most 4x4 posts take a 40-pound bag of concrete mix; 6x6 posts, at least an 80-pound bag.

After backfilling two-thirds of the hole with soil, fill the remainder with concrete, mixed stiffly. Make a slight mound on top to shed rainwater, where the concrete meets the post. After a year, check to see if a gap has opened up between the concrete and the post, and if it has, caulk it with silicone caulking.

When designing your gate, be sure to make the opening wide enough to allow a wheelbarrow, lawnmower and other garden equipment to pass through. It is often helpful to build a section of removable fencing next to the gate, as well.

STRUCTURES FOR CLIMBING VINES AND ROSES

BENTWOOD TRELLIS

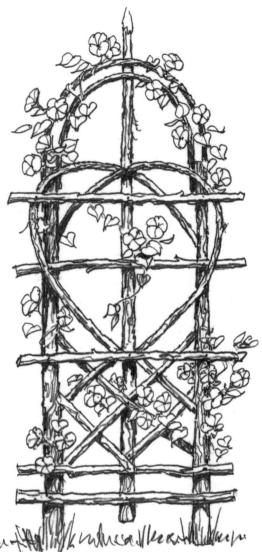

While a geometric, pristine pergola looks perfect in a formal setting, rustic garden structures made from trees, vines and branches may seem more suitable for an informal garden. In the last few years, "Adirondack" architecture has gained popularity with gardeners throughout the United States. This style originated in England, and was copied in the early 1900s in New York State, where wealthy estate owners, like the Rockefellers and Vanderbilts, employed local craftsmen to build outdoor structures for their elaborate camps. Garden furniture, gazebos, arbors, pergolas and trellises often were made from rot-resistant cedar, which was indigenous to the area.

MATERIALS

Quantity	Size	Description	Location or Use
2	78 inches	2-inch-dia. red cedar poles	uprights
5	40 inches	1-inch-dia. willow or maple	crosspieces
1	90 inches	1½-inch-dia. red cedar	center pole
4	5 feet	¾-inch-dia. grape vine or willow	heart pieces
2	3 feet	¾-inch-dia. maple	lattice pieces
4	2 feet	¾-inch-dia. maple	lattice pieces
1 lb.	1½-inch	galvanized finish nails	
1 lb.	2-inch	galvanized finish nails	

Since our own summer retreat is a renovated barn, this bentwood trellis fits perfectly with its rustic architecture. It looks at home whether covered with climbing roses or standing alone and bare in the dead of winter, silhouetted in the snow. A trellis is a perfect structure on which to train quick-growing climbing plants, such as morning glories, clematis or honeysuckle.

We learned how to build a trellis using "bentwood" by enrolling in an excellent workshop given by Cristina Spindler at the Peconic River Herb Farm, in Calverton, New York (see Sources). She teaches the method used by Jim Long, who is an herbalist and gardener from Arkansas and an authority on bentwood design and construction. (For additional information, write for his booklet, "Teacakes under the Trellis" — see Sources.) We have described, in abridged form, his building method with minor variations.

Unlike the other projects in this book, the materials for this design are free, provided you have access to and permission to cut fresh wood from a forest or woodlot. We agree with Jim Long when he says that the very best material to use is cypress. However, unless you live in the southeastern part of the United States, you may have difficulty locating it. Good alternatives are willow or red cedar. You can occasionally find red cedar in nurseries or farm supply stores, since the poles are often used in agriculture.

Gather your materials together the same day that you intend to build the trellis. It is important that the wood be as green and pliable as possible so it will bend easily without splitting. When selecting the wood for your trellis, don't worry if the pieces differ slightly in size and shape. These variations give your trellis a unique and natural quality.

FRAME

Lay the two uprights parallel on the ground, 22 inches apart, with the large ends toward you (see Fig. 2-1). Lay a crosspiece about 12 inches from the lower ends of the uprights, and drive a 2-inch galvanized nail into each intersection. Position and nail the fifth crosspiece 60 inches above the first, making sure the uprights are still 22 inches apart. Then position and nail the second, third and fourth crosspieces 4 inches, 26 inches, and 48 inches above the first crosspiece (see Fig. 2-1). Nail them in place, using 2-inch galvanized nails.

Fig. 2-1

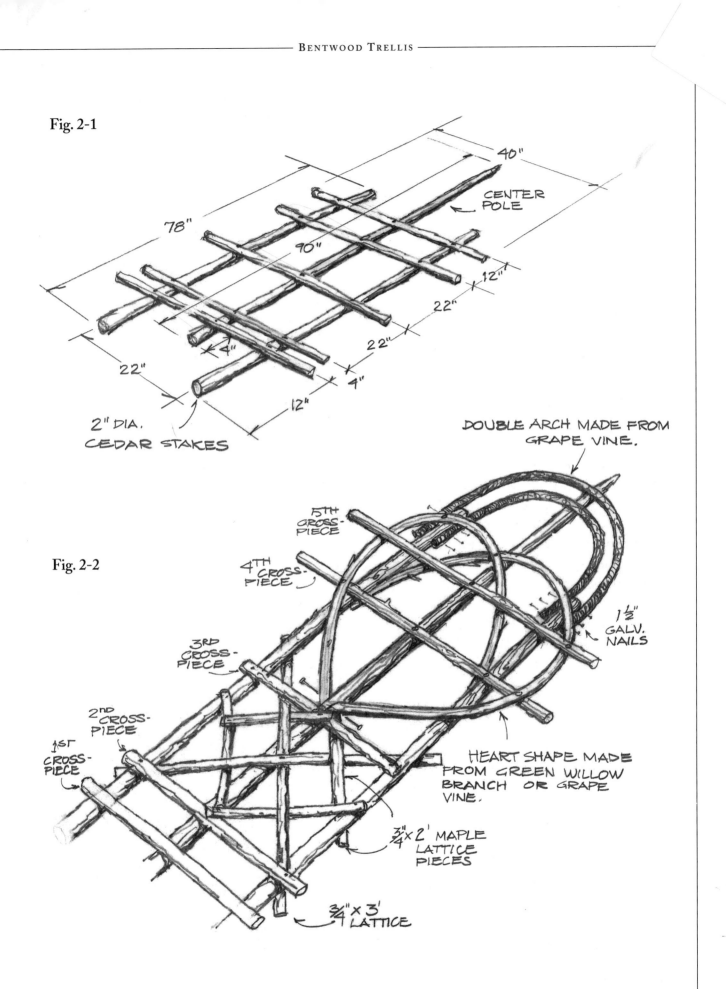

40"

CENTER POLE

78"

90"

12"

22"

22"

4"

4"

22"

12"

2" DIA. CEDAR STAKES

DOUBLE ARCH MADE FROM GRAPE VINE.

Fig. 2-2

5TH CROSS-PIECE

4TH CROSS-PIECE

3RD CROSS-PIECE

2ND CROSS-PIECE

1ST CROSS-PIECE

1½" GALV. NAILS

HEART SHAPE MADE FROM GREEN WILLOW BRANCH OR GRAPE VINE.

¾" X 2' MAPLE LATTICE PIECES

¾" X 3' LATTICE

ARCHES

According to Jim Long, young cedar saplings work best for the arches, but we had trouble locating these. Instead, we found grape vine to be an excellent source, since it is so pliable. It is often found winding its way up trees and if unchecked, can strangle them. This is a much better use for it! Cut two fairly straight pieces, 5 feet long. Nail one piece near the top of the left pole on the inside, and a second piece to the top of the same pole on the outside, using three 1½-inch galvanized nails to attach each piece. Bend the two pieces over to form two concentric arches, nailing them in the same fashion to the right pole (see Fig. 2-2). Cut off any excess grape vine.

CENTER POLE

Lay the 90-inch-long center pole under the frame so that the lower end extends about 4 inches below the first crosspiece. Center it between the two uprights, then nail through each crosspiece into the center pole. Nail the center pole to the arches where they intersect at the top of the trellis.

HEART

Using loppers, cut the large end of each heart piece at an angle. Estimate the angle by looking at Figure 2-2 and holding each piece in position to see how it attaches to the center pole. After cutting the ends, install the right-hand piece first. Hold it with the cut angle against the center pole, just above the third crosspiece and nail it to the center pole. Bend the other end, starting the bend where it crosses the fourth crosspiece and continuing it across the center of the trellis at the fifth crosspiece (see Fig. 2-2). Adjust the bend so the small end fits behind the fourth crosspiece, then nail the heart piece to the center pole, securing it in place. Repeat this process with the left-hand heart piece, nailing the grape vine securely at all intersections.

LATTICE

Place one of the 3-foot lattice pieces diagonally across the space between the second and third crosspieces, and tuck the ends under the crosspiece so the lattice piece is slightly bent over the center pole (see opening illustration, page 19). Hold the upper end of the lattice piece against the upright, 4 to 6 inches above the third crosspiece, and move the lower end left or right until the lattice piece is approximately parallel with one of the heart pieces, trimming the small end of the piece, if necessary. Using 1½-inch nails, nail through the crosspieces into the lattice piece and secure each end to the uprights. Using the same technique, install the other long lattice piece on the opposite diagonal. Nail through the lattice pieces into the center pole.

Nail the remaining lattice pieces in place, standing back and "eyeballing" your design now and then, making sure that it looks like the illustration before sinking in all the nails! Continue weaving shorter pieces of willow lattice into the structure, until you have a square of diamonds in the middle.

INSTALLATION

Since this trellis is not self-supporting, choose a location where it will be somewhat protected from the wind, such as the wall of a shed or against a fence or other existing structure, and nail or wire it directly to the supporting structure.

OBELISK

The obelisk — a tapering, four-sided shaft with a pyramidal apex — dates back to the ancient Egyptians, who cut them out of single blocks of granite and covered them with hieroglyphics. Today, they can be constructed much more easily out of posts and lattice!

An obelisk can be a focal point in the center of a garden, or quadrupled, they can become effective boundaries, marking the four corners of a formal garden. An obelisk can also be hidden in a special place, greeting you after a turn in a garden path.

MATERIALS

Quantity	Size	Description	Location or Use
4	8 feet	2x2 cedar posts	legs and pyramid corner posts
2	10 feet	2x2 cedar posts	base frame
4	8 feet	1x8 clear cedar T&G (V-groove)	base siding
3	8 feet	1x4 clear cedar	corner board and horizontal trim
1	12 feet	⁵⁄₄x6 cedar decking	top of base
1	8 feet	1x2 cedar posts	braces
1	8 feet	2x6 clear cedar	pyramid lattice
1	12 feet	¹¹⁄₁₆ x1⅜ solid crown molding	base trim
1	5½ -x5½ -inch	clear cedar cap	top
1	5-inch-dia.	finial ball	top
1 lb.	1½ -inch	galvanized finish nails	
1 lb.	2½ -inch	galvanized finish nails	
1 lb.	2-inch	galvanized deck screws	
1 bottle	8 oz.	waterproof yellow glue	
1 qt.		preservative or paint (optional)	

The lattice uncovered creates patterns of light in the early spring before vines cover it, and later in the summer, looks glorious filled with a mass of morning glories or scented wild clematis. Anything that climbs will thrive on an obelisk, winding its tendrils through the cedar lattice. We used one for vegetables and herbs and found that it helped protect the produce from rabbits and ground rot. We advise cutting back vines in the fall, and making any necessary repairs in the lattice. We oiled our obelisk, but it can also be stained or painted. Dark green, gray or white seem well suited to the garden environment, while not competing with the vivid colors of flowers.

BASE

Begin by building the base frame and legs out of 2x2 cedar posts (see Fig. 2-3). Taking four 8-foot-long 2x2 cedar posts, cut off 28 inches from each one for corner posts. (Save the leftover pieces for the pyramid corner posts.) Next cut eight pieces of 2x2, 25 inches long, for the frame. Drill ⅛-inch pilot holes about 4¾ inches up from the bottom of each leg, then glue and screw the four bottom frame pieces to the leg pieces. To avoid drilling into another screw, off-set the

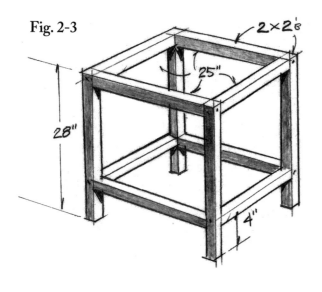

Fig. 2-3

2×2 8

25"

28"

4"

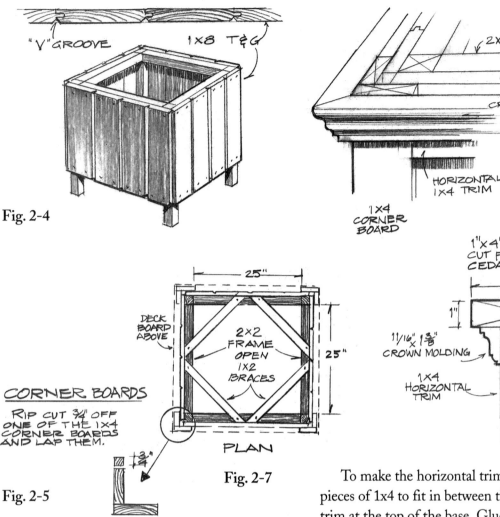

Fig. 2-6

"V" GROOVE   1X8 T&G

Fig. 2-4

2X2 FRAME

1X8 T&G
1X4

CROWN
MOLDING

HORIZONTAL
1X4 TRIM

1X4
CORNER
BOARD

1"X4" DECK BOARD
CUT FROM 5/4 X 6
CEDAR

4"

1"

11/16" X 1 3/8"
CROWN MOLDING

1X4
HORIZONTAL
TRIM

2X2

25"

DECK
BOARD
ABOVE

2X2
FRAME
OPEN
1X2
BRACES

25"

CORNER BOARDS

RIP CUT 3/4" OFF
ONE OF THE 1X4
CORNER BOARDS
AND LAP THEM.

PLAN

Fig. 2-7

1 3/4"

Fig. 2-5

screw holes by ¼ inch (that is, at 4⅞ and 4⅝ inches from the bottom). Do the same for the top four pieces of the frame, drilling pilot holes ⅞ and ⅝ inches down from the top.

To make the siding, cut 16 pieces of cedar 1x8 tongue-and-groove (T&G) with V-groove edges, each 24 inches long. Using glue and 2½-inch galvanized nails, attach the siding to the base frame, with the V-groove facing out (see Fig. 2-4).

Cut eight pieces of corner board from 1x4 clear cedar, each 24 inches long. Rip cut ¾ inches off every other piece of vertical trim and using a lap joint, glue and nail the pieces to the corners (see Fig. 2-5).

To make the horizontal trim, measure and cut pieces of 1x4 to fit in between the vertical corner trim at the top of the base. Glue and nail the horizontal trim to the base top.

Before cutting the four pieces of solid crown molding (sometimes called bed molding), measure the total distance across the top of the base (from corner board to corner board). Cut the four pieces of molding, mitering the ends at a 45 degree angle (see Fig. 2-6) and attach them to the top of the base, using 1½-inch galvanized finish nails.

To cover the crown molding and top off the base, rip cut the 12-foot-long 5/4 x6 cedar decking so it's exactly 4 inches wide. Then cut four pieces approximately 32 inches long, mitered 45 degrees at the corners. Glue and nail them to the tops of the posts, siding and crown molding.

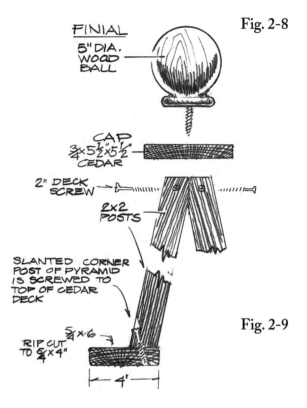

Fig. 2-10

PYRAMID

DETAIL

SPACE 2½"

⅜" x 1½"
SINGLE
LATTICE
CEDAR
STRIPS

2x2
CEDAR
POST

5' 3"

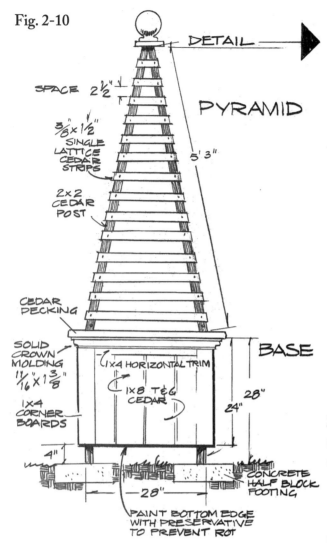

CEDAR
DECKING

SOLID
CROWN
MOLDING
1¹¹⁄₁₆" x 1⅜"

1x4
CORNER
BOARDS

BASE

1x4 HORIZONTAL TRIM

1x8 T&G
CEDAR

28"

24"

4"

28"

CONCRETE
HALF BLOCK
FOOTING

PAINT BOTTOM EDGE
WITH PRESERVATIVE
TO PREVENT ROT

FINIAL   Fig. 2-8
5" DIA.
WOOD
BALL

CAP
¾" x 5½" x 5½"
CEDAR

2" DECK
SCREW

2x2
POSTS

Fig. 2-9

SLANTED CORNER
POST OF PYRAMID
IS SCREWED TO
TOP OF CEDAR
DECK

RIP CUT
TO ¾"x 4"   ¾"x 6

4'

2-inch galvanized deck screws. Cut the bottom of each post at a slight angle and screw it into the decking (see Fig. 2-9).

LATTICE

Make your own lattice strips from an 8-foot-long 2x6. Begin by rip cutting ⅜-inch-thick strips. Then make a 2½-inch spacer to rest the lattice strips on while you are marking, cutting and nailing each strip to fit the pyramid (see Fig. 2-10). When nailing the lattice to the four corner posts, start from the bottom and work up. Do the same for all four sides of the pyramid.

CAP AND FINIAL

Top the obelisk off with a cedar cap piece and a wooden finial ball, which are sold at most lumberyards. If you are unable to find a ball, you can order it by mail (see Sources).

Finish the obelisk by giving it three or four coats of stain or paint, or by leaving it natural and allowing it to weather gray.

To keep the base square, make braces out of four pieces of 1x2, approximately 21 inches long, mitered 45 degrees at the ends. Nail them to the bottom 2x2 frame pieces (see Fig. 2-7).

PYRAMID

The pyramid consists of four corner posts, constructed from four pieces of 2x2, each cut 56 inches long. Cut these from the long off-cuts, which were set aside earlier.

Mark the angles where the posts will join at the top, and using a rasp, shave off the overlapping wood so that the four posts join together neatly at the top. Screw them together, using

PERGOLA

While working on a garden house in East Hampton, we happened to glance over to the yard next door and our eye caught one of the most beautiful garden structures we have spotted while researching this book. It was a pergola — a small arbor formed of horizontal trelliswork and supported on columns, made to train vines and other plants. The creator of this pergola, Mr. Whipple, was wearing a wide-brimmed straw hat and was hard at work in his garden. He reminded us of our imagined reader, neither a professional designer nor a professional carpenter, but an individual with an eye for good design and the will to create something with his own hands that would beautify his garden and last for many years. He calls it "Whipple's Folly."

MATERIALS

Quantity	Size	Description	Location or Use
4	8 feet	wood columns	posts
5	8 feet	2x6 #2 fir	beams
1	8 feet	cedar or redwood railing	top rail
1	8 feet	cedar or redwood railing	bottom rail
3	10 feet	2x2 cedar or redwood posts	railing balusters
1 pkg.	12 feet	redwood fillet	railing
12	6 feet	1x2 spruce	temporary braces
1 cu. yd.	1- to 1½ -inch	stone	footing and drain
2 bags	80-lb.	concrete mix	footing
4	16-x16-inch	pre-cast chimney blocks	footing
1 roll	30-lb.	tar paper	drain
8	4-inch	angle irons	column brackets
4	⅜-x8-inch	lag screws and washers	
8	3-inch	galvanized deck screws	
1 lb.	1½ -inch	galvanized deck screws	
1 lb.	2-inch	galvanized finish nails	
1 lb.	3-inch	galvanized finish nails	
1 gal.		preservative or paint	

A pergola like Mr. Whipple's can be quite expensive, but his cost next to nothing. He serendipitously discovered four wooden columns at a yard sale for $10 each. He also found two sections of railing left over from a former remodeling project. The only "store bought" pieces were the eight 2x6 beams and two bags of concrete mix, which he purchased from a lumberyard.

Whether it is to be an entrance to a formal bed of flowers, or a solitary structure placed in a clearing with a backdrop of firs, choose a spot for your pergola where it will look attractive from several angles. If you are going to train vines on the pergola, observe how much sun falls on it during different times of the day and year. If you want to grow sun-loving plants, like morning glo-ries or roses, make sure you build it where there is full sun. If you have only partial sun, plant something that is shade tolerant, like the fragrant wild clematis, a strong and fast spreading vine that will quickly turn the pergola into a shaded bower.

After you have picked the site for your pergola, find the post locations by measuring and marking a 4-x5-foot rectangle on the cleared ground. Compare the diagonal measurements to make sure they are equal (see Fig. 2-11). This will insure that the corners are square.

For proper drainage, dig a 12-inch-deep by 16-inch-wide trench connecting the four post locations. Fill the bottom of the trench with 8 inches of crushed stone, cover the stone with tar paper and backfill with soil.

Fig. 2-11

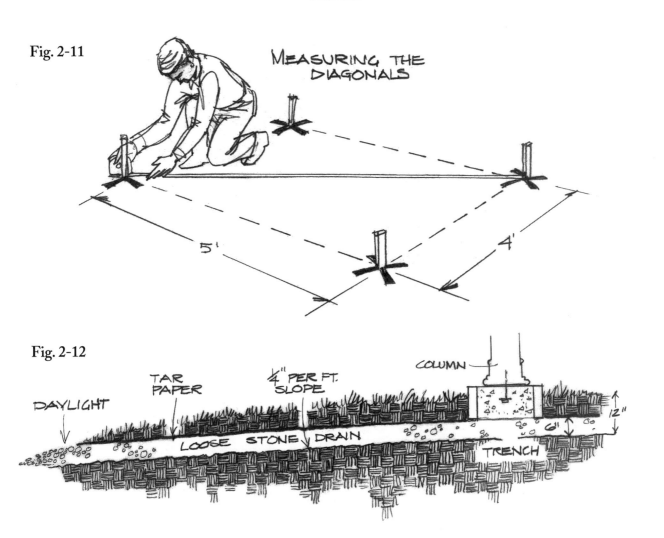

MEASURING THE DIAGONALS

5'

4'

Fig. 2-12

DAYLIGHT

TAR PAPER

¼" PER FT. SLOPE

COLUMN

LOOSE STONE DRAIN

TRENCH

12"

6"

Dig a second drainage trench, connected to the first trench. It should be 12 inches deep and 4- to 6-inches wide, and slope downward toward the lowest level of your garden. Angle the slope ¼ inch/foot and continue the trench until it meets grade level (see Fig. 2-12). Partially fill the trench with crushed stone, cover with tar paper and backfill with soil. The purpose of the trench is to help drain any standing water from under the column footings and to help prevent frost from heaving the columns out of alignment.

COLUMNS

If you are using solid wood columns for your pergola, secure them to the concrete base by boring a ¼-inch hole in the bottom of each column and partially screwing a ⅜-x8-inch lag screw (with a large washer on it) into the hole. To fur-

ther anchor the post to the concrete base, partially screw four 3-inch galvanized deck screws into the bottom of each column (see Fig. 2-13). Treat the bottom of each column with preservative and tar to prevent water from wicking into the column by capillary action.

If your columns are hollow, bore two ¼-inch holes at the bottom of each one to drain any water that might collect. Use two 1½-inch galvanized deck screws to screw two 4-inch angle irons to the inside of each column (see Fig. 2-14).

At each corner of the 4-x5-foot trench, bury a pre-cast hollow chimney block (see Fig. 2-15). Place a large rock in the center of each corner chimney block to support the column while the concrete is curing. Fill the space inside with wet

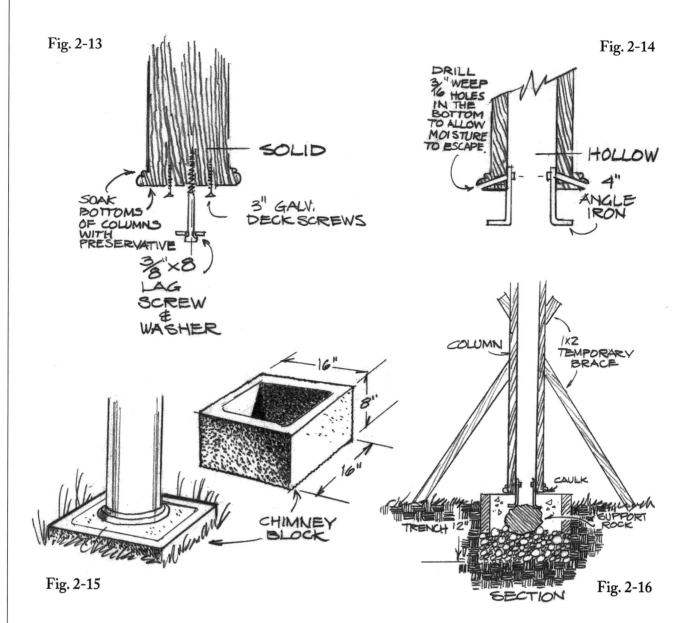

Fig. 2-13

SOLID

SOAK BOTTOMS OF COLUMNS WITH PRESERVATIVE

3" GALV. DECK SCREWS

3/8"x8 LAG SCREW & WASHER

Fig. 2-14

DRILL 3/16" WEEP HOLES IN THE BOTTOM TO ALLOW MOISTURE TO ESCAPE

HOLLOW

4" ANGLE IRON

16"

8"

16"

CHIMNEY BLOCK

Fig. 2-15

COLUMN

1x2 TEMPORARY BRACE

CAULK

TRENCH 12"

SUPPORT ROCK

SECTION

Fig. 2-16

concrete and carefully stand the columns up so that the protruding lag screws or angle irons are embedded in the concrete (see Fig. 2-16).

To make sure the columns stay plumb while the concrete cures, nail two temporary braces to each column. Using a level may be difficult since the columns are tapered, so tape a small sliver of wood to the top of the level, compensating for the taper of the column (see Fig. 2-17).

Once the first column is perfectly aligned, nail a crossbrace to the next column at the top.

Continue around until all four columns are aligned; plumb and square.

BEAMS

Allow the concrete to set for several days. In the meantime, cut out the decorative ends of the 2x6 beams, using an electric jig saw. Draw the profile on a piece of cardboard, 5½ inches wide (see Fig. 2-18). Measure in 1 inch from each corner and place a mark. Using a compass, scribe a 3½-inch radius arc down to a point, 1 inch up from the bottom edges. Draw a 1-x1-inch notch at one end of the arc. Using a utility knife, cut out

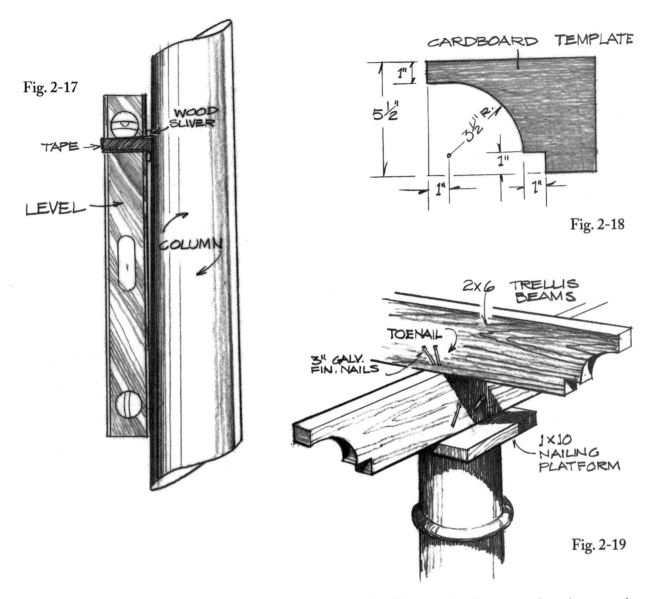

Fig. 2-17

WOOD SLIVER

TAPE →

LEVEL →

COLUMN

CARDBOARD TEMPLATE

1"

5½"

3½" R.

1"

1"

1"

1"

Fig. 2-18

2x6 TRELLIS BEAMS

TOENAIL

3" GALV. FIN. NAILS

1x10 NAILING PLATFORM

Fig. 2-19

this cardboard template and use it to mark where the 2x6 beams will be cut. Sand any rough edges on the curves with a rolled up piece of 60-grit sandpaper.

Make a square platform for the top of each column to support the beams by cutting four pieces of 1x10, each 10½ inches square. Join each piece to the top of a column, using waterproof glue and 2-inch galvanized finish nails (see Fig. 2-19).

Using a stepladder for support, nail the first two 2x6 beams in place with 3-inch galvanized

finish nails, centering them over the columns and toenailing into the platforms. Set the nail heads below the surface and fill the depressions with vinyl spackle. Nail the three remaining 2x6 decorative beams at right angles to and on top of the first two beams, centering the two outside ones over the columns and placing the middle one so it is equidistant from the two outside ones (see Fig. 2-20).

RAILING

Carefully measure the distance between the inside edges of the two sets of columns, and cut the top and bottom rails to this length. Be sure

Fig. 2-20

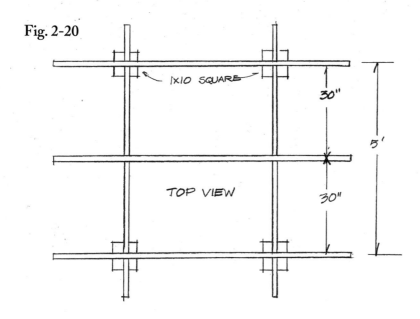

1x10 SQUARE

30"

TOP VIEW

30"

5'

you measure the distance between the columns where the inside edge of each rail will be. If you measure along the centerline of the railing, the piece will be short. Using an electric jig saw, shape the end of the rail so that it fits in between the curved columns perfectly. For the railing balusters, cut pieces of 2x2 cedar or redwood, each 28½ inches long. Position the balusters 6 inches on-center (see Fig. 2-21). Measure the distances between the balusters, and cut and nail fillet pieces to fit the spaces (see Fig. 2-22).

Finish by painting all surfaces with three to four coats of preservative or paint.

Fig. 2-21

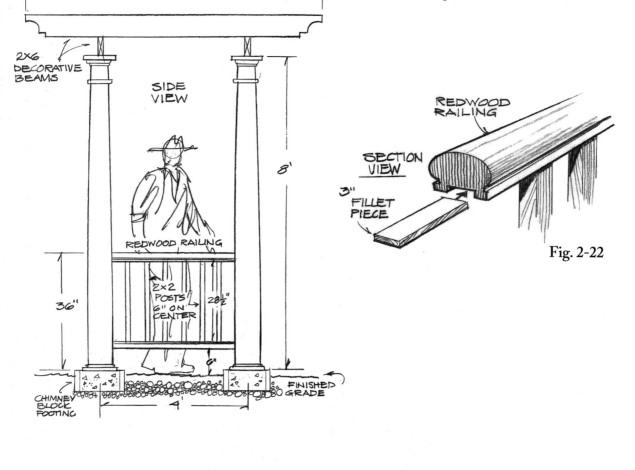

8'

2X6 DECORATIVE BEAMS

SIDE VIEW

8'

REDWOOD RAILING

2x2 POSTS 6" ON CENTER

28½"

36"

6"

CHIMNEY BLOCK FOOTING

FINISHED GRADE

4'

REDWOOD RAILING

SECTION VIEW

3" FILLET PIECE

Fig. 2-22

HEART GATE, PINECONE BIRDHOUSE, GARDEN TOOLBOX, HEART STOOL (PAGES 109, 66, 94 AND 45)

COVERED SEAT (PAGE 58)

POTTING BENCH (PAGE 82)

ROSE ARBOR (PAGE 37)

ROSE ARBOR

An arbor not only functions as an overhead support for climbing flowers or vines, but also creates a spot of shade in an otherwise sunny garden. When designing and positioning an arbor, consider both the layout of your garden and the architecture of your house. An arbor can cover a walkway or path or connect a row of low shrubs or fencing. The arbor that we built was designed to be the focus of the garden. It stands alone with no climbers planted below it, creating a frame for a palette of colors in the background.

MATERIALS

Quantity	Size	Description	Location or Use
4	8 feet	4x4 clear cedar	posts
1	4x8 sheet	MDO plywood	arches
2	8 feet	1x4 clear cedar	bases and capitals
1	8 feet	2x4 clear cedar	arch veneer and top slats
1	8 feet	2x4 clear cedar	crosspieces
1	4x4 panel	clear cedar privacy lattice	sides
3	8 feet	clear cedar lattice cap	sides
16	3½ -inch	galvanized deck screws	
1 lb.	2-inch	galvanized deck screws	
1 lb.	1½ -inch	galvanized finish nails	
1 qt.		epoxy glue	
1 pt.		waterproof yellow glue	
1	50 feet	heavy hemp twine	
3	sheets	coarse, medium and fine sandpaper	

POSTS

Begin by cutting four 4x4 cedar posts to exactly 7½-foot lengths. Sand the posts using coarse (60-grit) and fine (120-grit) sandpaper and fill any holes with wood filler. Using a sharp handsaw or rip saw, mark and cut out a notch 2 inches deep by 1½ inches wide from one end of each post. This is where the ends of the arches will be inserted. **Tip:** To make more accurate cuts, try to line up visually the top and end of the cuts as you are making them (see Fig. 2-23A). Don't worry if the notches aren't perfect, since they will be hidden by the capitals at the top of the posts. To remove the material between the two cuts, use a sharp chisel and a mallet. This is easily done by holding the chisel vertically over the bottom line of the notch and striking it with a mallet (see Fig. 2-23B). Remove the chisel and place it in the end of the post, and give the chisel a series of sharp blows. This will split out about ¼ inch of wood each time. (see Fig. 2-23C).

ARCHES

The arches are generally the most difficult section of any arbor to construct. Traditionally, they are made by cutting, clamping and gluing many little pieces of wood together and then shaping them into a semi-circle. The method we use is much easier, less time consuming, has no joints and is much stronger. The trick is to use a relatively new plywood called MDO (medium density overlay) or Duraply. This is a product originally developed for highway signs. It has a brown covering, which is actually several thin layers of paper impregnated with a phenolic resin, which makes it impervious to the weather.

Each arch consists of two pieces of ¾-inch MDO plywood, which are glued together. Lay the MDO plywood panel on two sawhorses and mark a line lengthwise down the center of the panel. Since the arches are 48 inches wide, mark a radius point 24 inches from each side and from one end of the panel (see Fig. 2-24) Drill a

Fig. 2-23A

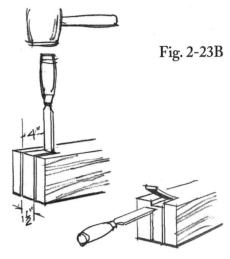

Fig. 2-23B

Fig. 2-23C

Fig. 2-24

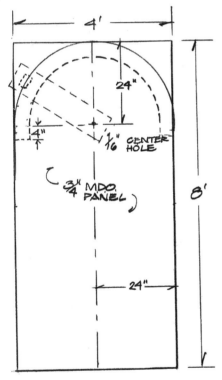

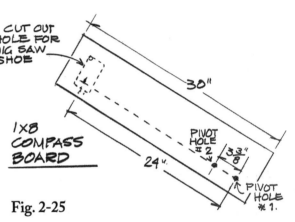

CUT OUT
HOLE FOR
JIG SAW
SHOE

1x8
COMPASS
BOARD

30"

24"

PIVOT
HOLE
#2

3 3/8"

PIVOT
HOLE
#1.

Fig. 2-25

¹⁄₁₆-inch pivot hole through the panel at this point.

To make the curves of the arches, cut a "compass board" out of scrap 1x8, 30 inches long. Remove the blade from your jig saw and trace the

outline of your saw shoe on the compass board, marking where the front edge of the blade fits into the shoe. Beginning at this mark, draw a line, parallel to the long edge of the 1x8 and continue it to a point 24 inches away (see Fig. 2-25). This will be your pivot point. It is essential that the pivot point and the front edge of the saw blade (once it's reinserted) are "in line" (equidistant from the side edge of the compass board). After reinserting the jig saw blade, use the electric jig saw to cut out the marked rectangular section, creating a hole inside which the jig saw shoe fits snugly (see Fig. 2-26).

Drill a ¹⁄₁₆-inch-diameter hole at the pivot point and insert a 1½- or 2-inch finish nail

Fig. 2-26

COMPASS BOARD

SCRAP

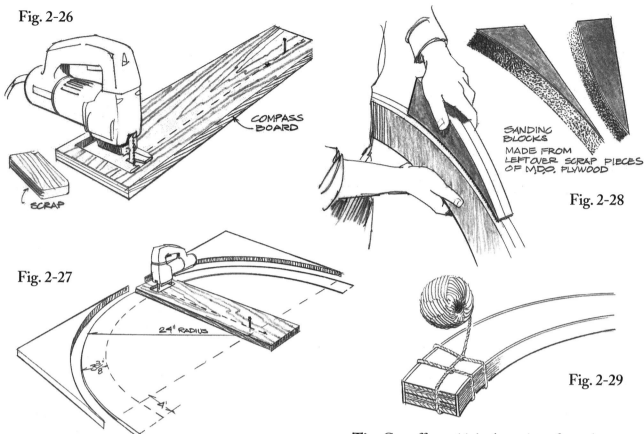

Fig. 2-27

24" RADIUS

3⅜"

4"

SANDING BLOCKS MADE FROM LEFTOVER SCRAP PIECES OF MDO PLYWOOD

Fig. 2-28

Fig. 2-29

through the compass board and into the hole in the MDO panel. Use this to cut the arches (see Fig. 2-27). As you make the curved cuts, keep in mind that the bottom of the saw blade will have a tendency to angle out away from the center. To prevent this, push the saw slowly along the curve, and keep the motor running at the highest speed. If you have set up your compass board correctly, these curved cuts should be extremely easy to make, and you should achieve a perfect semicircle each time. To cut the inside curve of the arches, make another ¹⁄₁₆-inch pivot hole 3⅜ inches from the first hole (refer back to Fig. 2-25).

Repeat this procedure to cut three more arch pieces. Then stack two pieces on top of each other, making sure they are exactly the same size, and glue them together with waterproof glue. When you are done, you should have two identical 1½-inch-thick arches.

Tip: Cut off two 11-inch sections from the waste pieces of MDO plywood — one from the top of the curve and one from the bottom — and glue 1½-inch-wide coarse (60-grit) sandpaper strips to the curved edges. These sanding blocks will come in handy when sanding the curves, eliminating any chance of flat spots in the curves (see Fig 2-28).

Using a table saw, rip cut four ³⁄₃₂-inch-thick strips of clear cedar from the 8-foot-long 2x4. (Set aside the remaining wood for the top slats.) Glue these veneer strips to the edges of the MDO plywood, to hide the end grain. To hold the strips in place while the glue is drying, you would need about 30 clamps. A better solution is wrapping the arches with heavy hemp twine. Apply waterproof glue to all the surfaces to be glued and wrap the cord around the strips and the arch. Keep the cord pulled tightly at all times, going back under each previous turn so that the cord can be cinched up securely (see Fig. 2-29). There

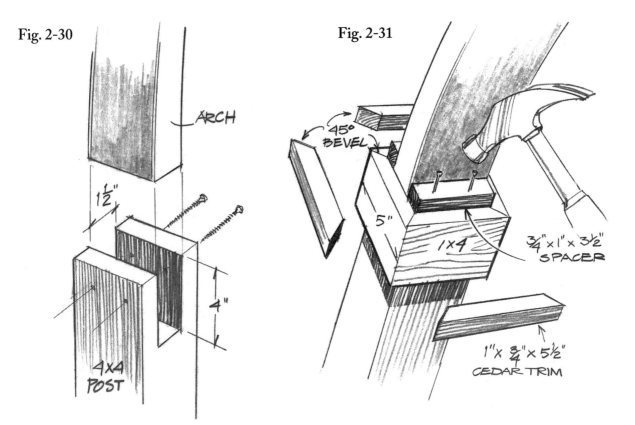

Fig. 2-30

Fig. 2-31

should be no gaps between the strips and the plywood arch. If gaps exist, place wooden shims under the cord.

Once the glue has dried, remove the twine and sand the edges smooth, using the sanding blocks. Test fit the ends of the arches to see if they fit into the notches you have made in the posts, then glue them in place with waterproof glue. Make sure both posts are parallel, and screw a temporary 48-inch-long brace across the bottom to hold them in place. Put two 2-inch galvanized deck screws in each joint where the posts meet the arches (see Fig. 2-30).

CAPITALS AND BASES

To hide the joints where each arch meets the post, cut four pieces of 1x4 clear cedar, approximately 5 inches long. Bevel each end and temporarily tack them to the post, checking the fit (see Fig. 2-31). File and sand until they fit perfectly and glue them in place. Do the same for the bottom of each post, placing the base pieces

exactly 5 feet, 3 inches from the top of the posts.

To "trim out" the top of the capitals, cut two 1-x3½-inch spacers for each capital and glue them next to the face of each arch, covering the end grain on the 4x4 post. Then cut 1-x¾-inch clear cedar trim pieces for each capital. Miter the end of each piece at a 45 degree angle and glue and nail them to the top of each capital (see Fig. 2-31).

CROSSPIECES

Cut four crosspieces of 2x4 clear cedar, each 19 inches long. To attach them to the posts, drill two ⅜-inch-diameter screw holes, 1½ inches deep (see Fig. 2-32A). Position the screw holes below the bottom of each capital and above each base so that the crosspieces are 50 inches apart. Continue drilling the pilot holes, using a ³⁄₁₆-inch-diameter drill bit, until you come out the other side. Lay the two sets of arches and posts on their sides, facing each other. Glue and screw the crosspieces in place, using 3½-inch

Fig. 2-32

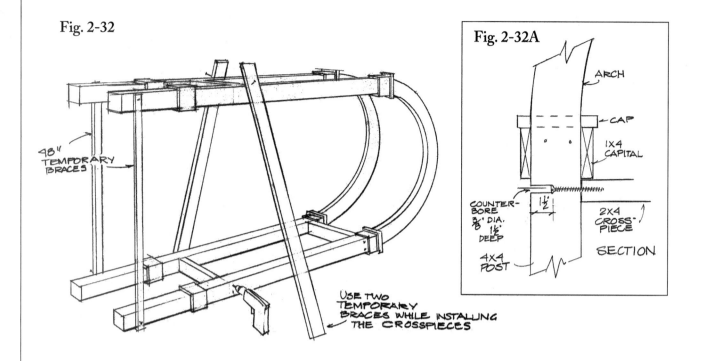

Fig. 2-32A

galvanized deck screws. Once you have two crosspieces attached to one pair of posts, turn the structure over and attach the other two crosspieces (see Fig. 2-32).

LATTICE

Cut four pieces of lattice cap, 19 inches long, and four pieces, 47 inches long. Cut two pieces of lattice, each 17x48 inches (see Fig. 2-33). **Note:** If you plan on painting this structure, paint the lattice and support pieces before they are assembled.

Glue all the pieces together to form a lattice frame. Fit the lattice frame into the side opening created by the crosspieces and the posts, and screw them in place, using 2-inch galvanized deck screws (see side view, Fig. 2-34).

TOP SLATS

Using the wood left over from cutting the veneer strips, rip cut three 8-foot-long pieces, each ¾ inch thick. Cut these into nine pieces, each 27 inches long. Place the first two pieces 1½ inches up from the top of the capitals. Align the remaining pieces equidistant from each other and screw

Fig. 2-33

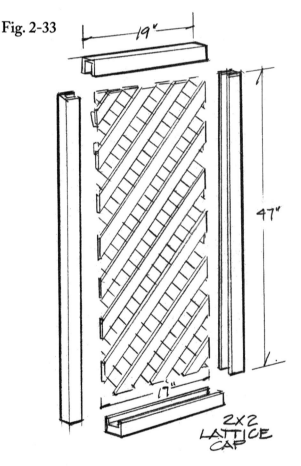

them in place, using 2-inch galvanized deck screws (see Fig. 2-34).

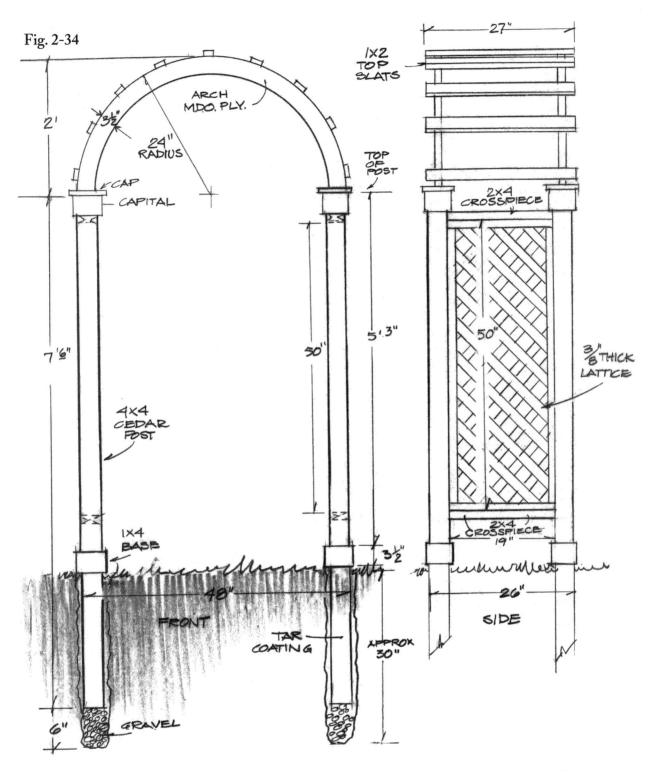

Fig. 2-34

2'

3½"

24" RADIUS

ARCH M.D.O. PLY.

1×2 TOP SLATS

27"

CAP CAPITAL

TOP OF POST

2×4 CROSSPIECE

7'6"

50"

5'3"

50"

3/8" THICK LATTICE

4×4 CEDAR POST

1×4 BASE

2×4 CROSSPIECE 19"

48"

3½"

FRONT

TAR COATING

APPROX 30"

26"

SIDE

6"

GRAVEL

INSTALLATION

To install the rose arbor, dig four holes approximately 30 inches deep, using a posthole digger. Fill the bottom of each hole with rocks or bricks (to allow for drainage) until they are 24 inches deep. To protect the posts, coat the bottom 24 inches with roofing tar before burying them in the ground. With an assistant, place the arbor legs in the holes and remove the temporary braces. Using a level, check to make sure everything is plumb and level before backfilling. Tamp the dirt down with a 2×4 as you are backfilling.

RELAXING IN THE GARDEN

HEART STOOL

Every now and then it's nice to sit down, relax and survey what you have accomplished in the garden while planning for the next season. It is also helpful to have a place to rest your tools where they won't be overlooked and mistakenly left outside overnight. This appealing garden stool serves both purposes. It also makes a handy stepping stool when pruning out-of-reach branches and can even serve as an extra seat for unexpected guests at the end of your picnic table. Sturdy yet lightweight, the stool can easily be moved about, using the heart shaped cut-out as a comfortable hand grip.

MATERIALS

Quantity	Size	Description	Location or Use
1	2 feet	1x12 clear cedar	seat
1	2 feet	2x4 cedar	support cleats
1	6 feet	2x2 cedar	legs
12	2-inch	galvanized deck screws	
1 qt.		water sealer	

SEAT

Make the seat by cutting the 1x12 piece of cedar 22 inches long. To cut out the heart-shaped hole in the seat, find the center of the board and drill two 1½-inch-diameter holes, each centered ¾ inch from either side of the center of the board (see Fig. 3-1). Draw two tangent intersecting lines, from the outside of the two circles, meeting below the circles. Cut out the remaining triangu-lar piece of wood, using an electric jig saw, and cut the seat corners at a 1½-inch radius, rounding off the edges with sandpaper (see Fig. 3-2).

SUPPORT CLEATS

To make the two leg support cleats, cut two pieces of cedar 2x4s, 10 inches long. Using a table saw or block plane, bevel the edges at an 11 degree angle. Mark where the center of the

Fig. 3-1

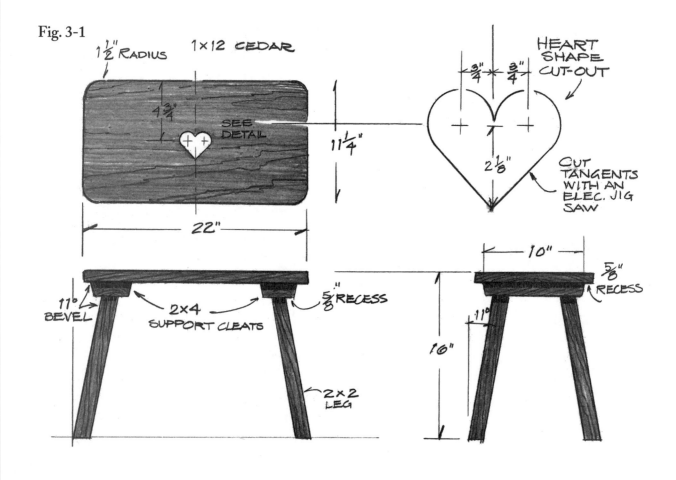

Fig. 3-2

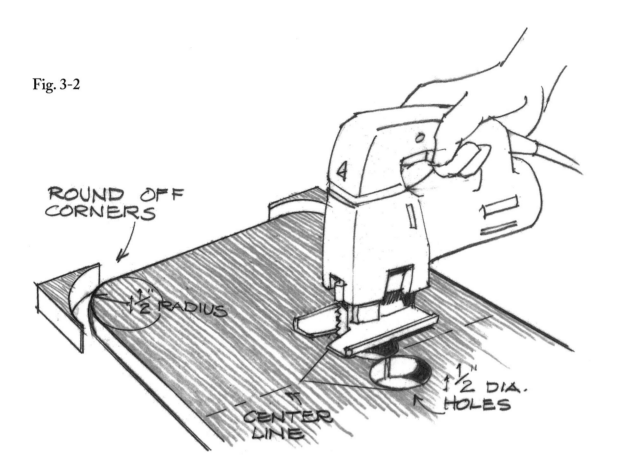

ROUND OFF CORNERS

1½" RADIUS

CENTER LINE

1½" DIA. HOLES

Fig. 3-3A

2"
2"

Fig. 3-3B

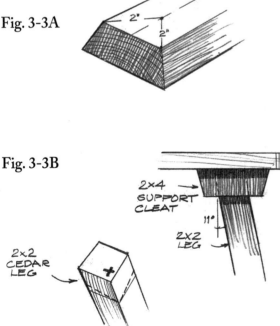

2x4 SUPPORT CLEAT

11°

2x2 LEG

2x2 CEDAR LEG

1½-inch-diameter leg holes will be by measuring in 2 inches from each corner to the centerline of each support cleat (see Fig. 3-3A). **Note:** The legs are attached to the 2x4 support cleats, so that they slant at an 11 degree angle on either side. Use a 1½-inch spade drill bit to make the four angled leg holes in the 2x4 support cleats. Use this book as a visual guide to help "eye ball" the angle of the drill while cutting (see Fig 3-4). Start the hole with the drill held vertically and then gradually slant the drill to an 11 degree angle, while drilling all the way through.

LEGS

Make the legs by cutting four pieces of 2x2 cedar, each 15 inches long. Draw a line around the perimeter of each leg, 1½ inches from one end. The object of this step is to make the ends of the square 2x2 legs round, with a shoulder that conforms to the 11 degree angle of the leg.

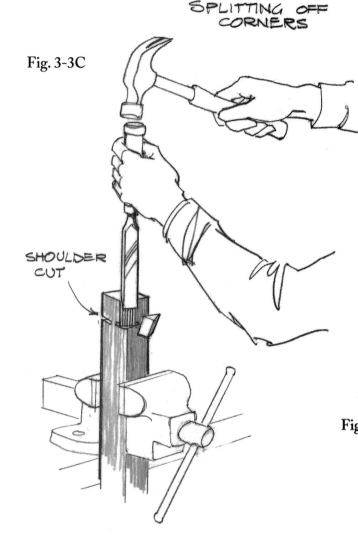

SPLITTING OFF CORNERS

Fig. 3-3C

SHOULDER CUT

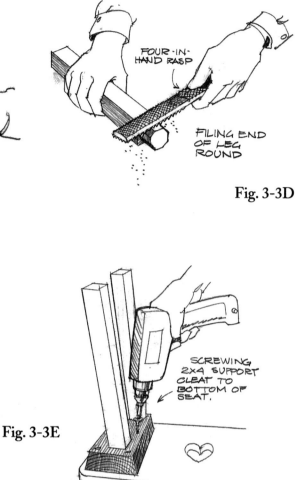

FOUR-IN-HAND RASP

FILING END OF LEG ROUND

Fig. 3-3D

SCREWING 2X4 SUPPORT CLEAT TO BOTTOM OF SEAT.

Fig. 3-3E

Place an X on what will be the top outside corner of each 2x2 to indicate which way the leg will eventually face once the seat is completed (see Fig. 3-3B). To make the legs fit into the angled holes, the corners of the 2x2 must also be cut off at an 11 degree angle. Draw a line, slanted 11 degrees from the existing line, and using a hand saw, crosscut the corners around the legs. Hold each leg up, and using a chisel and hammer, split off the corners of each one (see Fig. 3-3C). Round off the ends with a rasp until they fit in the 1½-inch-diameter holes (see Fig. 3-3D). You

should be able to twist them by hand into the holes, so that they fit snugly. Do not pound them in with a hammer, as you might split the 2x4 leg support. When you are satisfied that they fit together perfectly, glue the legs into the holes.

Join the four 2x4 support cleats to the underneath side of the seat, ¾ inch in from the outside edges of the seat, using six 2-inch galvanized deck screws (see Fig. 3-3E). Give the stool a coat of water sealer to protect it and to bring out the rich natural color of the cedar.

Fig. 3-4

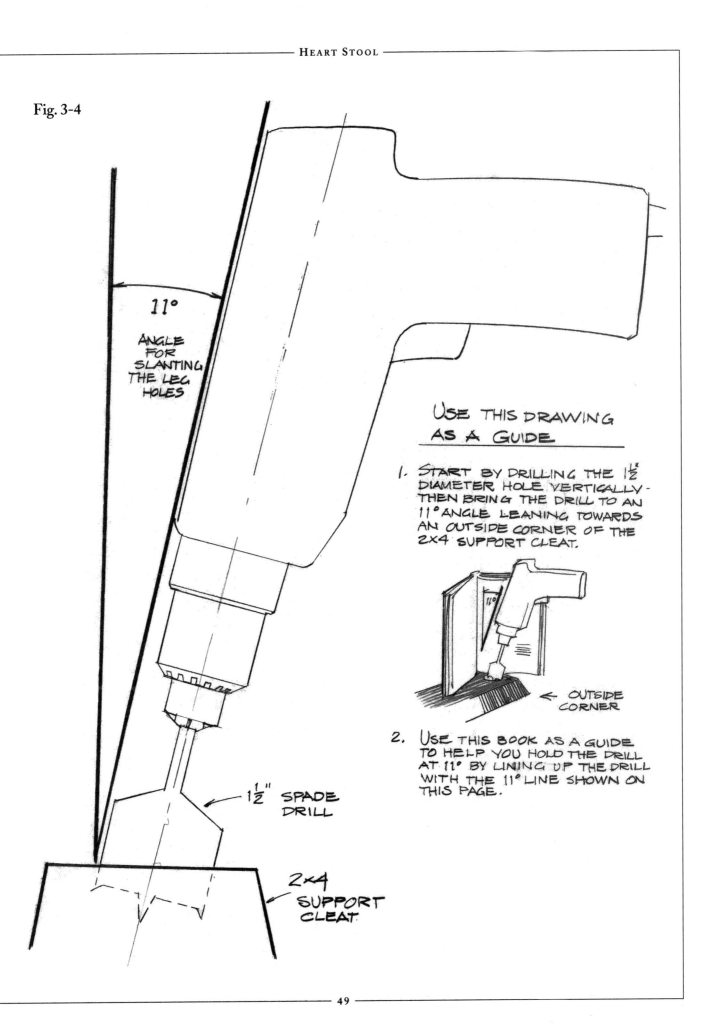

11°

ANGLE
FOR
SLANTING
THE LEG
HOLES

USE THIS DRAWING
AS A GUIDE

1. START BY DRILLING THE 1½"
   DIAMETER HOLE VERTICALLY -
   THEN BRING THE DRILL TO AN
   11° ANGLE LEANING TOWARDS
   AN OUTSIDE CORNER OF THE
   2×4 SUPPORT CLEAT.

← OUTSIDE
   CORNER

2. USE THIS BOOK AS A GUIDE
   TO HELP YOU HOLD THE DRILL
   AT 11° BY LINING UP THE DRILL
   WITH THE 11° LINE SHOWN ON
   THIS PAGE.

1½" SPADE
DRILL

2×4
SUPPORT
CLEAT.

PICNIC TABLE

After working in the city all winter, we celebrate the summer months by spending as much time as possible outdoors, working, relaxing and, of course, dining "al fresco." Most of our meals are eaten at the long picnic table that David built in our front yard. When night falls, we illuminate the table with hurricane lanterns, build a wood fire (no charcoal allowed) and cook out as often as possible. Friends and relatives join us on weekends, gathering together at what has become an indispensable landmark representing years of pleasant meals and memories. When the first chill sets in, we bundle up; and only when it becomes teeth-chatteringly cold, do we reluctantly head indoors to eat.

MATERIALS			
Quantity	**Size**	**Description**	**Location or Use**
1	10 feet	6x6 redwood or P.T.	legs
1	6 feet	2x8 redwood or P.T.	table supports
10	8 feet	2x4 redwood	table top
2 bags	80-lb.	concrete mix	base collar
1 lb.	3-inch	galvanized deck screws	
1 box	½-inch	wood plugs	table top
1 qt.		water sealer or stain	

We recommend redwood for this table, instead of the more usual option, P.T. lumber. When you call your local lumberyard to order the clear redwood 2x4s, you may be shocked to hear the price. However, consider what you are getting: a rot-resistant, sturdy table that (with a little care) will remain in good shape for many years. Left natural, without paint or stain, the clear redwood weathers to a soft shade of gray and blends in with the surroundings.

LEGS

Cut the two 59-inch-long legs out of 6x6 lumber. Hold up the butt end of each leg so it is at a slant, and heat with a propane torch. When it begins to smoke, drip candle wax onto the leg bottoms, sealing the wood and creating a moisture barrier which will keep water from wicking up the end grain (see Fig. 3-5).

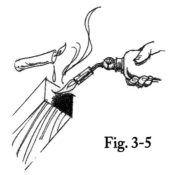

Fig. 3-5

The area where the post emerges from the ground is the most vulnerable to rot and insect infestation, so soak this part of each leg with wood preservative. Once it is dry, give it a coat of roofing tar.

Using a posthole digger, dig two holes, approximately 32 inches deep and 54 inches apart. Place a brick or stone in each hole for the legs to rest on. Do not backfill the holes until both legs have been positioned in the ground and you have checked to make sure that they are square. Do this by measuring diagonally from the outside corner of one table support to the outside corner of the other support. They should be an equal distance apart. Place a 2x4 across the two supports and check for level, as well. Make sure each leg is 27½ inches high from the ground and use the level to check that each leg is plumb, or vertical, to the ground. This can be frustrating and time-consuming, but is an important step to ensure that the table remains stable. After the legs are positioned perfectly, backfill the holes, tamping down and compressing the loose soil as you fill. Continue checking with a level to make sure the posts have not gotten out of alignment.

Don't fill the hole completely with dirt. The top portion should be filled with concrete. Measure out 4 inches from each side of each leg and dig a 3-inch-deep circular trench around the leg where it meets the ground. Pour a stiff mixture of wet concrete in the top portion of each hole and in this trench around the posts. The diameter of each trench should measure approximately 14 inches. Mound up the concrete with a trowel, so

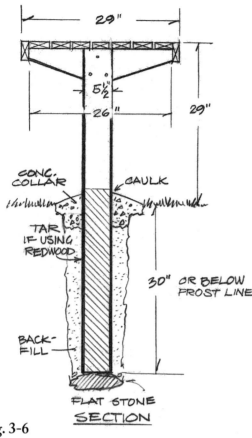

Fig. 3-6

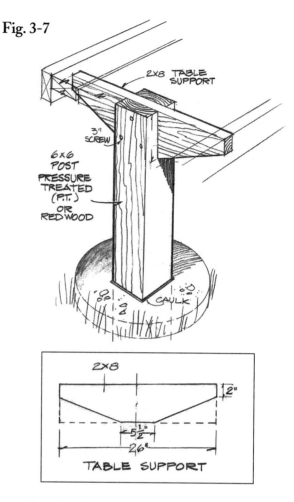

Fig. 3-7

that rainwater will be shed from the surface (see Fig. 3-6). Let the concrete set overnight. **Note:** After several months the wood may shrink away from the concrete, so apply a bead of silicone caulking where the two materials join.

TABLE SUPPORTS

Cut the two table supports out of the 2x8, each measuring 26 inches long. Taper (slant) the ends of each table support (see detail, Fig. 3-7). Center the supports in the leg slots and screw three 3-inch galvanized deck screws through each side of the legs and into the table supports.

Each table support forms a "T" across the top of one of the legs and provides a support for the 2x4s. Carefully mark a 1½-inch-wide slot, 7¼ inches deep, in the center of the top of each post to accept the table support. Do this by drawing two vertical lines, 7¼ inches down on the

outsides of each post. Using a (rip) hand saw, make two vertical cuts down each post (see Fig. 3-8A). Drill two ½-inch holes at the bottom of the cuts and using a ½-inch-wide chisel, cut out the inside of each slot (see Fig. 3-8, B and C).

TABLE TOP

Cut seven pieces of redwood 2x4s, each 93 inches long. For the table edging, cut two pieces, 29 inches long, and two pieces, 8 feet long. Precise measurements are important. Lay the seven 2x4s across the two table supports, so there is a ¼-inch space between each one. Draw a centerline across the 2x4s above the center of each table support, and drill a ½-inch-diameter counterbored hole, ½ inch deep in the center of each 2x4. After checking to make sure the ends are aligned evenly, screw all seven pieces to the table supports (see plan view, Fig. 3-9).

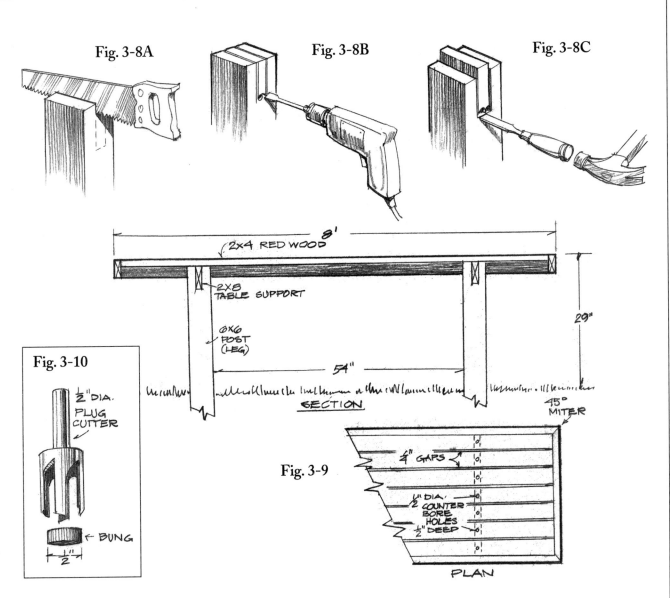

Fig. 3-8A

Fig. 3-8B

Fig. 3-8C

2X4 REDWOOD   8'

2X8 TABLE SUPPORT

6X6 POST (LEG)

54"

SECTION

29"

45° MITER

Fig. 3-10

½"DIA. PLUG CUTTER

← BUNG

1½"

Fig. 3-9

¼" GAPS

½" DIA. COUNTER BORE HOLES

½" DEEP

PLAN

Trim off the ends of the table edging at a 45 degree angle. After drilling ½-inch-diameter counter-bored holes ¾ inch down from the top edging, screw the side and end edging to the table top.

FINISHING

Fill the ½-inch screw holes with ½-inch plugs. It is easy and looks better to make your own plugs from a scrap piece of redwood, using a special bit called a "plug cutter" (see Fig 3-10), which can only be used with a drill press. If you don't have access to a drill press and a plug cutter, you can buy birch or cherry wood plugs to fit the holes. If these aren't available locally, you can or-

der them from any good woodworking supply catalog (see Sources). Glue and gently tap in the plugs, with a wooden mallet. Using medium (80-grit) sandpaper, sand off the tops of the plugs and the table surface.

Allow redwood to weather for a week or two and then give it a coat of sealer, such as CWF or Thompson's Weatherseal. Every year the table top will become a little grayer. If you don't like a weathered look, it can easily be lightly sanded and covered with a coat of sealer to keep the rich-looking redwood finish. If you use pressure-treated lumber, stain the wood with a color of your choice.

GARDEN BENCH

A garden bench has many uses. It can be situated at the end of a garden path, provide a place to rest after a few hours of weeding and planting or serve as a sturdy seat to accompany a picnic table. The following design is for a simple, durable, well-constructed bench that takes only a few hours to construct. The seat is 48 inches long and the legs are free-standing. Depending on your needs, however, you can change the dimensions of the bench or set the legs permanently in the ground.

MATERIALS

Quantity	Size	Description	Location or Use
		(FOR MOVABLE BENCH)	
1	8 feet	4x8 fir or P.T. timbers	seat
2	8 feet	2x6 P.T. lumber	legs and crosspieces
2	15 inches	⅜-inch-dia. threaded rod, with 4 washers and 4 nuts	
1 lb.	2½-inch	galvanized deck screws	
		(FOR PERMANENT BENCH)	
1	10 feet	4x8 fir or P.T. timbers	seat
1	8 feet	6x6 P.T. timber	legs
1	30 inches	⅜-inch-dia. threaded rod, with 4 washers and 4 nuts	

MOVABLE BENCH:

SEAT

Cut two pieces of 4x8, each 48 inches long. (You might have to use a handsaw if your electric circular saw does not reach all the way through the 4x8.) Make two marks on each 4x8, one 6 inches in from the end, and the other 10½ inches in from the end (see Fig. 3-11A). Mark the same dimensions on the opposite end of each 4x8. Cut two, 1½-inch-deep x 4½-inch-wide notches out of the inside face of each 4x8, where you have marked. This distance is the same width as the bench legs. Make the notches by resting the timber on edge and cutting several 1½-inch-deep cuts inside the marked area. Draw a straight line from the bottom of one cut to the bottom of the other cut. Lay the timber down flat and chisel out the notch, using a sharp ¾-inch-wide chisel (see Fig. 3-11B). **Note:** Chiseling out the notched material is best done by holding the chisel against the pencil line with the bevel side of the chisel facing the wood that you will be removing. Give two or three hard blows to the wood, incising a line aproximately ¼ inch deep. Turn the timber over and do the same on the other side. Turn the timber on edge and chip away the inside material (see Fig. 3-11C).

LEGS

Cut six pieces of 2x6 P.T. lumber, 16 inches long (four for the legs, and two for the crosspieces). Cut two pieces of P.T. lumber, 10½ inches long, for the inside pieces of the legs.

To cut the leg crosspieces, make diagonal cuts on two corners of each of two 16-inch-long 2x6s (see detail, Fig. 3-12 for the exact dimensions).

To construct each leg, sandwich a 10½-inch-long 2x6 and a base crosspiece between two 16-inch-long 2x6s. Fasten the pieces together using eight 2½-inch galvanized deck screws, placed in each leg support (see side view, Fig. 3-12).

Fig. 3-11A

Fig. 3-11B

Fig. 3-11C

MOVABLE BENCH

Fig. 3-12

FRONT VIEW

SIDE VIEW
2X6 P.T.
CROSSPIECE

Fig. 3-13

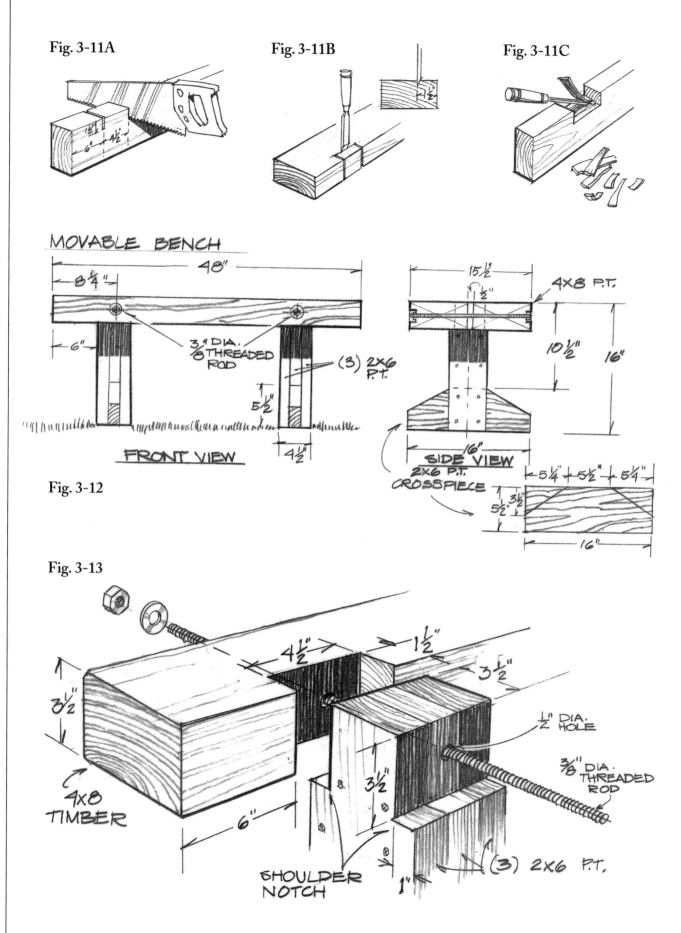

Fig. 3-14

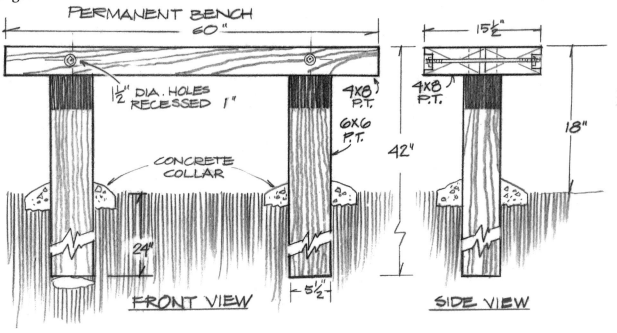

Cut out two shoulder notches in each leg support to support the bench seat. Using a carpenter's square, mark a 1-x3½-inch shoulder notch on each side of each leg. Make a 1-inch-deep crosscut 3½ inches down from the top, and chisel out the notch (see Fig. 3-13).

The leg supports are attached to the bench top by one 15-inch-long, ⅜-inch-diameter threaded rod at each end. Use a 1½-inch diameter spade bit to bore a 1½-inch-diameter by 1-inch-deep hole 8¼ inches in from each end of the bench. With the bench laid on its side, trial fit the two seat timbers to the legs and mark where the hole for the rod should go by tapping the threaded rod a few times to make a dent in the leg. Use this mark as a guide to drill a ½-inch-diameter hole through each seat timber and the top of the leg. Note that the larger (½-inch) hole is necessary to adjust for any misalignment. Assemble the pieces and slip the threaded rod through them, tightening the nuts with a socket wrench.

PERMANENT BENCH:

Follow the above directions for the movable bench, however, since the permanent legs are made from 6x6 timbers, which measure 5½x5½ inches (not 4½x5½), mark the notch on each seat timber at 6 inches plus 5½ inches. Also remember to drill the holes for the threaded rod 8¾ inches, rather than 8¼ inches, from the end. Cut the two 6x6 legs, each 42 inches long, and bury them 24 inches in the ground (see Fig. 3-14). To keep the bench from moving, dig a shallow, 3-inch-deep trench around the legs. After the legs have been buried, fill the trench with concrete, mounding it slightly. This concrete collar will help support the posts as well as shed rainwater.

If you have used pressure-treated lumber, you can either leave it to weather gray or stain it, as we did. If you use fir, we recommend allowing it to weather naturally, showing off the natural wood colors.

COVERED SEAT

This romantic-looking covered seat is called a "shadow box" because of the welcoming shade the lattice top creates, enabling you to sit outside even on the hottest of days. Constructed of clear cedar, it is both an elegant and practical design which could be the main feature of a summer garden, covered with tendrils of evening blooming vines and English ivy, or a seat for two on a porch or patio. This garden seat is a variation of a design by Abbie Zabar, an avid herb gardener and author of garden and children's books. Abbie's garden seat sits on her New York City terrace, overlooking Central Park, and commands a breathtaking view of the Manhattan skyline.

MATERIALS

Quantity	Size	Description	Location or Use
2	12 feet	4x4 clear cedar posts	corner posts
1	8 feet	4x4 clear cedar	horizontal side pieces
2	8 feet	4x4 clear cedar	crosspieces
8	12 feet	1x4 clear cedar V-groove	lower sides and back
1	5 feet	1x2 clear cedar	slats and cleats
1	4x8 panel	diagonal cedar lattice	sides, back
1	4x4 sheet	¾-inch exterior plywood	base
2	6 feet	2x4 cedar	rafters
2	8 feet	2x2 cedar	purlins, cross tie and ridge pole
3	8 feet	⁵⁄₄x4 clear cedar	seat
1	10 feet	2x6 clear cedar	cove molding
2	8 feet	1x4 clear cedar	fascia
1	36 inches	¾-inch-dia. dowel	plugs
18	⅜-x6-inch	lag screws	
2 lb.	2-inch	galvanized finish nails	

WALL FRAME

Cut the 4x4 cedar posts to 6-foot lengths. Sand them smooth, using several grades of sandpaper (60- to 120-grit: coarse to smooth). Number the top of each post and draw an arrow showing its relation to where the center of the structure will be (see Fig 3-15). **Note:** It is important to do this, since it is easy to mix the pieces up when assembling them.

Using a carpenter's square, mark the position where each lag screw will go, 1½ or 2 inches from the ends of each 6-foot-long post. Notice that the holes are staggered, so that the screws will not touch each other when they are installed (see Fig. 3-16). Drill ¾-inch-diameter holes, ¾ inch deep, followed by ⁷⁄₁₆-inch-diameter pilot holes that extend completely through the post.

Cut six horizontal side pieces out of 4x4 cedar, each 15½ inches long. Cut four crosspieces out of 4x4 cedar, each 41 inches long. Sand all the

Fig. 3-15

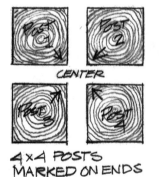

Fig. 3-16

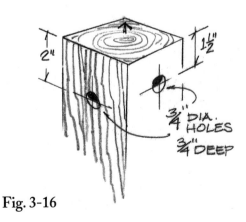

Fig. 3-17

Fig. 3-19

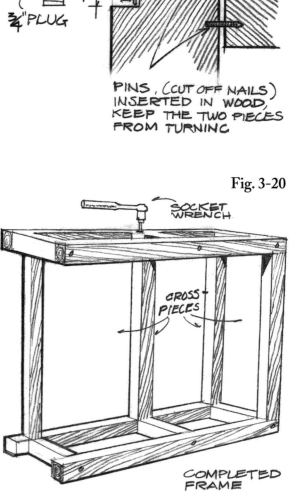

Fig. 3-20

Fig. 3-18

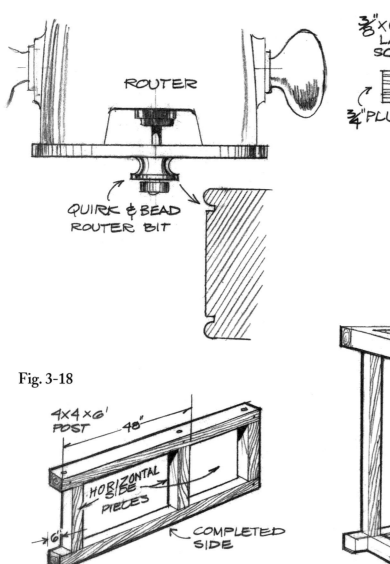

pieces, going from coarse to smooth. **Tip:** For a more classical look, route the top and bottom edges of all the horizontal members, using a quirk and bead router bit (see Fig. 3-17).

Assemble the sides as shown in Figure 3-18. To do this, stand three horizontal side pieces on end, position a 4x4 post on top of them and glue and screw one ⅜-x6-inch lag screw into each joint, using a socket wrench.

Note: To prevent the 4x4 horizontal side pieces from turning once installed, cut the heads off four 2-inch nails and hammer them halfway into the side grain of each vertical post. When you screw the post down, these points will press into the soft end grain and help lock the posts and beams together (see Fig. 3-19).

Lay one of the assembled sides flat on the ground, and stand up the three back and one front crosspieces, positioning them so that they

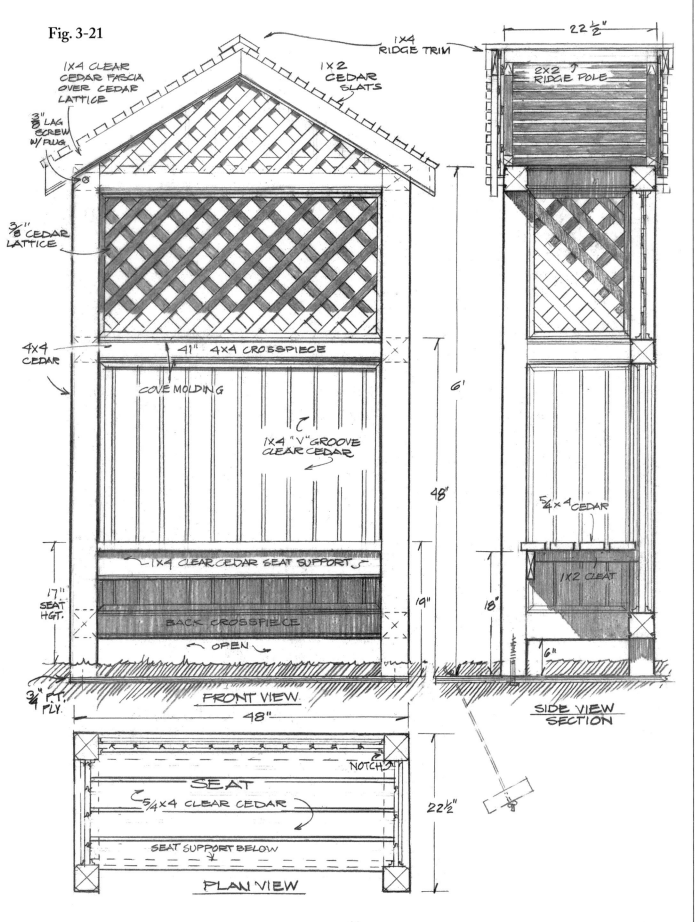

Fig. 3-21

1X4 CLEAR CEDAR FASCIA OVER CEDAR LATTICE

1X4 RIDGE TRIM

1X2 CEDAR SLATS

3/8" LAG SCREW W/ PLUG

2X2 RIDGE POLE

22½"

3/8" CEDAR LATTICE

4X4 CEDAR

41" 4X4 CROSSPIECE

COVE MOLDING

1X4 "V" GROOVE CLEAR CEDAR

6'

48"

5/4 X 4 CEDAR

1X4 CLEAR CEDAR SEAT SUPPORT

1X2 CLEAT

17" SEAT HGT.

BACK CROSSPIECE

19"

18"

OPEN

6"

3/4" FT. PLY.

FRONT VIEW

48"

SIDE VIEW SECTION

NOTCH

SEAT

5/4 X 4 CLEAR CEDAR

22½"

SEAT SUPPORT BELOW

PLAN VIEW

Fig. 3-22

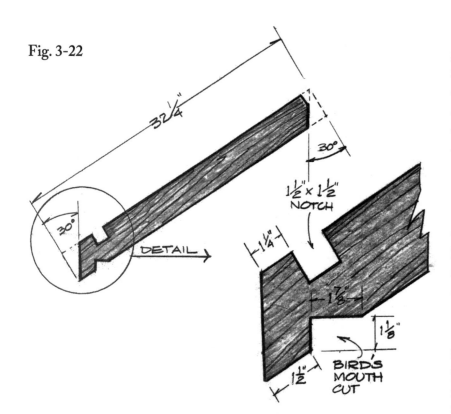

are aligned with the horizontal side pieces. Apply epoxy glue to the exposed ends. With an assistant, carefully position the second side over the ends of the crosspieces (see Fig. 3-20). Use three bar clamps to hold the assembly in place and screw ⅜-x6-inch lag screws through the side into the ends of the crosspieces. Turn over the assembly and follow the same procedure for the second side. Stand up the structure. For a finished look, plug the holes and sand them smooth.

LATTICE AND SIDING

Measure the uppermost openings in the sides and back of the covered seat. Then, using an electric jig saw, cut the lattice to fit inside the openings. Install the lattice, using ¾-inch cove molding nailed onto both sides. **Tips:** It is much easier to paint the lattice before installing it. If you own a router, it is cheaper and quite easy to make your own cove molding by routing, then ripping, a clear cedar 2x6 into ¾-x¾-inch strips (see Fig. 3-23). You will need about 120 feet of molding cut to the lengths shown in Fig. 3-23.

Install the 1x4 tongue-and-groove (T&G) vertical boards in the bottom side and back openings, using ¾-x¾-inch cove molding to secure them to the horizontal 4x4s (see plan view, Fig. 3-21).

ROOF FRAME

To make the roof rafters, cut four pieces of 2x4, 32¼ inches long. Cut both ends off each piece at a 30-degree angle (see Fig. 3-22).

Measure 1½ inches up from the bottom end of each piece and cut a right-angle notch (bird's mouth), 1⅛-x1⅞-inch (see detail, Fig. 3-22).

For the purlins, cut three pieces of 2x2 cedar, each 22½ inches long. Cut a 1½-x1½-inch notch in the rafters to accept the 2x2 purlins, 1¼ inches from the bottom ends (see Fig. 3-24). Cut a 1½-inch notch out of the peak, where the rafters

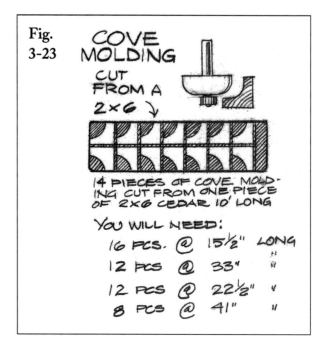

Fig. 3-23

COVE MOLDING CUT FROM A 2×6

14 PIECES OF COVE MOLDING CUT FROM ONE PIECE OF 2×6 CEDAR 10' LONG

YOU WILL NEED:

16 PCS. @ 15½" LONG
12 PCS @ 33" "
12 PCS @ 22½" "
8 PCS @ 41" "

Fig. 3-24

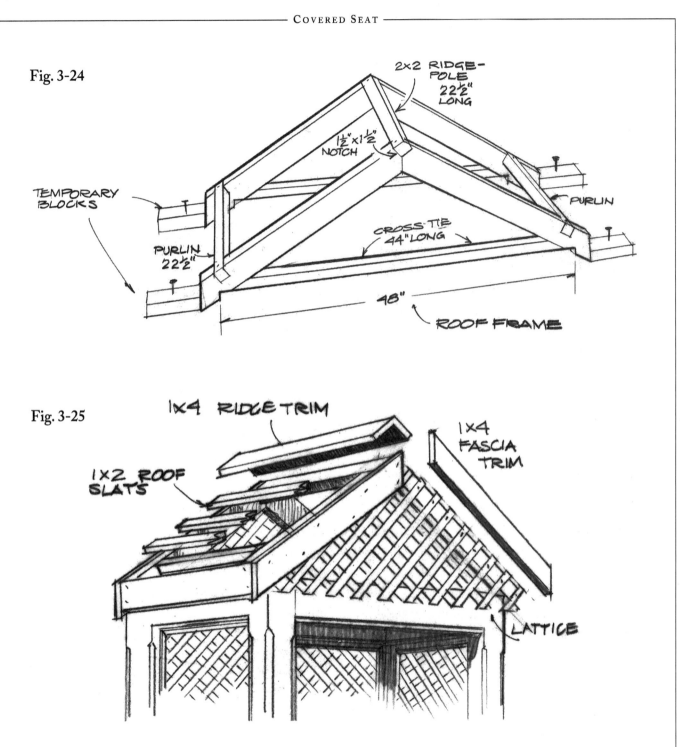

Fig. 3-25

meet, to support the 2x2 ridgepole. Glue and screw the pieces together using temporary blocks to keep the rafters from spreading. Make sure the pieces are square with one another and that the inside measurement between the bird's mouth cuts is 48 inches.

When the glue has dried, cut two 2x2 cross ties, 44 inches long, and cut the ends off at 30-degree angles. Glue and screw these two cross ties to the bottom of the rafters. Set the assembled roof frame on the main frame and secure it by screwing down through the 2x2 crosspiece into the top front and rear 4x4s of the frame.

ROOF TRIM
Referring to Fig. 3-25, cut, glue and nail diagonal cedar lattice to the front and back gables

Fig. 3-26

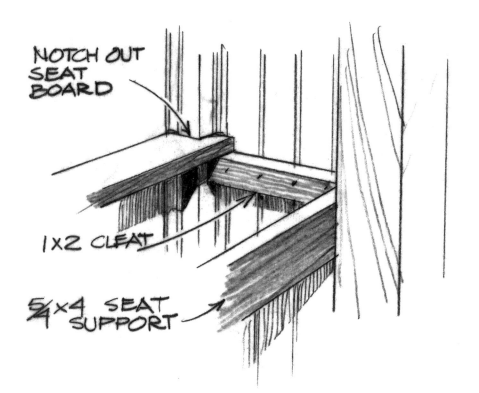

NOTCH OUT SEAT BOARD

1X2 CLEAT

5/4 X4 SEAT SUPPORT

of the roof frame, allowing each piece to overlap the top of the main 4x4 frame by 1⅛ inches. Cut the top of the lattice off flush with the tops of the rafters. Trim the front and sides of the roof with clear 1x4 cedar, using 2-inch galvanized finish nails. Begin with the side trim, nailing it to the ends of the rafters. Next, cut the front trim pieces to meet at the peak, each at a 30 degree angle, and trial fit them together. Hold the front trim pieces in place and mark on the back where the side pieces meet. Cut where marked, and nail in place, using 2-inch galvanized finish nails, spaced 8 inches apart.

Cover the roof with 1x2 cedar slats, 27½ inches long, spaced 1 inch apart and overlapping the front and back trim boards by 1 inch (see front and section views, Fig. 3-21).

SEAT

Measure the inside width from side panel to side panel (about 43 inches), and cut six pieces of 5/4x4 clear cedar for the seat. Screw one piece to the inside backs of the two front posts, 18 inches up from the bottom of the posts, so that it provides a lateral support for the seat (see plan view, Fig. 3-21). Nail one 1x2 cleat across each side, 18 inches up from the bottom to support the seat on the sides. Install the remaining 5/4x4 cedar boards for the seat, using 2-inch finish nails, nailed to the cleats and the supporting board (see Fig. 3-26). The front and back seat boards will have to be notched around the vertical corner posts.

For a final elegant touch, chamfer the outside edges of the corner posts with a 45 degree bevel router bit.

GARDEN ORNAMENTS, ACCESSORIES AND NECESSITIES

PINECONE BIRDHOUSE

T his project is, literally, for the birds! It requires only a few hours to make and will attract songbirds to your garden, blending in effortlessly with the surroundings, especially when hung in a pine tree or other evergreen.

If you find that the decorative roof is too time-consuming, a simple shingle roof is just as appealing to most birds. The house can be made out of scrap lumber and leftover or discarded cedar shingles or shakes. If you don't have any lying around your property, check with the lumberyard. They may give you a few loose shingles for free — the older and grayer the better.

MATERIALS

Quantity	Size	Description	Location or Use
6	18 inches	cedar shingles	sides and roof
1 dozen		pinecones	roof
1	3½-x3½-inch	1x4 scrap lumber	floor
1 qt.		epoxy glue	
1 lb.	1-inch	thin galvanized brads	
2	½-inch	eye screws	
1	36 inches	nylon string	
OR			
2	2-inch	galvanized deck screws	

Fig. 4-1

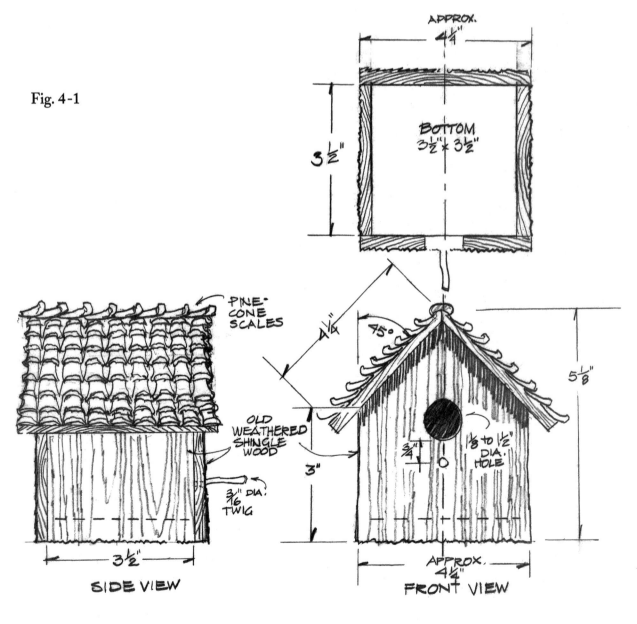

SIDE VIEW

FRONT VIEW

WALLS AND FLOOR

Using a handsaw or electric jig saw, cut the front and back walls of the birdhouse out of shingles, each 4¼ inches wide by 5⅛ inches high. Find the center and mark a vertical line on the front and back walls. Measure 3 inches up from the bottom of each side and make a mark. This is the bottom of the roofline (see front view, Fig. 4-1). Draw a diagonal line from this mark to the centerline at the top of the shingle, and cut the gables on each side of the front and back walls.

Measuring up 3 inches from the bottom, use a spade drill to bore a 1⅛-inch- to 1½-inch-diameter hole in the center of the front wall. Drill another hole ³⁄₁₆ inch in diameter, ¾ inch below the first hole. This lower hole is for the perch.

Cut two pieces of shingle for the sides of the birdhouse, each 3½ inches wide by 3 inches high. Angle each top cut 45 degrees where it will meet the roof.

From a piece of scrap lumber, cut a square 3 ½-x3½-inches for the floor. Place the floor piece on edge and glue and nail the front piece to the floor, using 1-inch, thin galvanized brads. **Tip:** Use one of the side pieces as a prop while you are nailing (see Fig. 4-2). After attaching the front to the floor piece, nail the front to the sides. Turn the structure over, and repeat the same steps for the back.

ROOF

Cut two roof pieces out of cedar shingles, each 4¾ inches wide by 4¼ inches long. Bevel the roof tops with a file or rasp, so that the pieces meet at the peak. Glue and nail the roof to the sides, front and back.

To "spruce up" the roof, find a dozen or so pinecones lying under a white-pine tree. (Don't worry about the sticky pitch that gets on your hands, as this can be easily removed with paint thinner.)

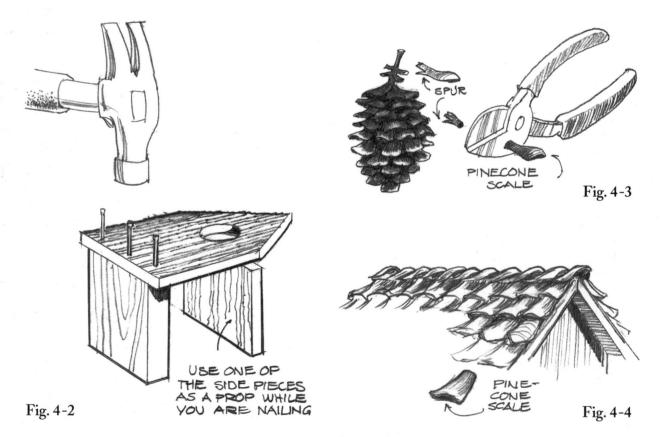

Fig. 4-2

USE ONE OF THE SIDE PIECES AS A PROP WHILE YOU ARE NAILING

SPUR

PINECONE SCALE

Fig. 4-3

PINE-CONE SCALE

Fig. 4-4

Potting Shed (page 132)

GARDEN HOUSE (PAGE 116)

GARDEN CART (PAGE 105)

GARDEN BENCH, BENTWOOD TRELLIS, OBELISK, PICNIC TABLE (PAGES 54, 19, 23, AND 50)

Starting from the stem end of each pinecone, remove the scales, discarding the smaller, odd-shaped ones and reserving the larger ones. You will notice that on the back side of each scale, there is a small spur where it was joined to the main part of the pinecone. Clip this off, using a pair of clippers (see Fig. 4-3). Starting with the bottom row, glue the scales to the roof, using epoxy glue, and overlapping the rows as you work toward the peak. Finish off the top ridge by adding a row of scales across the top (see Fig. 4-4).

You may be tempted (as we were) to add a perch for the birds to stand on, even though experts say this is not necessary. If you do have a perch, make sure it is small in diameter to discourage acrobatic squirrels from using it to gain access to the house. We found a weathered, crooked stick on the beach, which fit perfectly with the architecture of our birdhouse.

To hang the birdhouse, drill two small holes in the roof and screw two ½-inch-long eye screws into the roof ridge and into the front and back walls. Tie a nylon string to one eye screw, loop the loose end over a tree branch, under and over again, then back to the second eye screw.

Fig. 4-5

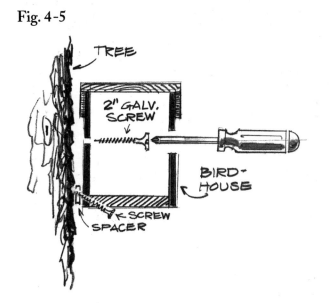

You can also screw the house to a tree by drilling a small pilot hole in the back, centered with the larger hole in the front of the house. Using a Phillips screwdriver, carefully insert a 2-inch galvanized deck screw through the larger hole, into the pilot hole in the back, and screw it into the tree branch (see Fig. 4-5). Add another screw, diagonally through the bottom, to prevent the birdhouse from turning.

WIND CHIMES

The subtle background tinkling of a wind chimes can be very inspiring while meditating on next year's plantings. To insure that the chimes move easily with a breeze, buy lightweight aluminum tubing. Bamboo also can be used to make wind chimes, but it will make a much different sound.

The following instructions are for a basic, simple wind chimes, but you should feel free to expand on the design, if you desire. Any type of wood can be used to make the spreader. We chose pine for both the spreader and clapper, but if you have a scrap of redwood or teak, either of these woods will look beautiful, sanded smooth and oiled. Experiment with different lengths of tubing to create different harmonies. Hang the wind chimes in a spot where the wind moves the paddle easily and enjoy nature's melodies.

MATERIALS

Quantity	Size	Description	Location or Use
1	7 inches	1x8 pine scrap	spreader
1	3 ½ inches	1x4 pine scrap	clapper
1	3x6 inches	¼-inch-thick cedar	paddle
1	9 feet	⅝-inch-dia. aluminum tubing	chimes
1 roll		braided nylon or Dacron string	
1	1-inch-dia.	metal ring	hanger

	Distance from top of aluminum tube to ⅛-inch hole:	Length of tubes:
#1	3¼ inches	14 inches
#2	3⅜ inches	15 inches
#3	3¾ inches	16¼ inches
#4	4 inches	17¼ inches
#5	4¼ inches	18¼ inches
#6	4½ inches	20 inches

SPREADER

To make the spreader, use a compass to inscribe a 7-inch-diameter circle on a scrap piece of 1x8 pine. With an electric jig saw, cut out the wooden circle. Round off the edges using 60- and 120-grit sandpaper.

To establish where the six sets of holes will be placed in the wooden spreader, draw a 3-inch-radius circle from the center. Starting at any point on the circle, walk the compass around the circumference, making six equidistant marks, each 3 inches apart (see Fig 4-6).

Drill two ¹⁄₁₆-inch holes, ¼ inch away from either side of each mark. These holes are for the string from which the aluminum tubes hang.

Drill six additional ¹⁄₁₆-inch-diameter holes in the spreader (three sets of holes) for the string that attaches the wind chime to the top ring. To locate these holes, draw an equilateral triangle

halfway between any two sets of the "chime" holes (see Fig. 4-7).

CHIMES

Using a hack saw, cut the aluminum tubing to the dimensions listed in the materials list. Smooth off the edges with sandpaper.

Drill ⅛-inch-diameter holes through each tube, according to the dimensions given in the table following the materials list above.

To assemble the tubes, tie a stop-knot at the end of a 7-foot-long piece of string. Thread the other end of the string down through one of the holes of the spreader and through the two holes at the end of the longest tube, then back up and down through the two adjacent holes in the spreader and through the next longest tube (see Fig. 4-8). Continue until you have strung the last tube. Thread the string up through the last hole of the spreader and tie a stop knot to pre-

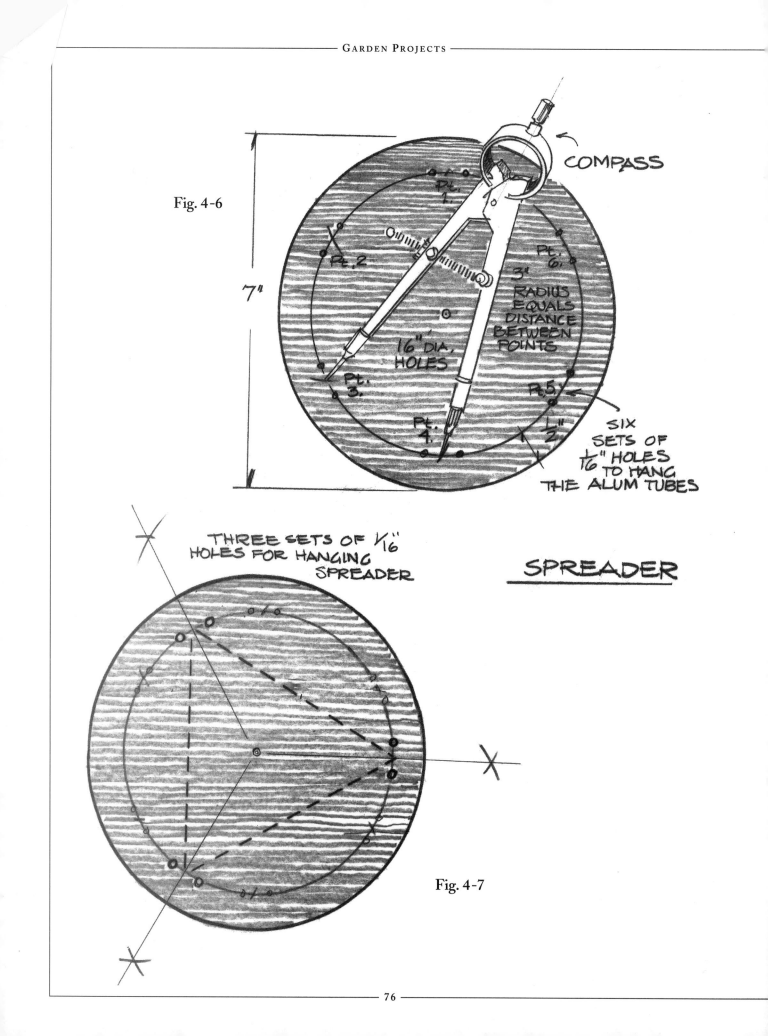

Fig. 4-6

7"

COMPASS

Pt. 1.

Pt. 2.

Pt. 6.

3" RADIUS EQUALS DISTANCE BETWEEN POINTS

$\frac{1}{16}$" DIA. HOLES

Pt. 3.

Pt. 4.

Pt. 5.

$\frac{1}{2}$"

SIX SETS OF $\frac{1}{16}$" HOLES TO HANG THE ALUM TUBES

THREE SETS OF $\frac{1}{16}$" HOLES FOR HANGING SPREADER

SPREADER

Fig. 4-7

Fig. 4-8

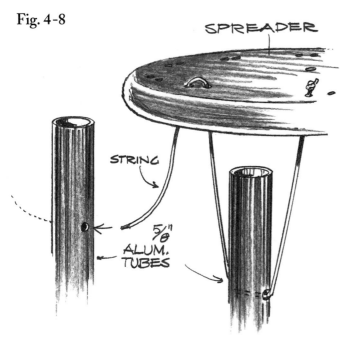

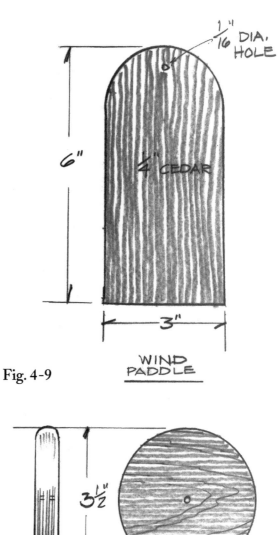

Fig. 4-9

WIND
PADDLE

CLAPPER

vent the string from slipping back down through the hole.

CLAPPER AND PADDLE

Cut out a paddle from a piece of ¼-inch-thick cedar (a shingle will work) and drill a tiny hole in the top (see Fig. 4-9). Thread a piece of string through the hole and tie a stop knot in one end. Allow enough string so that the top of the paddle will be 1½ inches below the end of the longest tube. Tie another stop knot and thread the string through the clapper, allowing 9 inches of string between the clapper and the spreader. Thread the string through the spreader, tying a third stop knot to keep the thread from slipping through the hole. Hang the wind chimes in a breezeway or from a tree limb where it will catch the maximum amount of wind.

HANGING THE CHIMES

To hang the wind chimes, make a stop knot in the end of a 40-inch-long piece of string and thread it up through the bottom of one of the six remaining holes in the spreader, through a 1-inch metal ring (placed about 6 inches above the spreader) and back down through the companion hole. Continue the string over to the next two holes, repeating the process two more times and tying the end of the string with a stop knot.

Kneeling Stool

As a boy, David used to watch his mother, an avid gardener, place a green mat down in front of her flowers, and carefully kneel down and begin weeding. When she was finished she would slowly get up — somewhat dizzy — and move the mat to another spot. If only she had had this kneeling stool back then!

Gardening, especially weeding, requires a lot of bending, stooping and kneeling; consequently, anything that makes this task easier will make working in the garden more pleasurable. This is an excellent garden accessory for anyone who has a bad back, since it takes the strain out of kneeling down and standing back up. It is so lightweight that it can easily be carried in one hand. It can also be turned upside down and used as a temporary seat.

MATERIALS

Quantity	Size	Description	Location or Use
1	6 feet	1x10 #2 clear cedar	sides and bottom
1	24 inches	2x2 clear cedar	corner cleats
6	2½-inch	galvanized deck screws	
1	8½x15 inch	½-inch closed-cell sponge-rubber pad	bottom
1 bottle	8 oz.	waterproof yellow glue	
1 box	¾-inch	brass brads	
1 pt.		water sealer	

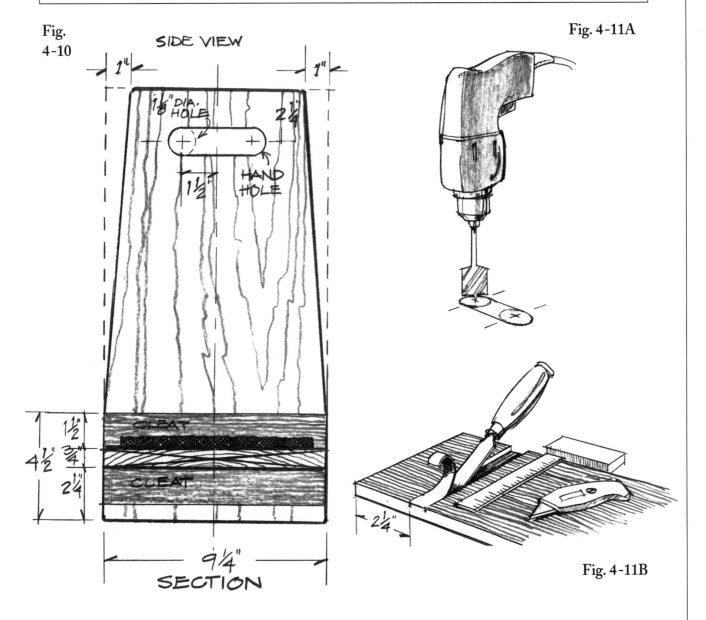

Fig. 4-10

SIDE VIEW

1"   1"

1⅛" DIA. HOLE   2¼"

1½"

HAND HOLE

1½"
¾"
2¼"
4½"

CLEAT

CLEAT

9¼"

SECTION

Fig. 4-11A

2¼"

Fig. 4-11B

Fig. 4-12

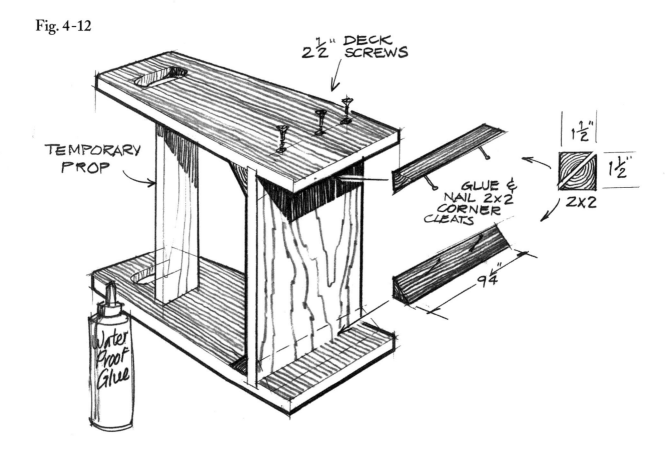

SIDES AND BOTTOM

Cut two pieces of 1x10 clear cedar 18 inches long for the sides, and one piece 20 inches long for the bottom. Sand all three pieces. Taper the sides, by starting 4½ inches up from the bottom edges and gradually slanting them 1 inch inward, at each top (see Fig. 4-10).

Each side of the kneeling stool has a hand hole for easy carrying. To mark the placement of the hand holes, find the center of each side and make a mark 1½ inches on either side of this point, 2¼ inches down from the top of the side. Draw an X at each of these points and drill 1⅛-inch-diameter holes at the marks (see Fig. 4-10). **Note:** When drilling the holes, use a 1⅛-inch-diameter spade drill bit (see Fig. 4-11A) and drill only halfway through the wood. Remove the drill and turn the board over, drilling through the wood the rest of the way. This helps prevent the

wood from "tearing out" when the drill emerges from the wood.

Cut out the material between the holes, using an electric jig saw. Roll up a piece of 60-grit sandpaper and sand the edges of the hand holes until they are smooth and rounded.

DADOES

To make a strong joint where the pieces meet at the bottom of the kneeling stool, it is necessary to cut one ⅛-inch-deep dado across the bottom of each side. Using a metal straight-edge and a utility knife, score a cut 2¼ inches above, and parallel with, the inside bottom of the side. Hold the end of the bottom piece against this line, and score another line parallel to and above the first line. Make several more passes with the utility knife until both lines are ⅛ inch deep. Use a sharp ¾-inch chisel to remove the wood between

Fig. 4-13

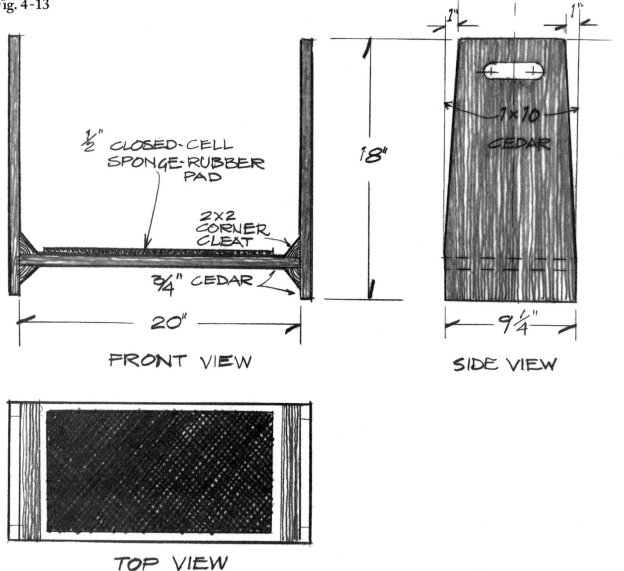

FRONT VIEW

½" CLOSED-CELL SPONGE-RUBBER PAD

2X2 CORNER CLEAT

¾" CEDAR

20"

18"

1" 1"

1×10 CEDAR

9¼"

SIDE VIEW

TOP VIEW

the lines (see Fig. 4-11B). Smooth out the dado with a rasp or file. Coat the dadoes with water-proof glue and place the bottom piece into the grooves. **Note:** Cut a piece of scrap wood, 19¾ inches long, and use it to hold the unsupported end while the glue is drying. Use bar clamps to hold the pieces together. Drill three ⅛-inch diameter pilot holes through the sides where they meet the bottom, and screw three 2½-inch galvanized deck screws through the sides and into the ends of the bottom piece (see Fig. 4-12).

To add extra strength to the two bottom joints, rip cut diagonally across the middle two 9¼-inch-long pieces of 2x2 cedar, creating four support cleats (see detail, Fig. 4-12). Glue and nail these four strips to the inside corners where the bottom piece meets the sides.

Finish the kneeling stool by gluing and nailing the closed-cell, sponge-rubber pad to the bottom piece, using waterproof yellow glue and ¾-inch brass brads (see Fig. 4-13).

POTTING BENCH

A lthough a potting bench may at first glance seem like a luxury, once you have built one, you will consider it a necessity. This design gives you a convenient place to pot plants without bending over, hooks to hang the essential potting tools on, and a storage shelf below for heavy bags of potting soil and fertilizer. The removable bin for soil frees up the rest of the bench top for plants and pots while you are working. This design is so attractive that our friend Virginia uses her redwood potting bench as a hutch in her pantry, lining the shelves with wicker baskets filled with pasta and canned goods and lining the backsplash with ornamental plates!

MATERIALS

Quantity	Size	Description	Location or Use
2	8 feet	2x4 redwood or P.T. lumber	legs and crosspieces
1	12 feet	2x4 redwood or P.T. lumber	crosspieces
8	8 feet	⁵⁄₄x4 redwood or P.T. lumber	top and bottom decking and trim
2	8 feet	⁵⁄₄x8 redwood or P.T. lumber	backsplash, top shelf and shelf backboard
1	6 feet	1x4 redwood or P.T. lumber	back braces
1 lb.	1½-inch	galvanized deck screws	
1 lb.	2½-inch	galvanized deck screws	
1	16-qt.	12¾-x15½-inch plastic dishpan (optional)	
1 bottle	8 oz.	waterproof yellow glue	

LEGS AND CROSSPIECES

Begin by cutting the 2x4 front and rear legs, 35 inches and 54 inches long, respectively. Cut four 2x4 crosspieces, each 22 inches long, to hold the legs together. Glue and screw the top crosspieces to the insides of the legs, 35 inches up from the bottom of each rear leg, and flush with the top of the front leg, using 2½-inch galvanized deck screws (see Fig. 4-14). Glue and screw the bottom crosspieces to the front and rear legs, so that their tops are 15 inches from the bottom of the legs. **Note:** Before attaching the crosspieces, use a carpenter's square to check that all the pieces are at right angles to each other.

DECKING, BACKSPLASH AND BACK BRACES

In preparation for building the top and bottom decking, cut fourteen pieces of ⁵⁄₄x4, each exactly 48 inches long. Stand up the assembled legs and attach the front and back ⁵⁄₄x4 decking boards to the crosspieces, using 2½-inch countersunk deck screws. The back decking board will have to be cut 3 inches shorter to fit between the two rear legs (see Fig 4-15).

To build the backsplash, cut a ⁵⁄₄x8, 48 inches long. Tip the structure over (see Fig. 4-16), and screw the backsplash to the rear leg posts, so that the bottom edge of the backsplash is 1 inch above the bottom edge of the crosspieces.

To build the diagonal back braces, cut two 1x4s, each 32 inches long. Find and mark the center of the bottom edge of the backsplash (see detail, Fig. 4-17). Hold each piece of 1x4 (one at a time) diagonally, one end touching the center of the backsplash, the other end touching the leg (see Fig. 4-17), and trace the angle where the pieces meet at the center. Also trace the angle where the bottom edge of each brace will overlap the rear leg, and cut the braces at these angles.

Using 1½-inch galvanized deck screws, screw the 48-inch-long ⁵⁄₄x4 decking to the bottom crosspieces, leaving approximately a ¼-inch gap between each board. Install the top decking in the same way. **Note:** If you are installing the dish pan, do not screw the top decking at this time.

Select the ⁵⁄₄x4 with the nicest grain for the front edge trim, and screw it every 10 inches to

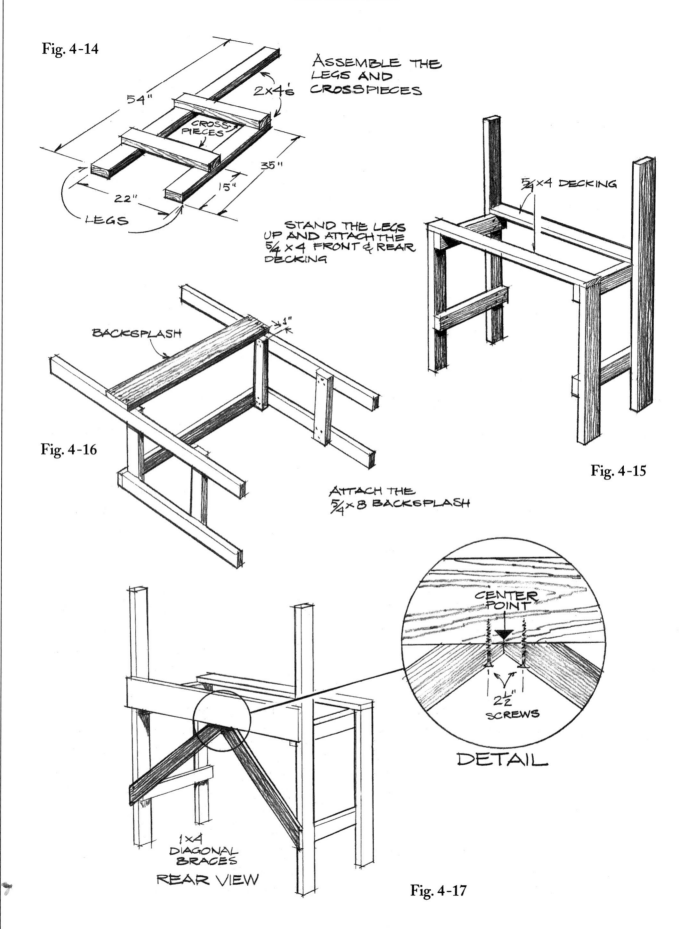

Fig. 4-14

ASSEMBLE THE
LEGS AND
CROSSPIECES

54"

2×4's

CROSS
PIECES

35"

15"

22"

LEGS

STAND THE LEGS
UP AND ATTACH THE
5/4 × 4 FRONT & REAR
DECKING

5/4 × 4 DECKING

Fig. 4-15

BACKSPLASH

1"

Fig. 4-16

ATTACH THE
5/4 × 8 BACKSPLASH

CENTER
POINT

2 1/2"
SCREWS

DETAIL

1×4
DIAGONAL
BRACES

REAR VIEW

Fig. 4-17

Fig. 4-18

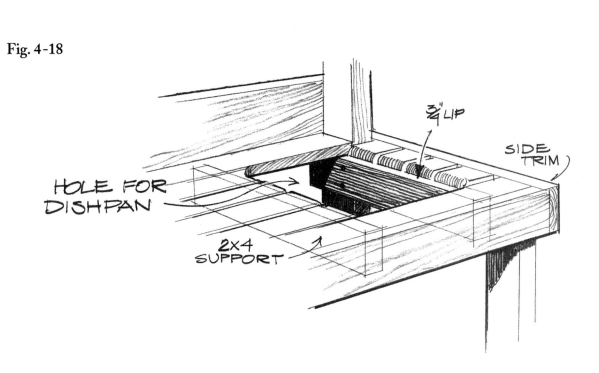

HOLE FOR DISHPAN

2x4 SUPPORT

¾" LIP

SIDE TRIM

the top front of the legs and the front edge of the deck board. Cut two pieces of ⁵⁄₄x4, approximately 24 inches long, to trim off the two sides of the top decking, and screw them to the 2x4 legs (see Fig. 4-18).

SHELVES

To build the top shelf, cut a piece of ⁵⁄₄x8, 48 inches long, and screw it to the tops of the two rear legs. To make the backboard for the top shelf, cut another piece, 48 inches long, from the same board, and screw it to the back of the shelf and to the backs of the two rear legs. Allow the backboard to extend 2½ inches above the top of the shelf (see Fig. 4-19).

To prevent pots from falling off the ends of the top shelf, cut two pieces of ⁵⁄₄x8, 8½ inches long, and make a diagonal cut, 4½ inches from the bottom corner and 3½ inches from the top front corner (see detail, Fig. 4-19). Screw these side pieces to each end of the shelf.

Gardening tools and implements can be hung on the backboard under the shelf by attaching wooden pegs, hooks and nails to the wood,

depending upon your gardening needs.

POTTING SOIL STORAGE
(OPTIONAL)

To provide a convenient container for soil while you are potting, buy a 16-quart plastic dishpan, 12¾x15½ inches (Rubbermaid makes these in an almond color). Cut off the small plastic tabs that are under the lip.

Turn the dishpan upside down on the top (loose) decking and line up the walls of the dishpan with the right inside edge of the crosspiece that can be seen through the ¼-inch gaps in the decking. Using a pencil, trace the dishpan edge.

Cut out the hole for the dishpan using an electric jig saw, and round off the edges. Then, cut a 2x4 support piece, 22 inches long, to fit from front to back and to act as a support for the top decking pieces after they are installed. Using 1½-inch galvanized deck screws, screw the support in place. Position it so that the centerline of the support lines up with the left-hand edge of the dishpan hole. This will leave a ¾-inch lip to support the dishpan.

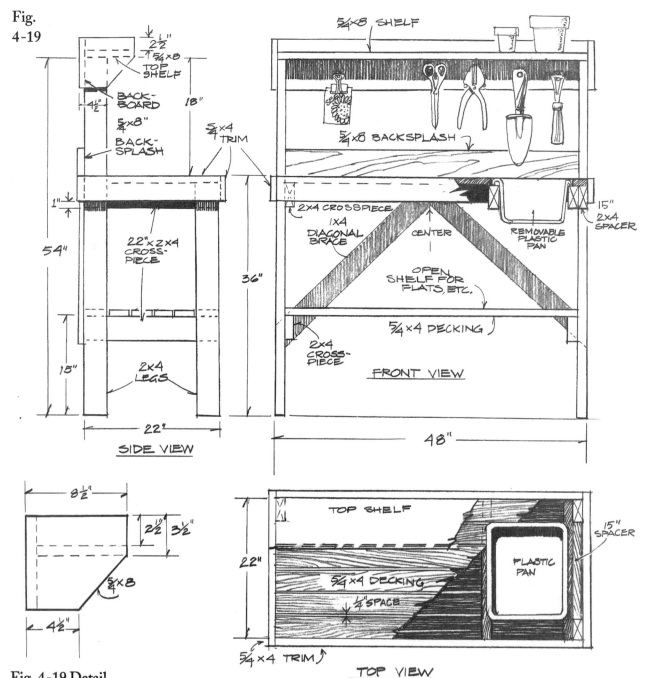

Fig.
4-19

SIDE VIEW

FRONT VIEW

TOP VIEW

Fig. 4-19 Detail

Also cut a 2x4 spacer, approximately 15 inches long, to fit between the front and rear legs. Screw it to the outside of the crosspiece (see Fig. 4-20), then screw down the deck boards. The spacer will help support the small pieces of deck boards on the right-hand side of the dishpan. Place the dishpan in the opening and your potting bench is ready for plants or pantry.

Fig. 4-20

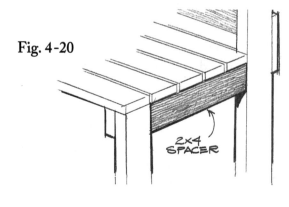

GARDEN SHOWER

There's nothing like showering outside for cleaning up and cloud watching. Open-air showering provides a wonderful way to relax after working in the garden or at the potting shed, and enables you to wash off thoroughly and enter the house feeling refreshed. The side of the garden shower can serve as a backdrop for flowers or greenery, such as brightly colored annuals or a fragrant rosebush surrounded by ivy. The plants will thrive on being watered regularly!

MATERIALS

Quantity	Size	Description	Location or Use
5	8 feet	4x4 cedar posts	frame posts
1	6 feet	2x4 cedar	side frame
1	10 feet	2x4 cedar	front frame
15	8 feet	1x6 clear cedar T&G (V-groove)	door, front panel and side panel
1	12 feet	1x4 #2 cedar	top trim
2	8 feet	1x6 #2 cedar	cap trim
1	14 feet	1x6 #2 cedar	front panel trim
2	10 feet	1x6 #2 cedar	door battens, braces and trim
1	12 feet	1x4 cedar	seat
5	10 feet	$\frac{5}{4}$ x4 redwood or P.T. decking	interior floor decking and seat cleats
1	12 feet	2x4 P.T. lumber	floor joists
2	3½-inch	galvanized self-closing hinges	door
1	6-inch	thumb latch	door
1	3-inch	hook-and-eye	door
1 lb.	2-inch	galvanized finish nails	
1 lb.	1¼-inch	galvanized deck screws	
6	⅜-x6-inch	lag screws with washers	
1	36 inches	1-inch wooden dowel	pegboard

This garden shower was originally designed and built by our good friend Bill Biery, a television newscaster by profession and an occasional weekend carpenter. We altered the design slightly by installing tongue-and-groove (T&G) boards diagonally, creating a herringbone effect, and adding an optional indoor shower bench. A brick walkway leads from the shower door to our deck.

In order to hold the cost of plumbing down, we attached the shower to the side of our house. If you do the same, try to match or complement the architecture of your house.

FRAME

This garden shower is built on five sturdy 4x4 cedar posts. To protect the bottoms from dry rot and insect infestations, soak them in wood preservative and coat them with wax or roofing tar (see Posts and Gates, pages 15-16).

Once you have decided where you want to build the shower enclosure, measure and mark where the first two postholes will be dug against the side of the house. They should be 5 feet apart and 18 inches deep. Measure out 3 feet from the first two postholes, and set two stakes 5 feet apart. Check to see if the stakes are square with the house by measuring the distance diagonally from corner to corner (see Fig. 4-21). Both mea-

Fig. 4-21

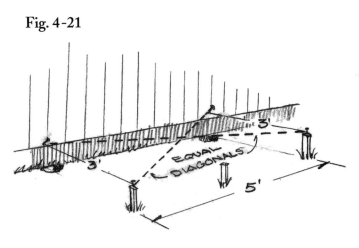

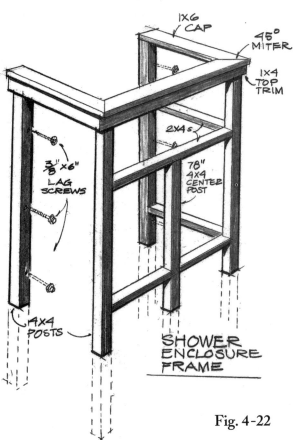

Fig. 4-22

surements should be the same (approximately 70 inches). Cut a third stake and place it equidistant between the two front stakes. Remove all three stakes and in their place, dig three 6-inch-diameter, 18-inch deep holes. Cut one 4x4 78 inches long for the front center post and place this in its hole. Place an 8-foot-long 4x4 in each of the other holes. Do not backfill until later.

To attach the first two posts to the house, drill three holes, each ½ inch in diameter, in both posts and screw ⅜-x-6-inch lag screws through the holes and into the house. **Note:** Always turn off the electricity when drilling into the wall of a house, and for convenience, use a battery-operated drill if you have one.

To connect and trim out the tops of the posts, cut a 61½-inch-long piece of 1x4, and nail it to the top front of the front two corner posts. Leave a ¾-inch overhang at each end. Cut two more 1x4 boards, each 36 inches long, and nail them to the top sides, spanning the distance between the posts attached to the house and the front two corner posts (see Fig. 4-22).

Cap the tops of the corner posts and trim pieces with 1x6 boards laid flat and mitered 45 degrees at the two outside corners of the shower enclosure (see Fig. 4-22).

To frame the top of the front panel, cut a 53-inch-long piece of 2x4, and toenail it between the two front corner posts, 5 feet up from the ground, and nail it into the top of the center post.

To frame the bottom of the front panel, cut two pieces of 2x4, each 24¾ inches long, and toenail them between the front corner posts and the center post, 12 inches up from the ground. Toenail two more 2x4s, each 29 inches long, between the two side posts opposite where the door will be (see Fig. 4-22). Check that the structure is square and plumb, then backfill the holes.

PANELS AND TRIM
Cover the front of the shower enclosure with 1x6 T&G cedar. Cut the ends off at 45 degree angles and nail them diagonally to the 4x4 posts and to the 2x4 horizontal frame (see front view, Fig. 4-23).

Fig. 4-23

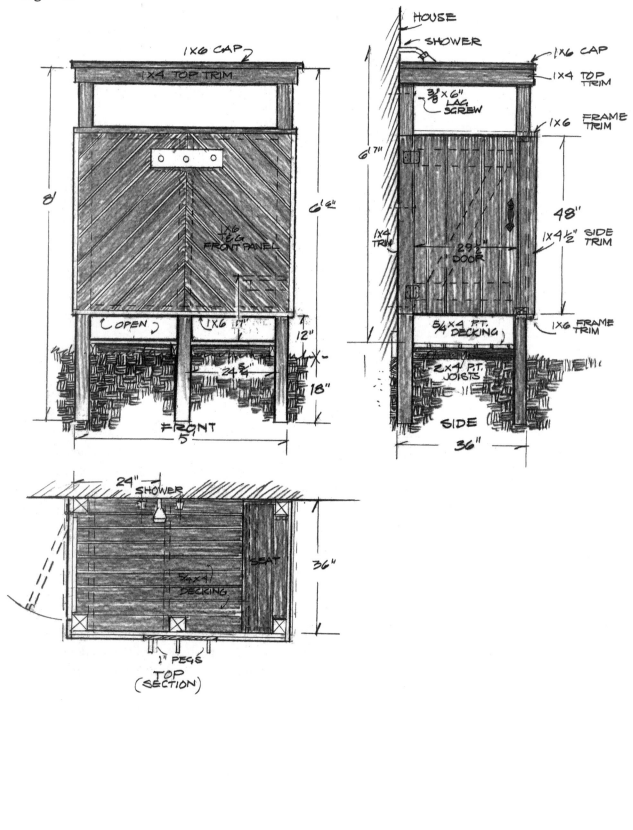

Fig. 4-24A

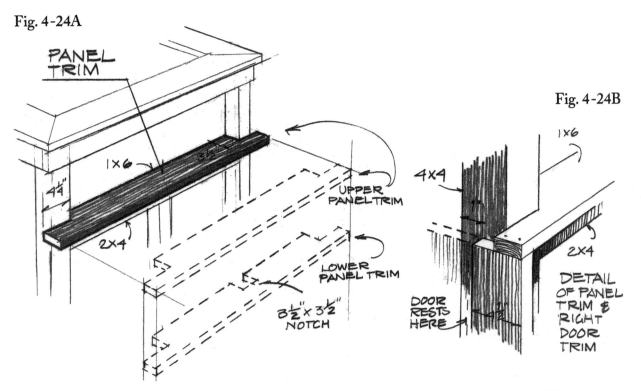

PANEL TRIM

1x6

4¼"

2x4

UPPER PANEL TRIM

LOWER PANEL TRIM

3½" x 3½" NOTCH

Fig. 4-24B

1x6

4x4

1"

2x4

DOOR RESTS HERE

2½"

DETAIL OF PANEL TRIM & RIGHT DOOR TRIM

Cover the right side of the shower enclosure with vertical 1x6 T&G boards, overlapping the front diagonal T&G boards by 1 inch.

To trim the frame of the front panel, install a 1x6, 61½ inches long, to the top and bottom of the panel. Cut a 3½-x4¼-inch notch out of the two back corners of the trim so that it can fit around the two corner posts (see Fig. 4-24A). Also cut a notch out of the middle of the bottom piece of 1x6 to accept the center 4x4 post.

In preparation for hanging the door, rip cut two 4-foot-long pieces of 1x6 T&G, one 3½ inches wide and another 4½ inches wide. These will be the left and right trim pieces. Nail the right trim piece in place, overlapping the front panel by 1 inch and making it flush with the front panel trim (see Fig. 4-24B).

Temporarily nail the left trim piece of the door enclosure to the post that is attached to the house. The distance between the two pieces of trim should be approximately 30 inches.

DOOR AND SEAT

Join together six pieces of 1x6 T&G, each 4 feet long. Rip cut the left and right boards square so that the total width of the six pieces measures about 29½ inches. Cut two battens from 1x6s, each 28¼ inches long, and screw them to the backs of the six 1x6 T&G, 4 inches from the top and bottom, using 1¼-inch galvanized deck screws. Place another piece of 1x6 diagonally across the door, with the ends overlapping the two battens. Mark where the diagonal brace meets the two 1x6 battens and cut the overlapping board off at these marks (see Fig. 4-25). Fit the diagonal brace between the two battens and screw it to the back of the door, using 1¼-inch galvanized deck screws.

Screw two 3½-inch galvanized self-closing hinges, 5 inches from the top and bottom of the door, and screw the door to the left trim piece and post. **Note:** The door will rest and close on the 1-inch-wide exposed lip of the 4x4 corner post.

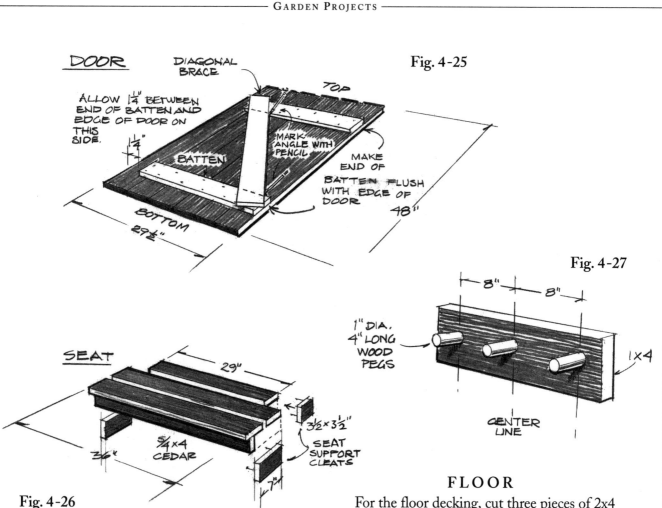

DOOR Fig. 4-25

ALLOW 1¼" BETWEEN END OF BATTEN AND EDGE OF DOOR ON THIS SIDE.

DIAGONAL BRACE

TOP

MARK ANGLE WITH PENCIL

MAKE END OF BATTEN FLUSH WITH EDGE OF DOOR

1¼"

BATTEN

BOTTOM 29½"

48"

Fig. 4-27

1" DIA. 4" LONG WOOD PEGS

8"   8"

1x4

CENTER LINE

SEAT

29"

3½ x 3½"

SEAT SUPPORT CLEATS

⁵⁄₄ x 4 CEDAR

36"

7"

Fig. 4-26

Install a thumb latch (operable from two sides) and a hook-and-eye for added security on the inside of the door.

Build a 36-inch-wide seat from ⁵⁄₄x4 cedar. For the seat top, cut three pieces, 36 inches long, and one piece, 29 inches long (see Fig. 4-26). Cut two cleats, 7 inches long and two cleats, 3½ inches long. Nail them to the house, front panel and 4x4 side posts (refer back to front view, Fig. 4-23). Nail the front of the seat to the front edge of the 7-inch-long cleats and nail the top pieces to the side cleats, using 2-inch galvanized finish nails.

Build an optional ledge for soap and shampoo out of a piece of scrap 1x4, toenailed between two of the front posts.

FLOOR

For the floor decking, cut three pieces of 2x4 P.T. lumber, 36 inches long, and nail them to the bottom of the 4x4 posts inside the shower stall (refer back to the section view, Fig. 4-23). Check to make sure they are level in all directions. Cut seven pieces of ⁵⁄₄x4 redwood or P.T. lumber, and screw them to the 2x4 joists, using 1½-inch galvanized deck screws. Cut one more piece of ⁵⁄₄x4 P.T. lumber 53 inches long to fit between the back posts, and two 24¾-inch-long pieces to fit between the front and center posts. Screw them in place.

As a final touch, build a pegboard from a left-over scrap of 2x4, measuring about 21 inches long. Drill a 1-inch-diameter hole in the center and 2 additional holes, 8 inches from the center peg. Cut three pieces of 1-inch-diameter dowel, 6 inches long, and glue them into the holes (see Fig. 4-27). Screw the pegboard to the center of the front panel, 6 inches down from the top.

CONTAINERS AND ENCLOSURES

GARDEN TOOLBOX

The garden toolbox is a simple project that requires only basic tools and a few hours to build, yet will last a lifetime and save you many steps back and forth from your garden shed to your garden. Take a look at the garden tools that you use most often and design your own compartments, so that your toolbox functions best for you.

One tool that we find particularly useful in gardening is a small 18-inch saw, which we use to cut branches and limbs when pruning trees and shrubs. We designed a special compartment along the inside of the box where the saw can be neatly stored and the saw teeth won't get dulled. Another small compartment at one end of the box holds seed packets and plant markers, leaving the remaining area open for trowels, clippers, pruning shears and other basic garden implements. The handle on top of the toolbox is flat, making it a useful support when cutting a piece of lumber, or a convenient place for a weary gardener to sit and catch his or her breath.

MATERIALS

Quantity	Size	Description	Location or Use
1	43 inches	1x10 clear pine	ends and bottom
1	60 inches	1x4 clear pine	sides and compartment dividers
1	20 inches	1x2 clear pine	top handle
1 lb.	2½-inch	galvanized finish nails	

Fig. 5-1

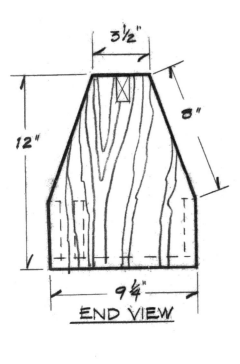

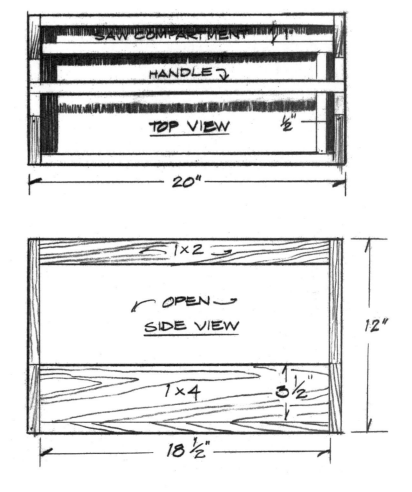

To make the box ends, cut two 12-inch-long pieces from the 43-inch-long 1x10 pine board. Cut the remaining piece 18½ inches long. This will be used for the bottom.

For the sides, cut the 1x4 pine board into three pieces the exact same length as the bottom piece (18½ inches). These will be used to make the two sides and a compartment divider.

Find and mark the center of each of the two end pieces, which is where the 1x2 handle will go. Measure and make a mark 1¾ inches from either side of the center of the end pieces. Measure 4¼ inches up from the two bottom corners of each side and make a mark. Connect the bottom marks to the top marks, forming diagonal lines (see end view, Fig. 5-1).

Fig. 5-2

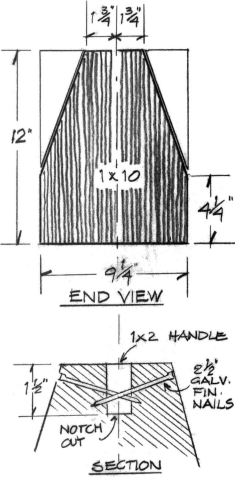

Fig. 5-3

TOOLBOX
USED AS
A SUPPORT
FOR SAWING

from the top corner edges of each end piece (see Fig. 5-2). Use 2½-inch galvanized finish nails to nail through the pilot holes and lock the handle in place.

Glue and clamp the ends and side pieces to the bottom. Once dry, nail the pieces together. Recess the nail heads with a nail set and fill the depressions with wood filler.

Make a compartment for the saw by fitting the last 18½-inch-long piece of 1x4 lengthwise inside the toolbox, 1 inch from the front side. Glue and nail it in place, using 2½-inch finish nails, spaced 3 inches apart. To hold seed packets and flower markers, cut a shorter piece of wood to fit perpendicular to the saw compartment, ½ inch from and parallel to one end of the box and glue it in place (see top view, Fig. 5-1).

Using the diagonal lines as your guide, cut off the four corners of the end pieces, using an electric jig saw or a handsaw.

Cut out the notch for the 1x2 handle, but make it slightly smaller than the 1x2. Use a file to gradually increase the width of the notch until the handle fits in the notch snugly. Be careful not to make too tight a fit which could cause the end pieces to split.

Position the handle in the two notches and drill ³⁄₃₂-inch-diameter pilot holes, ½ inch down

WINDOW BOX

Houses, apartments, even sheds can be enhanced with the addition of a flower-filled window box, spilling over with annuals and English ivy. The window box outside our dining room in New York City reflects the changing seasons and adds color to the room. In the summer, we fill it with white petunias and red geraniums and during the winter, we cover the soil with Christmas tree boughs, baby's breath and a few gold-tipped pinecones. For many people the total extent of their gardening is done in a window box. It's an easy and convenient way of enjoying a few flowers and vegetables without worrying about hungry deer, rabbits and many of the insects that plague the outdoor gardener.

MATERIALS			
Quantity	**Size**	**Description**	**Location or Use**
1	32 inches	1x6 #2 cedar	bottom
1	4x4 sheet	½-inch exterior V-groove plywood	front, back and sides
1	10 feet	½-x4-inch cedar	trim
1	8 feet	1x2 cedar	top trim
1	5-x32-inch	aluminum screen	bottom
1 lb.	1½-inch	galvanized finish nails	
2	6 inch	⅜-inch hanger bolts with washers and wing nuts	
1 bottle	8 oz.	waterproof yellow glue	

Measure the width of the sill under the window where the box will go. A common width is 34 inches. If you are spanning two windows, build a divider in the middle of the window box. Decide if you are going to use flowerpots, a plastic liner or simply fill the window box with soil. In warmer climates, the wood may tend to rot more quickly if the damp soil is in contact with it. If you are using pots or a liner, buy them before establishing the depth and width measurements of your window box.

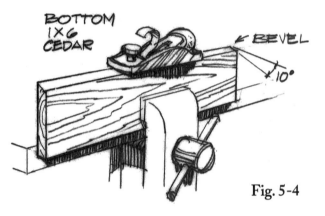

Fig. 5-4

The following directions are for a window box which has a slanted front and requires compound angled cuts. If this seems too difficult, adjust the measurements to make the front vertical.

BOX

To make the bottom of the window box, cut the 1x6 cedar, 32 inches long, and plane or cut one side at a 10 degree bevel (see Fig. 5-4). From the ½-inch exterior plywood, cut a piece for the back of the box that measures 7½ inches high by 32½ inches long. Cut the front piece out of the same exterior plywood, so that it measures 7¾ inches high by 32½ inches long. Plane or cut off the inside edge of the top front piece at a 10 degree angle. Make sure that the good (grooved) side of the plywood will face out when assembled.

Cut the two end pieces, 8 inches wide at the top, 6 inches wide at the bottom and 7½ inches high (see Fig. 5-5).

Cut a 45 degree bevel on all the edges that will join together. Glue and nail the sides, back and front together, and to the bottom of the box (see Fig. 5-6). Use 1½-inch galvanized finish nails and waterproof glue.

TRIM

Rip the 10-foot-long piece of ½-x4-inch cedar in half. Cut four pieces for the horizontal trim, each 33½ inches long, and bevel the ends at 45 degree angles. Glue and nail the trim pieces to the front and back of the window box at the top and bottom edges. Plane off the top front piece of

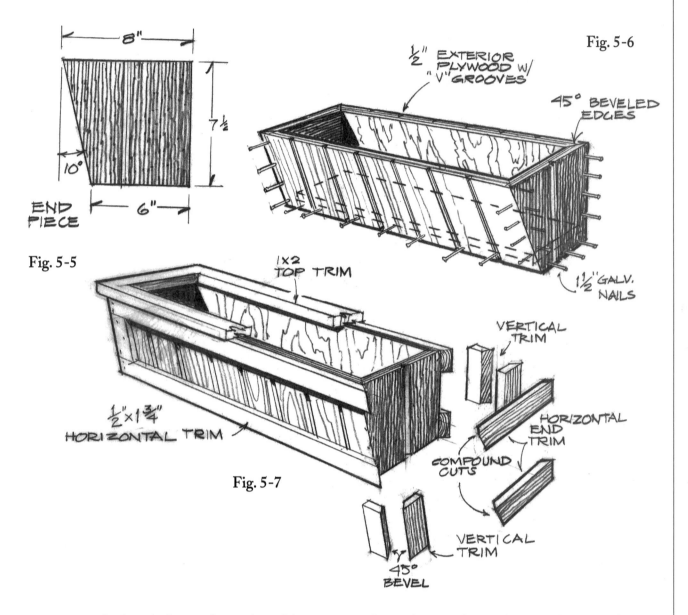

Fig. 5-6

½" EXTERIOR PLYWOOD W/ "V" GROOVES

45° BEVELED EDGES

1½" GALV. NAILS

Fig. 5-5

8"

7½

10°

6"

END PIECE

1x2 TOP TRIM

½"x1¾" HORIZONTAL TRIM

Fig. 5-7

VERTICAL TRIM

HORIZONTAL END TRIM

COMPOUND CUTS

VERTICAL TRIM

45° BEVEL

trim so it is flush with the top front edge of the plywood box.

Cut the four horizontal trim pieces for the ends, 9 inches for the top trim pieces and 7 inches for the bottom trim pieces. Make compound angle cuts on the ends that meet the front pieces of trim (see Fig. 5-7). Rip cut the remaining pieces of trim at a 45 degree bevel. Measure carefully the distances between the horizontal trim pieces, and cut the vertical corner trim pieces to fit between the horizontal trim.

Cover the top edges with 1x2 cedar, cut to fit so that it overlaps the plywood and trim pieces by ¼ inch on each side. This provides a lip that creates a shadow line on the outside of the box.

Drill ½-inch-drainage holes, approximately 6 inches apart, in the bottom of the window box (see top view, Fig. 5-8). Cut a piece of aluminum insect screen 5x32 inches to fit the bottom. This is used to cover the drainage holes and prevents insects from entering the bottom of the box. Break up an old flowerpot or cover the bottom with a thin layer of gravel before filling it with potting soil.

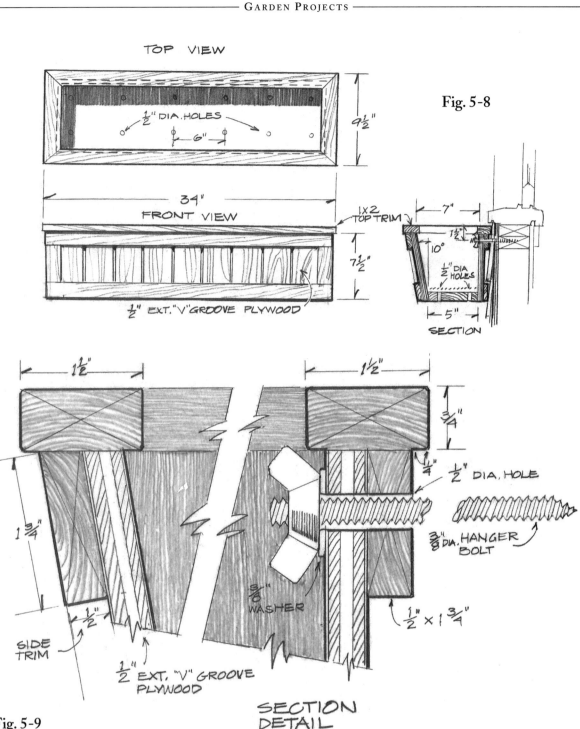

TOP VIEW

½" DIA. HOLES

6"

9½"

Fig. 5-8

34"

FRONT VIEW

1×2 TOP TRIM

7½"

½" EXT. "V" GROOVE PLYWOOD

7"

1½"

10°

½" DIA HOLES

5"

SECTION

1½"

1½"

¾"

¼"

½" DIA. HOLE

3/8" DIA. HANGER BOLT

1¾"

½"

3/8" WASHER

½" × 1¾"

SIDE TRIM

½" EXT. "V" GROOVE PLYWOOD

SECTION DETAIL

Fig. 5-9

INSTALLATION

Drill two ½-inch-diameter holes in the back of the window box, approximately 30 inches apart, and 1½ inches below the top edge of the top trim (see full-size detail, Fig. 5-9). Holding the window box in position under the window, hammer a ⅜-inch hanger bolt through the hole and into the side of the house to make a dent.

Remove the window box and drill two ¼-inch-diameter pilot holes into the side of the house where the dents are. Using locking pliers, or Vise-Grips, install the two hanger bolts, allowing 2 inches of the hanger bolt to protrude out from the house. Hang the window box on the hanger bolts and screw a ⅜-inch washer and wing nut onto the end of each bolt.

CEDAR PLANTER

This handsome cedar container looks elegant on a deck, or on a flagstone or brick terrace. Most planters of this size have a heavy, bulky appearance, but this one was designed with thinner supporting legs, giving it a lighter, slightly formal and almost oriental look. The contrast of the redwood legs and the cedar sides adds to the uniqueness of the design.

This type of planter is ideal for a person who doesn't have a lot of space or who doesn't have a lot of time for large-scale gardening. Whatever you are growing is up off the ground and in a more controlled environment. You can fill the planter with the best potting soil and mulch and pamper whatever flowers or vegetables you plant. Make sure to drill tiny holes every 6 inches in the base and cover the bottom with a layer of broken ceramic flowerpots or gravel for drainage. We use our planter to make a mini-vegetable garden, with tomatoes, arugula and fresh herbs, surrounded by marigolds for color and to keep the beetles away!

MATERIALS

Quantity	Size	Description	Location or Use
1	5 feet	2x2 redwood	legs
2	8 feet	1x8 T&G cedar	sides
1	8 feet	1x2 cedar	side trim
1	8 feet	1x3 cedar	top trim
1	2x2 sheet	¾-inch exterior plywood	bottom
1	20¼-inch-square	aluminum screen	bottom
1 lb.	1½-inch	galvanized finish nails	
1 dozen	2½-inch	galvanized deck screws	

LEGS

The legs of the planter have notches in them to hold the sides in place. To make these notches, use a table saw to rip cut a 5-foot-long piece of 2x2 redwood to the dimensions shown in Fig. 5-10. This is done with four passes of the saw. **Note:** You will only have to change the table saw fence once. However, make sure you take into account the thickness of the saw blade (kerf) when you set up your fence. After the 2x2 is notched, cut the wood into four 15-inch-long pieces.

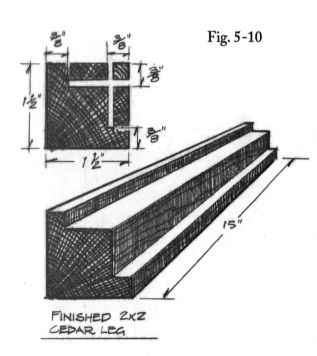

Fig. 5-10

FINISHED 2x2
CEDAR LEG

SIDE PANELS AND BOTTOM

To make the sides, cut the two 8-foot-long, 1x8 tongue-and-groove (T&G) boards into eight pieces, each 20¼ inches long. Rip cut the tongue off four of the pieces (about ½ inch) to create a flat surface on which the top trim can rest. Also rip cut ½ inch off the groove edge. Fit together two pieces of T&G to assemble each side.

Lay two of the legs flat on the floor. Apply waterproof glue to the grooves of the legs and to the ends of the side panels. Fit the side panels to the legs, allowing 1½ inches of the side panel to extend above the tops of the legs (see Fig. 5-11). This is to allow the 1x2 side trim to fit flat against the top of the siding. Use bar clamps, if you have them, to hold the pieces together while the glue is drying. Once the glue has dried, toenail 1½-inch galvanized finish nails through the ends of the T&G panel, into the 2x2 legs from the inside (see Fig. 5-11). Construct a second side/leg unit, following the same procedure.

While you are waiting for the glue to dry, cut a 20¼-inch-square bottom out of ¾-inch exterior plywood. Determining where the bottom of your planter is to be positioned depends on what you are planting. If you are going to fill it with an ornamental bush, place the bottom as low as possi-

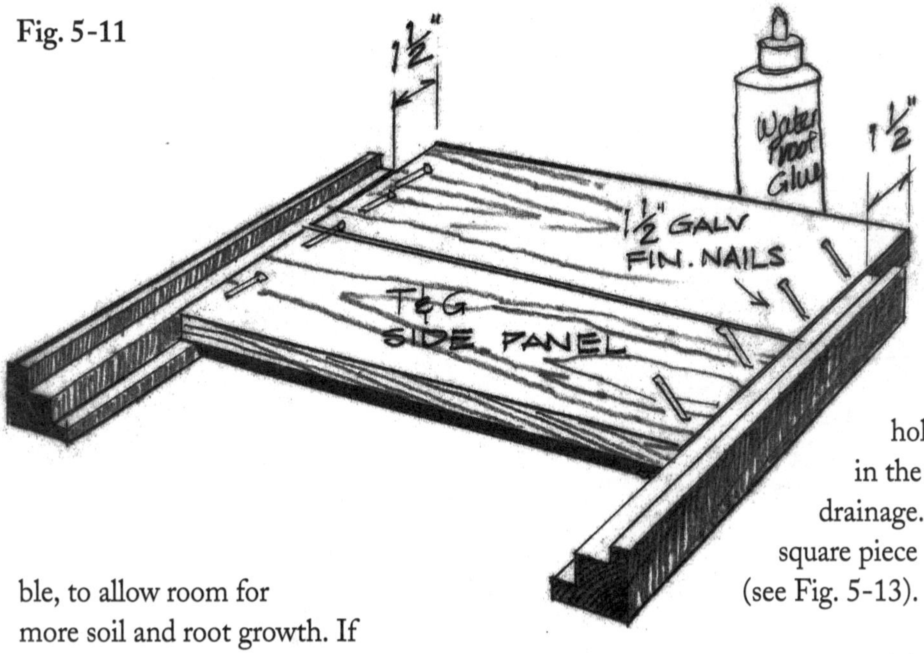

Fig. 5-11

ble, to allow room for more soil and root growth. If potted plants or annuals such as impatiens or Boston daisies are to be used, the bottom can be positioned higher, since not as much soil will be needed. Draw a line on the inside of the 1x8 side/leg unit to show where the top of the floor will go.

Place one of these units face down on your workbench, then lay a bead of glue inside the exposed leg grooves. Glue and fit the two remaining sides into the grooves. Lay a bead of glue around the outside edge of the ¾-inch plywood bottom and slip it in place where marked. Spread glue on the exposed ends of the upright sides and in the grooves of the remaining side/leg unit and assemble the final pieces. Make sure the side edges are lined up and level and that the box is square.

You will notice that there is a ¾-x¾-inch open space where the top of the T&G boards meet. Although it is not critical, you may want to fill these spaces by cutting four 1½-inch-long pieces of ¾-x¾-

inch cedar and gluing them in the corners (see Fig. 5-12).

When the glue has set, toenail the final side to the inside corner 2x2 legs, as you did previously. Drill nine ½-inch-diameter holes about 6 inches apart in the bottom to allow for drainage. Lay the 20¼-inch-square piece of screen on the bottom (see Fig. 5-13).

TRIM

To make the 1x2 side trim, cut four 24-inch-long pieces out of an 8-foot-long piece of cedar. Bevel cut the ends of each piece at a 45 degree angle. The inside of the bevel measurement, from one beveled edge to the other, should equal the measurement from corner to corner of the planter (23¼ inches). Carefully fit the pieces together at each corner and nail them in place, using 1½-inch galvanized finish nails.

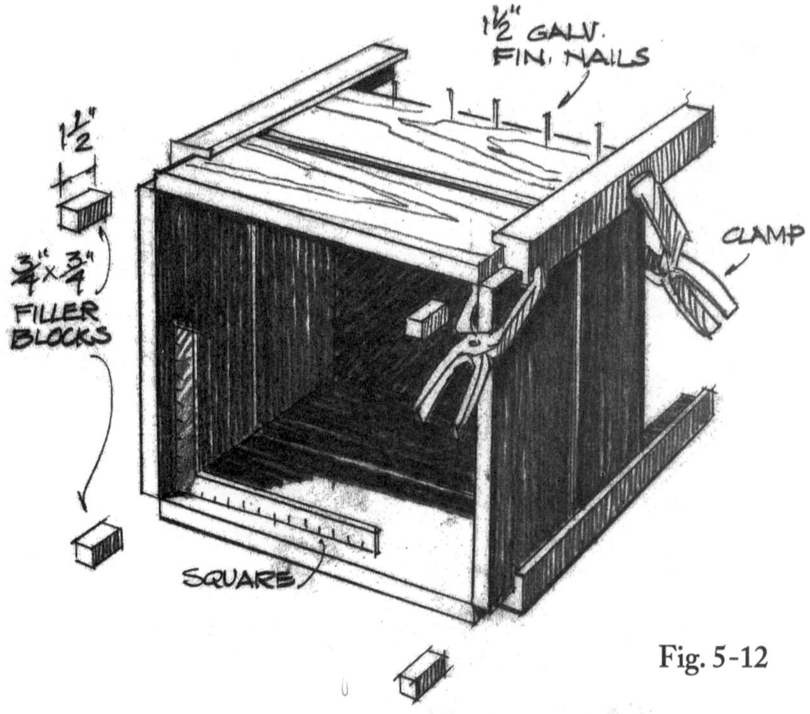

Fig. 5-12

Fig. 5-13

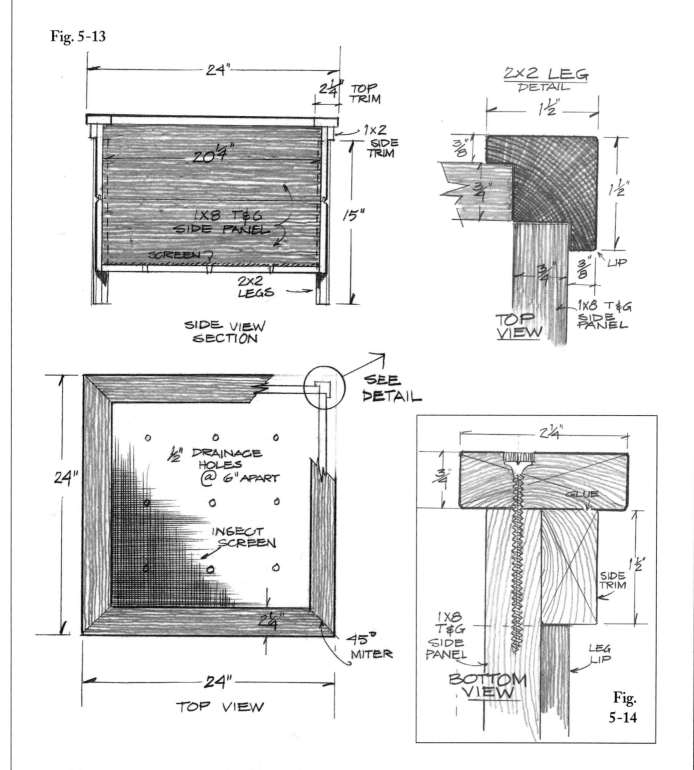

To make the top trim, cut four pieces of 1x3 cedar, each 24 inches long. Rip cut each piece so that the trim measures 2¼ inches across (see Fig. 5-13). Miter the ends at 45 degrees, so that they fit together perfectly at the corners. Glue the top pieces to the top edge of the T&G cedar and the

1x2 side trim. As an added measure of strength, counterbore and screw the top trim to the T&G panels, using 2½-inch galvanized deck screws, every 6 inches. Fill the remaining holes with wood plugs, which can be bought at a lumberyard or ordered from a woodworking supply catalog.

GARDEN CART

This garden cart has proved itself indispensable in working around the yard. It is rugged enough to haul stones, cordwood, topsoil or even balled trees. We have transplanted several small pine trees, transporting them from one location to another by tying them to the top of our cart. Because the front of the cart is angled, it can rest level with the ground, making it easy to rake up leaves, grass clippings and weeds. The 26-inch-diameter wheels allow plenty of clearance for high brush when you are carrying logs or branches through the woods.

MATERIALS

Quantity	Size	Description	Location or Use
1	4x8 sheet	¾-inch P.T. plywood	bottom, sides, front and back
1	8 feet	5⁄4x4 P.T. lumber	arms
1	4 feet	1½-inch-dia. pole	handle
2	26-inch-dia.	pneumatic tires	wheels
1	¾-inch-dia.*	steel axle	wheels
4	¾-inch	galvanized washers	axle
2		cotter pins	axle
1 lb.	2-inch	galvanized deck screws	
1 dozen	1½-inch	galvanized deck screws	

*Length depends on width of wheel hub. (Consult wheel manufacturer.)

The secret of this cart is that the weight of the load is balanced over the wheels, enabling you to easily push even heavy loads. David designed this cart long before the carts were commercially available. He got the idea from the Vietnamese, who transported 500-pound oil drums on bicycles along the Ho Chi Minh trail. Each of the garden cart wheels is rated at a 300-pound capacity, and can be mail-ordered from Northern Hydraulics Catalog (see Sources).

Begin this project by ordering the wheels and axle for the cart. Since dimensions may vary, it is advisable to wait until you have received the wheels to determine the exact width. You may have to adjust the width of the cart slightly to accommodate the axle. If you are only ordering the wheels, measure the width of the hubs (approximately 3 inches) and add ½ inch onto each end, plus the width of the cart and handles (32 inches). Using this dimension, have your local metal shop cut you a piece of ¾-inch-diameter steel rod, with a ⅛-inch-diameter hole drilled ¼ inch from the end, for the cotter pin (see arm detail, Fig. 5-16).

Referring to the cutting plan (see Fig. 5-15), cut out all the pieces from a sheet of ¾-inch

Fig. 5-15

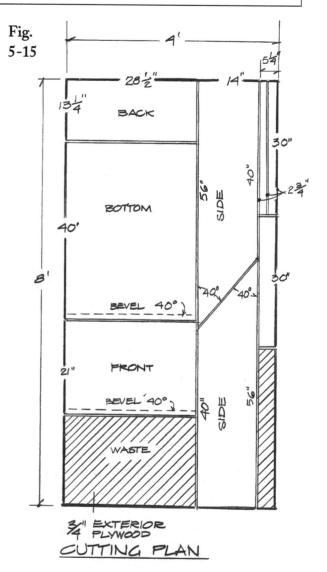

CUTTING PLAN

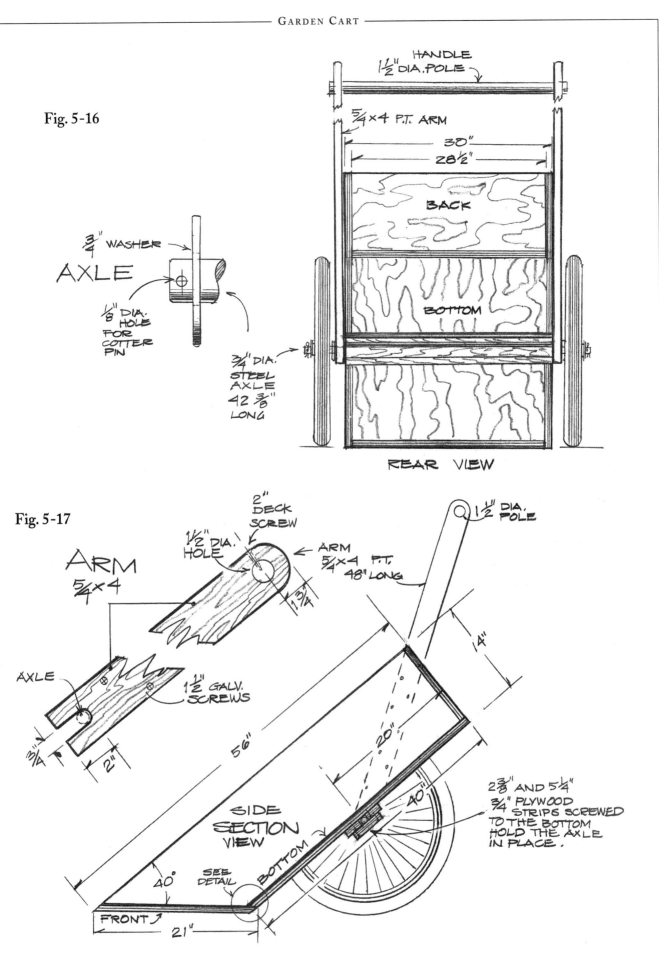

Fig. 5-16

HANDLE
1½" DIA. POLE

5/4×4 P.T. ARM

30"
28½"

BACK

BOTTOM

REAR VIEW

¾" WASHER

AXLE

⅛" DIA. HOLE FOR COTTER PIN

¾" DIA. STEEL AXLE 42⅜" LONG

Fig. 5-17

2" DECK SCREW

1½" DIA. HOLE

ARM 5/4×4 P.T. 48" LONG

1½" DIA. POLE

ARM 5/4×4

1¾"

AXLE

1½" GALV. SCREWS

3/4"

2"

56"

4"

20"

SIDE SECTION VIEW

BOTTOM

40"

2⅜" AND 5¼" ¾" PLYWOOD STRIPS SCREWED TO THE BOTTOM HOLD THE AXLE IN PLACE.

40°

SEE DETAIL

BOTTOM

FRONT

21"

Fig. 5-17 detail

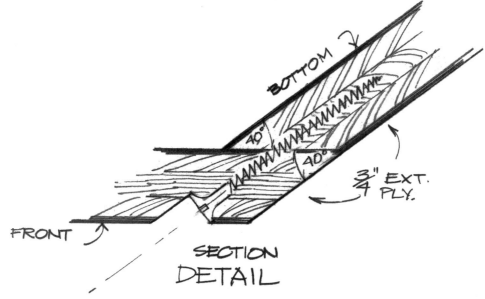

BOTTOM

40°

40°

3/4" EXT. PLY.

FRONT

SECTION DETAIL

exterior plywood. For the arms, cut two 48-inch-long pieces from the ⁵⁄₄x4 pressure-treated (P.T.) lumber. Round off the ends using an electric jig saw, then sand them smooth. Bore a 1½-inch-diameter hole in the center of each arm, 1¾ inches from the end, and make a ¾-x2-inch notch in the bottom end of each arm where it will straddle the axle (see detail, Fig. 5-17). Fit the 1½-inch-diameter pole (handle) into the hole at the top of each arm, and secure with a 2-inch galvanized deck screw.

Assemble the cart box by screwing the sides to the back, front and bottom, using 2-inch galvanized deck screws, every 4 inches. Note that the side pieces overlap the front, back and bottom pieces (see section detail, Fig. 5-16).

Mount the axle across the bottom of the cart, 20 inches from the back edge of the cart box (see Fig. 5-17). To hold the axle in place, glue and screw two 2⅜-inch-wide by 30-inch-long strips of ¾-inch plywood under the bottom of the cart. Position the strips 20 inches from the back, allowing a ¾-inch gap for the axle. Glue and screw a 5¼-inch-wide by 30-inch-long piece over the two strips, so there is a ¾-x¾-inch opening for the axle (see Fig. 5-17).

Fit the two arms over the axle, and screw them to the sides of the cart using six 1½-inch galvanized deck screws on each side.

Pump up the tires and you're ready to roll!

HEART GATE

A garden gate often serves as an introduction to a pathway or a protected garden area. It should be designed to attract the eye of the visitor and invite him or her to open it and walk inside. Sometimes, however, gates give the impression of a barrier, warning people not to enter. In an effort to dispel this feeling, a Connecticut gardener carved a heart in her gateway. The gate, painted white and enclosed by a post and an old stone wall, blends in with the environment while still defining an outdoor garden space.

MATERIALS

Quantity	Size	Description	Location or Use
GATE:			
3	8 feet	1x6 T&G cedar (center match)	front
1	10 feet	2x4 #2 cedar	crossbrace
1	6 inches	1-inch-dia. wood dowel	bolt handle
1	12 inches	1x2 #2 pine	wooden bolt
1 pair	12 inches	iron strap hinges	front
1	3 feet	¼-inch-dia. nylon rope	closing mechanism
1	12 inches	iron sash weight	closing mechanism
1	8 inches	1x2 #2 pine	hinge post and door stop
1	6 inches	black wrought-iron handle	
4	3-inch	galvanized finish nails	
1 lb.	2½-inch	galvanized deck screws	
1 lb.	1-inch	galvanized finish nails	
1 lb.	1¼-inch	galvanized deck screws	
1		compression spring for wooden bolt	
1	¼-x2-inch	eye screw	
1	¼-x4-inch	eye screw	
1 bottle	8 oz.	waterproof yellow glue	
1 qt.		water sealer	
POSTS:			
1	12 feet	4x4 P.T. lumber	inner post
2	8 feet	1x4 clear cedar	outer post trim
2	8 feet	1x6 clear cedar	outer post trim
1	8 feet	⅝-x⅝-inch cove molding	post base
1	14 inches	2x8 clear cedar	post caps

GATE:

Before beginning your garden gate, we suggest you review the section on Posts and Gates, pages 15-17.

Cut two pieces of 1x6 tongue-and-groove (T&G) cedar 32 inches long, two pieces 33 inches long and one piece 39 inches long. Glue the pieces together as shown in Fig. 5-18. When the glue has dried, cut off the exposed groove and tongue so that the final width of the gate measures 36 inches.

Make two crossbraces for the gate by cutting two 2x4s, each 36 inches long, and screwing them to the back of the gate, 2½ inches up from the bottom and 5 inches down from the top of the gate (measure from the 32-inch-long boards). **Note:** To install the wooden bolt later, you will temporarily remove the top crossbrace, so don't load it up with screws now. Place the remaining 2x4 over the corners of the crossbraces and mark the angle where they meet. (Make sure the diagonal 2x4 brace runs from the top latch side to the bottom hinge side, as shown in Fig. 5-19.) Cut the 2x4 off at the two marked angles and screw it to the back of the gate and the crossbraces, using 1¼-inch galvanized deck screws.

To lay out the top curves, first mark a vertical line down the center of the gate. Measure 9 inches down from the top and make a mark. Using a compass, draw an 8-inch-radius circle, us-

ing the mark as your pivot point. Measure 6 inches from the top corners of the gate, and make two marks. Draw two 3-inch-radius circles, using these marks as your pivot points. Hand draw two lines connecting the larger circle to the two smaller circles (see Fig. 5-19).

Fig. 5-18

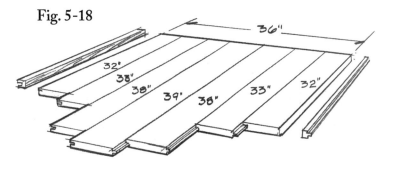

Fig. 5-19

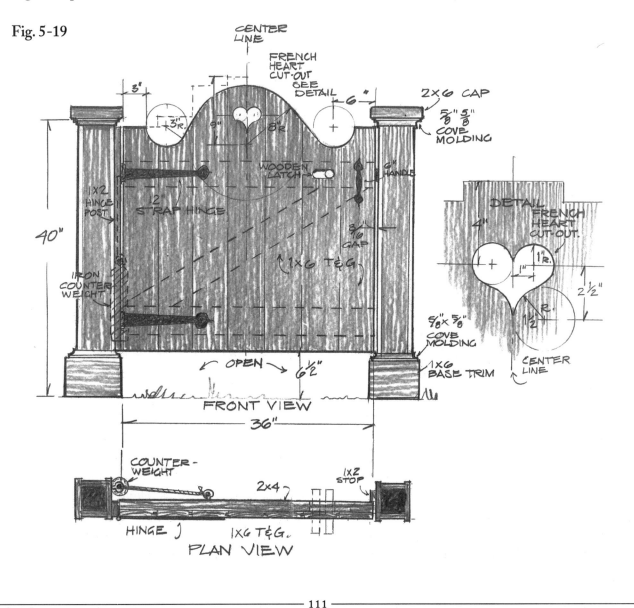

To lay out the French heart, measure 4 inches down from the top of the gate along the centerline and make a mark. Draw a horizontal line, extending 1 inch from either side of the mark and make a point (see detail, Fig. 5-19). Using these points as the pivot points for your compass, draw two 1-inch-radius circles. Measure over 1½ inches from either side of the centerline of the gate, and 2½ inches down from the horizontal lines. Mark these two points, then, using these as your pivot points, draw two 1½-inch-radius circles (see detail, Fig. 5-19).

Using an electric jig saw, cut the curved top of the gate and the French heart.

POSTS

Cut two 4x4 P.T. posts, each 72 inches long. To make the facing for the two posts, cut four 1x4s and four 1x6s, each 40 inches long, and nail them to the sides of the posts, beginning at the top of each post (see Fig. 5-20). **Note:** The bottom of these posts will be buried and do not need to be clad.

Use the leftover pieces of 1x6 to make the base trim. Cut eight pieces of 1x6, 7 inches long, with a 45 degree bevel on each end. Seal the backs and the edges of each piece with water sealer and nail them to the base of the posts, using 1-inch galvanized finish nails (see Fig. 5-20).

Cut eight pieces of ⅝-x⅝-inch cove molding to fit on top of the base trim. Notch out the edge of the 1x6 to accept the cove molding, and nail the molding to the trim, using 1-inch galvanized finish nails.

Make caps for the two posts out of two pieces of clear 2x8, each cut 7¼ inches long. Using construction adhesive and 3-inch galvanized finish nails, glue and nail a cap to the top of each post. **Note:** Drill ³/₃₂-inch-diameter pilot holes for the nails in order to prevent the cap pieces from splitting.

INSTALLING THE GATE

Dig two 6-inch-diameter holes, 42 inches apart on-center and 32 inches deep. Set the two posts in the holes, but do not backfill.

Screw the ends of the two strap hinges to the front of the gate, 5½ inches from the top and 3 inches from the bottom of the gate. Make a hinge post by cutting a 1x2, 32 inches long. Screw the other end of the two hinges to this 1x2. Screw four 2½-inch galvanized deck screws partway into the face of the hinge post (see Fig. 5-21). Hold the 1x2 hinge post and gate flush with the front of the post, and continue screwing the four screws into the post.

Close the gate and position the posts so there is a ³/₁₆-inch gap between the gate and the post. Cut another 1x2, 32 inches long, and nail it to the opposite post, to act as a stop for the gate. Check to make sure the posts are plumb on all sides and that the gate is level.

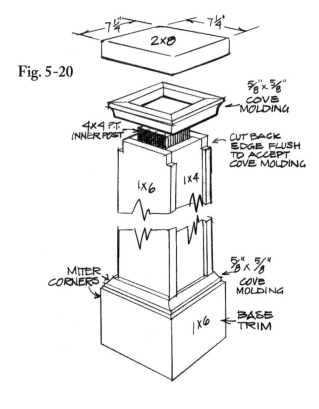

Fig. 5-20

2x8 — 7¼", 7¼"

⅝" x ⅝" COVE MOLDING

4X4 P.T. INNER POST

CUT BACK EDGE FLUSH TO ACCEPT COVE MOLDING

1X6   1X4

MITER CORNERS

⅝" x ⅝" COVE MOLDING

1X6   BASE TRIM

Fig. 5-21

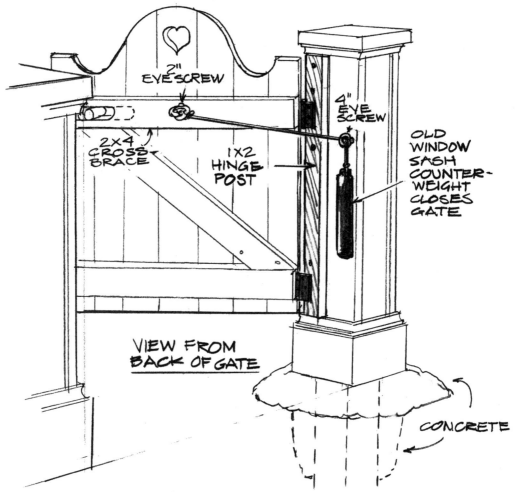

2"
EYE SCREW

4"
EYE
SCREW

OLD
WINDOW
SASH
COUNTER-
WEIGHT
CLOSES
GATE

2x4
CROSS
BRACE

1x2
HINGE
POST

VIEW FROM
BACK OF GATE

CONCRETE

Use braces if necessary to hold the posts in place while you backfill, tamping down the soil with a scrap 2x4. When you have reached 1 foot below ground level, fill the remainder of the hole with concrete (see Posts and Gates, page 17). Put a ⅜-inch-thick wedge between the top of the post and the gate while the concrete is curing (approximately three days), to allow for any "sagging" of the gate later on.

HARDWARE:

Screw a 6-inch black wrought-iron handle on the outside of the gate. Unscrew and temporarily remove the top 2x4 crossbrace, and cut a 1½-inch-wide by ¾-inch-deep mortise out of the end. Beginning 6 inches from the latch side of the gate, cut a 1⅛-x3-inch oval slot through the mortise groove (see Fig. 5-22). To make the wooden bolt, cut a 1x2, 12 inches long, and drill a 1-inch-diameter hole through the face of the 1x2, 8 inches from one end. Insert a 6-inch-long, 1-inch-diameter dowel, halfway through the hole and secure it in place by screwing a 1¼-inch screw down through the top edge of the 1x2 and into the 1-inch dowel.

Cut a corresponding 1⅛-x3-inch slot in the gate, 6 inches from the latch side. Spray silicone on the wooden bolt and place a very light compression spring (sold at hardware stores) at the end of the bolt. Re-attach the 2x4 crossbrace, with the wooden bolt and spring, to the back of the gate. Close the gate and mark where the bolt touches the post.

Fig. 5-22

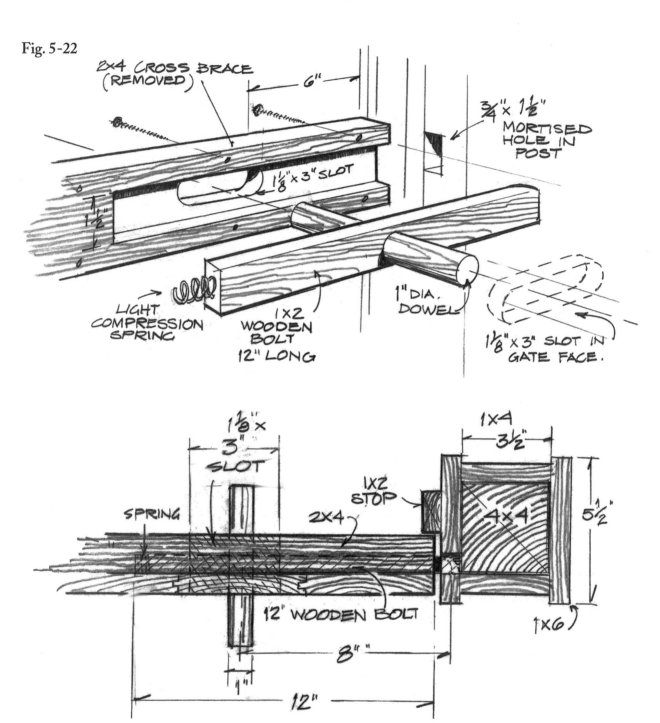

2x4 CROSS BRACE (REMOVED)

6"

3/4"x 1 1/2" MORTISED HOLE IN POST

1 1/8"x 3" SLOT

1 1/2"

LIGHT COMPRESSION SPRING

1X2 WOODEN BOLT 12" LONG

1" DIA. DOWEL

1 1/8"x 3" SLOT IN GATE FACE.

1 1/8"x 3" SLOT

SPRING

2x4

1X2 STOP

1X4 3 1/2"

4x4

5 1/2"

12" WOODEN BOLT

1X6

8"

1"

12"

Mortise out a 1½-x ¾-inch hole, ¾ inches deep, to accept the wooden bolt. Try closing the gate again. It should "snap" shut with a light push.

To make the gate self-closing, hang a counterweight from the hinge post. Screw the 2-inch-long eye screw into the top 2x4 cross-brace, 10 inches from the hinge side. Screw the 4-inch-long eye screw into the corner of the post (see plan view, Fig. 5-19). Tie the nylon rope to the 2-inch eye screw, thread it through the 4-inch eye screw and tie it to the counterweight.

GARDEN HOUSES

GARDEN HOUSE

This classic garden house was originally built by David's parents for his mother's garden in Summit, New Jersey, in 1937. Elegant and well suited for a formal garden, it was inspired by a Colonial garden shed built for George Washington's home in Mount Vernon. David recreated the structure for the corner of a brownstone backyard in New York City. Six feet wide, it is large enough to store all the essential tools for the garden and still leave plenty of room for kids to disappear in when playing hide-and-seek.

MATERIALS

Quantity	Size	Description	Location or Use
3	12 feet	2x6 P.T. lumber	base, floor joists and windowsill
2	4x8 sheet	¾-inch exterior plywood	floor deck
6	8-x-8-inch	concrete half blocks	base
2 or 3	assorted	gray slate	shims
3	12 feet	4x4 cedar posts	corners
4	10 feet	2x4 #2 fir	plates
2	8 feet	2x2 clear cedar	window sash
1	6 feet	1x6 cedar	window jamb
2	10 feet	2x4 nailers (cats)	
22	12 feet	1x6 T&G #2 cedar	siding and door
4	12 feet	1x2 cedar	dentils and bevel support strip
2	12 feet	4½-inch sprung crown	cornice molding
2	10 feet	1x6 #2 pine	crown support
1	10 feet	2x4 #2 construction fir	temporary post
3	10 feet	2x6 #2 construction fir	rafters
3	4x8 sheet	½-inch exterior plywood	roof
1 roll	36-inch	15-lb. tar paper	roof
3 bundles	36-inch	three-tab asphalt shingles	roof
1	12 feet	1x2 #2 cedar	doorstops
1	12 feet	⁵⁄₄x6 P. T.	door crossbraces and head jamb
1	12 feet	⁵⁄₄x4 #2 pine	door casing

HARDWARE:

Quantity	Size	Description	Location or Use
1 lb.	3½-inch	galvanized deck screws	
1 lb.	1½-inch	galvanized deck screws	door
1 lb.	2½-inch	galvanized finish nails	
3 lbs.	2-inch	spiral- or ring-shank siding nails	
2	2-inch	galvanized hinges	
1 dozen	1½-inch	copper nails	
2	18-inch	wrought-iron strap hinges	
1		thumb latch and handle	
1 sheet	24-x-24-inch	16-oz. copper sheet	
1 piece	9½-x21½-inch	window glass	
1 bottle	8 oz.	waterproof yellow glue	

BASE

Begin by making a level site for the garden house, 10 feet in diameter. Clear the area of any rocks or roots.

To build the base, cut six pieces of pressure-treated (P.T.) lumber, 36 inches long, and using a portable circular saw, bevel cut each end at a 30-degree angle (see Fig. 6-1).

Lay the pieces on a flat surface and assemble them, screwing the six corners together using 3½-inch galvanized deck screws at each joint (see Fig. 6-2). Check to make sure opposite corners are exactly 6 feet apart.

Cut three 6-foot-long pieces out of 2x6 P.T. lumber for the floor joists. Cut the ends of the first piece (cross joist) to fit into any two opposite corners of the base (see Fig. 6-3.) The next two pieces must be cut in half and shaped to fit the first piece where they intersect at the center. Screw them in place using four 3½-inch deck screws at each joint (see detail, Fig. 6-3).

To build the plywood floor, have someone help you lay the floor frame over the sheet of ¾-inch exterior plywood, tracing the shape of the outside edge onto the plywood (see Fig. 6-3). Do the same to the other side and using an electric jig saw, cut out the two pieces of plywood. Nail

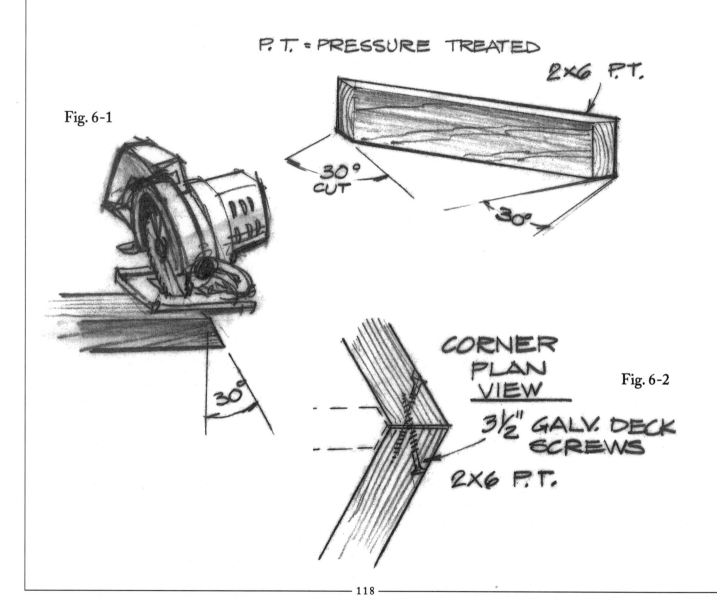

P.T. = PRESSURE TREATED

2x6 P.T.

Fig. 6-1

30° CUT

30°

30°

CORNER PLAN VIEW

Fig. 6-2

3½" GALV. DECK SCREWS

2x6 P.T.

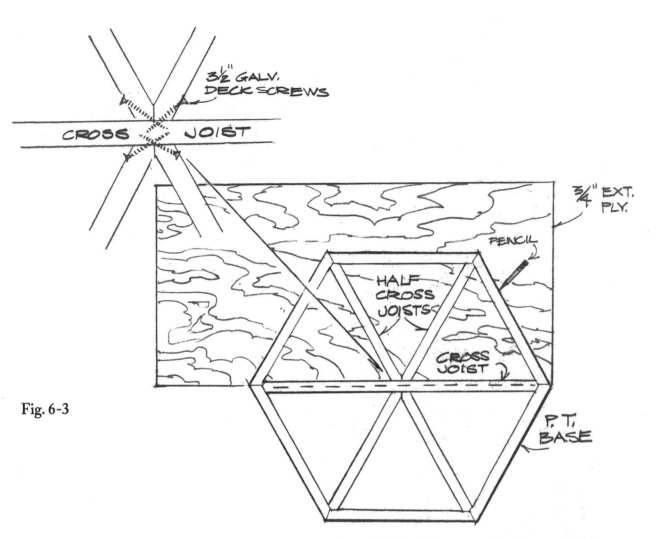

Fig. 6-3

the plywood to the base using 2-inch spiral- or ring-shank nails.

With help, move the floor base to where you want the garden house to be and lay it on the prepared ground. If the ground is not completely level (and it rarely is), bury a concrete block at the high side under the nearest corner and prop the low side up until the base is level. Place blocks under each corner until the base is level in all directions and is solidly supported at each corner. It is important to make sure the base is absolutely level since all subsequent work will depend on it.

During construction, it is possible that some of the blocks may compress into the soil, so it is a good idea to check the level of the floor each day before beginning work. If the base is not level,

buy a block of slate at your lumberyard (sold expressly for this purpose) and using a claw hammer, split off small thin slabs to use as shims between the blocks and the base (see Fig. 6-4).

WALL FRAMING

This garden house uses one 4x4 post at each of the six corners. To provide a good nailing surface for the siding, two edges of each post must be rip cut at 30-degree angles (see Fig. 6-5). Cut each post 68 ½ inches long and toenail them, or screw them to the base. (**Note:** There is no bottom plate as in conventional framing.) Connect the tops of the posts with 2x4 top plates laid flat. Cut each 2x4 top plate 36 inches long, and miter cut each end at a 60-degree angle (see plan view, Fig. 6-6). Screw them to the tops of the six posts. Check frequently to make sure the structure is

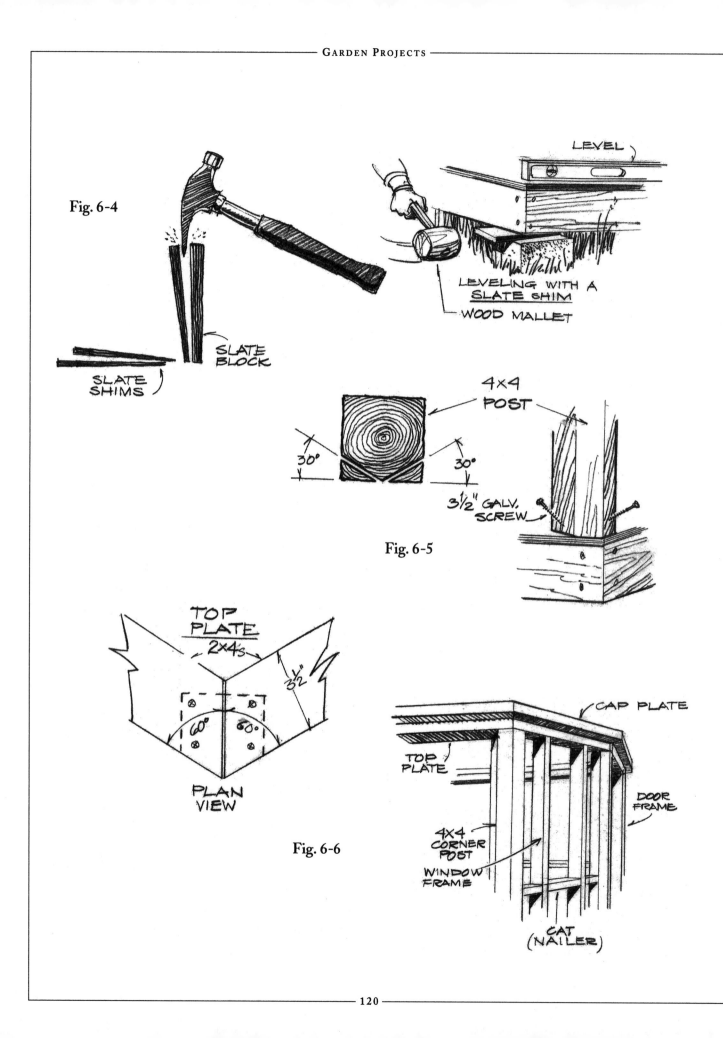

Fig. 6-4

SLATE SHIMS

SLATE BLOCK

LEVEL

LEVELING WITH A SLATE SHIM

WOOD MALLET

4×4 POST

30°   30°

3½" GALV. SCREW

Fig. 6-5

TOP PLATE 2×4's

3½"

60°   60°

PLAN VIEW

Fig. 6-6

CAP PLATE

TOP PLATE

4×4 CORNER POST

WINDOW FRAME

DOOR FRAME

CAT (NAILER)

positioned correctly by measuring the diagonals and checking for plumb (vertical) and square using a level and a framing square.

Add a second layer of 2x4s (called cap plates) over the top wall plate, so it is offset by ¾ inch, and protrudes out the same thickness as the siding you will install (see Fig. 6-6). This will allow the cap plate to cover the top of the siding and act as a solid base for the dentils. These pieces should also be cut at a 60-degree miter, but will be longer (approximately 38 inches along the outside edge) than the top plates because they protrude further.

Frame the window and the door using 2x4s. Measure and cut them to fit perfectly between the bottom of the top plate and the plywood floor.

Cut 2x4 nailers (sometimes called cats) approximately 34½ inches long, so they fit between each vertical stud and each corner post (see Fig. 6-6). Screw them to the studs and posts, 36 inches up from the floor.

WINDOW

Since the window can be built independently from the garden house, it is a good project to tackle on a rainy day. You may think that a 1-foot-wide window is a waste of time, since it provides only a little light to the interior; however, this is exactly the kind of extravagance that lends quality to this design and contributes to the elegance of the structure.

The window can be made very inexpensively and quickly if you have access to a table saw; otherwise, you will have to order a window custommade from your lumberyard. The reason this window is so easy to make is because it uses only one piece of glass instead of several small window panes. The muntin bars are applied to both sides

of the glass to give the impression of truly divided lights.

Since there is so little wood required, select only the best available clear stock. Buy 2x2 clear cedar from your lumberyard and use it to make both the window sash and the muntin bars.

Using a table saw, cut out the four pieces for the window sash from the 2x2 clear cedar. The two long sides (stiles) measure 24 inches long. The two short sides (rails) measure 12 inches long. Cut 45-degree bevels on each end (see Fig. 6-8).

Locate the center points where the muntin bars join the frame, and cut ⅜-x⅝-inch dadoes (see Fig. 6-9).

To hold the window glass, make a ⅛-inch-wide by ⅜-inch-deep groove in the center of the inside face of each piece of the window sash (see Fig. 6-10). Cut a piece of ⅛-inch-thick glass to fit into the groove. To cut the glass, score the surface several times with an inexpensive glass cutter, then place the scored line along a sharp edge and snap it apart.

To make the muntin bars, cut a piece of 2x2 in half lengthwise with a table saw. Place one of the two pieces cut-side down on the table saw, and make another cut lengthwise again; repeat with the second piece so that you have four identical ⅝-inch-square pieces (see Fig. 6-7). Test to make sure that they fit perfectly into the dadoes.

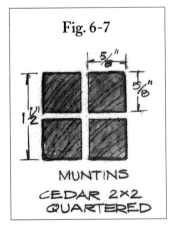

Fig. 6-7

MUNTINS
CEDAR 2×2
QUARTERED

Fig. 6-8

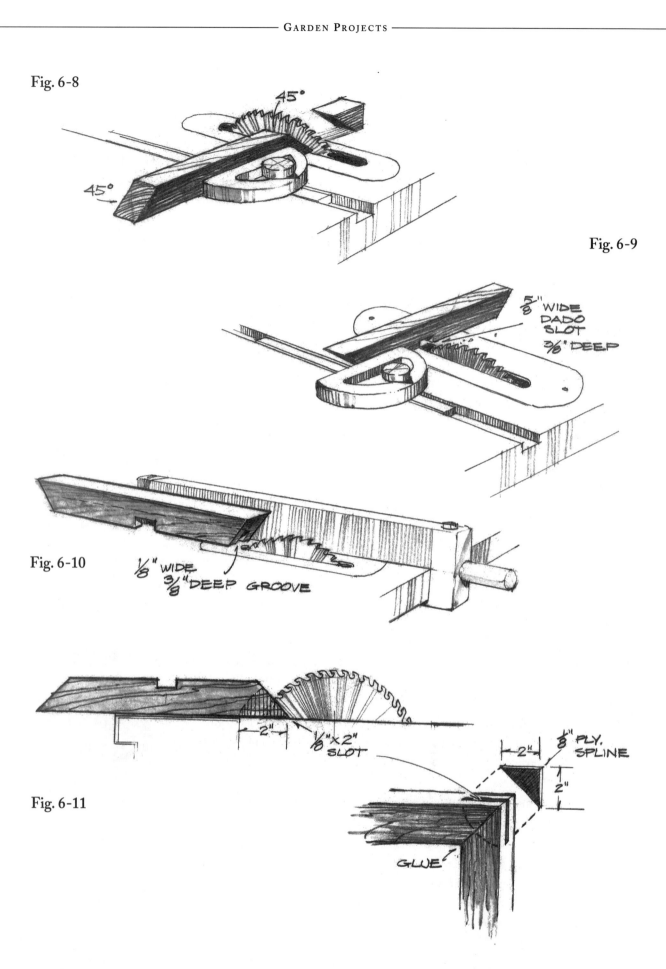

Fig. 6-9

5/8" WIDE
DADO
SLOT
3/8" DEEP

Fig. 6-10

1/8" WIDE
3/8" DEEP GROOVE

Fig. 6-11

2"

1/8" × 2" SLOT

2"

1/8" PLY. SPLINE

2"

GLUE

Fig. 6-12

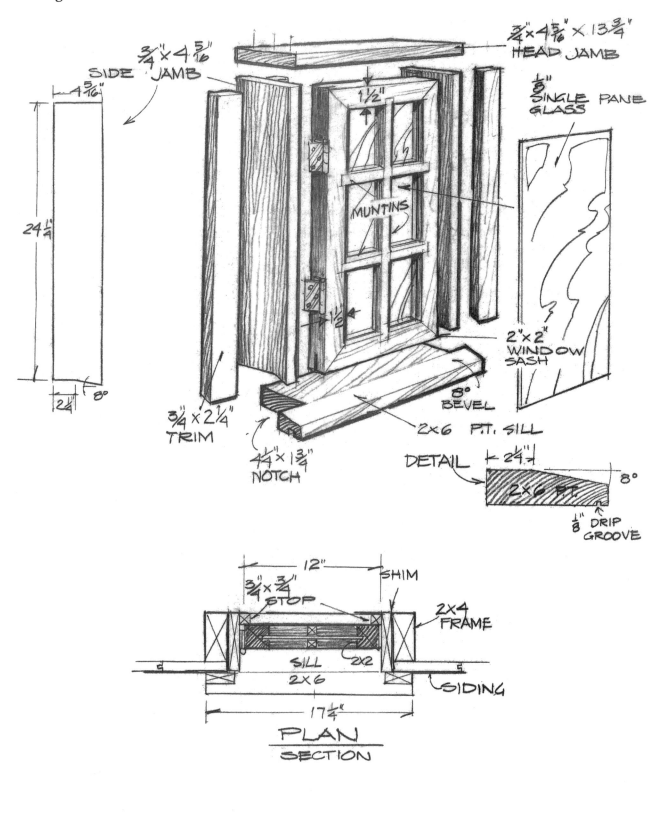

SIDE JAMB
$\frac{3}{4}$" × $4\frac{5}{16}$"

$4\frac{5}{16}$"

$24\frac{1}{4}$"

$2\frac{1}{8}$"

8°

$\frac{3}{4}$" × $2\frac{1}{4}$"
TRIM

$4\frac{1}{4}$" × $1\frac{3}{4}$"
NOTCH

HEAD JAMB
$\frac{3}{4}$" × $4\frac{5}{16}$" × $13\frac{3}{4}$"

$\frac{1}{8}$" SINGLE PANE GLASS

$1\frac{1}{2}$"

MUNTINS

$1\frac{1}{2}$"

2" × 2" WINDOW SASH

8° BEVEL

2×6 P.T. SILL

DETAIL

$2\frac{1}{4}$"

2×6 P.T.

8°

$\frac{1}{8}$" DRIP GROOVE

PLAN
SECTION

12"

$\frac{3}{4}$" × $\frac{3}{4}$"
STOP

SHIM

2×4 FRAME

SILL
2×6

2×2

SIDING

$17\frac{1}{4}$"

To join the window stiles and rails together at the four corners, cut a 2-inch slot in the end of each 2x2 (see Fig. 6-11). Make sure each slot is exactly in the center of the wood. Cut four 2-x2-inch right triangles out of a scrap piece of ⅛-inch plywood; they should be the width of your saw blade. Trial fit them into the corners (see detail, Fig. 6-11).

Temporarily assemble the window sash, including the scrap plywood triangles. Measure and cut the muntin bars to fit in the ⅜-x⅝-inch grooves in the window sash. Mark and notch out where the muntin bars intersect. After checking that all the pieces fit perfectly, squeeze a bead of silicone into the grooves in the window sash and set the piece of glass into the bed of silicone. Glue all the joints together using waterproof glue

(see Fig. 6-12). **Note:** If the window is going to be painted, you can achieve a more professional appearance by painting the muntin bars before installing them over the glass.

To make the finished window frame, begin by cutting a scrap piece of 2x6, 17¼ inches long. Cut a 1¾-x4¼-inch notch, leaving 1¼-inch-wide "ears" on the outside of the windowsill, then rip cut an 8-degree bevel along the top outside edge, and cut a ¼-inch-deep kerf along the bottom outside to create a drip line (see sill detail, Fig. 6-12).

Rip cut the 1x6 cedar to 4⁵⁄₁₆ inches wide, then cut two jambs to length, as shown in the side jamb detail of Fig. 6-12. Cut the head jamb 13¾ inches long, and nail the jambs together,

Fig. 6-13

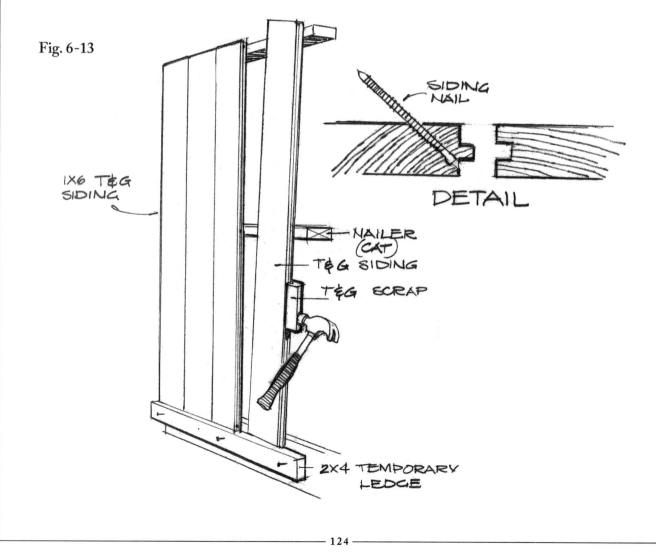

1X6 T&G SIDING

SIDING NAIL

DETAIL

NAILER (CAT)

T&G SIDING

T&G SCRAP

2X4 TEMPORARY LEDGE

Fig. 6-14

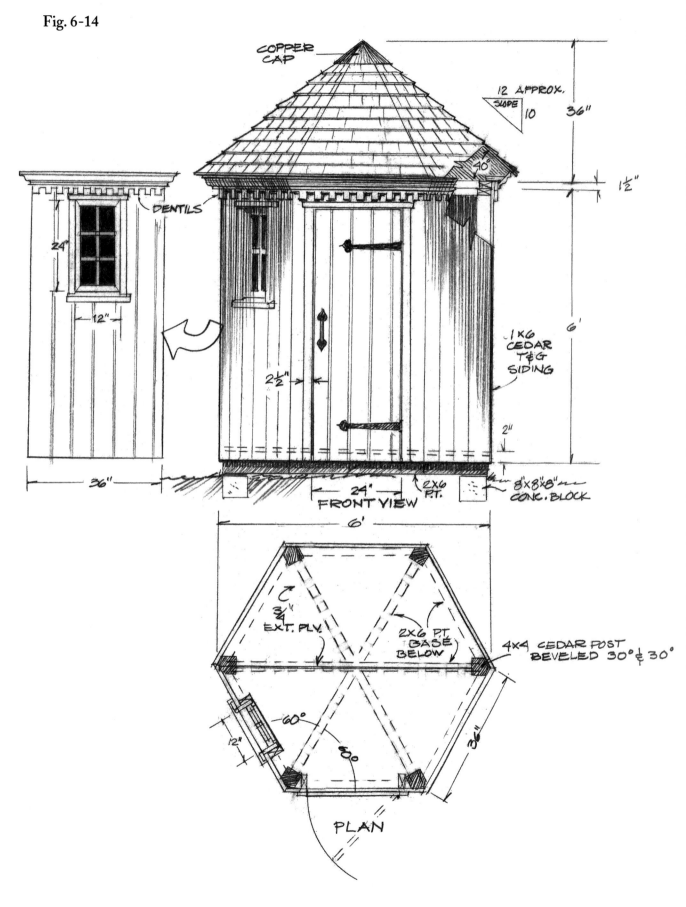

COPPER CAP

12 APPROX.
SLOPE 10

36"

1½"

DENTILS

24"

12"

1×6 CEDAR T&G SIDING

6'

2½"

2"

36"

24"

FRONT VIEW

2×6 P.T.

8"×8"×8" CONC. BLOCK

6'

¾" EXT. PLY.

2×6 P.T. BASE BELOW

4×4 CEDAR POST BEVELED 30° & 30°

60°

60°

12"

36"

PLAN

Fig. 6-15

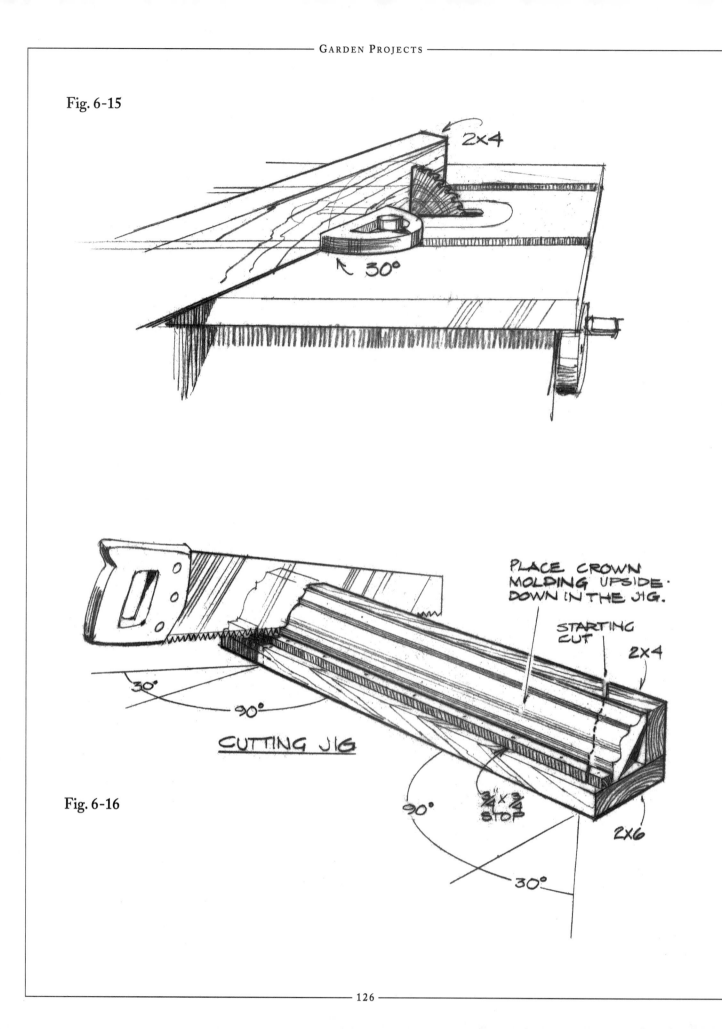

2x4

30°

PLACE CROWN
MOLDING UPSIDE·
DOWN IN THE JIG.

STARTING
CUT

2X4

CUTTING JIG

30°

90°

90°

30°

¾"x ¾"
STOP

2X6

Fig. 6-16

using 2½-inch galvanized finish nails. Install the 2-inch galvanized hinges on the window sash and hang the sash in the finished jamb. Using the offcuts left over from ripping the jamb, cut window stops to length (about 24¼ inches), and nail them along the inside of the sash (see plan, Fig. 6-12).

SIDING

This garden house can be sheathed in rough 1x6 tongue-and-groove (T&G) cedar, or, if you plan on painting it, smooth T&G cedar or pine. You will need approximately 37 pieces, 6 feet long, to cover the entire structure (see Fig. 6-13).

Starting at the right-hand side of the door, cut 1 inch off the groove side of one of the boards, so that the edge of the board is square, and face nail it along the door frame, using 2-inch spiral- or ring-shank nails every 6 inches. Nail a 2x4 so that it is parallel to and level with the base, to act as a temporary ledge on which to rest the boards (see Fig. 6-13). Slide each succeeding board onto the groove of the preceding one and pound it in place, using a scrap piece of T&G to protect the edge.

The boards are toenailed to the top plate, the bottom frame and the 2x4 nailer, using 2-inch siding nails. By toenailing the T&G boards through the tongue, you will avoid having any nails show (see detail, Fig. 6-13). There is no need to nail the left side of the board, since it is held by the tongue and groove. When you get to a corner, mark where the board extends past the post. Set your saw to 30 degrees and rip cut two boards. Join the boards so that the two boards fit neatly together at the corner. Continue around the garden house until you reach the other side of the door. Cut the last board (to the left of the door) off at right angles.

DENTILS

From a piece of 1x2 cedar, cut 72 pieces 1¾ inches long, and 72 pieces 3½ inches long. Glue and nail them vertically to the front face of the cap plate, overlapping the top of the siding, so that they alternate in size: long, short, long, short, etc. (see Fig. 6-14).

CORNICE

To make the cornice, cut six pieces of 4½-inch-wide sprung crown molding into 48 inch lengths. This dimension allows you a few extra inches at each end for adjustments. Using scrap lumber, make a miter jig to hold the molding while you are making your cuts. Since the roof is 6-sided, both ends of each strip of the cornice have to be cut off at a compound angle. To facilitate these cuts, build a simple jig with the correct angle cut in the jig to use as a cutting guide.

To construct the jig, use two 40-inch-long scrap pieces of lumber, one 2x6 and one 2x4. Measure in 6 inches from each end of the 2x4, and make a 30-degree cut, cutting into the wood as far as the saw blade will allow (see Fig. 6-15). Screw the two pieces of wood together at right angles. Nail a ¾-x¾-inch strip of wood, 40 inches long, to the 2x6, to hold the molding in place when cutting through it (see Fig. 6-16).

Before cutting the crown molding, measure the distance between each of the adjacent top corners of the shed. Turn the crown molding upside down in the jig and placing a hand saw in the "guide" cut of the jig, make a 30-degree compound cut at the end of each piece of cornice (see Fig. 6-16).

Our crown molding is "sprung" at a 45-degree angle (see Fig. 6-17), but in some areas of the country, only 38-degree sprung molding is available. Temporarily nail the crown molding onto a beveled (in our case, 45 degree) 36-inch-long 1x6

Fig. 6-17

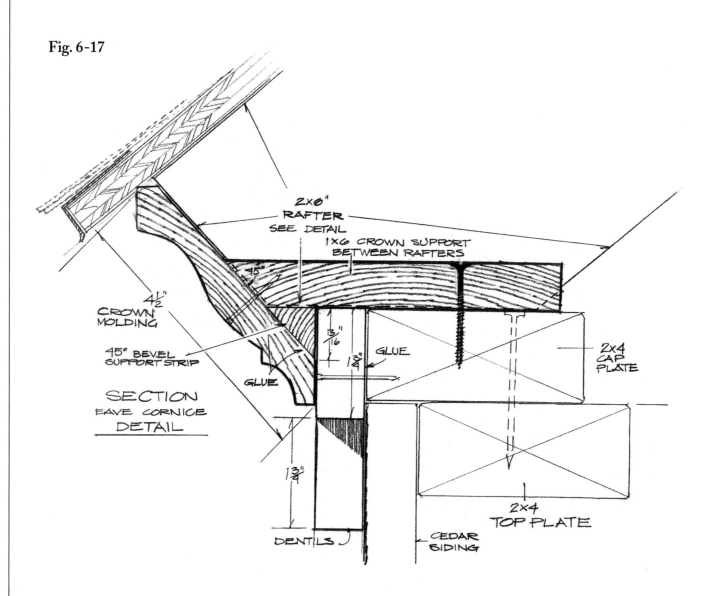

2x8" RAFTER SEE DETAIL

1x6 CROWN SUPPORT BETWEEN RAFTERS

45°

4½"

CROWN MOLDING

45° BEVEL SUPPORT STRIP

GLUE

SECTION EAVE CORNICE DETAIL

$\frac{13}{16}$"

GLUE

1$\frac{3}{8}$"

2x4 CAP PLATE

1$\frac{3}{4}$"

DENTILS

CEDAR SIDING

2x4 TOP PLATE

(crown support) and rest it on the cap plate to test it for fit. If the crown molding doesn't fit perfectly, make slight adjustments by shaving the ends with a belt sander. Make a triangular-shaped support strip, $^{13}/_{16}$-x$^{13}/_{16}$-inch, to fit in between the crown molding and the 1x6 (crown support), by cutting a piece of scrap lumber at a 45-degree bevel and gluing it to the back of the crown molding and the bottom front edge of the 1x6 crown support (see Fig. 6-17). When all the pieces of molding fit together perfectly, glue and screw the 1x6 crown support to the cap plate and to the outside of the dentils.

RAFTERS

Cut one end of a 5-foot-long 2x6 rafter, at a 40-degree angle. This will be the peak of the rafter (see Fig. 6-18).

To determine the final length of the rafter, you must first locate a point 8 feet 10 inches up from the center of the structure. Do this by temporarily toenailing a 9-foot-long piece of scrap 2x4 lumber to the exact center of the floor (see Fig. 6-19). Hold it in place by nailing a cross-brace to the cap plates. Measure up from the floor 8 feet 10 inches on the temporary center post and drive in a nail at this point. Measure

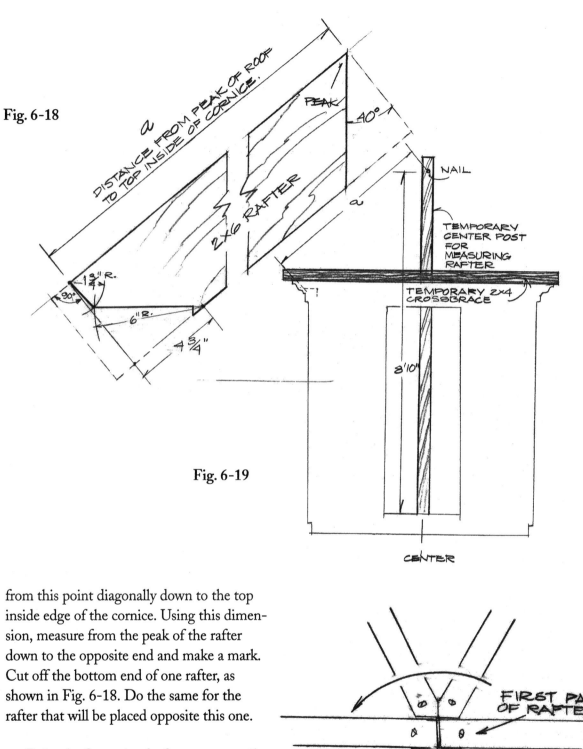

Fig. 6-18

Fig. 6-19

from this point diagonally down to the top inside edge of the cornice. Using this dimension, measure from the peak of the rafter down to the opposite end and make a mark. Cut off the bottom end of one rafter, as shown in Fig. 6-18. Do the same for the rafter that will be placed opposite this one.

Raise the first pair of rafters, temporarily nailing them together at the peak. Use the center post to hold them in place. The next two pairs of rafters join the first pair at the peak (see Fig. 6-20). These will be slightly shorter than the first pair and will have two

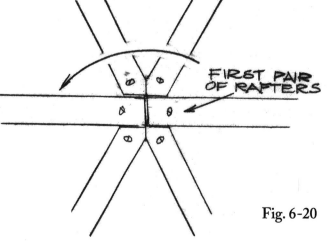

Fig. 6-20

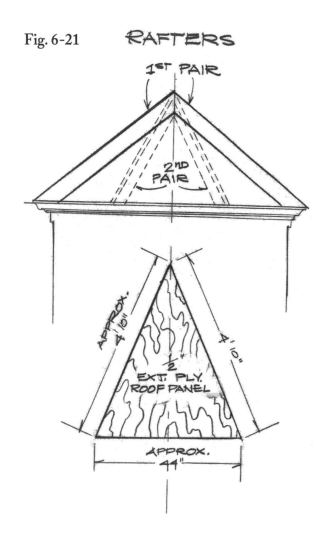

Fig. 6-21

RAFTERS

1ST PAIR

2ND PAIR

APPROX. 4'10"

4'10"

½"

EXT. PLY. ROOF PANEL

APPROX. 44"

beveled cuts on the end at the peak in order for them to fit together neatly. Remove the temporary center post and screw them together, using 3½-inch galvanized deck screws.

ROOF

The roof is sheathed with ½-inch exterior plywood. Each triangular piece will be approximately 4 feet 10 inches, allowing for a 1-inch overhang at the eaves (see Fig. 6-21). Check and adjust these dimensions to match your conditions. You will be able to cut two roof panels out of a single 4x8 sheet of plywood. Use a chalkline to mark the cut lines. Set your saw blade at 10 degrees and cut the pieces out. Nail the wedge-shaped panels to the rafters using 2-inch nails and cover the roof with 15-pound tar paper and asphalt shingles.

DOOR

Begin building the door by making a 29-inch-long head jamb out of ⁵⁄₄x6 P.T. lumber. Cut a notch out of each end, so that the head jamb will fit inside the door opening, yet extend ¼ inch past the 2¼-inch-wide door trim on each side. Install this head jamb under the 2x4 top plate, using 2-inch galvanized finish nails (see Fig. 6-22). To establish the height of the door, measure the

Fig. 6-22

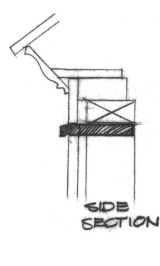

OVER-LAP ¼"

HEAD JAMB ⁵⁄₄"x6 P.T.

SIDE SECTION

distance from under the head jamb to the bottom of the siding. Cut five pieces of 1x6 T&G cedar to this dimension. Lay the pieces on two sawhorses, backside up, and join them together. Rip cut the two outside boards of the door, so that the door measures 23¾ inches, allowing clearance for the door to open and close (see front view, Fig. 6-14). Cut two ⁵⁄₄x6, P. T. crosspieces, each 21½ inches long, and screw them to the back of the door, using 1½-inch galvanized deck screws. For a perfect job, countersink each screw and bevel the edges of the two battens. Strengthen the door by running a ⁵⁄₄x6 diagonal brace from the top side opposite the hinges down to the lower hinge side (see Garden Shower, pages 91-92). Hang the door from two 18-inch black strap hinges.

Tip: To make hanging the door easier, attach the hinges to the door trim (casing) piece before attaching the trim to the house, screwing the hinges onto the door first and then onto the 2¼-inch-wide door trim (ripped from ⁵⁄₄x4 #2 pine). Attach a handle to the door to give you something to hold onto, while you are installing it. Support the bottom of the door with the toe of your boot, and when you are sure it is aligned properly, nail the door trim onto the siding (see Fig. 6-23).

To provide a surface for the door to rest against when it swings shut, cut two pieces of 1x2, 6 feet long, to act as a door stop. Cut them to fit the sides of the door. Stand inside the garden house with the door closed and nail them in place using 2½-inch galvanized finish nails.

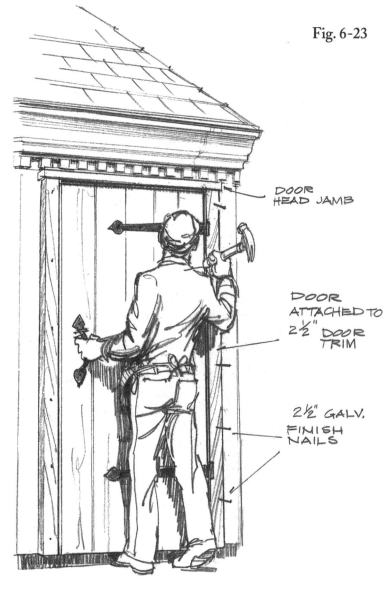

Fig. 6-23

DOOR HEAD JAMB

DOOR ATTACHED TO 2½" DOOR TRIM

2½" GALV. FINISH NAILS

CAP

To top off this elegant structure, it's easy to make a copper cap that fits over the peak of the roof and keeps out the rain. Find the center of a 24-inch-square sheet of 16-ounce copper and cut out a 24-inch-diameter circle. Mark and cut a straight line from one edge to the center (along the radius) of the piece of copper and bend it into the shape of a rough cone, overlapping the edges. After fitting the cone to the peak of the roof, nail it on securely, using 1½-inch copper nails.

POTTING SHED

Because of its simplicity, this garden shed can either be used as a potting shed or be converted into an artist's studio or a children's playhouse. It is especially attractive stained or painted white or a dark Charleston green. Another nice touch is to create a curving pebbled path leading up to the front door and ending with a piece of slate or bluestone.

When picking a spot on your property for the shed site, make sure that it conforms to the building code and obtain a building permit for an accessory structure from the building department (see Planning, page 10). Look for a level spot, free from roots and stones, that is easily accessible to your garden.

MATERIALS

Quantity	Size	Description	Location or Use
BASE:			
2	10 feet	2x6 P.T. lumber	base
1	14 feet	2x6 P.T. lumber	base
2	14 feet	2x6 P.T. lumber	floor joists
varies	4x8x16	solid concrete blocks	base
varies		slate shims	base
2	4x8 sheet	¾-inch exterior plywood	floor
WALLS:			
6	10 feet	2x4 construction fir	front and back plates
2	14 feet	2x4 construction fir	end plates
10	12 feet	2x4 construction fir	studs
3	12 feet	2x4 construction fir	horizontal nailers and window framing
384 lin. ft.		1x8 T&G #2 pine (V-groove)	wall sheathing
ROOF:			
5	10 feet	2x4 construction fir	rafters
1	4x4 sheet	½-inch plywood	gussets
1	10 feet	1x2	ridgepole
1 roll	6-inch-wide	insect screening	eaves
ROOF TRIM:			
2	10 feet	1x4 #2 pine	fascia boards
2	10 feet	1x4 #2 pine	gable trim
2	16 feet	11/16-x1⅜-inch solid crown	eaves molding
2	10 feet	1x6	eave boards
22	10 feet	1x4	spaced sheathing
ROOFING:			
5 bundles	18 inches	Premium red-cedar shingles	roofing
2	12 feet	1x4 #2 cedar	ridge trim
WINDOWS:			
2	8 feet	1x6 #2 pine	window jambs
2	10 feet	1x8 T&G	shutters
1	8 feet	1x4 #2 pine	shutter batten

MATERIALS CONTINUED

Quantity	Size	Description	Location or Use
DOOR:			
3	12 feet	1x8 T&G #2 pine	door
2	12 feet	1x6 #2 pine	door battens and jambs
2	10 feet	¼-x1⅛-inch lattice	insect screen
5	12 feet	1x4 #2 pine	door trim, diagonal door brace and corner boards
3	18-inch	wrought-iron strap hinges	
4 lbs.	3 ½-inch	common nails	
4 lbs.	2-inch	spiral- or ring-shank siding nails	
1 lb.	1¼-inch	galvanized deck screws	
SHELF:			
1	12 feet	1x12 #2 pine	shelf
1	10 feet	1x2 #2 pine	shelf front trim
1	8 feet	1x6	tool board
1	36 inches	1-inch-dia. wooden dowel	tool pegs

BASE

Begin by building a level base. Cut two pieces of 2x6 lumber, 9 feet long, and two more pieces of 2x6, 6 feet 9 inches long. Nail them together at the corners, using 3½-inch common nails (see Fig. 6-24). Cut four 2x6 P.T. floor joists, 6 feet 9 inches long, and nail them inside and at right angles to the 9-foot-long pieces, spaced 24 inches on-center. Place the last floor joist 12 inches from the end. **Note:** These measurements are made from the outside of each side of the 2x6 frame and to the center of each joist (see detail, Fig. 6-24).

Adjust for any unevenness in your building site by "shoring up" the base of the shed to make it level. Do this by laying the frame on concrete blocks at the low end of your building site. Use solid concrete half-blocks (4x8x16 inches), piled up on one another until the frame is approximately level. Then add slate shims in between the blocks and the frame, until the shed frame is perfectly level. **Note:** If you need more than three blocks to make the frame level, consider switching to 12-inch-diameter cardboard Sonotubes, buried 36 inches deep in the ground, and filled with concrete to form piers (see Fig. 6-25).

For several days, periodically check to make sure the frame has not settled "out of level," as this could cause problems in later stages of construction.

FLOOR

Cut two pieces of ¾-inch exterior plywood, 4x7 feet, and nail them on top of the 2x6 frame (see Fig. 6-26). Temporarily nail all four corners of each piece of plywood to the frame, to make sure the frame is square. Use the leftover plywood to cover the 12-inch-wide opening at the far end of the floor.

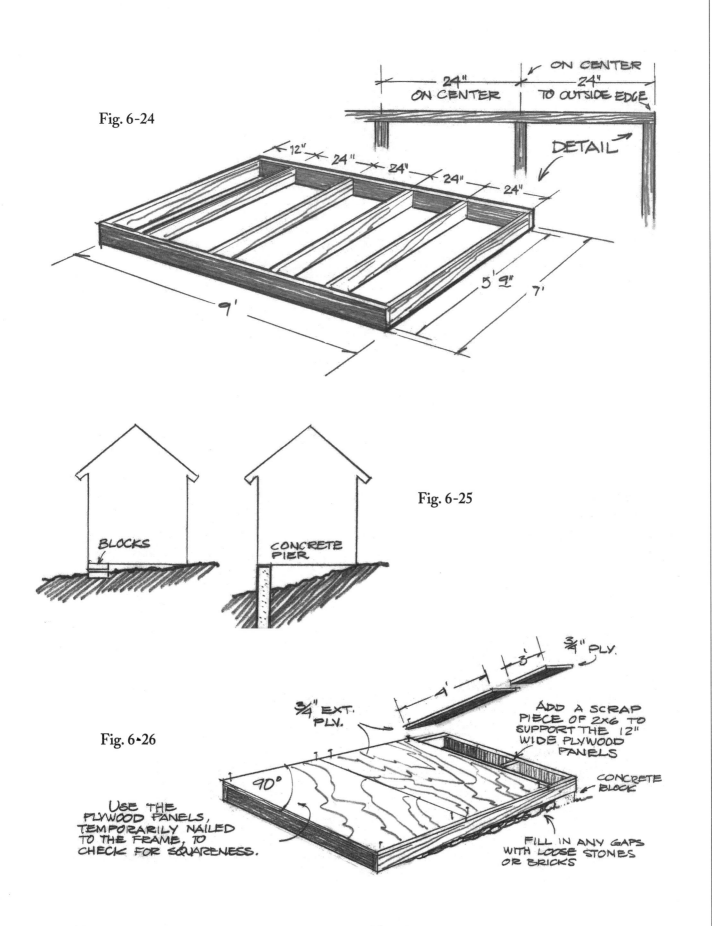

Fig. 6-24

24" ON CENTER

ON CENTER 24" TO OUTSIDE EDGE

DETAIL

12" 24" 24" 24" 24"

5' 9"

7'

9'

Fig. 6-25

BLOCKS

CONCRETE PIER

Fig. 6-26

3/4" PLY.

3' 1'

3/4" EXT. PLY.

ADD A SCRAP PIECE OF 2x6 TO SUPPORT THE 12" WIDE PLYWOOD PANELS

CONCRETE BLOCK

90°

USE THE PLYWOOD PANELS, TEMPORARILY NAILED TO THE FRAME, TO CHECK FOR SQUARENESS.

FILL IN ANY GAPS WITH LOOSE STONES OR BRICKS

Fig. 6-27

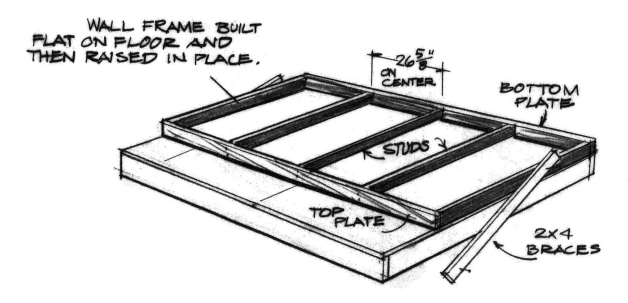

WALL FRAME BUILT FLAT ON FLOOR AND THEN RAISED IN PLACE.

$26\frac{5}{8}"$ ON CENTER

BOTTOM PLATE

STUDS

TOP PLATE

2X4 BRACES

Fig. 6-28

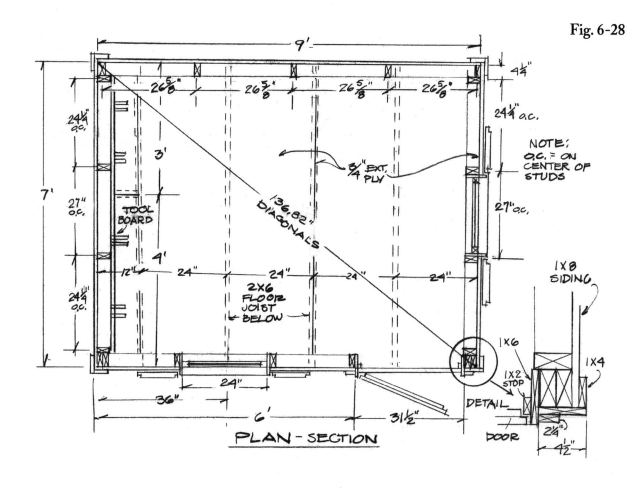

PLAN - SECTION

Fig. 6-29

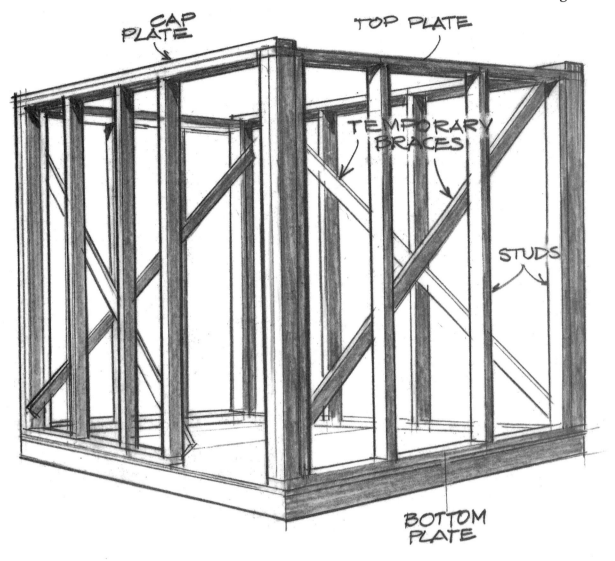

CAP PLATE

TOP PLATE

TEMPORARY BRACES

STUDS

BOTTOM PLATE

Double check for squareness by measuring the diagonals. They should measure 136⅞ inches. Nail the plywood to the frame, using 2-inch siding nails placed at 6-inch intervals.

WALLS

Build the back wall first by cutting two 2x4s into 9-foot-long plates, and five 2x4s into 69-inch-long studs. Using the floor deck as a work platform, nail the 2x4 top and bottom plates to the ends of the studs, 26⅝ inches on-center (measured from center of stud to center of stud [see Fig. 6-27]).

Lift the back wall frame up and secure it in place with two 2x4 braces nailed to the sides of the wall and to the sides of the floor frame.

Build the two end walls in the same way. Cut the top and bottom plates 77 inches long (which allows for the thickness of the front and rear walls). Cut four studs for each end wall 69 inches long. Once they are assembled, stand them up (one at a time) and temporarily nail them to the back wall frame.

Build the front wall to the dimensions shown

Fig. 6-30

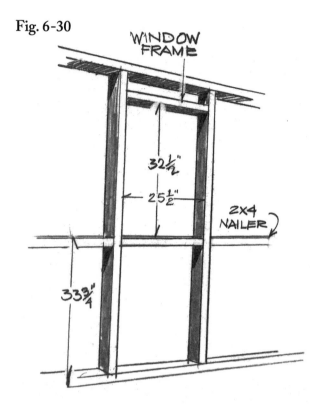

WINDOW FRAME

32½"

25½"

2X4 NAILER

33¾"

in the plan, doubling the number of corner studs for extra strength (see Fig. 6-28). After checking to make sure all the measurements are correct and the frame is square and plumb (vertical), nail the 2x4s together permanently with 3½-inch common nails.

To make sure the frame stays in alignment while you are completing the potting shed, temporarily nail 1x4 diagonal braces to the inside walls. Complete the frame by cutting and nailing a second layer of 2x4s (cap plate) on top of the end plates (see Fig. 6-29).

To strengthen the walls, toenail 2x4 nailers horizontally between the studs, 33¾ inches up from the floor (see Fig. 6-30).

¾" PLY.

1"

1x8 T&G SIDING

SUPPORT NAILS

Fig. 6-31

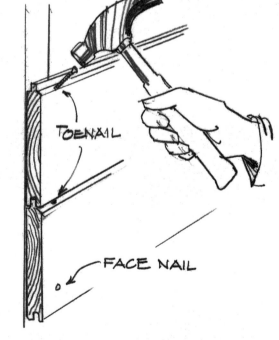

TOENAIL

FACE NAIL

Cut two pieces of 2x4, each 25½ inches long, and nail them between each pair of studs at each of the two window locations.

SIDING

To cover the walls with horizontal sheathing, you will need approximately 384 linear feet of 1x8, tongue-and-groove (T&G) V-groove #2 pine. Partially hammer in three nails to the 2x6 base of each side, 1 inch below the ¾-inch plywood floor. Use them as a ledge to rest the bottom of the first piece of 1x8 sheathing on (see Fig. 6-31). Start at the back and work around to the front, nailing on one course at a time, using 2-inch spiral- or ring-shank siding nails.

Face nail the first row of boards at the bottom, and toenail them at the top. The remaining boards are held at the bottom by the T&G, and toenailed into the "tongue" at the top of each successive board (see Fig. 6-31). Continue until you reach the top of the cap plate, rip cutting the last course as needed, so the sheathing board fits below the protruding cap plate.

RAFTERS

The rafters consist of five pairs of 2x4s, joined at their peaks by ½-inch plywood gussets. Begin by cutting a 10-foot-long 2x4 in half. Cut a 54-degree angle on one end of each piece. Using an electric jig saw, cut a notch (called a bird's mouth) for the rafters to sit on on the top plate. For the location of this bird's mouth, refer to Fig. 6-32.

Join the rafters at the top with 24-inch-wide triangular gussets, cut from a piece of ½-inch plywood. Make the gussets by cutting an 8½-inch-wide by 24-inch-long plywood rectangle, and cut off the two sides at 36½-degree angles (see detail, Fig. 6-33). Nail the gussets to the rafters, using 2-inch siding nails.

To make hanging the five pairs of rafters eas-

ier, cut a 1½-inch notch out of the center peak to accept a 1x2 ridgepole. Mark the ridgepole at 26 ⅝-inch intervals. With an assistant, set up the two outside rafters and install the three inside rafters, resting the 10-foot-long 1x2 ridgepole in the rafter notches (see Fig. 6-33).

Staple a 6-inch-wide piece of aluminum insect screening to the top edge of the front and rear siding and to the bottoms of the rafters (see Fig. 6-33 and detail, Fig. 6-34).

Finish nailing the siding on both gable ends of the shed. It is easier to let the ends of the siding overhang the tops of the rafters, then snap a chalk line and cut them off in one pass, using an electric circular saw. Do not allow any of the siding boards to stick up above the tops of the rafters as this will create a bump in the roof.

FINISHING THE ROOF

Nail two 10-foot-long pieces of 1x4 fascia to the ends of the rafters, allowing 6 inches to extend beyond each end of the gable-end wall. Nail a 10-foot-long 1x6 over the rafters and the fascia (see Fig. 6-35). Cut four 1x4s, each 5 feet long for the gable trim. Cut off one end of each 1x4 at a 54 degree angle, so that they will fit together neatly at the top. Notch out the tops of the 1x4 gable trim to accept the end of the 1x2 ridgepole (see Fig. 6-35).

To support the cedar roof shingles, nail two 10-foot-long 1x4s above each of the 1x6s along the eaves, using 2-inch siding nails. Allow a 2-inch space and add a second nailer, continuing up the roof until you reach the peak (see Fig. 6-34). Nail the ends of the nailers to the 1x4 gable trim.

Finish off the roof by adding ¹¹/₁₆-x 1⅜-inch solid crown molding to the eaves and the gables. For a professional, finished appearance, bevel the molding corners where they meet (see Fig. 6-36).

Fig. 6-32

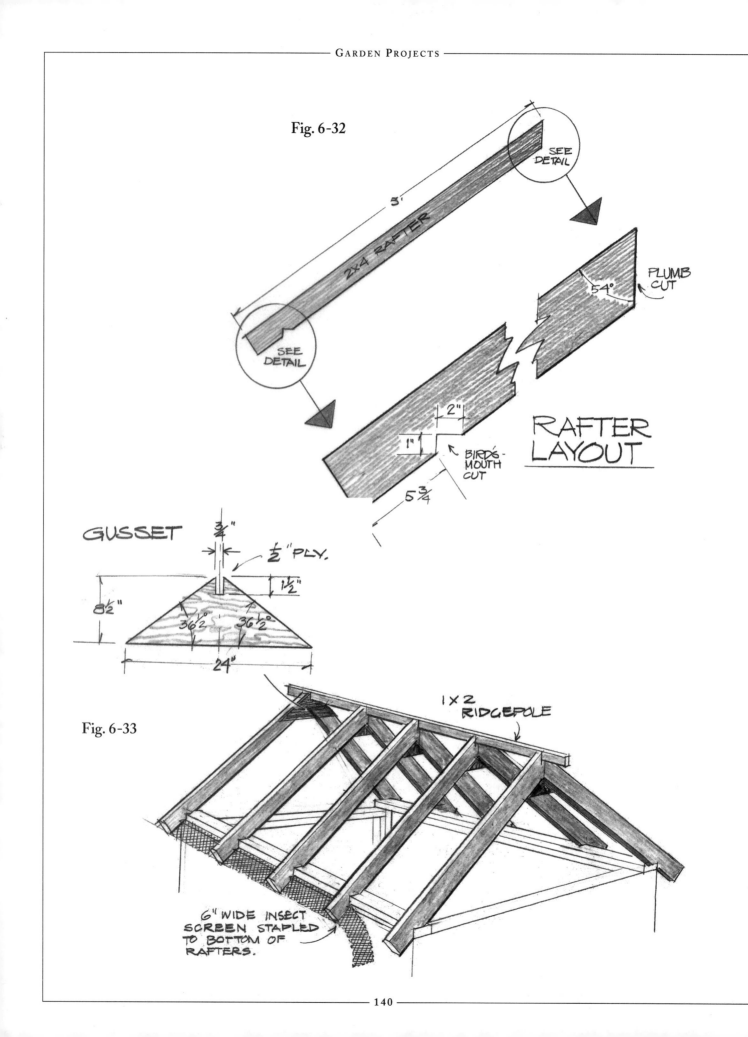

SEE DETAIL

5'

2X4 RAFTER

PLUMB CUT

54°

SEE DETAIL

2"

1"

BIRD'S-MOUTH CUT

5 3/4

RAFTER LAYOUT

GUSSET

3/4"

1/2" PLY.

1 1/2"

8 1/2"

36 1/2°   36 1/2°

24"

Fig. 6-33

1 X 2 RIDGEPOLE

6" WIDE INSECT SCREEN STAPLED TO BOTTOM OF RAFTERS.

Fig. 6-34

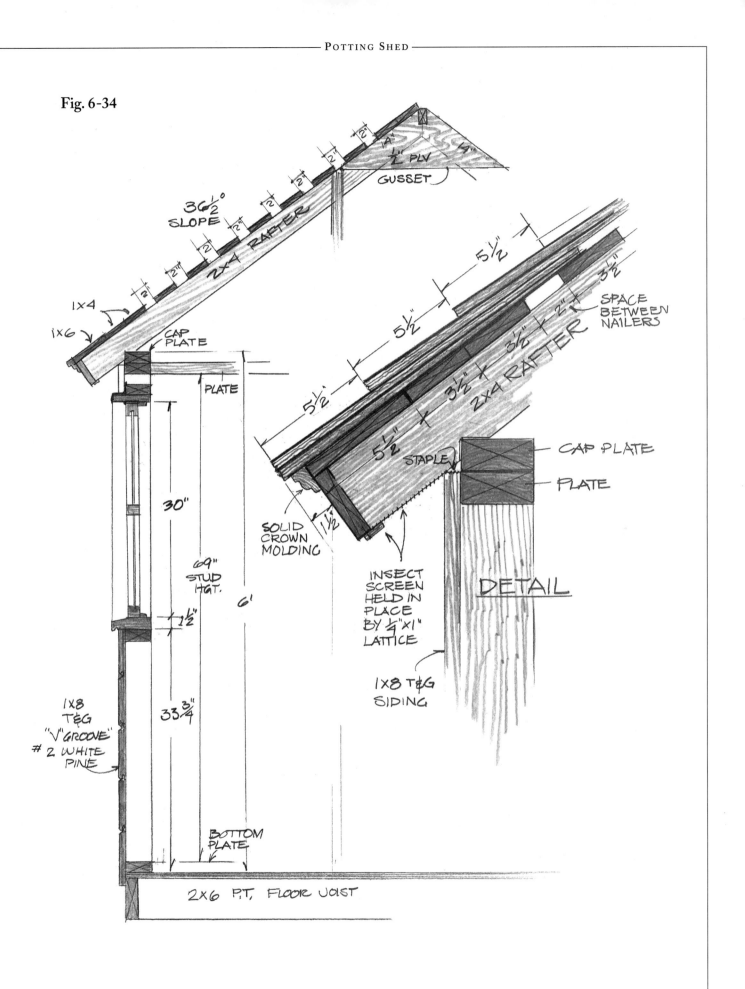

Fig. 6-35

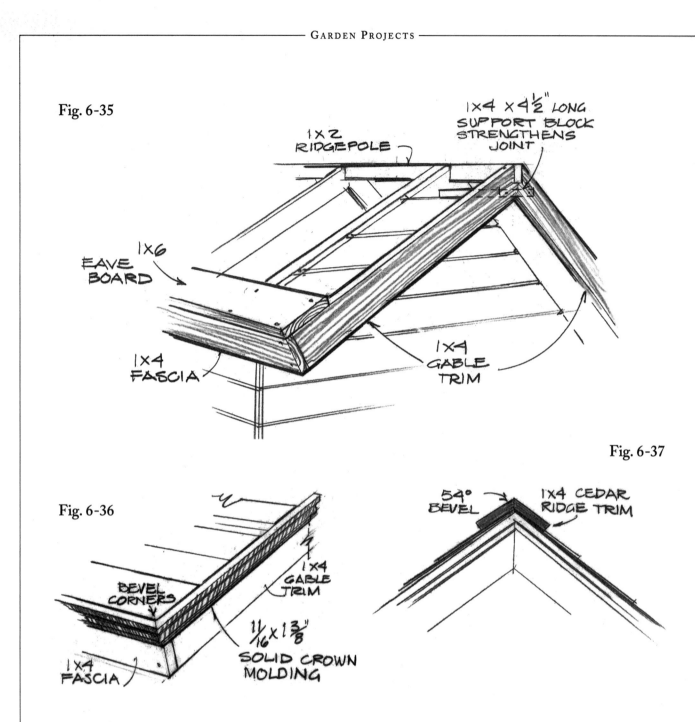

1x2 RIDGEPOLE

1x4 x 4½" LONG SUPPORT BLOCK STRENGTHENS JOINT

EAVE BOARD

1x6

1x4 FASCIA

1x4 GABLE TRIM

Fig. 6-37

Fig. 6-36

1x4 GABLE TRIM

BEVEL CORNERS

$\frac{11}{16} \times 1\frac{3}{8}$" SOLID CROWN MOLDING

1x4 FASCIA

54° BEVEL

1x4 CEDAR RIDGE TRIM

Use five bundles of red cedar shingles to cover the roof. Double the first two courses and overlap the gables and eaves edges by ½ inch (see detail, Fig. 6-34). Nail on each course 5½ inches above the preceding one, making sure to stagger the shingles so the joints don't line up. Use a chalk line or straight piece of 1x4 to keep the lines straight. Cover the peak with two 121-inch-long pieces of cedar. Rip cut each at a 54-degree bevel along one edge before they are nailed together (see Fig. 6-37).

WINDOWS AND DOOR

See Garden House, pages 121-127, for building the windows. Adjust the dimensions for a 24-inch-wide by 30-inch-high sash.

Frame the door opening in 1x6 #2 pine and add a piece of 1x2 to the front edge of the floor at the door opening (see Fig. 6-38). See Garden Shower, pages 91-92, for instructions on building the shed door. This door will be slightly larger, measuring 30 inches wide by 67 inches high.

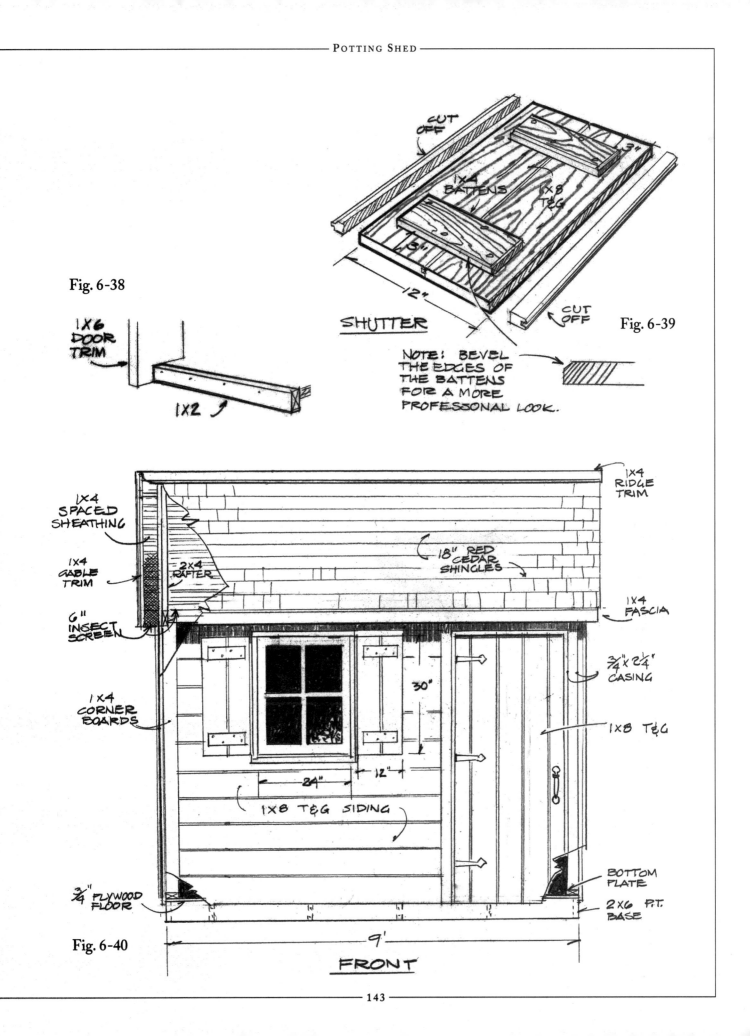

Fig. 6-38

1X6 DOOR TRIM

1X2

CUT OFF

3"

1X4 BATTENS

1X8 T&G

12"

3"

SHUTTER

CUT OFF

Fig. 6-39

NOTE: BEVEL THE EDGES OF THE BATTENS FOR A MORE PROFESSIONAL LOOK.

1X4 SPACED SHEATHING

1X4 GABLE TRIM

6" INSECT SCREEN

2X4 RAFTER

18" RED CEDAR SHINGLES

1X4 RIDGE TRIM

1X4 FASCIA

$\frac{3}{4}$" x $2\frac{1}{4}$" CASING

1X8 T&G

1X4 CORNER BOARDS

30"

24"

12"

1X8 T&G SIDING

$\frac{3}{4}$" PLYWOOD FLOOR

BOTTOM PLATE

2X6 P.T. BASE

9'

Fig. 6-40

FRONT

Fig. 6-41

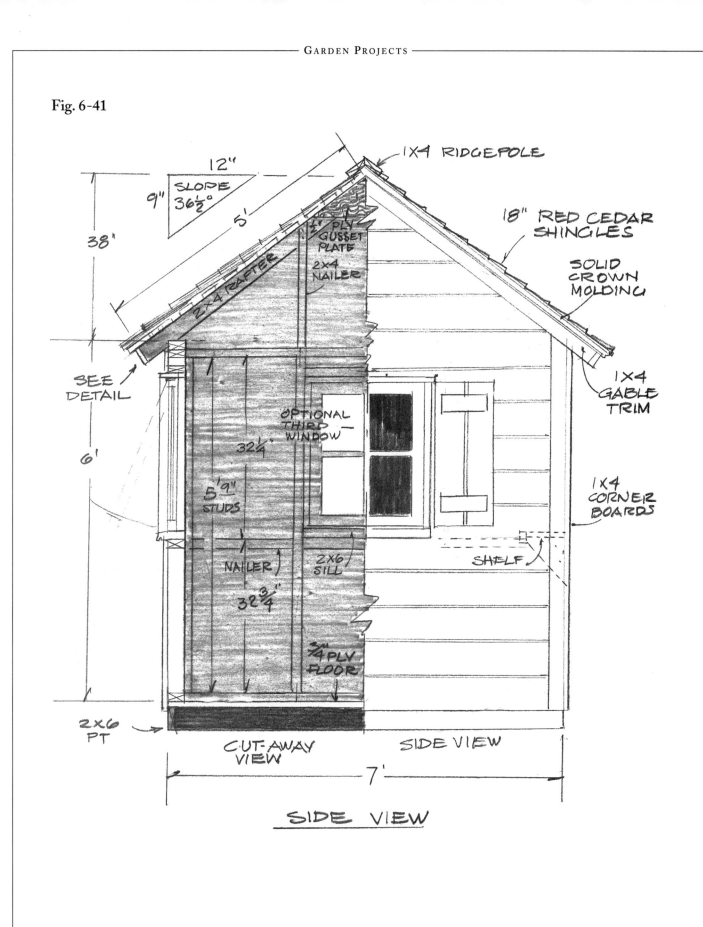

12"

9" SLOPE
36½°

5'

38"

1X4 RIDGEPOLE

18" RED CEDAR SHINGLES

SOLID CROWN MOLDING

2X4 RAFTER

½" PLY GUSSET PLATE

2X4 NAILER

SEE DETAIL

6'

OPTIONAL THIRD WINDOW

32¼"

5'9" STUDS

NAILER

32¾"

2X6 SILL

¾" PLY FLOOR

1X4 GABLE TRIM

1X4 CORNER BOARDS

SHELF

2X6 PT

CUT-AWAY VIEW

SIDE VIEW

7'

SIDE VIEW

Install three wrought-iron strap hinges to support it.

FINISHING TOUCHES

The shutters on this shed can be decorative or functional. Whether they are left natural, stained or painted, they give the shed a more finished appearance.

To build shutters for two windows, cut eight pieces of 1x8 T&G, 24 inches long. Cut 1 inch off the "grooves" of four pieces and 1 inch off the "tongues" of the other four pieces, so that the total combined width of each shutter panel measures 12 inches. To make the horizontal battens, cut eight pieces of 1x4, each 10 inches long, and position one 3 inches from the bottom and one 3 inches from the top of each shutter (see Fig. 6-39). Screw the battens to the shutters with 1¼-inch galvanized deck screws. For a more professional job, countersink the screws and fill the holes with wooden plugs. (For instructions, see Picnic Table, page 53.) Hinge or screw the shutters to both sides of each window.

To conceal the ends of the siding boards, add vertical 1x4 corner boards to the shed's corners (see Fig. 6-40). Notice that the corner to the right of the doorway requires a 1x6, ripped to 4½ inches, and nailed to the corner studs (see detail, Fig. 6-28).

The door is trimmed with ¾-x2¼-inch "casing" rip cut from a 1x4. Nail the trim next to both sides and to the top of the doorway.

As a finishing touch, nail up a 10-foot-long piece of ¼-x1⅛-inch lattice to secure the insect screen to the bottom of the fascia (see detail, Fig. 6-34). Add insect screen to the gable soffits, if desired, by stapling 6-inch-wide screening to the underneath side of the 1x4 spaced roof sheathing (see Fig. 6-40).

To make a shelf, cut a 10-foot-long 1x12, so that it lies on top of the 2x4 horizontal nailers inside the shed. Using an electric jig saw, cut out notches to accept the 2x4 studs. Support the shelf further by cutting a 1x12 diagonally to form a right triangle, and nail it to a stud under the shelf. Attach a 1x2 to the front of the shelf to give it more rigidity (see Fig. 6-41).

Build a tool board in the shed by cutting a 1x6, 77 inches long, and nailing it to the end wall studs. Hold each garden implement up to the board and mark the position of the supporting pegs. Bore ½-inch-diameter holes in the board and glue 6-inch-long, ½-inch-diameter wooden dowels in the holes.

GLOSSARY

A/C or A/D plywood: Plywood that is knot-free or clear on one side only.

Arbor: A latticework bower intertwined with climbing branches, vines and flowers to create a shady spot in a garden.

Batten: A piece of lumber screwed across the back of doors or shutters to strengthen them.

Beveled cut: An angled cut.

Block plane: A small hand tool used to shave off or smooth lumber. Usually has a low-angled blade specifically designed to smooth the endgrain.

Bower: An arbor or leafy shelter.

Bird's-mouth notch: A right-angle notch made in a rafter where the rafter meets the wall.

Butt hinges: Standard hinges.

CDX plywood: An inexpensive, exterior-grade plywood.

Chalk line: An instrument with colored chalk and string used to mark a straight line between two points.

Chamfer: The edge of a board beveled at a 45-degree angle.

Clapboards: Horizontal siding boards applied with an overlap.

Collar tie: A horizontal piece of lumber that connects rafters opposite each other and prevents them from spreading apart.

Counterbore: To enlarge a hole in order to recess a screwhead. The hole is often filled with a wooden plug.

Countersink: To bore a conical hole in order to recess a screwhead.

Dado: A rectangular groove cut in wood across the grain.

Eaves: The overhanging edges of the roof.

Electric jig saw (or saber saw): An electric portable saw used to make curved cuts.

Exterior plywood (ext. ply.): Plywood in which the plies are bonded together using exterior or waterproof glue.

Fascia board: A board nailed to the ends of the rafters, below the roof edge.

Folly: A whimsical or extravagant structure erected to suit a fanciful taste, lending interest to a view or serving as a conversation piece.

Framing square: A large (2-foot by 16-inch), L-shaped metal tool used when measuring and marking boards for framing.

Frieze board: The highest board directly above the siding and below the soffit.

Gable end: The triangular wall between the sloping ends of a roof.

Galvanized: A zinc coating used to prevent rusting.

Gusset: A piece of plywood nailed over a joint to reinforce it.

Header: A horizontal beam above window and door openings.

Joist: A horizontal beam that supports the floor.

Kerf: The groove made by the cut of a saw blade, or the width of the cut itself.

Lag screw: A large screw with a hexagonal head that is used to join heavy pieces of lumber.

Lap joint: A joint made by lapping one piece of wood over another.

MDO (medium density overlay) or Duraply: A plywood sandwiched between several thin layers of paper, impregnated with a phenolic resin. This brown covering makes it impervious to the weather.

Mortise: A groove or recess cut in a piece of wood.

Muntin bar: A strip of wood that divides window panes.

Nail set: A small tool used to hammer nail heads beneath the surface of the wood.

Obelisk: A vertical, tapering, four-sided shaft with a pyramidal apex. These structures are often covered with foliage in a garden.

On-center (O.C.): The distance from the center of one piece of lumber to the center of another.

Pergola: An arborlike structure supported on posts or columns, over which vines or plants may be trained.

Phillipshead screwdriver bit: An attachment for an electric drill used to drive Phillips (cross-head) screws.

Pilot hole: A small hole drilled into a piece of wood to help prevent the wood from splitting when a screw or nail is driven into the wood.

Plate: Horizontal lumber on the top or bottom of a wall to which vertical studs are nailed.

Plumb: Absolutely vertical. Can be determined by using the plumb vial on a level.

Pressure-treated lumber (P.T. or C.C.A. lumber): Lumber that has been chemically treated to resist rot and insects.

Purlin: A horizontal roof beam supporting the rafters of a roof.

Rafters: Lumber that slopes from the roof ridge to the eaves and supports the sheathing and shingles.

Rail (window): The horizontal members of a window sash.

Rasp: A rough-edged file used to shape wood.

Ridgepole: A horizontal board at the peak of a roof to which rafters are nailed.

Router: An electric tool used to cut grooves and shape lumber into various profiles for moldings.

Section: A drawing that shows the "cut-through" view of a building or object.

Soffit: The underside of the roof overhang.

Spade bit: A flat drill bit used for making holes.

Speed Square: A triangular-shaped metal tool used as a guide for cutting lumber at right angles with an electric saw.

Stile (window): The vertical members of a window sash.

Stud: Lumber used for the vertical framing members in a wall.

Toenail: To drive a nail at an angle.

Tongue-and-groove (T&G): Boards in which the tongue of one board fits into the groove of another.

Trellis: A lattice structure used to support growing vines or plants.

Utility knife: A thin-bladed cutting tool used to cut shingles and other thin building materials.

SOURCES

CYPRESS LUMBER

Griffis Lumber Co.
Gainsville, FL 32654
904-372-9965
All types of cypress—rough cut to finished

Quality Millwork
2570 Franklin Ave.
Fort Meyers, FL 33901
813-334-2800
Lumber shipped common carrier

RAILINGS

Mansion Industries, Inc.
14425 East Clark Ave.
Industry, CA 91745

BENTWOOD WORKSHOP

Peconic River Herb Farm
Cristina Spindler
310-C River Rd.
Calverton, NY 11933

BENTWOOD TRELLISES

Jim Long
Long Creek Herbs
Rt. 4, Box 730
Oak Grove, AR 72660
417-779-5450

GARDENING TOOLS

Walt Nicke Gardening Tools Catalog
36 McLeod Lane, P.O. Box 433
Topsfield, MA 01983
508-887-3388

POST CAPS

Island Post Caps
118 Long Lots Rd.
Westport, CT 06880

STAINS FOR PRESSURE-TREATED WOOD

Osmose Wood Preservative, Inc.
P.O. Drawer O
Griffin, GA 30224-0249

LANDSCAPE GARDENING

Gardenscapes
Virginia Conklin
Fireplace Road
East Hampton, NY 11937

CART TIRES

Northern Hydraulics Catalog, Inc.
P.O. Box 1499
Burnsville, MN 55337-0499
800-533-5545

TOOLS AND HARDWARE

Sears Power and Hand Tools
20 Presidential Dr.
Roselle, IL 60172

Garrett Wade
302 Fifth Ave.
New York, NY 10001

Harbor Freight
3491 Mission Oaks Blvd.
Camarillo, CA 93011

Trendlines
375 Beacham St.
Chelsea, MA 02150

The Woodworkers' Store
21801 Industrial Blvd.
Rogers, MN 55374-9514

Defender's Industries, Inc.
225 Main St., P.O. Box 820
New Rochelle, NY 10801-0820
Epoxy resin: West System

SPONGE RUBBER

Canal Rubber Supply Co. Inc.
329 Canal St.
New York, NY 10013

ABOUT THE AUTHORS

RICHARD D'ALONZO

DAVID STILES is a designer/builder and illustrator, and the author
of eight other how-to books, including *Sheds* and *The Treehouse Book*
(which won the ALA Notable Children's Book Award). A graduate of
Pratt Institute and The Academy of Fine Arts in Florence, Italy, he is the
winner of two awards from the New York Planning Commission.
His articles have appeared in *House Beautiful*, *Country Journal*,
Home Mechanix and the *New York Times*.

JEAN TRUSTY STILES, a graduate of Wheaton College, lives in
New York City, where she is an actress/model and an instructor
of English as a Second Language at Baruch College. Jeanie and David
have written *Playhouses You Can Build* and *Kids' Furniture You Can Build*,
and have appeared on numerous television programs, including
the "Our Home" show. They have a 20-year-old daughter,
Lief-Anne, who is a student at Duke University, and divide their
time between New York City and East Hampton, New York.